That Bloody Hill

D1559964

That Bloody Hill

Hilliard's Legion at Chickamauga

LEE ELDER

McFarland & Company, Inc., Publishers
Jefferson, North Carolina

ISBN 978-1-4766-6958-8 (print)
ISBN 978-1-4766-3126-4 (ebook)

LIBRARY OF CONGRESS CATALOGUING DATA ARE AVAILABLE
BRITISH LIBRARY CATALOGUING DATA ARE AVAILABLE

Front cover drawing on tan paper, Chinese white and black
ink wash 17.4 × 25.3 cm, *Chickamauga*, artist
Alfred R. Waud (Library of Congress)

Printed in the United States of America

*McFarland & Company, Inc., Publishers
Box 611, Jefferson, North Carolina 28640
www.mcfarlandpub.com*

To my family.
My parents, my wife, and my children
all had a role in making this book possible.
It will be a tremendous thrill to put a copy
of this book in their hands.

Table of Contents

Acknowledgments

The author has many people and organizations to thank for their help during the process of writing and producing this book. Their help has been all over the map; virtually every part of the journey has been with someone's help. I am grateful and hope to mention, with thanks, everyone here.

My wife Amy put up with long absences during the research and even longer blank and silent stares into the air as I tried to figure stuff out. Her sense of humor is world class, which was especially evident while I completed the Legion's roster.

Our children Sean and Regan have played a role. Sean helped with photographic advice, and he and his wife Mindy were supportive when I ran into research issues. Regan has tramped around battlefields with me, not to mention our visit to the site of the gunfight at the OK Corral.

It was a family project that started me down the Chickamauga research path. While I was working on genealogy information required for an education grant for Regan, the story of Hilliard's Legion got itself front and center on my desk. Regan was eventually awarded the grant and the Legion's story has been on this desk ever since.

My warm and loving parents, Leon and Dorothy Elder, instilled in me an appreciation of history, particularly American history. They also emphasized the importance of learning to write.

The wonderful ladies of the United Daughters of the Confederacy not only provided information for this book; they also repeatedly offered suggestions for how to proceed on the rare occasions when I asked for information they could not provide.

The Alabama Department of Archives and History is a treasure lode of historic booty for Civil War researchers. Check their website (http://www.archives.alabama.gov/) for a list of the information available. A veteran of many visits to the research room, I can tell you that Southern Hospitality is alive and well at the ADAH.

The same is true of the wonderful folks at the Auburn University Library in Alabama. Their remarkable helpfulness will not be forgotten. Here, too, was found a wonderful sense of humor. The author was in the Auburn Library, plodding through microfilmed copies of some Confederate medical files, when the term Vulnus Sclopet began popping up. Listed in the Disease columns of each page, it became obvious that, whatever this illness is, it was deadly in 1863. The author suddenly saw his way to acceptance in the world of Civil War research—a serious study of the deadly illness. Rushing to the research desk, the author asked the librarian to use the internet to discover what sort of killer Vulnus Sclopet was. "It's short for Vulnus Sclopeticum," the librarian informed. "That's Latin for gunshot wound." As the visions of a best-selling book dissolved, the author blurted out the obvious question: "Why didn't they [the doctors] just write 'gunshot wound' on the form?" The librarian answered, "I guess they were snobby even then."

Marilyn Levinson is the Curator of Manuscripts at Bowling Green State University's Center for Archival Collections and was also very helpful. Mrs. Ouida Starr Woodson of Alabama was kind enough to let me use the information compiled by her great grandfather about Company D of the Legion's 5th Battalion.

I am particularly indebted to James Ogden and his co-workers at the Chickamauga National Military Park in northern Georgia. Ogden made his Gracie Battalion file available and then gave terrific advice about further avenues to follow on the research trail. The Rangers at CNMP are perfect hosts. It turns out that when bumbling visitors from California manage to get lost on Park property and walk five miles down the wrong path when the intended course was a few hundred yards, the Rangers manage to keep a straight face and give the requested directions when contacted via cellular phone.

For a rookie writer, turning a manuscript into a book can be a trying effort. I had help from two great friends. Carole Swartz jumped in and edited the manuscript, making a huge difference. Teri Schott of Sure Schott Design made the maps in this book easy to understand. Both Carole and Teri helped me turn my manuscript into something acceptable for my publisher.

Introduction

The men of Hilliard's Legion played a major role in the Confederate victory in the American Civil War battle of Chickamauga. They were members of Brigadier General Archibald Gracie's brigade, along with the 43rd Alabama and the 63rd Tennessee infantry regiments. In the dwindling twilight of September 20, 1863, the men of the Legion helped push a stubborn force of Union defenders away from their defensive positions and eventually off the top of Horseshoe Ridge. Through the years, Gracie's command has been credited with that accomplishment and then is also said to have been knocked off the side of the hill due to suffering heavy casualties and running out of ammunition.

The Legion's men actually accomplished a good deal more than that. Their full participation in that victory has never been explored or credited. The book you hold does that for the first time. By reading letters from veterans of the fight that are usually ignored by historians who write about this battle and then comparing those veterans' comments with facts found in the usual sources, this author has determined what Gracie's men in general and the Legion's men in particular really accomplished that bloody afternoon. They not only forced Union defenders away from the defense of the Ridge's Hill 1; a small group of Gracie's men participated in the capture of a few hundred Union soldiers who were among the last defenders still atop that ridge. Gracie's men held their position overnight, having never been driven away from their perch on the edge of the hillside.

This author originally sought only to better understand the wording of the tablets along Horseshoe Ridge at the Chickamauga/Chattanooga National Military Park after a visit there. Those markers seemed to be at variance with what had been written about the battle when he visited the park for the first time in 2006. That confusion led to more reading and then to a search for first-person information from veterans of the fight, especially those of Hilliard's Legion. The mother lode came in the form

1

of the Archibald Gracie Papers, primarily letters from the general's son to surviving members of his father's command. Through the length of this book, the general's name is sometimes written as Archibald Gracie III and his son is sometimes referred to as Gracie IV as a way of reducing confusion.

Gracie III died in 1864 when Gracie IV was still a small boy. Decades later, Gracie IV's research into the battle became extensive. The book that resulted from that effort, *The Truth about Chickamauga,* is universally credited in bibliographies of Chickamauga-related studies, but his papers are almost never referenced. Gracie IV did something we cannot do today: He talked to veterans of the fight and exchanged letters with them. This first-person research should not be ignored by historians and it is not ignored by this author. The world lost a good researcher when Gracie IV succumbed to illness in December of 1912. His illness and death were hastened by the harrowing night he spent standing atop an upturned lifeboat after the sinking of the RMS *Titanic.*

In today's research world, sources are increasingly available via the internet. The author used Ancestry.com to access the muster rolls of Hilliard's Legion. The Alabama Department of Archives and History contracted with Ancestry to make the records available for researchers, and even researchers who visit the ADAH in Montgomery would be directed to use a computer to view those records. The originals remain with the ADAH but they have become fragile and are not available for viewing. The author accessed the muster cards for the Legion's soldiers through Fold 3.com. The muster rolls, muster cards, and the ADAH Civil War Soldiers Database were the primary sources for the Legion roster at the end of this book.

A note on spelling: This book quotes many primary sources, some in letters written under trying conditions by individuals who lacked formal education. The spelling is, at times, very poor. The author has used the original spelling to give the reader a better feel for the people and the time in which they lived.

The story of the fighting on Horseshoe Ridge is very complicated. It involves numerous regiments, battalions and brigades in both the Union and the Confederate armies. Some of those units fought, withdrew and returned to the fighting. Some officers reported that they pulled their commands off the Ridge, thinking the fighting was over, hours before the shooting finally ended. Determining what happened when and in what order was a challenge. The goal was to accurately follow the Legion's role in the fighting all the way to the end, and that has been accomplished.

For those readers not familiar with Civil War military nomenclature, a brief note about the units described in these pages: In simple terms, companies are identified by letter (Company A, for example) and usually started the war with about 100 soldiers. Regiments in both armies typically had roughly four to seven companies and were identified by number and state (such as the 43rd Alabama Infantry Regiment). For the purposes of this book, consider battalions the rough equivalent of regiments. There were usually two or three regiments in a brigade, though some brigades were larger. Divisions were made up of brigades.

In the following pages, the origin of Hilliard's Legion will be detailed as well the steps the Legion followed as a part of Gracie III's command. The Legion was like every other command on both sides of the Civil War. Its men suffered illnesses and frequently died before experiencing combat. Some deserted, others died in combat, and a few lucky ones survived the war, surrendering at Appomattox. One is buried at the Arlington National Cemetery and another played a starring (and nearly fatal) role as a Union soldier, earning the Medal of Honor near the end of the war.[1] Others played important roles in post-war Alabama, and some moved as far away as Brazil after the war ended.

This is their story.

1

Crossing
the Chickamauga

Hilliard's Legion crossed Chickamauga Creek at Dalton's Ford, heading north in the growing darkness of evening on September 18, 1863. Crossing some farmland owned by a family named Hunt and then walking toward a wooded area, the Legion marched less than a quarter mile before stopping for the night.

An Alabama unit in the Confederate States Army, the Legion had been formed little more than a year earlier and was now the largest part of Brigadier General Archibald Gracie's Brigade. The brigade was one of three in Brigadier General William Preston's Division. The division's other two brigades, under the command of Colonel John Kelly and Colonel Robert Trigg, would cross the Chickamauga the next day. Preston's Division was attached to Major General Simon Buckner's Corps.

It was dark before Gracie's entire brigade was in position and in a defensive posture. The moon would not reach its first quarter until September 20, so there was little light for use in the fields.[1]

Gracie's men formed a line that ran roughly east and west and faced north. They were roughly parallel to the creek and on land owned by the Hunt family. The land is largely flat there, as befits a farm.

For the night of the 18th Gracie's Brigade was the forward element of Preston's Division.

Crossing the Chickamauga marked the end of a marathon 18-day march for the soldiers of the Legion. The Legion had been on hand for the non-fight at McLemore's Cove days earlier, and the soldiers knew the enemy was somewhere nearby as they crossed the Chickamauga on the 18th.

Braxton Bragg, the commanding general of the Confederate Army of Tennessee, wrote of his men after the battle, "For two weeks most of them had been without shelter, on short rations, in a country parched by

Dalton's Ford, where Gracie's Brigade crossed Chickamauga Creek in the early evening of September 18, 1863. The Brigade came toward the photographer's position. Gracie's men were the first of Preston's Division to cross the creek. The brigades of Colonel John H. Kelly and Colonel Robert C. Trigg crossed the next morning (author's photograph).

drought, where drinking water was difficult to obtain.... During the action, and for a day or two before, and up to this time, all were on short rations and without cooking utensils."[2]

The Union's Army of the Cumberland and the Confederate Army of Tennessee had marched and countermarched for weeks, occasionally coming into contact with each other. Now they were in very close proximity. In fact, around the middle of the afternoon on the 18th, Buckner's artillery traded shots with a Federal unit. Those cannon blasts and other minor skirmishes were preludes to what became the deadly Battle of Chickamauga.

The battle lasted two full days and part of another, cost many lives, raised some commanders on both sides to hero status and negatively impacted the careers of others. At the end of three days of fighting, much of it among the fiercest of the Civil War, the Confederates held the field and were thus credited with a victory. But the Federals retreated into the nearby city of Chattanooga, a major prize they had captured earlier in the month. Determining the victor of the battle of Chickamauga is best summed up as a question of viewpoint.

As the soldiers of Hilliard's Legion rested in the woods near the banks of the Chickamauga and the Hunt farm over the night of September 18/19, they had no way of knowing what was ahead of them. It was probably just as well.

2

The Founding
of the Legion

Henry Washington Hilliard was born in Cumberland County, North Carolina, on August 4, 1808. The family relocated to South Carolina where Hilliard attended college and was eventually admitted to the bar. He became a professor of Elocution and English Literature at the University of Alabama before moving to Montgomery, Alabama, and returning to his practice of the law. He was later elected to the state legislature, lost a bid for a seat in Congress, and accepted an assignment to serve a mission as the Chargé d'Affaires to Belgium. Two years in Belgium were enough and Hilliard returned to Alabama where he again ran for Congress in 1845. This time he won and went on to serve three terms.

Hilliard did not seek a fourth term in office and instead returned to his legal career. At the time of the 1860 Federal Census, Hilliard owned real estate valued at $30,000 and his personal estate was valued at $26,500. He owned 14 slaves.[1]

Hilliard reportedly did not agree with the secession movement, but eventually came to support the Confederate cause after Abraham Lincoln called for volunteers to join the United States Army to overcome the Confederacy. Named Commissioner of the Confederate States, he was sent to Tennessee to push that state's leaders to leave the Union. Finally, on April 24, 1862, Hilliard was made a colonel in the Confederate States Army and commissioned to recruit a legion of about 3,000 men.

Hilliard's Legion was organized at Montgomery, Alabama, on June 25, 1862. Formally known as Hilliard's Legion, Alabama Volunteers and alternately known as Hilliard's Alabama Legion, the original Legion included five battalions. The 5th Battalion was a cavalry unit and it quickly was split from the Legion and made part of the 10th Confederate Cavalry.

The 4th Battalion was an artillery unit, but its soldiers fought mainly as infantrymen. One company from the 4th Battalion became R. F. Kolb's

Battery and was also split away from the Legion. By the time of the battle of Chickamauga, Kolb's command was part of the Reserve Corps of Artillery under the command of Major Samuel C. Williams in the Army of Tennessee.

The 1st, 2nd and 3rd Battalions were infantry units. Combined with the remainder of the 4th Battalion, the Legion was about 3,000 strong by the time it left Montgomery.

In some cases, companies already raised by other men came to the Legion. In other cases, men joined the Legion as individuals. An advertisement typical of the time was placed in the *Montgomery Daily Advertiser* on March 8, 1863. It read as follows[2]:

Volunteers Wanted.

I have been detailed for the purpose of obtaining recruits for Company G, (Capt. Middleton) and other companies of the 1st Battalion Alabama Legion. You have the right to volunteer before being conscripted and will receive all the benefits which are secured by law to volunteers. I can be found at the store of Blount & Hale, next to Central Bank. During my absence Major John H. Holt will act for me.

Lieut. ROBERT H. MOLTON

Co. G, 1st Bat. Ala. Legion[3]

The *Daily State Sentinel* in Selma, Alabama, carried an ad seeking cavalrymen for the Legion on May 11, 1862. The ad read as follows:

ATTENTION CAVALRY.

I have been authorized by the War Department to fill up a Cavalry Company, which is now in service, for 12 months. I desire to obtain a few more recruits to fill up the Company, and make it ready to repair immediately to the field of action, either in Tennessee or Kentucky, and will belong to the 5th Alabama Battalion.—I appeal to the brave men of the South to come forward and give your country your services when they are so much needed.—

Our Government calls for more men, and they must be had.

This Company is in for 12 months service, and each man is only required to furnish a double barrel shot gun, the Governor will furnish sabres.

For information or application for membership, apply to me at Fayetteville Talladega County, or D. W. Caldwell, Columbiana, or R. R. Hardy, Selma.

J. W. Perkins

Com. Company[4]

Most of the volunteers who came to serve in Hilliard's Legion were inducted into the Confederate States Army during the first week of July 1863. Many of the men had registered prior to that time but did not report until that busy week.

On July 8, 1862, the Legion headed by rail for Atlanta.

John Massey, the Adjutant for the 1st Battalion, wrote later: "When we left Montgomery … we did not know where we were going. We rather thought we were going to Virginia, as it was then the most active field of operations."[5]

From Atlanta, the Legion moved on to Chattanooga. The Legion's members were armed in Chattanooga and remained there for more training over the next three weeks. From Chattanooga, the Legion eventually joined the investment of the Cumberland Gap on September 18.

On the following October 2, the Legion joined General Braxton Bragg's invasion of Kentucky. Twenty days later, the Legion was back at the Gap, having marched roughly 300 miles to and from Kentucky without seeing combat.

If the Legion was not fighting the enemy, its men were at least getting lots of aerobic exercise. The Legion was on the move again on November 4, heading through Knoxville and eventually to Bridgeport, Alabama, where the Legion stayed briefly. Then it was back to Knoxville, where the Legion arrived on November 25.[6]

From that point until the following April, the Legion's battalions moved to different locations and did not serve together. During this period, on December 1, Hilliard resigned as commander of the Legion and Colonel Jack Thorington, who had led the Legion's 1st Battalion, was elected as the leader of the Legion. Lieutenant John H. Holt took command of the First Battalion.

Massey wrote, in a manner that might be termed politically correct in today's society, that Hilliard was not much of a military leader. "But military genius was not one of the brilliant parts in the make-up of this many side man," Massey wrote. "He appeared to much better advantage in the court room, on the hustings, in the halls of Congress, and in the courts of kings than he did in the role of a soldier on the tented field."[7]

The 1st and 4th Battalions were ordered to Big Creek Gap, Tennessee, on December 27, while the 2nd Battalion went to the Cumberland Gap and the 3rd was sent to Clinton, Tennessee. Some companies were detached from their battalions and scattered. For example, Company A of the 1st Battalion spent part of the winter at Bristol, Tennessee, and Company E of the 3rd Battalion was in Knoxville, Tennessee during this time.

Army life was difficult in those days. Just staying healthy was a trial that many young men did not survive. While the Legion was not in combat during this period, it was already suffering casualties. Letters home from Legion soldiers seem matter of fact in their descriptions of life in the Confederate Army.

Benjamin Mason was a private in the Legion's Company A, 1st Battalion. His September 29, 1862, letter to his wife described how four men died nearly a year before the Legion experienced combat. At the end of the letter, in a postscript, Mason wrote, "There has been four men killed out of our Legion Since we have been in the gap. Three of them were killed by the striking of fire in a powder house and firing the powder. The other was shot by seven Indians who were on picket and the white men had on yankey cloths and went to pass their lines. They halted him and he did not stop and they shot him. There is two hundred and fifty of these Indians here and they belong to a north Carolina regiment and make very good soldiers."[8]

Mary Allin Loftis was an attractive young Alabama woman as the war started. She famously wrote letters to and received many wartime letters from a variety of Confederate soldiers. Among her correspondents was Corporal James Pritchett of the 3rd Battalion's Company B. Pritchett wrote to Loftis from camp in Claborn County, Tennessee, on September 16, 1862, "I enjoy tolerable health this morning.... There is a good many of this company sick now, but not many deaths. L. W. Moore and L. S. Reaves died since we have bin her which makes six out of this company."[9]

The most common Confederate ailment was present in every Confederate camp: diarrhea. Mass sanitation was not a Confederate strength, particularly early in the war, and that fact contributed mightily to the spread of the misery. Other diseases cost the Legion men as well.[10]

By April 25, 1863, the Legion was still under the command of Thorington but it was now attached to Brigadier General Archibald Gracie's Brigade, which was stationed at Bean's Station, Tennessee. Three of the Legion's battalions were stationed at the Cumberland Gap by that time, but by August 3,

Brigadier General Archibald Gracie. This is an image of a painting produced after the war from a war-era photograph (Alabama Department of Archives and History, Montgomery, Alabama).

the full Legion was ordered to join Gracie's command at Strawberry Plains, Tennessee.

Mason, the Company A, 1st Battalion private, in a March 24, 1863, letter to his wife, wrote, "There is an order just in for us to report to General Gracy [*sic*] next day after tomorrow at [unclear word] cross rodes [*sic*] between [unclear] and Big creek gap and from there I don't know where. I fear this is the beginning of trouble with us."[11] Just days short of six months later, Mason would be proven correct.

James Pritchett, of Company E, 3rd Battalion, wrote to Loftis from Strawberry Plains on August 15, 1863, that he was in good health. "There is not much sickness her now. This Betalion is in better helth now than hit has bin in sum time."[12]

Shortly after Pritchett wrote that letter, the Legion, now part of Gracie's brigade, headed off toward Chickamauga.

Archibald Gracie III was born to a successful family in New York City in 1832. After five years of study abroad, he attended the United States Military Academy at West Point, graduating in 1854. He ranked 14th in a class of 46.[13] After serving in what are now the northwestern states of Washington, Oregon and Idaho, Gracie resigned his commission and entered the banking business in Alabama. The family had cotton farming interests there.

Gracie married Josephine Mayo of Richmond, Virginia, in November of 1856. Josephine's father owned a home in New Jersey, near the home where Gracie had spent part of his youth. When the war drew near and obvious, Gracie's father moved the majority of his family back to New Jersey. The elder Gracie was a Union supporter and did not want to be caught behind the lines when war broke out. The Gracies were just another family split apart by the Civil War.[14]

The young couple, Mr. and Mrs. Archibald Gracie III, lived in Mobile, Alabama. Gracie continued his banking career and joined the local militia unit, the Washington Light Infantry. A captain in the militia by 1861, Gracie became a major in the 11th Alabama Infantry shortly after the war started. He was later promoted to colonel of the 43rd Alabama Infantry regiment and then to brigadier general in November of 1862. Gracie's Brigade joined Braxton Bragg's Army of Tennessee as part of Preston's Division.

Massey had a more positive opinion of Gracie than he did of Hilliard, the man who raised the Legion. Massey wrote of Gracie, "He was a fine drill master, a brave officer, and made one of the best brigade commanders in the army."[15]

The Legion's strength by the time it crossed the Chickamauga was less than a third of its original muster. The 1st Battalion is generally listed with 238 men, the 2nd with 230, the 3rd with 229 and the 4th with 205. That totals 902 men and officers.

Gracie's Brigade included the Legion's four battalions, plus the 43rd Alabama (with 400 men) and the 63rd Tennessee (402 men) regiments. The brigade's full strength is generally accepted to have been 1,704 men and officers when it fought at Chickamauga.

To reach the Chickamauga, Gracie's command marched constantly for nearly three weeks. In his book *A History of the Sixtieth Alabama Regiment*, Sergeant Major Lewellyn A. Shaver of the Legion's 1st Battalion, A Company, wrote, "Here were 18 days of almost constant marching. The heat and dust contributed much to the inconvenience of the troops during the whole march, and the suffering from these and other causes was intense."[16]

John Forbes Davenport, a private in the Legion's 1st Battalion, wrote home to his wife and children, "My Dear we had a very heard werisom march for Cumberlin Gap to Ringold Georgia and to Lefayett Ga."[17] It was a long, hot march and it was accomplished by soldiers who were not well fed.

Private Mason, of the Legion's 1st Battalion, Company A, wrote home as early as April 30, 1863, "I don't know how long this sort of fair [fare] is to last but if it lasts long we will have very serious times times [sic] in the command for I for one wont stay in the army long and live on dry bread and but little of that."[18] Mason wrote later to his wife that he and his comrades used their own money to supplement the meager offerings from the Army.

Then again, in a May 12, 1863, letter, Mason wrote, "There is a great deal of complaint now about rations we don't get but about half rations now and that is generally of poor beef and course meal Some days we get one meal a day and some times more and some times less."[19]

Three days before the battle, Bolling Hall, Jr., a captain in the 2nd Battalion, wrote to his father, "We have marched several hundreds of miles going day & night. We have faced the enemy several times in line of battle but they have always ran."[20]

The Hall family had five brothers in uniform at Chickamauga, four of them as members of the Legion. The Legion brothers all wrote brief letters for inclusion in a packet with the letter from Bolling Jr., mentioned above. John Elmore Hall, a lieutenant in the 2nd Battalion, wrote, "We have had hard times lately marching. The dust is worse than I have ever seen."[21]

It was as such that the men of Hilliard's Legion settled down on the night of September 18. Most of their number were privates, just ordinary foot soldiers. It was the ordinary foot soldier, more than any officer or even group of officers, who turned the tide of battle at Chickamauga. In truth, it was *these* foot soldiers who changed the history of the battle.

In the Confederate States Army, the term "foot soldier" had a special meaning, as about a third of the CSA men were usually without shoes on any given day during the war. The modern day visitor to the Chickamauga National Military Park is invited to consider that fact during a walk through the area where Gracie's men spent the night of September 18–19.

One of those individual foot soldiers was Henry Hilliard Hines of Alabama, a private in Company F of the 1st Battalion of Hilliard's Legion. Hines officially mustered in and enrolled on May 14, 1862, at Evergreen, Alabama. He enlisted for a three-year hitch in Captain Nicholas Stallworth's company. During the summer of 1862, Hines' service record shows him sick and in an Atlanta hospital. Hines returned to his unit in time for the next pay period and was active when his unit arrived at Chickamauga. Hines never achieved a greater rank than that of private. He was typical of men of his era: A farmer, he stood five feet, six inches tall, had gray eyes and light-colored hair. He was about 20 years old when he enlisted. He was born near the Burnt Corn settlement in southern Alabama. Hines was not married when he went to war.

The Civil War was the single biggest political, military and social event in the history of the United States and Hines was one of the millions of Americans who somehow participated in that event. Not all participants in the struggle were soldiers or sailors. Some were farmers, like the family and friends Hines left behind when he joined the Confederate States Army. Farmers and ranchers on both sides, those who stayed behind when the call to fight went out, grew the food and other crops that fed the armies and the rest of the country. Some farmers and ranchers found themselves in the way of the war and lost everything. Factory workers, carpenters and railroad men built the means to wage war: the guns and ammunition, the horse-pulled wagons, the trains and train rails. Other workers created ways to measure the cost of war, such as by making tombstones.

And, of course, it took politicians to decide to go to war in the first place.

You can't write effectively about the military aspects of a specific battle without mentioning the actions of large units and decisions made by the commanders of those units. After all, those decisions place the common soldier in history's line of fire. In Hines' case, those decisions also placed him in the *Yankees'* line of fire. Some of those decisions will be considered in these pages.

This narrative covers the three days of the battle of Chickamauga and their impact on the life of men like Henry Hines, September 18–20, 1863. They were three unforgettable days.

3

Chasing the Confederates
Out of Tennessee

The Union Army had been trying to kick the Confederate Army of Tennessee out of eastern Tennessee since late in 1862. In the weeks leading up to the fight at Chickamauga, the Union target was the Southerners' railroad center in Chattanooga. If the Federals could take Chattanooga out of the already flawed railroad system that was the lifeblood of the Confederacy, then the rebel army would be in deeper trouble than it already swam in.

The Battle of Stones River represented the first Union attempt to take control of the region. The Union Army of the Cumberland, headed by Major General William Starke Rosecrans, traded blows with the Confederate force headed by General Braxton Bragg. Both sides claimed victory but nothing was really decided. Bragg's Southern army lost about 10,000 men at Stones River, men not easily replaced. Rosecrans' force suffered casualties, too, or the Federals would not have left the battlefield. But the Union armies had a deeper pool of resources than did the Confederates and Rosecrans could more readily replace losses than could his rebel counterpart.[1]

That ability to make good on losses probably contributed to the ensuing game of feint and dodge between the two commanders. When summer came and Rosecrans marched again, Bragg was out-maneuvered and forced to abandon Murfreesboro, Tennessee. The same thing happened when Rosecrans threatened Tullahoma, Tennessee. Rosecrans was winning without cost and steadily marching closer to Chattanooga as he did so. After Tullahoma, Bragg's army fell back to defend Chattanooga. Rosecrans' Army of the Cumberland got across the Tennessee River by September 5, 1863, and threatened to move far enough south and east to block a potential escape route for Bragg's Army of Tennessee. By moving south and east, Rosecrans also exposed the state of Georgia in general and the city of Atlanta, in particular, to invasion. Rosecrans forced Bragg to leave Chattanooga without a fight and the Confederates started their evacuation on September 7.

By the next day, September 8, 1863, there weren't many Confederates left in Chattanooga. The Legion, now in Gracie's Brigade, Preston's Division and Buckner's Corps, was generally to the north of Chattanooga and near the right flank of Bragg's force before Chattanooga was abandoned. By the 8th, the Legion was part of the Confederate movement to the south. Bragg had done a terrific job of saving his army while giving up virtually the entire state of Tennessee.

The Union army's movements after the capture of Chattanooga, when Rosecrans believed the Rebels were still retreating and he was chasing after them, caused parts of his army to split into differing routes as they filtered through mountain passes in the region around Chattanooga. Those pathways, or gaps, created opportunities for the Confederate force to pounce on separate segments of the Union army. General James Negley's division was the leading portion of the Union's XIV Corps and was far ahead of the remainder of that command when Rosecrans' men began chasing the Confederates. Negley was far enough in front of his corps that he inadvertently created an opportunity for Bragg and the Confederates.

McLemore's Cove is really a valley between Lookout Mountain to the west and Pigeon Mountain to the east. The Cove is roughly 20 miles south of Chattanooga. Negley's command passed through Stevens Gap to cross Lookout Mountain and penetrate eastward to a spot near the opening to Dug Gap, which leads across Pigeon Mountain. The Confederates had a numerical advantage in that area and had a chance to capture or kill Negley's entire division. Negley eventually got reinforcements from the XIV Corps, but not enough men to make up the manpower difference. Bragg had a golden opportunity to hurt Rosecrans, and he knew it.

Recognizing an opportunity is one thing. Taking advantage of an opportunity is something else. And life in the Army of Tennessee was, well, something else. Bragg's command structure was dysfunctional. Professional jealousies, personality conflicts and similar problems were rampant among Bragg's subordinates. Braxton Bragg was not a popular leader within his army. A favorite of Confederate President Jefferson Davis, Bragg was frequently unable to convince his subordinates to follow his orders, even when the plans were good ones. Such was the case of the trap Bragg hoped to spring on Negley's division at McLemore's Cove. When Confederate commanders dithered with a chance for a battlefield victory at hand, the trap Bragg wanted to spring could not be properly triggered, either on September 10 or the following day. Negley eventually figured out for himself that his command was in trouble and was able to pull his men out with time to spare.

In his outstanding essay on the McLemore's Cove incident, Steven E. Woodworth concluded that the Confederates enjoyed a three-and-a-half-to-one manpower advantage at the Cove on September 10 and still had a two-and-a-half-to-one edge after Negley's reinforcements arrived.[2]

The Legion played a supporting role at McLemore's Cove, although John Davenport wrote his wife that the Legion was very involved with the affair. In his September 30 letter, Davenport said of events at McLemore's Cove, "On Sept the 11 we was throun out rit to skirmish in McLemors Cove. We drove the enemy back to Pigen Mountain and encamped near the foot of the mountain that night."[3]

Davenport's letter makes the engagement seem like a Confederate victory when it was, in fact, a classic example of the insubordination that raged among Bragg's sub-commanders. Negley's entire command marched into a trap at McLemore's Cove, a chance Bragg recognized and wanted to take advantage of. Negley's division was enclosed by both geography and Confederates. But the door was never closed and Negley got away.

In a September 15, 1863, letter home, Bolling Hall, Jr., told his father, "We once thought we had a whole corps of over 10,000 cut off in McLemore's Cove but by bad management they escaped."[4]

Bragg's plan for an attack on Sept. 10 failed due to the extremely slow movement of his army. His renewed order for an attack on Sept. 11 called for a division from Lieutenant General Leonidas Polk's corps to attack Negley at dawn in connection with an attack by Major General Thomas C. Hindman's division. No attack happened on either day. In fact, there was very little movement on either day by the Confederates, despite the direct orders from the commanding general of the Army of Tennessee.

Polk again failed to act on September 13 when, under direct orders from Bragg, he was to attack a segment of the Union army that was to his front. Polk's force out-numbered the Union men, but Polk apparently did not feel like fighting that day. He did not attack. "Thus Bragg failed to crush the center of Rosecrans's army through the delay of his generals," wrote Massey.[5]

Bragg had requested that the Confederate government send supplemental forces to help his army. Those requests were finally answered when a part of Robert E. Lee's Army of Northern Virginia was sent to Bragg's aid under the command of Lieutenant General James Longstreet. The addition to Longstreet's force started coming to fruition when the lead elements of

Longstreet's corps arrived a few days after the McLemore's Cove failure. Longstreet's men were still arriving when the fight at Chickamauga started and Longstreet himself came on the scene on the night of September 19/20. Longstreet, as Bragg learned, brought a 12,000-man force to help the beleaguered Army of Tennessee. Rather than wait for this powerful force to complete its arrival, Bragg tried to attack on September 18.

Whether it was poor planning by Bragg, poor execution by Confederate commanders, alert soldiering by some units of Federal cavalry or a combination of all those things, Bragg's surprise attack on the 18th did not accomplish much.

General Leonidas Polk (Alabama Department of Archives and History, Montgomery, Alabama).

The perspective of time is important here. The Union victory at Gettysburg, Pennsylvania, and the fall of Vicksburg, Mississippi, had both happened in early July of 1863. New Orleans had fallen to the Federal Navy. The loss of the railhead at Chattanooga was another stunning blow to the Southern cause. Bragg hoped to reverse the loss of Chattanooga. The Battle of Chickamauga was the result of that hope.

George Washington Sexton, a private in Company D of the Legion's 1st Battalion, in Gracie's Brigade, was a diarist of unsurpassed brevity. Years after the battle, he summed up the events leading up to the fight at Chickamauga this way:

Sept. 1, 1863   Left Tennessee with Buckner's Corps and participated in the chase of the enemy in McLemore's Cove.
Sept. 15, 1863   Arrived at Lafayette, Georgia, completing a 300 mile march. Rested before giving chase.
Sept. 18, 1863   Found the enemy on the banks of the Chickamauga.[6]

Through the years, historians have debated whether Rosecrans fought needlessly at Chickamauga. A long series of bloodless maneuvers had already gained him the goal he sought, some say. There was no need to chase an army Rosecrans believed was retreating. It is legitimate fuel for debate, but the question does not serve us here. The only thing that matters here is that Rosecrans' army *did* become embroiled in the fight near Chickamauga Creek.

It was a hard time to be a foot soldier. Every soldier in every army in every era of history knows about waiting. Soldiers wait to be told what to do, wait for the proper time to do what they are told and then wait for someone to judge the quality of their work. They wait for food, wait for supplies and wait for the enemy. In the woods near Chickamauga Creek, the soldiers of Hilliard's Legion tried to sleep as they waited for daybreak.

Who were these Legion members? Many of them were farmers and most were from Alabama, but their professions and birthplaces frequently differed. Hilliard's Legion, like many military outfits of the time, was an interesting social cross-section of the people of the state of Alabama in 1862. Their ages spread across several decades but most were in their twenties. Most were single but a few were married men. The soldiers included successful professionals with everything to lose if the war was lost, and they risked everything by joining the military. There were young men just starting out in life. The oldest enlistee, the author believes, was 61-year-old Davis Whitted, a private in the 5th Battalion's Company C. Robert Craft, who was enrolled in the 5th Battalion's Company E, was 56 when he joined. Several others were as young as 15.

At the company level, the rosters frequently included multiple members of the same family. Companies were drawn from a given community. Virtually every member of the 3rd Battalion's Company F, for example, was a farmer born in Georgia who joined the Confederate Army on May 9, 1862.

If America can be called the great melting pot, then soldiering is the great melding process. Regardless of age, professional or personal background, personal habits or date of enlistment, soldiers have to learn to accept training and come to understand how to follow orders. They must act cohesively and can only learn to do so through strenuous training.

For many enlistees, this was easier said than done. There were desertions, lots of them, throughout the Confederate Army and the Legion was no exception. A portion of the desertions can, of course, be attributed to the Confederacy's inability to properly feed and clothe its soldiers. Nothing generates unhappiness in a soldier more than an empty belly and ragged clothing (see Appendix 4). Whatever the reasons, the Legion suffered from desertions.

The 3rd Battalion's Company D lost privates Burns Nibblett (age 17) and Walker Nibblett (26), who left the Army shortly after they joined. Both enlisted on May 9, 1862, and deserted five weeks later, on June 18.

George F. Owens, a Georgia-born machinist, was 30 and single when he enlisted on May 9, 1862. He deserted at Cumberland Gap on September 16, 1862. Henry M. Owens, 24 when he enlisted, was also a machinist born in Georgia; he enlisted on the same day as George Owens and also deserted at Cumberland Gap on September 16.

Some deserters served awhile before leaving their comrades in the field. Thomas C. Conron, a private in Company C of the 1st Battalion, was 22 when he enlisted. He was a bookkeeper prior to the start of hostilities. He suffered a finger wound at Chickamauga that kept him out of the battles at Knoxville and Bean's Station. He is listed as a deserter from the trenches in front of Petersburg. William G. Oliver enlisted on June 10, 1862. Another Georgia-born farmer, Oliver served in Company F of the 3rd Battalion. He was wounded at Chickamauga, is listed as sick during the battles of Knoxville and Drewry's Bluff, and then is listed as a deserter on December 22, 1863.

There were plenty of different walks of life represented on the muster rolls beyond farming. John Arnold was 24 years old and single when he enlisted and he listed his occupation as "jockey." Others were ministers, bookbinders, doctors, painters, laborers, carriage trimmers, lawyers and students.

The odds of these soldiers returning home at war's end to resume their careers were not good. The statistics for the 1st Battalion's Company D are illustrative. Keep in mind this unit eventually became Company I of the 60th Alabama Infantry Regiment, an outfit created by adding companies A, B, C and D of Hilliard's 1st Battalion to the remainder of the 3rd Battalion. As members of the 60th, the men in this company fought through the battles of Knoxville, Bean's Station and others before digging into the trenches in front of Petersburg in 1864. The 60th surrendered with Lee at Appomattox.

And yet, better than 40 percent of the original muster of 109 officers and soldiers survived the war. The Legion's 1st Battalion, Company D file belonging to the Alabama Department of Archives and History, which is available at www.ancestry.com, has a statistical breakdown of the history of the company. There were six commissioned officers and 103 enlisted men for a total of 109. Of that total, there were 65 casualties. Nine men were killed and one died of wounds for a total of 10. Disease killed 13 more. There were 31 wounded. The army discharged 26 men from the company, five were transferred and six others deserted. Two men resigned and three others retired. None were listed as disabled, captured, exchanged, escaped or died. Records are not perfect. Though the recapitulation of records shows no disabled, a muster roll from July 2, 1862, at the Federal Prisoner of War camp at Camp Mary in Ohio shows that Private J. W. Loftin, who enlisted at age 29, was "Disabled from accidental wound to the hand."

And then there was Captain Westley D. Walden, of the 2nd Battalion's B Company. Walden was 43 years of age and a successful man by the time he enlisted in 1862. He lived in the Coosa County, Alabama, town of Nixburg, which was served by the Mount Olive post office at the time. Married, widowed and married again, Walden had four children and a 900-acre farm valued at $3,950, according to the 1860 Productions of Agriculture Schedule 4 for the 2nd Subdivision of Coosa County. Walden's farm included a horse, two asses or mules, five milch [*sic*] cows and 11 other cattle, plus 30 swine. His livestock's value totaled $800. The farm also produced 10 bushels of rye and 400 bushels of Indian corn, according to page 15 of the form.

Clearly then, Walden had the means to pay a substitute to serve in the Confederate Army rather than serve in it himself. Instead, he enlisted as a captain. As will be seen, Walden suffered multiple wounds within the Federal works on the crest of Horseshoe Ridge. He died on October 10, 1863 and is buried in Nixburg.[7]

General Gracie's report after the battle stated that Walden deserved special mention.

4

September 19, 1863

Preston's report located Gracie's brigade on the night of September 18 as "established in line of battle running almost east and west, near Hunt's house and a few hundred yards north of the river."[1]

By 8 a.m. on September 19, both Kelly's and Trigg's brigades were across the Chickamauga. They passed Gracie's formation to put themselves in the more forward positions. The farmland and surrounding woods were teeming with Confederate soldiers that morning.

Preston's report after the battle is among the finest of its kind this author has read. In it, Preston wrote that his command went into battle with 4,078 officers and soldiers. Gracie's brigade made up nearly half of Preston's strength.

After meeting with other commanders in the area, Preston adjusted Gracie's position by conforming it "to the general line of battle, and moved westwardly toward the main road that runs north from La Fayette to Chattanooga. After advancing about 600 yards it arrived near a sharp curve of the Chickamauga, which impeded farther progress. I halted the command on the brow of the hill overlooking the stream and plain below."[2]

Soon some of Gracie's men were fighting the enemy. Major John D. McLennan of the 4th Battalion, Hilliard's Legion, wrote, "On Saturday, the 19th, when the brigade formed line of battle on the Chickamauga, my battalion was thrown forward as skirmishers, taking position on the bank of the river. In the evening we fired a few shots at straggling Yankees. Two are known to have been killed; 2 others were captured. We remained in this position during the night."[3]

Major John A. Aiken of the 63rd Tennessee Infantry Regiment wrote in his report that his unit was also active on the 19th. Aiken reported that,

The line established, we remained until 9 a.m. the 19th, when we were moved in column about 1 mile distant and to our left, and again formed [...] overlooking the enemy's battery. We had been formed about one hour when the enemy opened upon us with shot and shell, severely wounding 1 lieutenant and 1 man. After some time,

Gracie's Brigade crossed this field in the direction indicated on the morning of September 19, 1863. Chickamauga Creek is generally to the left of the path Gracie took (author's photograph).

and the firing from that battery had ceased, we were moved in column by a circuitous route to the right and formed 300 yards in rear of Colonel Triggs brigade, where we remained exposed to a fire of shot and shell until dark.[4]

Massey, the 1st Battalion Adjutant, wrote that some Legion members attracted the artillery fire about which Aiken wrote:

All was quiet along the Chickamauga until about eight o'clock the next morning, when some of the First Battalion while lighting their pipes started a fire in the dry leaves in our front. The smoke revealed our position and drew the shells from a battery of the enemy. They burst in our front and over our heads, doing some damage. Lieutenant Colonel Holt ordered me to detail some men to put out the fire. The men started, but hesitated when the shells came think and fast with startling explosions. I said to them, "Well, if you can't put the fire out, I will do it myself." They could not stand this reflection on their courage and promptly went with me and extinguished the fire.[5]

Shaver wrote that,

The shells of the enemy, and not unfrequently their Minnie balls, fell in our midst, dealing death in many instances. Litters were constantly passing to and fro through our line, bearing from the scene of action the wounded and the dying. The tide of battle ebbed and flowed incessantly: now there was a lull; now the sharp, continuous rattle of small arms broke upon the ear; now there came a burst of thunder-sounded, and each individual noise was lost in a tumultuous outburst of artillery.

Then the storm would subside, and an enthusiastic cheer from the victors in the charge would rend the air. During each lull, there were distinctly audible, the wails of the dying and the heart-piercing shrieks of strong men in agony. The storm and lull succeeded each other.[6]

In his report written on September 26, 1st Battalion Captain George W. Huguley wrote in simpler terms: "On the morning of the 19th, we formed line of battle near Dalton's Ford, on Chickamauga Creek. We remained in that position, with slight changes, during the day, occasionally being shelled from the enemy's batteries, but without any loss."[7]

Other units were not so lucky. Preston wrote, "I lost a commissioned officer killed and a few men of the Sixth Florida, with Lieutenant Lane and others, of the Sixty-third Tennessee, wounded.... My troops remained in ranks ... patiently enduring the fire."[8]

Shaver continued in his book, "There was silence in the ranks. Each heart had its own burden. At any moment the command 'forward' might be given; and though nerved for the contest, and anxious to strike for our country, we realized the fact, that death was present."

The reader is invited to imagine the Lafayette Road as a straight line, with Gracie's command near the close end of the straight line and to its right. Major General Alexander P. Stewart's three-brigade division was immediately north of Gracie's men and the commands of Brigadier General Bushrod R. Johnson and Brigadier General Evander Law were still further north, parallel to and about 1,000 yards east of Lafayette Road. Directly behind Preston's and Stewart's divisions, its left flank very close to Dalton's Ford, was the division of Major General Benjamin F. Cheatham.

Preston and Stewart made up Buckner's corps while Johnson and Law were part of John Bell Hood's corps.

By mid-morning of the 19th, Braxton Bragg had a fluid and developing situation on his hands and he sent Cheatham's large force north to aid with the fighting generally along the Brotherton Road. The area of concern was roughly 2,500 yards due north of Cheatham's location and Cheatham's force was in perfect position, with no Confederate units between it and the problem spot, to march toward the shooting. Sometime after 11 a.m., Cheatham's men marched north.

The wooded and farming areas behind Preston and Stewart were destined to become field hospitals and, with the meandering Chickamauga to contend with, many of the Confederate wounded had to walk or be carried through the area where the reserve units waited. Water was an important asset to a Civil War–like hospital and the creek made an excellent source.

At about noon on the 19th, Major General Buckner ordered Preston to shift his command about half a mile to the north. Kelly and Trigg also shifted, placing Trigg closest to the enemy and Kelly behind Gracie.[9]

The area where most of Gracie's brigade was located during this time is marked by several markers and a cannon today. There is a narrow footpath that leads to the indicators. There is also a steep path which leads 100 yards or so down to the banks of the Chickamauga. The location is quiet nowadays and is a little way off a much larger trail. It is heavily wooded and probably not often visited. It is easy to let one's imagination picture a large, orderly military unit clad in ragged gray, waiting for the call to duty.

Mostly, here was more waiting for the Legion, with the added evidence of the price of battle. The few additional commands that *were* given the men of the Legion during the 19th were to step "double-quick" to the right or to the left, according to Shaver's account. Small movements notwithstanding, the men of the Legion and Gracie's other men remained in this position for the rest of the 19th.

From the north, the Legion's soldiers heard the caustic sounds of battle that Shaver wrote about. Cheatham's men, and those of Law and Johnson, were a part of the heavy work of driving the Yankees out of the Brock field, toward Brotherton Road to the north and back toward Lafayette Road to the west.

During the afternoon, Trigg's Brigade became the next of Preston's Division to be in position to go to the fighting.[10] From its position between

The location where Gracie's Brigade spent most of the day and night of September 19, 1863 (author's photograph).

the Park farm and the Viniard field, Trigg's brigade was probably a bit less than 600 yards from the enemy, and Trigg's men exchanged shots in a long-range duel with the Federals in the Viniard field.

By 3:45 p.m., Trigg's men had moved up to the edge of the woods on the eastern side of the Viniard field and were attacked by an oblique angled Union force that was aimed toward the north and east. The Federals' angle of orientation gave Trigg's soldiers a devastating opportunity and the southerners from Florida and Virginia took advantage of the chance presented them.

The Union men who were able to do so retreated. One of Trigg's regiments, the 6th Florida, chased the retreating Federals, then were turned back themselves when the 100th Illinois turned back and fired.

By the end of the day, Viniard's field was a no-man's land.

A few hundred yards north, the armies kept shooting at each other, even after dark. The Confederates missed a chance for a big breakthrough after dark when a group of Federals was routed and the rebels did not pursue. But finally, the heavy shooting ended with the Confederate forces generally holding positions in advance of where they had been in the morning.

During Civil War battles, the fighting normally ended around the time darkness came to the battlefield. Things could be confusing enough when the sun was up, but when the sun was down nothing was certain. The Confederacy lost one of its most capable soldiers when General Thomas "Stonewall" Jackson was shot by friendly fire after dark at Chancellorsville four months before the battle of Chickamauga.

If the shooting on September 19 mostly stopped in the dark, it was far from quiet in the area where Gracie's men were staged. Again, from Preston's report:

> Night coming on Trigg bivouacked in the woodland near the edge of the cornfield, while Gracie and Kelly occupied a position in front of a little hut near which Major-General Buckner had established his headquarters.... During the night Gracie's and Kelly's brigades were vigorously engaged in constructing defenses to strengthen the left, and in the morning Williams' and Leyden's battalions of artillery were supported by my infantry under cover of good field entrenchments.[11]

According to letters written by General Gracie's son, Archibald IV, more than 40 years after the war, the defenses constructed during the night of the 19th were built by a group of 50 to 100 privates, four noncommissioned officers and two commissioned officers. The privates, at least, came from both Gracie's and Kelly's brigades. These men were detailed to what Lieutenant John W. A. Sanford of the Legion's 3rd Battalion termed "fatigue duty" and directed to create defensive breastworks and the like. Gracie IV's March 20, 1908, letter to E.F. Comegys, who served in Company I of the 43rd Alabama, says the "fatigue duty" soldiers came from every regiment and battalion in Gracie's command.

Brigadier General Bushrod R. Johnson commanded a division that operated within a short distance of Preston's. He wrote in his report, "[f]inding my line now ... quite irregular in its formation, I proceeded immediately to reform it in the wood about 660 yards east of the road ... by order of Major-General Hood, temporary breastworks of timber were put up along the line, behind which my command rested."[12] John B. Fuller, a private in Company D of the 3rd Battalion, wrote that the detail was assembled at 3 a.m. on the 20th to "build breastworks." Fuller wrote Gracie IV on June 17, 1905, from Fuller's home in Louisville, Kentucky. It is a remarkable letter which also describes some of the climactic moments of the fighting on Horseshoe Ridge.[13]

Sanford's report includes a note about the so-called "fatigue" detail and puts the count at 50 privates, plus the commissioned and non-commissioned officers, a total of 56 of Gracie's men for the special detail. Sanford does not specifically list which commands the men of the detail came from, and Fuller wrote that he was joined in the work by "a number of others from the Brigade." Fuller is apparently the source for Gracie IV's contentions about both the size of the detail and the idea that its members came from various units in the brigade. Gracie IV lists 3rd Battalion members Fuller and W. C. Athey as members of the detail, which seems to have been under the direct command of Lieutenant David Hughes of the 43rd Alabama Regiment's Company F. With Hughes in command, it seems likely that soldiers from his regiment, the 43rd, were included in the detail. Fuller's letter mentions a Lieutenant Owen as assisting Hughes in command of the detail. This might have been William T. Owens, who was originally a first sergeant in Company B of the 3rd Battalion and was promoted to second lieutenant during the war.

Eventually, this "fatigue duty" command went to the fighting with the 6th Florida Regiment, which was part of Trigg's division, but the timing is a little confusing. More on this matter later.

As fate would have it, the Hughes Detail was building defenses in support of a group of former members of the original Hilliard's Legion. The reader will recall that R. F. Kolb's Battery was split away from the Legion shortly after the Legion was formed and that Kolb's men went to Chickamauga as members of the Reserve Corps Artillery. The Williams command mentioned in the quote above from Preston's report is the same Major Samuel C. Williams mentioned in the second chapter.[14]

The fighting was over for the day (the 19th), Shaver wrote, but sleep was nearly impossible for the Legion's fighting men:

All through the night a sharp fire was kept up between the pickets, and, ever and anon, the booming of a cannon, startling us in our troubled slumber, reminded of the carnage of the past day, and the coming horrors of the morrow. After nightfall, too, the shrieks and groans of the wounded, lying on the battle-field between the two lines, were more clearly heard. Add to all this the facts, that the night was cold, our supply of blankets and clothing scanty, and the orders prohibited fires and you will readily understand that "tired nature's sweet restorer, balmy sleep," visited but few eyelids in the Legion, for any length of time during the night of that stirring day.[15]

Reportedly, the temperature dipped into the 30s overnight as Sergeant Horace McLean, a quartermaster in Company B of the Legion's 2nd Battalion, noted in a letter home to his wife. McLean wrote, "I had like to forgot to write about sleeping on the battle field two nights and that in the [unclear word] of the wounded both of the enemy and our men that could not be taken off the field before night. The nights were quite cold and frosty and the wounded lay and hallowed and groaned all night long. The most horable fritful groans that I ever heard."[16]

Massey also recalled that cold night: "We had been forbidden to kindle any fires. We had nothing to eat except cold beef and tough biscuits made of flour and water three days before."[17]

Few letters written home by soldiers after a major engagement during the American Civil War fail to mention the sounds of the wounded as they lay on the battlefield. The soldiers injured so badly as to be unable to make their way back to the safety and aid of their own lines could do nothing but moan or call out in the dark for help. They often called for water. The experience of being unable to go to the service of wounded comrades marked every soldier who went through it.

Davenport wrote home in his September 30 letter, "But the crye of the wounded was anuf to melt the heart of the most hard foragers hart. I could not sleepe for lisning to ther pitiful crye and mornes for too nights. I was glad when we moved off the Battlefieald so I could not hear them."[18]

Shaver mentioned longing for his loved ones back home and thoughts of "deep solicitude for the issue of the severe struggle pending in their immediate front that the men of the Legion passed the 19th of September, 1863."[19]

The common foot soldiers in Hilliard's Legion and the remainder of Gracie's Brigade had an appointment with history the next day, but they did not know that as they waited for sleep to come on the night of September 19/20 in a wooded area near Chickamauga Creek. The waiting was almost over.

5

Hurry Up and Wait

The common soldiers were not the only men who found sleep elusive deep into the Chickamauga night of September 19/20. The commanders of both the Federal and Confederate armies were consulting with their divisional and corps commanders about the plans for the following day.

Rosecrans met with his key subordinates all at one time and set the plans clearly. The quality of the Union leader's planning and the execution of the battle plan might be called into question by historians. Most Civil War commanders have had their planning and battlefield decisions questioned in the years since the war. But every one of Rosecrans' senior commanders knew and understood his responsibility for the following day. Rosecrans' behavior on September 20 can be questioned, as we will see, but his activities the night before were to his credit.

Things were more complicated for CSA commander Braxton Bragg. Much of his force was still arriving late that night. He could not meet with generals who were not yet on the field. Bragg met with his commanders and depended upon their professionalism to spread the plan to *their* subordinates. Bragg appointed Longstreet, who had yet to arrive, as the commander of the Confederate left wing on the night of September 19/20 and placed Lieutenant General Leonidas Polk in command of the right wing. Polk had already been one of Bragg's commanders.

Bragg's report states that,

Upon the close of the engagement on the evening of the 19th, the proper commanders were summoned to my camp fire, and there received specific information and instructions touching the dispositions of the troops and for the operations of the next morning. The whole force was divided for the next morning into two commands and assigned to the two senior lieutenant-generals, Longstreet and Polk—the former to the left, where all his own troops were stationed, the latter continuing his command of the right. Lieutenant-General Longstreet reached my headquarters about 11 p.m., and immediately received his instructions. After a few hours' rest ... he moved at daylight to his line, just in front of my position.[1]

In his report, Longstreet wrote about his delayed arrival at Bragg's headquarters and the subsequent meeting with the commanding general:

> Our train reached Catoosa Platform, near Ringgold, about 2 o'clock in the afternoon of September 19. As soon as our horses came up [about 4 o'clock], I started with Colonels Sorrel and Manning, of my staff, to find the headquarters of the commanding general. We missed our way and did not report till near 11 o'clock at night. Upon my arrival, I was informed that the troops had been engaged during the day in severe skirmishing while endeavoring to get in line for battle. The commanding general gave me a map showing the roads and streams between Lookout Mountain and the Chickamauga River, and a general description of our position, and informed me that the battle was ordered at daylight the next morning, the action to be brought on upon our right and to be taken up successively to the left, the general movement to be a wheel upon my extreme left as a pivot. I was assigned to the command of the Left Wing, composed of Hood's and Hindman's divisions, an improvised division under Brig. General B. R. Johnson, and Buckner's corps, consisting of Stewart's and Preston's divisions.[2]

Bragg's decision to alter his command structure overnight in the midst of a major engagement has been discussed by historians through the years. It was an unusual move. Bragg has been criticized for the decision. But was it uncalled for? The reader is encouraged to consider the following points:

- Polk was put in command of the right wing, where he had already been in command. No change there.
- What else could Bragg do with Longstreet? He had to be in command somewhere.

The Confederate army had many fine commanders with West Point training who served the Southern effort well. Archibald Gracie was one, as were Robert E. Lee and many others. But the Confederate States Army was also populated with a number of other officers who frequently dithered when they should have followed orders. The reader will recall what happened at McLemore's Cove. Delays or inattention to orders on the battlefield can be as costly as poor planning. The Confederate attack was supposed to have started shortly after sunrise, but it did not. Command-level dithering froze the Army of Tennessee in its tracks again. General Leonidas Polk's assignment was to attack at dawn and he did not. There is an explanation, of course, and arguments can be made about where the finger of blame might be pointed between Polk and his subcommanders. But where the finger might point is immaterial and the bottom line is that the attack was not launched by the right wing of the Confederate Army.

Historians have at times blamed Longstreet's delayed start on July 2 at Gettysburg for the loss there (ironically, Longstreet was on the right at Gettysburg). But both Bragg and Longstreet wrote in their reports after Chickamauga that Longstreet was up around dawn to get a feel for the battlefield where he commanded but which he had never seen.[3]

Massey wrote that Gracie used Longstreet's presence as a rallying point for his brigade. The 1st Battalion's Adjutant wrote in his *Reminiscences* that Gracie rode along the line of his men shortly after sunrise and called to his troops, "Alabamians, you will be led in battle to-day by General Longstreet. Show yourselves worthy of your native state." Massey wrote that Gracie's men, who included a regiment from Tennessee, cheered Gracie's words.[4]

Whether Braxton Bragg was an astute military professional or the miserable failure to be expected from a political favorite is a discussion for a different time. What is clear is that Bragg was not well served by Leonidas Polk and Polk knew better. The result was a stalled Confederate Army. And as the Confederates wasted time, the Federals gained time to prepare. How much all this mattered to the Alabamians of Hilliard's Legion is open to question, but it certainly did not help them any. Sometime between the end of fighting on September 19 and the delayed resumption of combat on September 20, the Federals, stationed along a ridge that wiggled along a southeast-northwest axis near the Snodgrass family farm, threw together an informal series of log and fence rail breastworks. The rough defensive barriers were hastily muscled into place on the edge of the heights, looking downhill and toward the south. Numerous sources recalled hearing trees being chopped down during the night and Massey wrote that the barriers were between two and three feet tall.

This was Horseshoe Ridge.

Interestingly, Gracie now stood in support of a veritable all-star team of Confederate commanders. Longstreet's presence has been discussed above. John Bell Hood ran the show in the center of Longstreet's line and Lafayette McLaws was also on the way. There were all-stars on the opposing side as well. Major General George H. Thomas was hours away from earning the nickname he'd carry through the remainder of his life: The Rock of Chickamauga.[5]

According to Lieutenant Colonel J. W. Bishop of the 2nd Minnesota Infantry Regiment, "The sun rose clear and soon dissipated the lazy mist that had settled over the field during the night" on the morning of the 20th.[6]

The Legion had been generally stagnant on September 19, but early in the morning of the 20th, the brigades of both Gracie and Kelly moved. By 6:30 a.m., Gracie's line had anchored its southern (left) end very near the bend in the Chickamauga, pointing due north a short piece and then turning northeast before its right end reached the Park farm. Kelly's line started at the Park farm and pointed a bit west of north until just before the end, where it was bent east as a defensive posture.

The change put the two commands in position to march to the support of the rest of the Confederate fighters and left them as the southernmost Confederate units on the battlefield. The only Confederate soldiers south of Gracie's brigade now were the doctors, orderlies and wounded in the battlefield hospitals, plus the fatigue detail.

But it was another case of hurry up and wait. The two brigades stayed in their new positions for six more hours. Finally, at about 12:30 p.m., the

Modern day Lafayette Road, facing north from modern day Viniard-Alexander Road. Gracie's and Kelly's commands walked roughly a mile north from here before stopping at a staging area along the road (author's photograph).

orders came to move out. Gracie's men led Kelly's as the brigades marched north along Lafayette Road. Shaver wrote about the Legion's march toward the sound of the guns:

> Until about 3½ p.m. the Legion advanced with the advancing army, encountering a constant stream of wounded, who bore witness to the sharpness of the conflict, and also to the cheering fact that the Confederate flag was being borne onward in triumph.... On all sides, they viewed "with shuddering horror pale, and eyes aghast," heaps of silent slain—friend and foe, man and beast, in one promiscuous slumber![7]

Remember the Lafayette Road and straight line the reader envisioned on a piece of paper earlier? The Legion and the rest of Gracie's Brigade now marched toward the north end of that same line. Both Gracie and Kelly marched in lines perpendicular to the direction of the road. The

The spot along the Lafayette Road where Gracie's Brigade stopped prior to its march toward Horseshoe Ridge, facing north. While here, the Brigade came under light artillery fire. This location is a few hundred yards north of the Brotherton cabin and Brotherton Road, where Kelly's Brigade stopped (author's photograph).

brigades marched for more than a mile before stopping between 3 and 4 p.m. Gracie's men stopped in an area next to the Lafayette Road and between the Brotherton cabin (to the south) and the Poe cabin (north), facing north. Kelly's men were just behind Gracie's.

The 63rd Tennessee's Aiken described the movement thusly: "We were marched by the right flank into and along the Chattanooga road in the direction of heavy musketry and artillery firing when we again formed in line of battle to the right of the road, where we remained for about one hour."[8] The approximate location where the brigades stopped is marked today by a plaque on the west side of the roadway. The same marker relates that in this location, the brigades came under artillery fire from Union cannons situated in the Kelly Field.

A short distance south, part of Trigg's Brigade was supporting a Confederate artillery unit at the Brotherton cabin. Remember that, up to this time, Trigg's Brigade was the only unit in Preston's Division, the majority of which had seen serious combat since the division crossed the Chickamauga. As a whole, the division was rested and ready. This time the soldiers did not have to wait long. At about 4 p.m. Gracie's men, and Kelly's, were ordered to move out. They were headed for Snodgrass Hill and Horseshoe Ridge.

6

Horseshoe Ridge

Horseshoe Ridge is well named because it is shaped like a set of horse-shoes sitting side by side. There are three hills. Hill 3 of the ridge is furthest to the west, at the Legion's left as it marched toward battle. Hill 2, the tallest of the three, is the point in the middle, and Hill 1 is the furthest right. The hills are quite steep to walk up and there are more trees on them now than back in 1863. The Snodgrass cabin was a little more than 200 yards north and east of Hill 1 on the ridge, and the Snodgrass field was further right from the cabin. The Snodgrass family grew corn in the field that year, which the Federal army augmented with artillery pieces during the battle. The trees on the steep sides of the ridge in the modern day are much thicker than in 1863, and there is much more undergrowth now. At the time of the battle, farm animals and wild animals munched upon the plant life and kept the growth down so that the trees formed a canopy at the taller levels. It was much easier to see in the wooded areas in those days than now.

Easier to see, that is, when thick layers of smoke from artillery pieces and small arms fire did not fog the woods and limit vision. The Horseshoe Ridge area had been under attack for several hours by the time the Gracie, Kelly and Trigg battalions were called to action, with smoke severely ham-pering the gunmen on both sides. Today's peacetime views from above or at the base of the ridge are not much better than what the men of the Legion faced on September 20, 1863, except that today's trees would have offered some protection for the attacking Confederates as the Union rifle-men fired at them.[1]

The morning of September 20 generally went well for the Confeder-ates, despite the late start. They gained ground, although they paid a bloody price for every yard. About the time Preston's Division began mak-ing its way up Lafayette Road away from the creek, the Confederate attacks had started herding the western-most Federals toward the direction of

Snodgrass Hill and Horseshoe Ridge. A Federal mistake had opened a large gap in the Union line, just about the time Longstreet's front advanced. The resulting flood of Confederates into Union territory changed everything for Rosecrans. The commanding general of the Army of the Cumberland eventually panicked, left the area and headed for Chattanooga, following the big southern breakthrough in front of his position. Other Federal leaders were leaving the field as well, taking their soldiers and supplies with them.

At about that time, around 12:30 p.m., rebel General John B. Hood was wounded as he sat on his horse a few strides inside a wooded area adjacent to Dyer Field. The wound was severe, shattering his right femur, and marking the second time Hood was badly hurt in six weeks. He would eventually have the leg amputated. Not content with his service, Hood would return to active duty months later. It took a while for word to filter through to James Longstreet that Hood was out of the fighting. As a result, there was some confusion and disagreement among some of the Confederate commanders where Hood had been in charge.

By 12:45, the rebel division of Brigadier General Joseph Kershaw had gained the northern end of the Dyer field and was climbing up a hill toward a wooded area. Kershaw's division, which had been at Gettysburg, still numbered about 1,500 men. The division moved within about 100 yards of the Union force at the north end of the field, just inside the woods, and opened fire.[2] The Federal soldiers in Colonel Charles G. Harker's 3rd Brigade (of the Union's 1st Division and XXI Corps) were a few yards away from the modern day monument to South Carolina soldiers. By 1:15 p.m., Harker's command had fled behind the Federal artillery in Snodgrass field and Kershaw's men were attacking the Union positions atop Horseshoe Ridge. Kershaw's men were stopped and driven back, but this attempt to scale the hills was mostly a continuation of their chase of Harker's men.[3]

A word about the Federal line atop Horseshoe Ridge is appropriate here. We narrowly define Horseshoe Ridge to include Hills 1, 2 and 3 as shown on most maps of the battle because that specific explanation deals more clearly with the actions and struggles of Hilliard's Legion. With our narrow focus upon that area, we know which Union units faced the Confederate efforts on those hills. However, it will become important later to understand that the ridge continues in a westerly direction from the area of Hill 3. As the ridge is aligned more or less in a straight direction at that point, it is really not a horseshoe formation anymore. Events west of Hill 3 had an impact on the fighting in the Horseshoe area, as will be seen.

The ridge also extends better than 200 yards east of Hill 1 and the Legion was heavily involved on the slope of that extension.

As Kershaw's Division rushed up the hills for the first time at about 1:30 p.m., it was confronted by the 21st Ohio spread between Hills 3 and 2, the fragmented remains of three regiments (14th Ohio, 4th Kentucky and 10th Kentucky) on Hill 2, and a collection of other units spread along the top and to the Union left of Hill 1: Walker's Brigade, the 19th Illinois, the 11th Michigan, and the remnants of the 53rd Ohio, 17th Ohio and 58th Indiana.

Kershaw's men tried again at about 1:45 p.m. and they were joined by the soldiers of the 15th Alabama, commanded by Colonel William C. Oates. This was the same regiment that had tried so valiantly to push the men of the 20th Maine off the Union left at Little Round Top during the battle of Gettysburg roughly 10 weeks earlier. This latest rebel attack was repulsed by the Federals along the crest of Horseshoe Ridge. Oates simply never had any luck with uphill attacks.

The Confederates had additional forces on their own left, to the left of Hill 3, and an attack there failed at about the same time that Kershaw's rush at the ridge failed. Two divisions of Tennesseans fought over the crest of the ridge a little less than a quarter mile west of Hill 3.

This was a little after 2 p.m. A Union counterattack drove the Tennessee men back down the face of the hill. But the pulling back by the Tennessee fighters did not change the fact that they had reached the crest and made trouble while they were there.

Union Brigadier General James B. Steedman directed a counterattack at the Confederate left, where Brigadier General Bushrod Johnson was in command. Steedman restored order along his line by about 2:30 p.m., but by then things were happening to the east, along Hills 1, 2 and 3.

Kershaw attacked again, but this time more Federal units, flush with ammunition, had rushed to the Union line on Hill 2. The ridge was now defended by the same units listed above as defenders in the first attack, along with (from west to east) the 35th Ohio, 2nd Minnesota, 87th Indiana and 9th Ohio.

Kershaw's far right nearly took part of Hill 1. The 7th South Carolina regiment reached the breastworks thrown together earlier in the day and planted the regimental flag in front of the defenders. But the 7th was driven back, as were the rest of the exhausted men in Kershaw's command.

One of the great combat stories of the Civil War comes from that particular South Carolinian rush toward the summit of the ridge. The

Confederates' regimental flag bearer was wounded as the Federals regrouped to repulse the Confederate charge. Struggling with a mortal wound but concerned about the safety of the regimental colors, the flag bearer, a man named Alfred D. Clark, jerked the flagpole from the earth and tossed it back over his head to the protection of his comrades below. Then Clark died. The drive up the side of the ridge by the 7th South Carolina would become a confusing point for historians for reasons to be made clear.[4]

The large Confederate force to the left of Kershaw's men moved ahead again against Steedman's line between 3 and 3:30 p.m. That attack also failed. Kershaw's men were fought out. Three attempts against a well-defended position atop a steep slope was enough to drain the attacking soldiers of energy and resulted in high combat losses. Kershaw's Brigade suffered 504 men killed, wounded and missing out of an original complement of 1,591.

It was at this time, about 4 p.m., that Hilliard's Legion and the other two regiments of Gracie's Brigade, a part of Preston's Division, moved toward Horseshoe Ridge.

7

Another Uncoordinated Confederate Attack

Longstreet, as left wing commander, delayed the use of Preston's Division, explaining in his post-action report:

> About 3 o'clock in the afternoon I asked the commanding general (Bragg) for some of the troops of the Right Wing, but was informed by him that they had been beaten back so badly that they could be of no service to me. I had but one division that had not been engaged (Preston's), and hesitated to venture to put it in.... I therefore concluded to hold Preston for the time, and urge on to renewed efforts our brave men, who had already been engaged many hours.[1]

At 4 p.m., Preston's Division was ordered into the fight.

It is interesting to note that in his 1896 book *From Manassas to Appomattox, Memoirs of the Civil War in America*, Longstreet said he proposed to Bragg a sweeping movement by Preston's Division that could have encircled the Federal lines during the early afternoon. Longstreet said in his *Memoirs* that the movement proposed would leave open other attacking possibilities as well. But in his report, which was written shortly after the battle, Longstreet puts the same conversation as happening in the morning of September 21.[2]

In his terrific essay "Bull in the Woods? James Longstreet at Chickamauga," William G. Robertson, Director of the Combat Studies Institute and a Command Historian, U.S. Army Combined Arms Center, wrote that Longstreet, the commander of the Confederate left wing on September 20 at Chickamauga, had three options for the use of the Preston's Division. Two of the options were flanking maneuvers and the third was the choice taken.[3]

Longstreet, who had experienced the costly failure from Robert E. Lee's decision to mount a frontal assault on the final day at Gettysburg just six weeks earlier, might have considered another option at Chickamauga. Longstreet's report made no mention of options he considered for the employment of Preston's Division in the mid-afternoon hours of September 20, after his meeting with Bragg. His main consideration seems to have been the importance of removing the Yankees from the top of Horseshoe Ridge. Whatever options Longstreet pondered before Preston's Division was committed to the fighting at Horseshoe Ridge were erased. Preston's Division, including Gracie's Brigade and Hilliard's Legion, was sent toward the Ridge.

"The heights extending from the Vidito house across to the Snodgrass house gave the enemy strong ground upon which to rally," Longstreet wrote in his after-action report.

> Here he gathered most of his broken forces and re-enforced them. After a long and bloody struggle, Johnson and Hindman gained the heights near the Crawfish Spring road. Kershaw made a most handsome attack upon the heights at the Snodgrass house simultaneously with [Brigadier General Bushrod] Johnson and [Major General Thomas] Hindman, but was not strong enough for the work.

Longstreet continued,

> It was evident that with this position gained I should be complete master of the field. I therefore ordered General Buckner to move Preston forward. Before this, however, General Buckner had established a battery of 12 guns, raking down the enemy's line which opposed our Right Wing, and at the same time having fine play upon any force that might attempt to re-enforce the hill that he was about to attack. General Stewart, of his corps, was also ordered to move against any such force in flank. The combination was well-timed and arranged.[4]

We have already observed at the end of the second chapter that decisions by commanders in charge of large units eventually have an impact on the individual foot soldier. Such was the case for the Confederate soldiers of Hilliard's Legion. Instead of a flanking maneuver, which might have bagged a tremendous number of Federal prisoners and could have invited Rosecrans to consider abandoning Chattanooga, Longstreet and Bragg sent the men of Hilliard's Legion toward another bludgeoning attack upon the Federals on Horseshoe Ridge, continuing the afternoon-long struggle there.

Gracie's men spent the first hours of the day listening to the sounds of battle. The shots, shouts and cannon blasts were all around them. We know from Shaver's colorful account, among others, that there were incoming artillery shells and the occasional Minie ball that zinged through the ranks as well. Then came the order to move toward the sounds of the fighting. By 4 p.m., Gracie's was the northernmost brigade of Preston's Division, still stationed along Lafayette Road between the Brotherton and Poe cabins. Kelly's Brigade was a short distance down Lafayette Road to the south, near Brotherton's cabin. Trigg's Brigade was further south, near Viniard's field, and was giving infantry support to Williams' Reserve Corps Artillery, the group of big guns that included Kolb's Battery.[5]

During their march up Lafayette Road, Gracie's line straddled the road in a straight perpendicular line. The brigade stopped at the spot between the Brotherton and Poe cabins in the same formation. Now Gracie's men basically turned left and walked single file through some woods until they reached the Dyer Field of open farm land.

In the Dyer Field, Gracie's Brigade stopped and turned right face. The brigade was now looking at the hills and trees of Horseshoe Ridge. Standing

The approximate location where Gracie's Brigade came out of the woods and saw Horseshoe Ridge for the first time. The modern day South Carolina monument and other markers top the first hill the Confederates climbed before stepping into a dip in the hill and then climbing again toward the Union defenders (author's photograph).

roughly shoulder to shoulder and facing approximately to the northeast, the brigade marched forward, toward the sound of the guns. The Gracie and Kelly brigades walked about 1,500 yards from the Lafayette Road to the battle zone. They marched north through the field. Gracie's left-most soldiers eventually walked up a fairly steep hill at the north end of the field before leaving the clear area. The right flank had a more gradual grade to move over. The entire brigade eventually disappeared into the trees.[6]

Aitken, of the 63rd Tennessee, described the march toward combat this way: "the command 'left face' was given and we marched at double-quick across the Chattanooga road west about one-half mile, when we were thrown into column of companies and then into line on the right of the brigade and near the left of Barksdale's [Humphrey's] (Mississippi) brigade, and on the right slope of the hill occupied by the enemy. The line was formed under a heavy fire of musketry."[7]

Trigg's command had a longer distance to cover. After crossing Lafayette Road, these men walked through some woods before coming into the south end of Dyer Field, a bit east of the Tan Yard and a few hundred yards west of Brotherton's cabin. This group was headed to the Confederate left side of Hill 3 for another attack on Steedman's line.

The Gracie and Kelly commands reached their destinations first. Preston wrote in his report that he formed Gracie's line of battle with Gracie's left wing resting near a tall tree on the summit of the hill near the edge of the field. Then fate and a new piece of poor battlefield leadership upset Preston's plan, as Preston wrote in his report:

> While engaged in bringing Kelly into position, Gracie's brigade disappeared in the wood, advancing against the battery hill. I ordered Captain Blackburn, my volunteer aide-de-camp, to follow and ascertain from General Gracie by what authority he had moved. General Gracie replied that he had been ordered to advance by Brigadier-General Kershaw, who was in the ravine just beyond the field. The movement was slightly premature, as Kelly was not formed, but I at once ordered his brigade forward, and sent Captain Blackburn to direct him to oblique to the right again, so as to press toward the slope of the hill in the rear while Gracie was attacking in front. The enemy had kept up a rapid artillery fire from the hill and across the field, but Gracie, passing through Kershaw's ranks, which were halted in the first ravine beyond the field, dashed over the ridge beyond and into the hollow between it and the battery hill.[8]

The result was another uncoordinated Confederate attack.

Here again we can pause to wonder about the decisions and actions of ranking officers and the results of those actions upon the individual foot soldiers. Kershaw's regiments had spent most of the afternoon chasing the Federals and then battering themselves against the informal but fixed defenses atop the three hills of Horseshoe Ridge. The attacks were costly and exhausting. Gifted with fresh troops to continue the attack, he ordered Gracie forward.

Kershaw's version of the event places himself in charge of Preston's men. He wrote:

> About 4 o'clock Gracie's and Kelly's brigades came up **and reported to me.** I directed them, the former to form on my rear and the latter to form on Gracie's left. General Hindman informed me that he was about to attack on Anderson's left, well on the right flank of the enemy, with two brigades of infantry with artillery. Soon after he opened heavily in that direction, but sent me word the attack was likely to fail unless a demonstration was made along the front. I determined on an attack, combining all our forces; McNair's brigade, which had come up, on my right, Gracie's, Kelley's, Anderson's, my own, Eighth, Fifteenth, and Second Regiments participating.[9] (The emphasis is the author's.)

Gracie's report also indicates that he reported to Kershaw and was told to move forward. Based upon all available reports, it seems likely that Gracie's was the only brigade not already attacking the ridge that was moving forward at that moment. Certainly, Preston's report indicates that he, Preston, was in the process of putting Kelly's men in place to launch the attack when Gracie's men started moving. What impact this miscue had on the men of Hilliard's Legion is open to conjecture. A coordinated attack, such as that planned by Preston, would have meant more Confederate soldiers aimed at the Union-held crest of the ridge at one time and would have allowed for companies, battalions and brigades to protect each other. Union defenders would have had more wide-spread targets and might have been unable to bring so many guns to bear on the Legion when Gracie's men came into view. The left side of Gracie's Brigade was uncovered without Kelly's Brigade in place.

Here, Gracie himself could have made a difference. Had he conferred with his own commanding officer, Preston, before following Kershaw's order to march forward, Gracie could have avoided some of the trouble his brigade ran into on the hillsides at Horseshoe Ridge.

As Gracie's men passed into the tree line behind and slightly to the right of the present day South Carolina Monument, they crested the hill, then walked a brief distance downhill. It was somewhere in the woods that they passed through Kershaw's bloodied soldiers. The brief downhill respite ended and the Legionnaires' paths reached a point where Gracie's men began moving up hill again. It was in the so-called saddle, the segue between the downhill and uphill directions, that Gracie's men first came under fire from the Union soldiers atop the ridge.[10]

Massey wrote, "In order to reach the breastworks where the Federals were posted we had to pass over the top of a ridge several hundred yards from their position, then go down a slope into a ravine, and up the steep side of Snodgrass Hill. The moment we appeared on this ridge we were greeted by a ferocious volley of musketry."[11]

According to the *Montgomery Weekly Advertiser*, "Having to down a hill and up another, the enemy had every advantage, they lying on top of the ridge secure and safe behind their breastworks. General Gracie, who showed himself both brave and cool, ordered a charge, and the men with a yell went forward."[12]

Gracie's Brigade headed toward both sides of Hill 1 and the area between Hills 1 and 2. Kelly's men would aim themselves at Hills 2 and 3 a short time later.

It was a noisy and confusing location. Small arms fire mixed with the deep booms of field guns blasting away in the near distance. Gunsmoke and the smoke from small fires at ground level thickened the air and clouded vision. Even as they listened to the orders from their own officers, the Legion men could hear the shouts and shrieks of the warriors from both sides as they struggled to kill each other.

Gracie's report did not specify the order in which he set his two regiments and the battalions of the Legion. But the reports of battalion commanders in the Official Records, with statements from other soldiers, lend some clues. The casualty reports also shed light on the question. The author concludes that Gracie originally organized his command in this manner: From left to right, the 43rd Alabama, the 3rd and 4th Battalions (Legion men from Alabama) aimed at positions between Hills 2 and 1. Then came the 1st and 2nd Battalions (also Legion men from Alabama) aimed at the center of Hill 1 and further right. Finally, to the far right was the 63rd Tennessee, which was supposed to be aimed at the right side of Hill 1.

Major John A. Aiken, in command of the 63rd Tennessee, wrote in his report that his regiment was on the right of the brigade as Gracie's men went under fire. Colonel Young M. Moody, commander of the 43rd Alabama Infantry Regiment, wrote in his report that his command was on Gracie's left flank when it was discovered that the 43rd overlapped the right-most unit of Kelly's Brigade. Gracie ordered Moody's men to halt briefly and wait for orders, which they did. It was almost as if the 43rd was held in reserve. A short time later the 43rd was inserted in line between the 63rd on the right and the Legion's 2nd Battalion to the left. The 1st Battalion marched between the 3rd Battalion (to the left) and the 2nd (right).

Horseshoe Ridge, Gracie's Original Plan

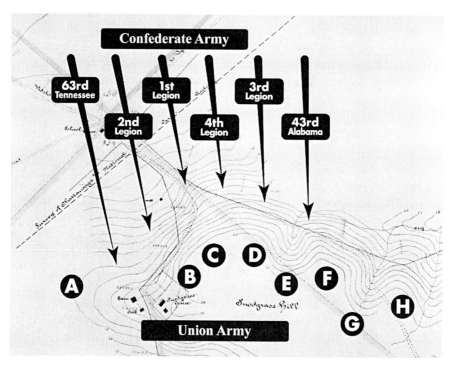

A Harker and Hazen
B 58th Indiana, 17th Ohio, 31st Ohio
C 11th Michigan
D 19th Illinois
E Walker and 9th Ohio
F 87th Indiana and 2nd Minnesota
G 35th Ohio
H 22nd Michigan and 89th Ohio

Gracie's original formation is shown here. Note the 43rd Alabama on Gracie's left (reader's right). When Preston, the Divisional Commander, aligned the brigades of Gracie and Kelly, the commands overlapped. Gracie ordered the 43rd Alabama to take a position behind the remainder of Gracie's men in order to fix the problem. Note also the intended direction of the 63rd Tennessee to Gracie's right (courtesy Teri Schott).

Charles S. Malloy, a lieutenant in Company D of the 3rd Battalion, said after the war that the Legion's 4th Battalion was to his left. Malloy, who eventually became a captain, also said the slope of the hill in the area of the ridge where his battalion ascended was at a gradual angle.[13]

Major General Buckner, the corps commander, wrote in his report that Preston's men "with great impetuosity assailed the enemy in his almost impregnable position."[14] The task at hand was a tough one. It was made more difficult by Kershaw's interference and then by the action of the 15th Alabama, which had attacked the ridge along with Kershaw's men. Now, as Gracie's men and Kelly's commands started their push toward the berm of the ridge, the 15th suddenly pulled out of its attack and retreated. This movement blocked and delayed some of Gracie's men as they moved to their assigned locations.

Major John D. McLennan, commander of the 4th Battalion, wrote in his report: "The advance commenced with spirit and determination. We

4:30 pm Horseshoe Ridge

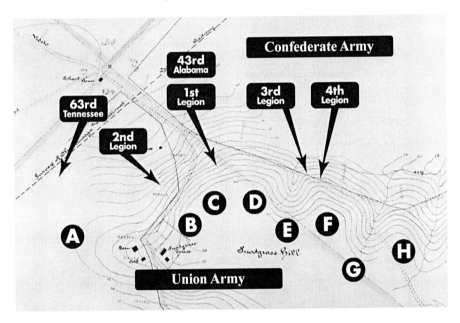

A Harker and Hazen
B 58th Indiana, 17th Ohio, 31st Ohio
C 11th Michigan
D 19th Illinois
E Walker and 9th Ohio
F 87th Indiana and 2nd Minnesota
G 35th Ohio
H 22nd Michigan and 89th Ohio

Gracie's men moved forward at about 4:30 p.m., before Kelly's Brigade was ready. Because the 43rd Alabama overlapped Kelly's right flank, Gracie repositioned the 43rd behind his line, giving the Brigade a reserve force of sorts. At this time, the four battalions of Hilliard's Legion were the only parts of Gracie's force attacking Horseshoe Ridge because the 63rd Tennessee somehow broke off from its intended course and attacked the Snodgrass cornfield (courtesy Teri Schott).

had gone but a short distance when we were ordered to lie down in order that Kershaw's brigade [probably the 15th Alabama] might retire. Being under a telling fire, the withdrawing of this brigade necessarily caused some confusion and partly broke my lines, which I could not afterward perfectly restore."[15]

Gracie wrote in his report: "Passing through Kershaw's command, the brigade found itself suddenly in the presence of the enemy, strongly posted behind breastworks of logs and rails on the crest of an opposite hill. The fury of musketry, grape, and canister immediately commenced."[16] Most of the grape and canister Gracie mentioned came from the Federal artillery in the cornfield to the right of Gracie's Brigade.

Some of the ordinance may have come from a battery atop Hill 2. In a letter he wrote in 1909, Isaac Cusac (Captain of Company G, 21st Ohio Volunteer Infantry) wrote about two pieces of Union artillery that were briefly in that location. "Soon after we had taken our position on the ridge, two pieces of artillery [sic] took position to our left … where the steel observatory west of the Snodgrass house is located," Cusac wrote. "I do not know where they belonged, but they remained but a short time, firing a few shots and then disappeared."[17]

The steel observatory Cusac wrote about was built on Hill 2 as part of the creation of the national military park. The structure is no longer in place.

Preston wrote:

> The 2nd Alabama Battalion stormed the hill and entered the entrenchments. Here an obstinate and bloody combat ensued. Brigadier-General Gracie, while bravely leading his men, had his horse shot under him. Lieutenant-Colonel Fulkerson, commanding the 63rd Tennessee; Lieutenant-Colonel Jolly, of the 43rd Alabama; Lieutenant-Colonel Holt, of the 1st Alabama Battalion, and Lieutenant-Colonel Hall, of the … 2nd Alabama Battalion, were severely wounded while gallantly leading their respective commands in the assault on the hill. Many brave officers and men here fell.[18]

Massey was hit twice, first in an ankle and then later in his chest. The ankle, he learned, was not broken and so he continued his duty. Minutes later, a Federal bullet hit him slightly below his left collarbone. However, as luck would have it, Massey had rolled his coat and extra shirts that morning, slung them over his shoulder, and then tied them to his belt on the opposite hip, so the Minie ball did not seriously wound him. Once more, having discovered that his injury was not serious, he continued on.[19]

Preston added, "The brigade advanced with splendid courage, but was met by a destructive fire of the enemy from the cover of their field-works on the hill."[20] The destructive nature of the Union soldiers' defense was partially due to Gracie's early departure during Preston's preparations. Rather than a solid line moving as one toward the crest of the ridge and the Union line, Preston's Division went at the hill in uncoordinated groups, first Gracie and then Kelly. This gave the Union fighters on Hill 3 no direct attackers. Those Union defenders on Hill 2 temporarily had different firing angles. Rather than shoot just downhill at basically a right angle, the defenders on Hills 3 and 2 did not have attackers at their front. Some of the defenders on Hill 2 could fire at the left side of Gracie's line.

The modern-day visitor to the ridge is reminded that there were fewer trees to shoot between in 1863. At the very least, the Union defenders on Hill 2 had the opportunity to shoot at Gracie's attackers until Kelly's men advanced. It would have been longer range for the defenders on Hill 3 to fire effectively at Gracie's men. Remember, too, that McLennan's men had to stop and allow the 15th Alabama to retreat, temporarily narrowing even further the width of the attacking Confederate line.

On the right of Gracie's line, the 63rd Tennessee went off course and mistakenly charged at an area armed with Union cannons and infantry riflemen: the Snodgrass cornfield. The artillery squarely faced the Tennesseans. The men of the 63rd were mauled by the initial Union volley and very quickly found themselves pinned down. Aitken wrote of the 63rd's plight, "By some means the regiment became separated from the brigade and was subjected to a heavy fire in front and from the right. As soon as information could be communicated to the commander of the brigade of our exposed position, the 43rd Alabama Regiment was sent to support us on the left. The two regiments charged up the hill very near the enemy's position, but the fire of shot, shell, and musketry being so heavy, were compelled to retire."[21]

Moody's report differed slightly from Aiken's on one point. The 43rd, Moody wrote, was positioned by Gracie between the right side of the 2nd Battalion and the left of the 63rd Tennessee. The 43rd did not fall back with the 63rd, according to Moody. The 43rd was hit hard, though. Moody wrote in his report that Lieutenant Colonel John Jefferson Jolly and the six company commanders on the right side of the 43rd were killed or severely wounded, "almost at the very beginning of the engagement."[22]

Moody wrote in his report that the retreat of the Tennessee regiment, which happened at about 4:45 p.m., caused some confusion for the Alabama regiment, but the confusion did not last long. The 43rd continued its attack against the portion of Hill 1 closest to the Snodgrass farm buildings.[23]

Aitken's report noted that the 63rd's participation that afternoon marked its first experience under fire. He wrote in his report: "It was the first fire to which the regiment was ever exposed, and considering everything—that it formed under fire and was subjected to a heavy fire of artillery and musketry from the front and a rapid cross-fire from the right—too much praise cannot be awarded to the officers and men of the regiment for the manner in which they conducted themselves." Aitken added: "No troops during the entire engagement were exposed to a more deadly fire or withstood the shock with more coolness and determination."[24]

The 63rd's mistaken path toward the Snodgrass cornfield as opposed to the side of Hill 1 is more easily understood when visiting the ridge. The reader can imagine Gracie's men walking toward the ridge. The terrain rolls and dips as you approach the ridge line from the location where Preston staged Gracie and Kelly before sending those men toward the front. About half of Gracie's men, those of the 3rd and 4th Battalions, went straight at the area between Hills 2 and 1. But Hill 1 juts out from the ridge and forms an angle at the top of about 90 degrees. Down the side of the hill, the angle is less noticeable.

The reader can imagine a line of people walking shoulder to shoulder toward the corner of a building. Some of those walkers will move face first into the side of the building. Others, those who are in the line beyond the corner of the building, can continue walking and must turn left in order to smack into the side of the building.

The paths of Gracie's right-most soldiers, elements of the 1st Battalion, the 2nd Battalion and the 63rd Tennessee, had to veer left to attack the far side of Hill 1. The Legion's men veered left at the Federals atop Hill 1 and along the line toward the Snodgrass buildings. Alongside of the Legion men who *did* veer left, the soldiers of the 63rd Tennessee, who were on the far right of Gracie's line, walked into a bowl lined with ridges to their front and their left. They probably became confused by the surroundings and determined that the ridge in front was their intended point of attack. Rather than veer left, the 63rd moved straight ahead. Regardless of the reason for the confusion, the 63rd continued north toward the Snodgrass cornfield. Waiting for them was a rude reception committee: Parts of the 3rd Brigade of Colonel Charles G. Harker and elements of the 2nd Brigade, led by Brigadier General William B. Hazen. Two artillery units supported the infantry.[25]

The combination was deadly for the 63rd when it uncovered the waiting Federals. Within minutes, the 63rd had taken heavy casualties. The

The marker for the left flank of the 63rd Tennessee after it retreated from the Snodgrass cornfield, seen from the modern day road below the point of Hill 1. The regiment extended to the right of the road in this view. To the left of this view is the rise toward Hill 1. On the far side of the rise is the cornfield where the 63rd met with disaster at the hands of Union artillery and rifle regiments (author's photograph).

men pulled back into the geographic bowl where the same rise in the ground that had confused them and probably sent them marching in the wrong direction, now offered a modicum of protection.

The location where the 63rd Tennessee lost contact with the Legion's 2nd Battalion is approximately southeast of battlefield tablet number 81, which gives a version of Gracie's attack and sits below the spur of Hill 1. The area where the 63rd broke away sits in the lower part of an undulation in the ground; thus, looking in the direction the Tennesseans walked, there appears to be a continuation of the ridge that the brigade was assigned to attack. Perhaps that topographical feature confused the men of the 63rd.

Whatever the cause of the confusion, it should be noted that the Tennessee regiment continued due north toward the Snodgrass cornfield, while the Second Battalion swung to its left and headed to the north of due west and attacked the side of Hill 1.

Had the 63rd swung left with the men of the 2nd Battalion as Gracie no doubt expected, the Tennessee attackers would probably have been subjected to artillery and small arms fire from the cornfield for a time. Had the 63rd followed its intended path, the regiment would have taken heavy losses anyway, to be sure. But in this theoretical attack up the side of Hill 1, the 63rd might have suffered fewer losses than it did in the actual event. The Union fighters in the cornfield eventually would have been forced to stop firing at Hill 1 for fear of hitting the blue-clad defenders as the 63rd climbed closer to the crest of the ridge.

Years later, veterans of the battle placed a position marker for the 63rd's location after it pulled back. That marker sits behind a minor roll in the ground on the far side from the cornfield that masked the Tennesseans from the deadly fire from Harker's and Hazen's men. Heavily shot up, the men of the 63rd were now out of the fight. Of the 402 men available as the regiment started the day, 200 were killed or wounded.

To the left of the 2nd Battalion, Shaver and his mates in the 1st Battalion went right at Hill 1. Understandably proud of his unit, Shaver wrote with characteristic color: "The first volley of the enemy, who were lying in wait behind a fortification of logs in an excellent position, bore with

View of the left flank marker for the 63rd Tennessee looking up toward Horseshoe Ridge from a position that would have been held by members of the regiment after their pullback from the Snodgrass cornfield (author's photograph).

fatal precision upon our line, and created many a gap in our heretofore intact ranks; but it was responded to by an answering volley and a rousing cheer, which rose high above the din of conflict."[26]

H. H. Barganier, Company D of the 1st Battalion, wrote simply, "My Captain [Richard N. Moore] was wounded and died. The whole company was cut to pieces and but 4 or 6 was able for duty." Barganier himself suffered an ankle wound and never returned to service.[27] The 1st Battalion was stopped. The 2nd, exposed to fire from above on Hill 1 and from the same units which had abused the 63rd Tennessee (to their right) also stopped. The 2nd Battalion pulled back slightly to regroup. The 3rd and 4th were exposed to fire from both sides because the draw they charged had Federal men along the tops of both sides. The advances of the 3rd and 4th were stopped.

Sergeant John L. Odom, who served in Company F of the 3rd Battalion, wrote of having his "knapsack shot off." Of such near things is life made. Odom survived the war.[28]

Brigadier General Thomas J. Wood, commander of the Union's 1st Division at Chickamauga, was on the receiving end of the Legion's rush toward the crest of Hill 1. Wood's command included the 3rd Kentucky, as well as the 64th, 65th and 125th Ohio regiments. Those units were fighting on the far Union left on Horseshoe Ridge. Wood wrote about the fierce nature of the attack on the Union left side in his report:

> I deem it proper to signalize one of these attacks specially. It occurred about 4 o'clock, and lasted about 30 minutes. It was unquestionably the most terrific musketry duel I have ever witnessed. Harker's brigade was formed in two lines. The regiments were advanced to the crest of the ridge alternately, and delivered their fire by volley at the command, retiring a few paces behind it after firing to reload. The continued roar of the very fiercest musketry fire inspired a sentiment of grandeur in which the awful and the sublime were intermingled. But the enemy was repulsed in this fierce attack, and the crest of the ridge was still in our possession.[29]

Given the time noted, which was actually closer to 4:30 p.m., and the location, Wood likely alluded to his division's confrontation with Gracie's Brigade in general and the men of the Legion and the 43rd Alabama in particular.

Lieutenant Colonel J. W. Bishop of the 2nd Minnesota said after the war, "Preston's Division … with courage and enthusiasm, stimulated to the utmost, advanced to their fate."[30]

By about 4:45 p.m., Archibald Gracie had his hands full. He tried to rally his men, who were struggling to cope with the fierce Union defense of the ridge. Some rallied, others did not. The 63rd Tennessee, smaller by half than when it first came under fire, did not rally and return to the attack.

At about this time, Williams' artillery reserve, which included Kolb's Battery, was moved a few hundred yards north up the Lafayette Road to a location in front of the Poe cabin. The Poe cabin is sometimes called the "burning cabin" in the Official Records.

Kelly's Brigade—the reader will remember that Kelly's men were supposed to move in concert with Gracie's—began marching toward Hill 3 at about 4:30, but, in the confusion, ended up attacking the west side of Hill 2 and the area between Hills 3 and 2. Kelly's 58th North Carolina, led by Colonel John B. Palmer, very nearly reached the crest of Hill 2, but here again uncertainty in the smoky confusion of battle slowed the Confederates. The 58th North Carolina was slammed by ripping fire from its front by the 35th Ohio and on the right from defenders of the 2nd Minnesota. The right end of the 58th North Carolina gave a bit of ground as the remainder of the unit returned fire. Then Kelly ordered his men to stop their shooting, fearing the North Carolinians were actually shooting at the Confederates on Gracie's left. Palmer knew better and tried to keep his men firing, but could not do so. The Minnesotans had no such confusion, knowing that if they fired downhill, they were shooting at the enemy. The Minnesota men kept firing.

At this time the 63rd Virginia, led by Major James M. French, was moving up the hill to the left of the 58th North Carolina. The Virginians fired and may have been about to charge the crest of the hill when Kelly's stop-fire order arrived. Their momentum stopped. Both the North Carolina and Virginia regiments pulled back.

The Union's 21st Ohio was stationed between Hills 3 and 2 and fought bravely, but its soldiers began running low on ammunition. As they ran out of bullets, the men of the 21st retired to a spot away from the crest of the ridge, where they hoped to be resupplied. French's Virginians believed they were making headway and probably were rushing at the 21st Ohio. As the 21st Ohio's ranks pulled back from the crest, an opening yawned in the Union line. (The reader should envision the letter M. The 21st Ohio's position was at about the top of the left upright in the letter, where the writer's pen would change directions to move down toward the lower point of the letter.) The Confederates' 5th Kentucky had gone uphill toward the ridge on the left side of the 58th North Carolina. Under the command of Colonel Hiram Hawkins, the Kentuckians somehow braved the murderous fire from both the 35th Ohio on their right and the 22nd Michigan to their left and pushed into the gap left by the ammunition-challenged 21st Ohio. The 5th Kentucky may have been the first Confederate unit to reach the crest of Horseshoe Ridge between Hills 3 and 1.

Gracie was pushing his stalled brigade forward. Having rested through the day of September 19th and a good part of the 20th, this was a fresh unit and, at about 4:45 p.m., it tried again to move the Federals off the top of Horseshoe Ridge.

This time the 2nd Battalion fought its way to the edge of the Ridge's crest and forced the defenders out of their informal breastworks. It was the first unit of Gracie's Brigade to reach the goal, and most students of the fighting along the ridge believe the soldiers of the 2nd Battalion of Hilliard's Legion were the first men of Longstreet's wing to get there. If the 2nd Battalion didn't beat the Confederate Kentuckians to a spot on the crest of the ridge, it was a close thing.

4:45 pm Horseshoe Ridge

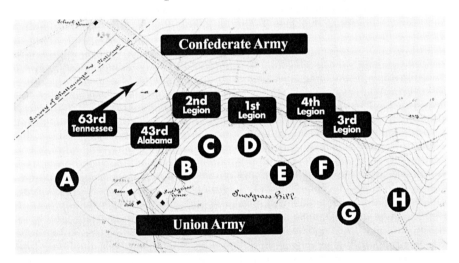

Ⓐ Harker and Hazen
Ⓑ 58th Indiana, 17th Ohio, 31st Ohio
Ⓒ 11th Michigan
Ⓓ 19th Illinois
Ⓔ Walker and 9th Ohio
Ⓕ 87th Indiana and 2nd Minnesota
Ⓖ 35th Ohio
Ⓗ 22nd Michigan and 89th Ohio

Gracie's attackers were stalled by 4:45 p.m. Gracie plugged the 43rd Alabama into the gap between the Legion's 2nd Battalion and the 63rd Tennessee. The Tennessee regiment pulled back, having been severely mauled by the defenders in the cornfield. The 43rd Alabama attacked the left flank of the ridge in concert with the 2nd Battalion (courtesy Teri Schott).

Gracie ordered the 43rd Alabama to shift slightly to its left, toward the men of the 2nd Battalion, so as to shield the men of the regiment from some of the killing fire coming from the cornfield. The men of the 43rd still suffered through heavy fire as they advanced, but they eventually joined the men of the 2nd Battalion on the crest of Horseshoe Ridge. Lieutenant Crenshaw Hall, the 2nd Battalion's Adjutant who wrote the Battalion's after-battle report, wrote, "On the right at this juncture Brigadier-General Gracie and Colonel Moody led up a part of the 43rd Alabama."[31]

Given the tenacity of the Federal defense, the daunting difficulty of the steep hillside and the informal physical barriers that the Union men had erected during the night to aid in their defense of the ridge, Gracie's pushing the defenders away from the crest of the ridge was a truly great martial achievement. Gracie summed up the action: "Undaunted, the brigade scaled the precipitous heights, driving the enemy before it, and took possession of the hill."[32]

Archibald Gracie had served with the 43rd Alabama. He knew the

View of Hill 1 from the Snodgrass Cabin, showing the Union positions and looking toward Hill 1. The 43rd Alabama attacked from the far left of the image. The defenders would have been looking toward the left. The highest point of Hill 1 is at right (author's photograph).

men and their leader, Colonel Young M. Moody. Using the 43rd as Gracie did, as a sort of reserve regiment, paid off when the Yankees pulled away from their protective cover at the edge of Hill 1, near the Snodgrass home, in order to escape the charging Alabamians. Moody, commander of the 43rd Alabama, wrote in his report: "I succeeded … with the assistance of Brigadier-General Gracie, in rallying my men under the enemy's fire, and we again moved forward, changing front forward … and charging up to the enemy's works on the hill, and with the Second Battalion, Alabama Legion, succeeded in holding the works, although exposed to a heavy fire of grape and shell and an enfilading fire of small-arms."[33]

Horace McLean, a sergeant and quartermaster in Company B of the 2nd Battalion, wrote home to his wife, Mary:

> … allow me to say to you without bosting [*sic*] that I acquited [*sic*] myself very well indeede [*sic*] upon the battle filed when I (word unclear, could be reached) their brest works I got a fair aim at one blue coat about thirty or forty feet and I threw him the highest fall I ever saw I killed three of them beyond a doubt I have a splendid gun and I tell you that I used it the very best I could but I must say to you that it is any thing but pleasant work.[34]

Crenshaw Hall, the adjutant and one of the aforementioned Hall brothers, wrote the report of the Legion's 2nd Battalion after the battalion's commander, Lieutenant-Colonel Bolling Hall, Jr., was wounded. Hall wrote that after stalling,

> The battalion again reformed, the men collected and fully possessed, officers at their posts, the advance was ordered, and Lieutenant-Colonel Hall, while leading the command under the fiercest fire, was shot down at a time when, by hard fighting, we had almost reached the enemy's works. Many brave men had now fallen. Captain Walden assumed command, and bravely led the still advancing line until shot down within the enemy's lines. Lieutenant Fisher, a brave officer, of Company C, about this time was mortally wounded. The enemy fiercely opposed our entrance. The effort was useless—the works were carried, the enemy driven before us in confusion.[35]

Walden was Captain Wesley D. Walden of the 2nd Battalion's Company B. Fisher was First Lieutenant William F. Fisher. Both men died of their wounds.

Lieutenant Colonel Bolling Hall, Jr., the 2nd Battalion's leader, is among the most revered figures in the long history of Alabama's military experience. At 18, he joined the Autuaga Rifles and with the group became a part of the 6th Alabama Infantry Regiment. Hall was a member of the 6th when it served at 1st Manassas. He was promoted to Corporal on December 1, 1861, before his enlistment ended the following February 10.

He was granted permission to raise another company, which he did, and that unit became part of Hilliard's Legion on March 16, 1862.[36]

Bolling Hall, Jr., apparently led from the front, because he reached the berm of the ridge before he suffered a severe knee wound in front of the Union's hastily-erected breastworks. In a letter written two years later, Ben Fitzpatrick, a former Alabama governor and multiple-term United States Senator, wrote to the Confederacy's Assistant Secretary of War, John A. Campbell, that Hall "led the desperate charge on what was called by some 'Battery Hill'—our flag you remember was pierced by 80 balls in that charged [sic] … Col. Hall's regiment carried the works he himself being shot down & severely wounded in the very act of taking the works."[37]

Nicholas Stallworth, a captain in the 1st Battalion who was wounded at Chickamauga, exchanged letters with Gracie IV decades after the war. In a 1907 letter to Stallworth, Gracie IV quotes from a letter Stallworth had written to him earlier: "About the moment I was hit I saw General Gracie going down the front of the line cheering his men. He was afoot leading his horse, which I learned afterward had been shot."[38]

General Gracie himself has been underserved by historians through the decades since the war. True, he is generally credited with using great energy on the afternoon of September 20, 1863. Historians such as Peter Cozzens (in his excellent book *This Terrible Sound: The Battle of Chickamauga*) acknowledge that Gracie redirected the movement of the 43rd so that the regiment could go to the aid of the 2nd Battalion, then encouraged the other units of the brigade during the most dangerous moments of the fighting. Gracie drove his brigade up that hill with great personal energy, losing two horses from under him in the process.

Gracie's decision to shift the 43rd a short distance to its left was a key to the successful attack on the Rebels' right. The undulations that made it so difficult for Confederate leaders to maintain command and control over their forces that afternoon probably played a role, too. When Gracie shifted the 43rd to its left, the regiment gained a bit of protection from the murderous artillery and small arms fire due to a rise in the ground. That rise was enough to cover Gracie's right from the Union fire for a time. Once the Confederates of the 2nd Battalion and the 43rd Regiment reached close proximity to the defenders of Hill 1, the Union men in the cornfield could no longer direct their fire at the attackers for fear of killing their Federal comrades.

The *Montgomery Weekly Advertiser* wrote: "The Second Battalion, having gained the breastworks were in a great measure protected after having reached them. As an evidence of the position they gained, its battle flag, which is a small one, has eighty-five distinct bullet holes, the staff was cut down twice and the color bearer bruised all over though fortunately not wounded dangerously."[39]

Most treatments of Chickamauga credit Gracie's work during that battle. But few discussions of the war in general mention Gracie outside of references to this one engagement. Gracie gave the Confederacy solid service until his death in front of Petersburg in 1864. One could argue, as this writer does, that Gracie's work at Chickamauga (and later) put to shame the mulish, lackadaisical non-effort of men like Leonidas Polk and Daniel H. Hill.

Bolling Hall, Jr., wrote of Gracie, "I think he inspires universal confidence in all the Alabamians under him & also most of the Tennesseans of whom he has one Regt [the 63rd] only."[40] The Advertiser also had strong words of credit for Gracie. "Indeed, the chief fault of his generalship, was a reckless exposure of his own person. He had two horses killed under him, but escaped unharmed. After the battle was over, his labors did not cease—he visited the hospitals to have his wounded comfortably disposed of and properly treated. Gen. Gracie should be appointed a Major General."[41]

It is easy to see the father in the son. While aboard the sinking ocean liner *Titanic,* Archibald Gracie IV saw to the safety of several women he had befriended during the voyage and loaned a pocketknife to crewmen, that those crewmen might be able to cut loose a collapsible lifeboat. After the *Titanic* slipped beneath the surface, Gracie IV swam to an upturned boat and stood on it for hours with a few other survivors, with freezing water up to their knees, until transferring to another lifeboat shortly before the rescue ship *Carpathia* arrived. Had they been aboard the *Titanic,* whether they survived or not, Polk and Hill might have spent their time after the ship struck the iceberg arguing over whose fault the whole thing was and refusing to move until each was given command of a lifeboat.

At the southern edge of Horseshoe Ridge, some of the Alabama men from Gracie's brigade now had the Federals' makeshift breastworks in their front. The Union defenders who had been on the crest fell back to a position a short distance away, and the two sides now began a steady rifle duel. The Union men had been forced back, but they now gave as good as they got. The flag of the Legion's 2nd Battalion, planted firmly next to the breastworks, famously collected 83 bullet holes and was later presented to Confederate President Jefferson Davis.

General Gracie wrote of the flag, and the man who carried it, in his report, "Its colors bear marks of over eighty bullets. Its bearer, Robert Y.

Hiett, though thrice wounded and the flag-staff thrice shot away, carried his charge throughout the entire fight. He deserves not only mention, but promotion."[42]

Interestingly, the Confederate president's wife, Varina Davis, returned the flag favor. In an April 28, 1908, letter to Albert Patterson of Jemison, Alabama (care of Jesse A. Caddell), Archibald Gracie IV alludes to a letter he had received from Patterson. Gracie IV wrote to Patterson, "An interesting point of information which you have given, which I have never heard before, is the statement that Mrs. Davis sent your Company a new flag."[43]

By this time Union General George Thomas had reached the conclusion that his position on the ridge would not be held. Having rendered more effective service than any other general officer in the Union cause that day at Chickamauga, and having earned a terrific nickname in the process, Thomas left the ridge to begin the process of withdrawing the remaining Union forces from the battlefield. But Thomas' leaving the immediate area did not make things easy for the attacking Confederates.

Gracie's 3rd, 4th and 1st Battalions were pinned down on the slopes of the ridge. Gracie energetically attempted to get the three groups moving forward again but he was unable to do so. Again, from McLennan's report:

> When ordered forward again the battalion advanced steadily under a murderous fire in our front from the enemy's well-selected and partially fortified position, returning the fire as we advanced until we came within 40 paces of their works (a few of my officers and men went within a few yards of the enemy's position). At this point a heavy fire was poured into us from the left, being on a line with the battalion on my right. A heavy fire pouring upon me from the front, right, and left, and my ranks being almost decimated, to have advanced farther without support would have been reckless in the extreme.[44]

Thus, most of their commands were pinned down but both Gracie and Kelly had footholds, tenuous though they were, on Horseshoe Ridge.

It appears the detail of 50 to 100 privates and officers charged with building defenses in the area where Gracie's brigade spent the day and night of September 19th were still doing their assigned "fatigue duty" when their comrades marched up Lafayette Road that afternoon. The exact spot where the work was done is up for speculation. General Bushrod Johnson's men did the same kind of work in an area roughly adjacent to the modern day Viniard-Alexander Road, and there is scanty evidence to suggest the Hughes Detail may have been working in the same area.

Gracie IV was in contact with John B. Fuller, a private in Company B of the Legion's 3rd Battalion. As the reader will recall, Fuller, who became a judge after the war, told Gracie IV that the Hughes detail was building breastworks for defense when the wounded and injured from Gracie's brigade began coming back from the front. In his June 17, 1905, letter to Gracie IV, Fuller wrote, "This detail worked until about four o'clock that afternoon, when some of the wounded of Gracie's Brigade passed out [probably 'our'] detail going to the rear and we were informed that our Brigade was then engaged in the fight. The detail threw down their picks and spades and double-quicked to the front, intending to rejoin the Brigade."[45]

Any wounded men from Gracie's Brigade that the men of the Hughes Detail saw at the time mentioned, 4 p.m., likely suffered their wounds while waiting in the area between the Brotherton and Poe cabins when Yankee artillerists sent a few shells their way.

It appears that Gracie IV was also in contact with another member of the Hughes detail, Private W. C. Athey of the 3rd Battalion's Company D. His conversations with Fuller and Athey led Gracie IV to conclude that the detail consisted of about 100 men. However, Lt. Colonel Sanford's statement in the Official Records, that the detail consisted of two commissioned officers, four non-commissioned officers and 50 privates, seems so specific that the author is inclined to accept this number as more probably accurate. Sanford's report was written shortly after the battle, another important consideration.

As they hustled toward the sounds of the battle, the men of the Hughes Detail fell in with the 6th Florida Regiment, under the command of Colonel J. J. Finley. The 6th was part of Trigg's Brigade and it eventually reached Horseshoe Ridge in time to play a role in the final bit of fighting.

Major Samuel C. Williams' artillerists got busy at about 5 p.m. Firing north approximately along the path of the Lafayette Road, the Reserve Corps Artillery aimed at Federal soldiers observed crossing the road from east to west, some of whom were probably on their way to join the fighting on Horseshoe Ridge.

Things on Horseshoe Ridge started changing drastically at about 5 p.m. Steedman's Federal units, which had fought so hard for so long against a determined opponent that day, collectively used up its available ammunition and began departing the premises. Steedman apparently tried to stop the retreat, ordering the men to use their bayonets. The 115th Illinois briefly turned back to face the attacking Confederates before rejoining the rush to the rear.

Here, there is an urge to compare the behavior of Steedman's force to the 20th Maine during the aforementioned Little Round Top engagement of the Gettysburg fight. It is not a fair comparison.

Steedman's command, like J. L. Chamberlain's men of the 20th Maine, ran critically low on ammunition. Steedman, like Chamberlain, ordered his men to stand and defend their ground with bayonets. Indeed, Chamberlain's men affixed their bayonets to their rifles and rushed down the rocky slope of Little Round Top at the Confederates.

But at 5 p.m. on September 20, Steedman was confronted by a numerically superior force, which Chamberlain was not, and by a foe that had been reinforced periodically during the day, which Chamberlain's opponent was not. And, though Chamberlain was probably not aware of this, his Confederate attackers had also used up their supply of ammunition. Finally, Chamberlain was instructed to hold his ground at all cost, whereas the Union Army was in retreat behind Horseshoe Ridge and Steedman's command merely joined that movement.

Eventually, three of the four battalions of Hilliard's Legion fought their way to the edge of Horseshoe Ridge. It was an expensive yet amazing feat of arms. In a May 27, 1907, letter to Joe Rayburn, Esq., Gracie IV quotes Private William T. Gillian, of the 1st Battalion's Company D, this way: "My battalion charged up Snodgrass's [Horseshoe] ridge, receiving the enemy's cross fire from the left and right and in front also. The fire from the left was, to my best recollection, the hottest. The slope of the ridge where we ascended was graded but to our right it was very precipitous. We had to oblique to the left to avoid the steep slope."[46]

Gillian's description of the ground he climbed puts Company D of the 1st Battalion slightly west, to Gillian's left, of where the point of Hill 1 juts forward. The edge of the Ridge running from Hill 1 north toward the Snodgrass cornfield runs basically straight. The side of the Ridge running west in the direction of Hill 2 undulates. The hillside toward the point of Hill 1 is quite steep but one of those undulations a few yards to the west allows for an easier climb.

As it marched toward the ridge, Gracie's front had five pieces: The four battalions and the 63rd Tennessee (with the 43rd Alabama held in reserve). The 1st Battalion was the middle unit. We know that the 1st Battalion had seven companies (A through G) and veterans of the battle said the center of Gracie's line struck the point of Hill 1.

Numerically, the center of Gracie's 1,306-man line (with the 43rd Alabama still acting as a reserve unit) works out to be somewhere in the 1st Battalion. The 63rd Tennessee, with its 402 soldiers, added to the 2nd Battalion, with 230 members, makes 632 men. That total is just short of the 653 needed to reach the mid-point of the line. We know the 1st Battalion was to the immediate left of the 2nd Battalion.

The plaque posted below the point of Hill 1, next to the modern day road which takes the visitor past the Snodgrass farm site and up to the top of Horseshoe Ridge. After listing the units that made up Gracie's command, the sign reads, in part: "This Brigade, with its Division was moved from the vicinity of the Brotherton House about 4 o'clock, and passed to the front of Kershaw's line on this ground. It at once assaulted Stanley's and Brannan's lines and carried the high spur in front of this position, holding it about an hour. Shortly after sunset, by rallying all available men the point was recaptured by Stanley's Brigade" (author's photograph).

Hardee's Rifle and Light Infantry Tactics, the organizational guide used by the Confederates, dictates that the company led by the senior captain will be the first company and will take the right or left flank position, as ordered by the commanding officer of the regiment or battalion. The company led by the next most senior captain will take the opposite flank and the line will then be filled in that manner, so that the least experienced captain will fight in the middle of the battalion line.[47]

Crenshaw Hall's 2nd Battalion report comments that his battalion was unsupported on the left, except for a few members of the 1st Battalion's Company A. That places the 1st Battalion's Company A on the right flank of the 1st. It also tells us that the companies of the 1st Battalion went up the side of the ridge in the following order from the left: B-D-F-G-E-C-A. The theoretical center of Gracie's Brigade would be the 23rd man from the right flank of the 1st Battalion, probably one of the left-most members of Company A or the right-most portion of Company C. By this time in the war, most of the companies in Hilliard's Legion were down to roughly 25 available men.

Thus, Company D of the 1st Battalion should have been to the west of the bend on the side of Hill 1. Gillian's testimony to Gracie IV that "we

The path described by Private William T. Gillian, 1st Battalion, Company D of Hilliard's Legion. Gillian described making an oblique to the left because of the steep grade. The point of Hill 1 is to the upper right of the image. The marker at the bottom of the image indicates the advance of the 7th South Carolina earlier in the fighting (author's photograph).

had to oblique to the left to avoid the steep slope" makes sense. Gillian's Company D would have been on the far side from the cornfield or around the corner of Hill 1 from the big guns.

Hall's 2nd Battalion probably lined up differently. Crenshaw Hall, the adjutant, wrote that he was located near his battalion's left flank and could only recommend honors for soldiers in his battalion that were near him during the fighting. Hall complimented the captains of companies F and C. This indicates the 2nd's companies lined up A-C-E-F-D-B. C would be on the left side and F would at least be in the middle.

The order in which the 1st Battalion's companies attacked the Ridge is important because it seems to verify Gillian's statement. The information we have about the 2nd Battalion seems to verify the information we have about the 1st.

We know now that a small number of Confederates advanced beyond the crest of the hill. Gracie IV, the general's son, attended at least two reunions of Confederate soldiers, one in 1907 and the other a year later. At the 1907 event in Montgomery, Alabama, Gracie IV met Gillian. Gillian told Gracie IV that he, Gillian, and a few others, continued beyond the area where the Union defenders had fought on the crest of the hill and chased Union soldiers toward the area of the buildings of the Snodgrass farm. Gracie IV wrote to Gillian later and summarized Gillian's statement in the form of an affidavit, which Gracie IV then sent to Gillian to sign. Gillian apparently signed a copy of the affidavit, according to later letters Gracie IV wrote on the subject.

An unsigned copy of the affidavit reads this way, in its entirety:

AFFIDAVIT

This is to certify that I, William T. Gillian, was a member of Co. D., 1st Battalion, Alabama Legion, commanded by Major Holt, in the battle of Chickamauga.

On this occasion, after having charged up the hill of Snodgrass Ridge, and driven the enemy from the summit and north through the thick woods, I, with other comrades, pursued them. We pressed through the woods into the open garden south of a log-house, which I intended taking shelter behind. As I double-quicked along I stopped and picked up a small pumpkin, which I put into my haversack.

I had not fired a shot from my gun and had roved but a few steps when I received a wound in my right arm. At this time I was very close to the log-house. I remember seeing there Comrade Hub Tillery, a few paces in front, between me and the log-house, when I turned back on account of my severe wound.

I sliced and ate this pumpkin that night, offering some to my comrades. They laughed at me and joked me about it from that day to the surrender, and called me pumpkin thereafter.

I further recall the fact that Lieut. Gilchrist of our company, just after I was shot, called out: "Come back, you boys, you are getting too far." These were his exact words.[48]

Tillery is probably Herbert Carey Tillery, also listed as a private in Company D of the 1st Battalion. Tillery, about a month beyond his 23rd birthday at the time of the battle, was born in Alabama's Butler County. Gracie IV seems to have been in contact with Tillery within the same time frame during which Gracie IV met and wrote letters to Gillian. Tillery seems to have told Gracie IV that he, Tillery, advanced far enough to take a position using the Snodgrass cabin for cover. Tillery pointedly backed up Gillian's statement.

Gilchrist is probably John Gilchrist of Lowdens County, Alabama.

In his letter to Rayburn, Gracie IV's quote from Gillian continues: "We passed over two temporary works of logs and rails obliquing to the right in the direction of the enemy's flight, driving the enemy before us. We pursued him out of the woods into the cornfield beyond.... My recollection is perfect as to our reaching the cornfield near the log house.... I was wounded within 25 or 30 feet of the said log house, and then withdrew from the right."[49]

According to James Ogden, the historian at the Chickamauga National Military Park, there is no reliable surviving description of the Snodgrass

Looking toward the peak of Hill 2 from the peak of Hill 1. Note the low spot to the left of the image. That is the approximate position where the 1st Battalion's Company D came up the side of the ridge after making its oblique movement. From there, Gillian, Tillery and others advanced toward the right side of the image toward the Snodgrass farm (author's photograph).

farmhouse, adjacent buildings or gardens as they were in 1863. The description in the affidavit fits with what is known about the property and the surrounding topography. It seems possible that the object of the daring penetration of the Union line was the Snodgrass garden. Remember that Braxton Bragg's report mentioned that his army had marched without food or eating utensils for days. Even water was hard to come by for the thirsty Army of the Tennessee as it walked toward the Chickamauga area. Whether the pumpkin vine was part of an organized garden, which the Snodgrass family certainly must have had, or whether it was what Ogden termed a "volunteer" vine, the growing gourds would have been an enticement for a hungry soldier.

Of course, in order to be a true "Volunteer" vine, the plant would have had to be located a few miles to the north, in Tennessee.

The central point of the pumpkin story is that the men of Brigadier General Gracie's 1st Battalion of Hilliard's Legion drove the Union troops from the crest of Horseshoe Ridge, and a smattering of those same Legion men pushed beyond the crest of the ridge by way of the left side of Hill 1. At least two of those Confederates, and possibly more, approached the Snodgrass cabin. Gillian, Tillery and the others must have gone beyond the rough breastworks on the edge of the ridge sometime after 5 p.m. and before the Federals departed for their retreat. The probe of the area near the Snodgrass cabin very probably happened shortly after the 1st Battalion secured its berth on the lip of Hill 1, and certainly happened before 6 p.m. The sides were exchanging rifle fire at the time.

There might not have been breastworks, informal or otherwise, in the area in front of Gillian, Tillery and others in the 1st Battalion. J. W. Bishop, the Lieutenant Colonel with the 2nd Minnesota, said in his "Van Derveer's Brigade at Chickamauga" presentation that there was no such protection for his comrades when the 2nd reached the Union line on the ridge.

Gillian's description of the steepness of the grade, of his company moving to its left in order to find easier climbing, fits with the idea that the 1st Battalion's Company A fought on the battalion's right flank and that Gillian, Tillery and their Company D comrades were near the left flank. The left flank would have been near the area that had been defended by the 2nd Minnesota.

Davenport, the 1st Battalion letter writer, described the battle to his wife:

> My Dear it would take a gret volum to relait all I saw in that fight.... My Dear in the early part of the engagement I was struck with a graip shot glancing my chest

and cutting my coat vest and shirt from the front of my right shoulder across my brest slitely graining the skin. Tho it bruised my chest smartly it knocked me to the ground and parilised my right arm. For a short time I thought I was shot through but soon recovered from the shock and went on in to the fight. We drove the enemy from his first line of Breastworkes and ocipied them ourselves. Our officers and men all seamed to vie with each other in ther deades of novel daring. General Gracey flue from wing to wing between the fire of both armeys giving command and encerageing his men to more desret deads. He had too horses killd under him and meney meney shot went throu his clothing. I had seven shot in throu my coat but non more than grained the skin.[50]

As Davenport was a private in the 1st Battalion's Company D, the same company as Gillian and Tillery, the author has wondered if Davenport was referring to that pair when he wrote, "Our officers and men all seamed to vie with each other in ther deades of novel daring."

It is interesting to note that neither Gillian nor Tillery were voted to represent Company D as members of the Confederate Roll of Honor for their service at Chickamauga. That honor went to Private B. A. Davis. Davis was killed in action at Chickamauga.

Ammunition eventually became a problem for Gracie's men, as it had

From Hill 1 with the Snodgrass cornfield in the distance. This is the approximate path taken by William T. Gillian and Hubert "Hub" Tillery when they advanced along the top of the hill. The Snodgrass Cabin sits to the left in this image (author's photograph).

been for the Union men along the ridge, because Gracie's men ran out. To make matters worse, some of their rifles fouled from overuse. Gracie was forced to recall his men, even those who had fought so heroically to establish themselves on and penetrate beyond the crest of the ridge. It must have been a bitter decision for Gracie to direct his men back down the slope. But that he did at about 6 p.m.

Davenport wrote home to his wife:

… fought untell sunset when our aminshon gaiv out and our brigade was relieved by another brigade. If we only had of had a little more of that noisy kill dead we would have had the honer of capturing the enemeys brigade. Tha say tha was just redday to surrender when tha heard us calling for more catredges. That encuredged them to fight on untell we was relieved. When tha surrendered to our succesers and the enemy gaiv way all along the line and the shout of victry was heard for miles along the line.[51]

Moody, of the 43rd Alabama, wrote in his report, "from want of ammunition, and my guns from frequent firing becoming unfit for use, we fell back to a point in the woods near which we first formed for attack."[52]

General Gracie, whose writing style was slightly less dramatic than Davenport's but still more complete than the succinct work of the 1st Battalion's diarist Sexton, wrote in his report:

Holding these heights for nearly an hour, and ammunition becoming scarce, I informed Brigadier-General Preston, commanding division, that unless supported the brigade could not much longer hold out. Trigg's and Kelly's brigades were ordered to my relief. Though with ammunition nearly exhausted, the brigade held its own till the scattering fire of its musketry betrayed its condition to the enemy. Trigg's and Kelly's brigades arriving, the command withdrew to replenish its empty cartridge boxes.[53]

It is interesting to note that Gracie IV's book, *The Truth about Chickamauga,* strives to prove that Gracie's command never completely left the crest of Horseshoe Ridge once elements of the brigade drove the Yankee riflemen away. Gracie IV spent a great deal of time and energy trying to settle the matter. His papers show he wrote many letters to soldiers on both sides of the battle, trying to elicit testimony and, sometimes, to argue his case. The letters indicate that Gracie IV was convinced that some soldiers of the brigade, especially from the 43rd Alabama, may have clung to some part of the crest of the hill.

Gracie, the general himself, stated plainly in the report cited above that he ordered his men to pull away from the top of the hill after their ammunition was expended.[54] Other officers wrote the same story in their reports, that having driven the enemy away from the strong point, and with relief on the way, Gracie's men pulled away for want of ammunition.

Longstreet summed up the action: "Preston dashed gallantly at the hill. ...Preston's assault, though not a complete success at the onset, taken in connection with the other operations, crippled the enemy so badly that his ranks were badly broken..."[55]

From within the brigade, the reports were much the same. Captain George W. Huguley of the Legion's 1st Battalion wrote in his report, "After a desperate fight of an hour and 50 minutes, our ammunition was exhausted and we retired."

Lieutenant Crenshaw Hall of the 2nd Battalion reported reaching the crest of the ridge and being joined by Gracie, Moody and the balance of the 43rd Alabama. He wrote in his report, "Together we resisted the enemy and still held the position. The hill was finally abandoned, but not until every cartridge was expended, when we retired to the opposite crest and reformed."

The 3rd Battalion's Lieutenant Colonel John W. A. Sanford wrote that his command reached the crest of the ridge after being initially stopped. Then, "A little after 6 o'clock several captains reported that many men had entirely exhausted their ammunition. They were instructed to hold their position. About twilight, the fire of the enemy having nearly ceased, we were ordered to retire, and did so in good order."[56]

Things were a little different for the hard-pressed 4th Battalion. Remember, the 4th was stopped short of the crest of the ridge. Major John D. McLennan reported: "Taking advantage of whatever protection could be found, we maintained our position until our ammunition and what cartridges could be obtained from the dead and wounded were nearly exhausted; the battalion then retired in good order." The men of the 4th Battalion, according to McLennan's report, were within about 40 paces of the enemy line when their advance was stopped.[57]

The advance of the Confederate regiments on the 20th of September was too fast for supplies to catch up to the leading units. Unable to hold their position without ammunition and in some cases unable to shoot rifles which had fouled due to overheating, Gracie's men fell back.

The author calls the reader's attention to the final line of the portion of Gracie's report quoted above. The General wrote, *"Trigg's and Kelly's brigades arriving,* the command withdrew to replenish its empty cartridge boxes" (emphasis added). It can be argued that the survivors among Gracie's men were not driven off the brow of the ridge, but that they fell back upon seeing the arrival of their relief. If elements of the

Trigg and Kelly brigades were moving into position to replace Gracie's gallant attackers, the argument might go, Gracie's men were not retreating. McLennan and Sanford wrote that their battalions *retired* from their position on the hill and Hall wrote that his men *retired* and *reformed*.

The reader could argue that the Legion men and their comrades in Gracie's Brigade were *ordered* to pull back but not *forced* to retreat from the crest of Horseshoe Ridge. Remember the wording of Sanford's report. He wrote that the Union defenders were not firing too many bullets when his battalion obeyed orders and pulled back. Sanford said, "About twilight, the fire of the enemy having nearly ceased, we were ordered to retire, and did so in good order."

Then there is Davenport's letter. He said the enemy heard the Alabamians calling for ammunition and "that encuredged them to fight on untell we was relieved. When tha surrendered to our succesers." Davenport indicates that he and his mates remained on the edge of the ridge until "we was relieved." While Davenport appears to have followed orders and left the ridge to go back down the hill he had climbed under such difficult conditions, he and his mates were not chased off and were not replaced by Union troops. They were to be relieved by Confederates.

Either way, Gracie's men were ordered to come back down the hill.

Traditionally, Gracie's Brigade is credited with the monstrous accomplishment of driving the Federal defenders away from the rough defenses of the ridge crest and holding the positions for about an hour and a half or a bit longer. Gracie's men are then excused for pulling back after exhausting their supply of ammunition and using their guns to the point where the firearms ceased to operate. We have seen in the Official Records where even General Gracie himself states that the Brigade pulled back. Gracie had reason to believe his order was followed.

The Brigade's officers, those who still lived by this point in the fighting, pulled back and most of the soldiers followed. But some Legion men and some members of the 43rd Alabama stayed on the edge of the ridge.

Maybe the men who stayed on the brow of the hill did not receive the order to retreat. Communication was difficult during Civil War battles. Here the heavy loss the Brigade's officers suffered probably played a role. According to the Official Records, Gracie's Brigade went into action on the 20th with 134 officers. Six of them were killed attacking the ridge and 30 more were wounded. That's a 20 percent loss in officers, making communication more difficult.[58]

Maybe some of the holdovers chose to remain out of pride or due to the rage of battle. These men may have been conservative with their

ammunition and still had enough cartridges on hand to mount a continued defense of their area. Most soldiers of the Legion had not seen combat
before crossing the Chickamauga two nights earlier. Many of them fired
wildly in the first moments of combat on the slopes of Horseshoe Ridge.
That probably contributed to the overuse of the rifles that eventually
fouled many of the Legion's weapons.[59] It is an under-reported fact that
many Union soldiers also reported that their rifles overheated and fouled
during the frantic defense of Horseshoe Ridge on the 20th.

The soldiers of the 43rd were probably more selective with their
ammunition that afternoon, and they got a later start after Gracie briefly
held them in reserve before sending them to the right side of the attack.
Still, many of the soldiers of the 43rd who had not been wounded going
up the hill ran out of ammunition and retired when ordered to do so.
Whatever their individual situations, some Legion men and others from
Gracie's Brigade remained on the crest of the ridge after the order went
out to pull back. They were still there when their relief appeared, and a
few stubborn survivors from Gracie's Brigade stayed the night. They were
not the only Confederates on the hill that night. Kelly's report testifies
that some of his men also stayed the night on the ground they so valiantly
stormed. From Kelly's post-action report: "The night being far advanced,
I made arrangements to replenish my supply of ammunition, and went
into bivouac on the hill which the brigade had so gallantly won."[60]

There are assertions that Preston's men were driven off the hills of
Horseshoe Ridge. William L. Stoughton, commander of the Federal Army's
11th Michigan regiment, wrote in his report that his brigade, with assistance from Brigadier General John Beatty, succeeded in driving Confederates from their positions. The timing and probable position of the
Stoughton/Beatty force indicate their attack was against a portion of Gracie's Brigade.

From Stoughton's report:

> At 6 p.m. the enemy still held his position, and as a last resort, I ordered up the
> Eighteenth Ohio, and rallying every man that could be got, charged forward with
> a cheer upon his colors. His flag went down. His lines broke and fell back from the
> hill. During the fight Brigadier General John Beatty rode up on the hill and assisted
> materially in sustaining and inspiring the men. His assistance there, and also in
> sending men forward, was timely and very valuable.[61]

Stoughton's report states that the Confederates he and Beatty drove
off the ridge had planted their colors "within 100 feet of our own," meaning
this particular group of attackers were stopped short of the edge of the
ridge. Three of Gracie's four brigades reached the edge, as did Moody's

43rd Alabama Regiment. The 63rd Tennessee did not approach the top. By process of elimination, Stoughton could thus be referring only to the 4th Battalion of Hilliard's Legion, the only battalion that did not make it to the top.

But the 4th Battalion was located too far to the right of the 18th Ohio (from the Union perspective) to have been attacked by the Buckeyes, led by Lieutenant Colonel Charles H. Grosvenor. Here the confusing conditions of combat played a role in the reporting. Stoughton reported accurately that the 18th Ohio drove Confederates from the side of the ridge, but this did not happen at 6 p.m. As will be seen, the 18th Ohio attacked earlier in the afternoon.

Brigadier General John Beatty's report contends that the regimental flag of the Confederate unit opposing the Stoughton/Beatty-led Federals was saved when the flag bearer threw it back down the hill behind himself. This action actually involved a South Carolina regiment during fighting earlier in the day, as has been mentioned. There is no record of a similar action by another Confederate soldier in a location and time frame that could have been part of Gracie's command.

Gracie IV was adamant about the fact that the desperate act of the Confederate flag bearer was committed by the South Carolina soldier, Clark. In *The Truth About Chickamauga,* Gracie IV quoted from a letter he received from Grosvenor: "The South Carolina troops had climbed over the little wooden works that we had built and were encountering a hand-to-hand fight. We ... drove the poor fellows over the works outward down the hill."[62]

Grosvenor described seeing the Confederate flag bearer get shot and said,

> ... he turned partly around and threw his flag, saving it, over the works down the hill. ... I did not know his name, but I am satisfied that he is the young man you are talking about. Whoever he was, whatever he was, and whichever he was, he is one of the most excellent young men I ever saw. No one of the war showed greater courage and bravery in a greater degree than this young fellow did.[63]

In his May 20, 1907, letter to Major Nicholas Stallworth, Gracie IV wrote, "From General [*sic*] Grosvenor himself I obtained the information that the incident mentioned happened before four o'clock, and as Gracie's Brigade did not move to the assault of Snodgrass's Ridge until after that hour, it did not come in contact as mentioned with Col. [*sic*] Grosvenor."[64]

Time frames are difficult to establish in most battles, and few Civil War engagements were as complex as the struggle for Horseshoe Ridge. The Union defenders had regiments arrive and pull out, only to get resupplied and return. There were regiments and fragments of regiments on top of that ridge. Most time references in the Official Records are estimates.

J. W. Bishop, the lieutenant colonel with the 2nd Minnesota, wrote after the war about fending off the final Confederate attack and then moving down the hill to rescue wounded Union fighters before the regiment retired. The idea that Bishop rescued injured comrades after the end of the fighting conflicts with what we know happened at the end of the fighting.[65] But Bishop could have, and probably did, go down the hill to tend to and retrieve wounded Union soldiers. This is where time estimates and the confusion about individual experience get in the way of understanding the bigger picture. Bishop's trip down the side of the ridge and his retreat from the area certainly happened after Kershaw's attackers were driven off and before Gracie's attack.

In Bishop's mind, the fighting must have ended because his men left the field after saving a few of the wounded. Thus, his report is accurate from his experience but it does not reflect the actual end of the battle. James Ogden, the historian at Chickamauga/Chattanooga National Military Park, frequently talks about battles within battles when describing the battlefield experiences of soldiers in different regiments or even different companies. Bishop's battle had ended and his report reflected that.

Gracie's men, some of them, were on the edge of the ridge top after the end of the bloody battle. Gracie IV reported receiving letters from Winfield Wolfe, John Nixon, and William B. Doyle, surviving members of Company A of the 43rd Alabama Regiment, who said they remained overnight on the brow of the hill and were willing to sign an affidavit to that effect.

Gracie IV, in a June 20, 1907, letter to Joseph E. Smiley, quoted Doyle as telling him that Doyle's company, Company A, was on the extreme right of the 43rd Regiment during the attack on the ridge. Company A, according to Doyle, through Gracie IV, attacked the steepest area of the ridge and reached the top, "where I know that the right of the 43rd, which was my company, slept that night after the fight. I well remember that we had to move dead men so that we could spread down our blankets to sleep."[66]

From the Confederate point of view, it was a good thing those Legion men and the soldiers from the 43rd Alabama who stayed on the edge of the ridge did so. They were not, in fact, relieved. Their first replacement group, the 1st Florida Cavalry (dismounted) with Colonel G. Troup Maxwell in command, served in Trigg's Brigade and inadvertently arrived in Gracie's area while looking to join the balance of Trigg's outfit while the fighting still raged.

Maxwell's regiment must have arrived in Gracie's area before the 6th and 7th Florida Regiments and the 54th Virginia attacked the western end of the Ridge. Maxwell wrote in his report that at the time he reached a position where he could be in support of Gracie's efforts, his regiment was subjected to brisk fire from the bluecoats on top of the ridge. Those Union rounds had to come from the area of Hills 2 and 3 or perhaps from the cornfield to Maxwell's right. The only men up on the edge of Hill 1 by then were a few of Gracie's Confederates who still had enough ammunition to remain in front of the informal breastworks erected by the Union men earlier in the day.

After first reporting to Preston, Maxwell was ordered to support Gracie. Maxwell found Gracie and was directed to join Gracie's force in attacking a hill, possibly meaning the Snodgrass cornfield, as that was the most active Federal area in Gracie's location at the time. Maxwell wrote in his report:

> Not being able to find my own brigade commander, I put myself under his (Gracie's) orders. He (Gracie) at first directed me to take the hill, but upon my suggestion that it was hardly possible for my small regiment to do what his large brigade had failed to accomplish, he ordered me to remain where I was until he could reform his brigade, the locality of which he did not then know. Being exposed to a severe fire to which they could not reply, I ordered my regiment to fall back to the cover of a fence in the corn-field, which they did in good order.[67]

Having "put myself under his orders," Maxwell then excused himself from following Gracie's directions and retreated to a safer location. The regiment's losses for the day came to one man killed and nine wounded, according to Maxwell's report. The day before, the 1st Florida had two men killed and 15 more wounded.

The Union troops still atop the ridge, who benefitted from a superior logistical program, exhausted their ammunition. After a while, most of the remaining Federals left, too, in order to avoid capture. By 6:00 p.m. the fight for Horseshoe Ridge was not over, but the most important characteristics were established: The fighting was fierce; both sides had run out of ammunition at crucial moments; debatable leadership decisions on both sides proved to be costly; examples of leadership excellence were evident in both armies; and both the Confederate and the Federal side suffered from communication failures.

The Confederates had a communications handicap at Horseshoe Ridge: Their lines were longer and many officers were either dead or wounded and out of the fighting. To visualize what that means, consider a traffic cone, the orange markers used everywhere to direct travelers on roads. The Union soldiers were perched at the top of three connected cones, mostly stayed in place and communicated around a small area. The Confederates were at the bottom of the cones and had a wider or longer base of operations, moved around a lot and had major units joining and leaving the fighting. The Federals had units retreating and then leaving the battlefield. The senior Union commander on the ridge, George Thomas, had left the area by the time we now consider to direct his army's overall retreat.

Fairly said, both sides suffered leadership casualties during the duration of the fighting and the loss of important commanders impacted the flow of the battle. But the three Federal divisions still fighting on Horseshoe Ridge by 6:00 p.m. had their leadership generally intact. The 21st Ohio lost only one officer during the fight for the ridge, the mortally wounded Lieutenant Colonel Dwella M. Stoughton. Four other officers also suffered wounds. Eleven officers were captured or otherwise classified as missing. Two officers of the 89th Ohio were killed or mortally wounded, Lieutenants Granville Jackson and Stephen V. Walker. Two other officers were wounded and 13 more were captured or missing. The 22nd Michigan had no officers killed during the fighting, although two who were wounded and later died were Captains William A. Smith and Captain Elijah Snell. Three others were wounded and 14 were reported missing or captured.

Gracie's Brigade lost six officers killed and 30 others were wounded.[68]

8

The Final
Confederate Threat

And what of Henry Hilliard Hines, the young, unmarried farmer in Company F of the Legion's 1st Battalion? Hines was wounded in his left ankle sometime on the 20th. It is reasonable to assume Hines marched with his unit to the scene of the fighting on Horseshoe Ridge and incurred his wound there. There is an unsupportable assumption by some of his descendants that Hines was hit as the Legion strode across the saddle area between the short downhill stretch immediately before the climb up the face of Horseshoe Ridge. Regardless of where he was at the time he was hit, Hines was one of many to fall wounded on that blood-soaked hill. The Legion's 1st Battalion, Hines' battalion, suffered heavy casualties at the hands of the Federal men above them. Hines was one of the 144 soldiers in the 1st who were wounded in that action. Twenty-four others were killed.

Also among the members of the 1st to be wounded was Benjamin Mason, the private who had written home about food shortages the previous spring. Mason suffered a hand wound and did not return to his comrades until the following October 28.

Mason and Hines were luckier than some. Another private, Michael Kief (1st Battalion, Company A), was wounded in *both* legs, as was Sergeant Fredrick Crusins of the same company.

But battlefield fortune is not predictable. Corporal James Jenkins, for example, survived the fighting at Chickamauga and later became part of the 23rd Alabama Sharpshooters, which joined the Army of Northern Virginia. Jenkins surrendered with Robert E. Lee at Appomattox.[1]

At 6:00 p.m. on September 20, 1863, the battlefield around Horseshoe Ridge was a very confusing place to be. Much of the Union command was in retreat, but a small piece of the Union force, the 21st Ohio, had returned to the fight. The Confederates were generally moving forward, but Gracie's ammunition-starved soldiers were forced to pull back—indeed, they were ordered to pull back—from their hard-won ground atop the ridge as reinforcements were arriving.

Various accounts of the fighting paint the picture: There was heavy gun smoke in the air and, in spots, small clumps of brush had caught fire, adding more smoke to the blinding air quality. Dead and wounded lay scattered everywhere, denser in some places than others. Darkness was nearly at hand. The combination of gathering darkness and the light and smoke from the fires must have added to the confusion. The fires were frequent happenings on Civil War battlefields. The weaponry, large and small, required a spark from one source or another in order to fire, and the ammunition frequently left the barrels of small arms and the tubes of cannons trailing sparks. The Horseshoe Ridge area was wooded and tinder rich.

At Chickamauga, as at other battlefields of the era, the results were ghastly. The seriously wounded often died on the fields and those already dead were sometimes burned beyond recognition. The smell of charred human flesh is ugly and it permeated the battlefield.

Gracie's units had been ordered to pull back from their positions on the hillsides, mindful that some of the enemy was still firing. Most of the Brigade's men followed the pullback order. The sojourn down the steep hill was difficult, made more so by trying not to trip over dead and injured comrades. Many of the Confederate men were shoeless, and though some were probably accustomed to that, their shoelessness must have made it harder to deal with tree trunks, roots, rocks, fires and weaponry left lying on the ground, the usual detritus of battle.

Elements of the Union Army were still fighting at 6:15 p.m. The 21st Ohio, which was not resupplied immediately after pulling back, was sent back toward the fighting on Hill 2 with one round of ammunition per man. The 21st joined the men of the 89th Ohio and the 22nd Michigan on the hill where all were under threat from Kelly's men of the 58th North Carolina, the 5th Kentucky and the 63rd Virginia. Captain Isaac Cusac of the 21st Ohio's Company G wrote in a 1909 letter to E. A. Carman that an unidentified Federal officer ordered the men of the 21st to move forward after the regiment had pulled back for want of ammunition. The officer ordered the men of the 21st to fix their bayonets and go back to the front line. They followed orders, Cusac wrote.[2]

But the final Confederate threat, the balance of Trigg's command, had just arrived.

Trigg described his actions:

6:00 pm Horseshoe Ridge

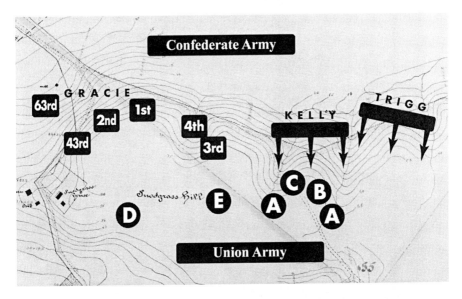

- **A** 21st Ohio *(Posted in Two Positions)*
- **B** 89th Ohio
- **C** 22nd Michigan
- **D** 9th Indiana
- **E** 35th Ohio

By 6 p.m., elements of three of the Legion's four battalions had positions on the top of the ridge from a spot between Hills 2 and 1 and around Hill 1 toward the Snodgrass farm buildings. There were few Union defenders atop either Hill 1 or Hill 2, but three regiments still defended Hill 3. Kelly's Brigade had attacked and the largest part of Trigg's Brigade was arriving (courtesy Teri Schott).

The battle was raging furiously when I arrived with the Seventh Florida Regiment, which I formed on the left of the 54th Virginia, which, with the 6th Florida Regiment, was already formed on the left of Kelly's brigade. ... Without wavering or faltering, these two brigades, marching over some of our own troops who were lying down, drove the enemy steadily before them until his right was forced from its strong position ... protected by breastworks. When near the base of this ridge I learned from Colonel Kelly the precise locality of the enemy, and immediately determined with him to attempt the capture of that part of his force in my front, my position being particularly favorable for the attainment of this end.[3]

On Hill 3 of Horseshoe Ridge, the 21st Ohio was split in two, acting as the left and right ends of the Union line, while the 89th Ohio and 22nd Michigan fought in the center. But the Confederate 7th Florida (of Trigg's Brigade) and 63rd Virginia (Kelly), acting like defensive ends rushing a quarterback, looped around the opposing sides of the Union line and completed a surrounding movement.

Cusac, the captain in the 21st Ohio, described how and where he and his comrades came to be captured this way in his 1909 letter to Carman:

> The result was that as we moved straight forward ... we struck on the left of the 89th, and I with Co. G and B went straight forward to the line and halted ... where the center of the 21st had been all afternoon. The regt [sic] with the exception of Co. G and B swang to the right and rear of the 89th and were captured ... at the same time with the 89th while I with Com. G and part of Co. B were taken near to the line the regt [sic] had previously occupied....[4]

Trigg explained:

> I immediately wheeled my brigade to the right, which brought me in rear of the enemy, and moved rapidly up the hill to within 20 paces of his lines. This movement

6:15 pm Horseshoe Ridge

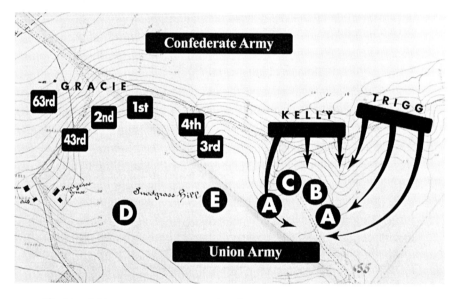

A 21st Ohio *(Posted in Two Positions)* **D** 9th Indiana
B 89th Ohio **E** 35th Ohio
C 22nd Michigan

At about 6:15 p.m., Kelly's and Trigg's brigades surrounded members of the 21st Ohio, 89th Ohio and 22nd Michigan and captured them. At roughly the same time, unsure what was happening to their right, the 9th Indiana and 35th Ohio fired a volley toward Hill 3 and left the area (courtesy Teri Schott).

surprised him and resulted in the capture of the twenty-second Michigan, the eighty-ninth Ohio, and part of the 5 stands of colors, and over 1,500 small-arms of the latest and most approved pattern. Darkness having fallen ... no farther movement was attempted.[5]

The "latest and most approved pattern" of weapon must have referred to the Colt revolving rifles that the 21st Ohio carried. There are reports that some soldiers in the 21st attempted to smash their revolving rifles against trees in order to destroy the weapons and make them useless for the Confederates. They probably needn't have bothered, as the Confederate government could not have supplied ammunition for the guns anyway.

Fuller, the 3rd Battalion private who was a member of the Hughes detail, was there with Trigg's men. He wrote to Gracie IV that the Hughes' detail joined the 6th Florida on the march toward the ridge and then "Our detail took position on the right of this regiment, and aided and assisted in driving the Yankees over one of the range of hills on the western end of Snodgrass Ridge. After being engaged some little while we were ordered to fix bayonets and charge a battery located on a little knoll to our front, but the battery was moved to the rear by the Yankees before we got to it."[6]

Notice how a common foot soldier, Fuller, did not describe grand, sweeping movements by the Confederate force. Fuller reported that the 6th Florida and the men of the Hughes detail were moving north and then east as together they all moved toward the fighting on the ridge. Then, Fuller said, "by some movement which I do not understand, our position changed to a ravine at the foot of Snodgrass Ridge on the north side. My recollection is that at that time we were facing South."

Fuller's 1905 letter to Gracie III continued, "It was then a little later than twilight—almost dark,

Unknown Union soldier holding a Model 1855 Colt revolving rifle. Some Union defenders on Horseshoe Ridge were armed with Colt revolving rifles (Library of Congress, Prints and Photographs Division, Reproduction No. LC-DIG-ppmsca-37042).

and the Yankees on Snodgrass Ridge then surrendered to us. We opened ranks, the Yankees marched in and we marched them down the ravine South."

One of the Union officers swept up by Trigg's encirclement effort was Major Arnold McMahan of the 21st Ohio Volunteer Infantry. McMahan remained a prisoner until he was paroled in 1864. After his parole, McMahan wrote his report on the fighting at Horseshoe Ridge. Before submitting that report, he wrote a letter to Major General James S. Negley and asked plaintively why he, McMahan, had received no order to retreat. "I would be pleased to have my report accompanied by a letter from you," McMahan wrote to Negley, "showing why I received no orders from you before night, or in time to prevent so severe a loss of my command on the 20th of September."[7]

The severe loss McMahan reported makes for an interesting review. The 21st Ohio went into the fighting at Chickamauga with 539 effectives, 22 of them officers. Of that total, 48 were killed (one an officer) and 101 were wounded (three officers). Of the remaining 390 enlisted men and officers, 265 were taken prisoner, leaving 125 survivors of the battle. The regiment lost the use of 76.8 percent of the soldiers it had at the start of the engagement. However, only 27.6 percent of the original total were killed or wounded.[8]

On Hill 2, the remaining Union regiments on the ridge still not captured—the 35th Ohio and the 9th Indiana—may not have been sure what was happening on Hill 3. The Indiana regiment fired a volley anyway and the two regiments left the area a short time later.

The commands of Trigg and Kelly did not pursue the fleeing Ohio and Indiana men. The Confederates had a healthy bag of captured Yankees, nabbed by the encircling movement, to keep an eye on.

Fuller wrote to Gracie IV that the Florida men moved the captured Federals south until "we found a road at the foot of Snodgrass Ridge on the South side.... I went with the detail probably a quarter mile from this ravine. I dropped out of ranks and returned to the foot of the ridge on the South side, where I found Gracie's Brigade encamped."[9]

Trigg stated:

> Before beginning the movement last alluded to, I requested two brigades which were in my rear to form on my left and co-operate with me. They declined for the want of ammunition. It is greatly to be regretted that they were not in a condition to give me assistance. Had they formed on my left our line would have extended nearly, if not quite, to the Chattanooga road, and being in rear of the enemy, all his forces occupying the ridge would have been completely cut off.[10]

Given his location, Trigg probably did not request cooperation from Gracie's men, who were closer to the area of Hills 1 and 2. Kelly's men were in the area, but they were already working with Trigg to encircle the remaining Union forces up on the ridge. Kershaw's men were not too far away, but the men of Anderson's command probably were closer to Trigg's location prior to his move up the side of the ridge.

Trigg apparently did not know the location of his dismounted cavalry regiment, the 1st Florida. That outfit was, as we have seen, largely unscathed by the fighting and probably had its full complement of ammunition, as the regiment did not exchange fire with the defenders of Horseshoe Ridge.

Longstreet concluded the Horseshoe Ridge portion of his report:

> … and by a flank movement and another advance the heights were gained…. The enemy broke up in great confusion along my front, and about the same time the Right Wing made a gallant dash and gained the line that had been held so long and obstinately against it. A simultaneous and continuous shout from the two wings announced our success complete. The enemy had fought every man that he had, and every one had been in turn beaten.[11]

Fuller's letter to Gracie is perhaps the most compelling evidence in the matter of whether Gracie's Brigade was forced off the brow of Horseshoe Ridge. The encircling movement by Trigg's men and those of Kelly came from the west, capturing the Union soldiers in front of it. Fuller and his mates moved south and uphill, climbing the backside of the ridge. These men more or less acted as a large dustpan while the broom, comprised of the other Confederates, swept the Yankees their way.

The men whom the Trigg and Kelly commands captured came from Hill 3, the westernmost of the Horseshoe Ridge hills, and the prisoners were among the final Union men still fighting on the ridge. Numerous sources in both Union and Confederate reports allude to this point.

If the Union soldiers captured by Trigg and Kelly (not to mention the Hughes detail) were the last Federals on the ridge, then there were none on the edge of Hill 1 by then. That means that no Federal force pushed Gracie's men off the edge of Hill 1. The Yankees did not reclaim the edge of Hill 1 before the Confederates rolled in from the Union right and emptied the ridge of the bluecoats.

Remember the time of day. Gracie ordered his brigade to pull back about 6 p.m. or near dark. Fuller said the 6th Florida and the men of the Hughes detail captured the enemy shortly after twilight, or "almost dark." A lot of things happened at almost the same time on that ridge.[12]

The events were close together. By this time, the largest part of the surviving mass of Union men was not moving forward. Those men were retreating. There were no Union men left to rush to the crude breastworks on Hill 1. The Federal men left to fend for themselves by the Union exodus from the fighting did not have time to rush toward Hill 1, even if they had been so inclined, before Trigg's men effected their capture.

The Federal retreat from Chickamauga jammed Dry Valley Road, according to George S. Canfield, the 15-year-old drummer for the 21st Ohio. Canfield's father, Captain Silas Sprague Canfield of Company K of the 21st, sent the teenager to fill canteens shortly before the 21st went into action on the 20th with the warning that if the younger Canfield became somehow separated from the regiment, he should head for Chattanooga. The younger Canfield did indeed become separated from the unit and ended up following a scary route while searching for his regiment.

The teenaged Canfield found himself

> ... in flight along with the broken right of Rosecrans' army! ... It was Dry Valley road that I was on, and it was rapidly becoming no road, but a sea of fleeing men.... The woods full of men, all in retreat and becoming more and more demoralized.... It was blockaded with teams of a wagon train. The soldiers forced the teams out of the way, here and there, breaking up the train.... We were running right into the battle line, where it was forced back by the now victorious enemy.... The road was now condensing again, with routed men. They poured from every part of the west side of the road, coming most from a point opposite what I learned was Snodgrass Hill.[13]

Daylight, even twilight, had been replaced by steadily darkening conditions. It was probably difficult to see Hill 1 from Hill 2, which is only about 150 yards away. Hill 3 is further away and impossible to see from Hill 1, even in daylight. There was no way for the stranded Union fighters to ascertain whether or not Hill 1 was a safe place for a Union soldier to be at that moment.

And, in fact, Hill 1 was decidedly *not* a safe place for Union soldiers by that hour. The reader will recall that the 43rd Alabama Regiment was a veteran outfit, one that did not waste ammunition. The 43rd had men on Hill 1 when darkness fell. Indeed, some men from at least one company of the 43rd, Company A, never left the crest of Hill 1 on the night of September 20/21.

As has been noted, Gracie IV met and corresponded with at least four men from Company A who told him they spent the night in the positions they assumed when they drove the Yankees off the edge of the south side of Hill 1. Those men, privates Winfield Wolfe, William B. Doyle, E. C. Martin and John Mixon, told Gracie IV that their company did not exhaust its supply of cartridges during the rush up the side of the hill, the Union retreat and the subsequent shooting contest.[14]

We can say with confidence that no Union group rushed forward to resume their positions on the berm of Hill 1 after Gracie recalled his brigade due to the lack of ammunition. Gracie's men were not chased from that position. Most of those who could leave did so when the order went out because of the lack of ammunition. But some who could still use their weapons stayed. There was no relief force for the hard-pressed Confederates on Hill 1.

It is impossible to overstate how confusing the conditions were for the Union soldiers atop Horseshoe Ridge. We have seen the conditions on the side of the hill where the Confederates relentlessly drove at the positions held by the Army of the Cumberland. The same smoky, tree-lined and bullet-filled environment that Gracie's men struggled with also made the job difficult for the Union soldiers. The author believes that the nature of the situation contributed to the heretofore held belief by some historians that Gracie's men, including the Legion, were *driven* off the edge of the ridge.

First, there is the fact that most of the surviving men of Gracie's Brigade pulled back off the ridge only when their ammunition ran out and they were ordered to pull back. The Official Records, letters and other sources make this point clear.

But finding a credible report that a unit of Thomas' force attacked the positions the Union soldiers had formerly defended anytime near nightfall is a challenge. There is no report which can be shown to prove that a Union unit drove Gracie's men off a position once the Gracie Brigade took possession of said position. The closest the author has come to a credible report that the Legion was driven from the berm of the ridge is the following. It comes from Brigadier General John Beatty, commanding the Union's First Brigade.

> Once during the afternoon the enemy succeeded in planting his colors almost on the crest of the ridge on our immediate front, and for a moment drove our men from the summit. An extraordinary effort of the officers present was successful in again rallying them to the crest, and the timely arrival of a detachment of the Eighteenth Ohio, led by Lieutenant-Colonel Grosvenor, drove back the enemy, who only saved his colors by throwing them down the hill.[15]

But note Beatty's reference to "the afternoon." The actions concerning the colors, presumably regimental colors, were those of the brave South Carolinian mentioned earlier, not an Alabama man. We have seen in both Grosvenor's letter to Gracie IV and from Gracie IV's May 20, 1907, letter to Stallworth that Grosvenor told Gracie IV about 40 years after the war that the flag in this action was a South Carolina regimental flag, not one from Alabama.

Earlier in the day soldiers on both sides had contended with visibility-limiting conditions, including gun smoke and artillery smoke, more smoke from small fires where the undergrowth and fallen leaves caught fire, trees and branches, shadows and steep terrain. By the closing minutes of the battle the surviving soldiers also had to contend with the dark of night.

It was difficult to determine friend from foe in the dark. One Union officer wrote of being confused by a body of men who advanced through the gloom wearing "blue jeans." The Union troops did not fire, but the men advancing in the gloom turned out to be Confederates and the Union men were captured.

Horseshoe Ridge, dearly bought with a heavy investment of men and ammunition, was now under Confederate control.

In his post-battle report, Confederate Major General T. C. Hindman wrote of the fighting on Horseshoe Ridge, "I have never known Federal troops to fight so well. It is just to say, also, that I never saw Confederate soldiers fight better."[16]

9

Was There
a Fake Surrender?

The fog of war, smoke of battle and falling of darkness all combined to make things very confusing for the foot soldiers and their officers fighting along the heights of Horseshoe Ridge as night closed in on September 20, 1863.

And this war was fought by two armies made up of men who spoke the same language. While it is true that an Alabamian can immediately discern the accent of a Mainer in the quiet of a library, the same cannot be said of the same two men a short distance from one another in the midst of a major battle. The shots, booms, groans and shouts of a military engagement make words easier to detect than regional accents. Send a few bullets whizzing by a soldier's ears and even a steady combat veteran can be confused by what he hears. Given that situation, anyone can run into trouble.

The reader is asked to keep these thoughts in mind as we briefly step away from the men of Hilliard's Alabama Legion and explore an enduring question about the deadly fighting at Horseshoe Ridge.

Was there a fake surrender by a group of soldiers who then leveled their arms and fired upon their would-be captors after the latter group dropped its guard? Most texts covering the Battle of Chickamauga mention this matter, if only in passing. It is a dramatic story with deadly consequences and it points toward the grizzly nature of the fighting on and near the ridge. There are several versions, and the author is convinced that any version *could* be true.

From the Union side, Captain Charles H. Vantine of the 21st Ohio wrote in his official report:

At about half past 5 p.m. the enemy sent up messengers to Brannan's men stating that some of them were waiting for them [our men] to cease firing in order to give themselves [i.e., the enemy] up. The firing ceased and the enemy came up, but instead of a giving themselves up they fired a volley and charged up the hill, gaining possession of it entirely.

A bit later, there was this in Vantine's report:

> While we were waiting a column was observed filing in a small ravine on our right flank. Supposing they were our men (they being dressed in blue jeans) we took no notice of them until they formed line of battle facing toward us. They formed and commenced advancing on us; when asked who they were, said they were "Jeff. Davis' men;" supposed they were some of J. C. Davis' division. When they were within a few rods of us they called upon us to "surrender," "lay down," &c. A portion of the men jumped up to retreat toward General Brannan's division, when they poured in a heavy volley, wounding and killing a great many.[1]

The cynical reader will note that Vantine's version of both the incidents happened at key points in the struggle to maintain a Union position on the front of Horseshoe Ridge. The statements would have us believe that it was Confederate deceit, or at least Federal troop confusion, not martial skill, daring and courage that gained a foothold on the tip of the ridge. Vantine was among those Ohioans who escaped the Trigg/Kelly pincer sweep that gathered up McMahan and so many other soldiers of the 21st. Vantine's report was written a day or two later. McMahan's report does not mention either incident, but his was written after two years as a prisoner of war.

There are Confederate versions of same the story, reversing the roles, wherein a Union unit asks to surrender, then kills the kindly Confederate soldiers that stand patiently waiting an honorable retirement by said Unionists. The stories can't all be true, but if anything like the above described did happen, it may have been born of the fog (not to mention the smoke) of war.

Once again a report from the Official Records is relevant, this one from Confederate Colonel John H. Kelly. Kelly wrote that at about 5 p.m.,

> I determined to attempt to dislodge him (the enemy) by assault, and for this purpose transferred the Fifty-eighth North Carolina from the right to the left of my line and moved forward, swinging somewhat to the right. When I arrived at the base of the hill the enemy was heard to cry, "We surrender! we surrender!" I immediately stepped to the front, my horse having been previously killed, and called upon the officer who seemed to be in command and demanded that if he proposed to surrender he should lay down his arms. He came to the front and said, "Wait a minute." I replied, "No, sir; lay down your arms instantly, or I will fire upon you," and turned to my command, but before I could give the command "ready," he poured upon it a terrific fire, which, on account of its suddenness, threw the brigade for the instant into confusion; but it rallied and was reformed within 30 yards of this position. I am confident that the enemy intended to surrender, and that his fire was drawn by an unauthorized shot from his ranks.[2]

Kelly, a Brigade commander at the front of his men, turns his back on enemy soldiers who have stated they wish to surrender but have yet to give up their arms. Then, when the treacherous enemy reveals the real intent of the encounter with "a terrific fire," Kelly somehow escapes injury.

What really happened? We don't know. But Kelly's version, that one group of enemy soldiers wanted to surrender and another group did not, rings true. It really doesn't matter which side had which role in the event.

If it happened.

10

An Expensive Victory

General Gracie wrote in his report, "Early the next morning the brigade resumed the position it had so nobly won."[1]

Nobly, perhaps. But the spot on the ridge won by Gracie's men was a *costly* victory. The author has culled a variety of sources for the purpose of finding the best numbers of men killed and wounded from Gracie's Brigade. The Legion's four battalions and the two regiments in the brigade went into battle with 1,870 soldiers and officers, according to Gracie's report. Preston's report shows the Brigade's complement at 2,003, but the author assumes that total includes surgeons, soldiers with illnesses and other non-combat members. It appears that Gracie took 1,704 fighting men into action on September 20. Of that total, 90 men were killed and 615 more were wounded, meaning that 41.3 percent of the brigade's attackers were killed or wounded.[2]

The cost for Hilliard's men alone was far higher by percentage. The four battalions that came from the original Legion had 415 casualties (67 men killed and 348 wounded) out of the 902 that went into battle, or 46 percent. The 1st Battalion went into the fight with 238 men and officers and suffered 24 killed and 144 wounded for a stunning 70.5 percent casualty rate.

That figure compares with the losses suffered by the 63rd and 69th New York regiments, two parts of the Union's famed Irish Brigade, during the battle of Antietam. The 63rd and 69th both suffered roughly 60 percent losses in that engagement. The brutal carnage inflicted on the Union army, and the Irish Brigade in particular, in that bloody engagement was a generator in the growing tide of anti-war sentiment in the North in 1862.[3]

After Chickamauga, families in Alabama felt the same crushing sense of loss.

It is interesting to note the impact the carnage had on a single company in the Legion's 1st Battalion. Company F went into the conflict with

26 effective soldiers. Of the 26, 18 were killed or wounded, a 69.2 percent casualty rate. The author searched various sources to compile an accurate list of the Legion's members and has found 84 original members of Company F. Disease, desertions and other problems drained the company of about 70 percent of its manpower before the unit ever saw combat.[4]

Captain Nicholas Stallworth, in the same 1907 letter quoted above, is quoted by Gracie IV: "My company suffered terribly, an aggregate of twenty-eight or thirty went into the charge and twenty-four of us were hit." Stallworth himself was wounded, but he returned to the army and eventually commanded the 23rd Battalion, Alabama Sharpshooters. The 23rd was made up of some of the survivors of the 1st Battalion's fighting at Chickamauga.[5]

Another combat loss comparison is in order. Wood's 1st Division of the U.S. Army went into battle on September 19 with 2,965 soldiers, including officers. After two days of fighting, Wood reported, 34.9 percent of those men were killed, wounded or missing. In his report, Wood said those figures "show an almost unparalleled loss. They attest the severity of the conflicts through which my command passed on the 19th and 20th."[6]

Wood's was a sad casualty report, to be sure. He concluded his report:, "The record of [the 1st Division's] participation in the great battle of the Chickamauga is written in blood."[7] Still, it paled when stacked next to Gracie's. The losses Wood detailed were inflicted over two days of fighting.

The 21st Ohio Regiment, with its large number taken prisoner, suffered as well. Of the 22 officers and 517 enlisted men that the 21st took into battle at Chickamauga, 49 percent were lost. Remember, this regiment used up the ammunition it was issued on the 20th and retired. It scrounged up enough ammunition for each surviving man to go back to the fighting with one round and used *that* supply before Trigg's pincer movement wrapped the 21st into a bundle of blue-clad prisoners. Some escaped, as we have seen. Few Union regiments fought with more courage than that shown by the 21st. Subtracting those taken prisoner, the casualty rate after two days of hard fighting was still 28.8 percent.

The losses incurred by the two non–Legion regiments in Gracie's Brigade were also ugly. According to the Official Records, the 43rd Alabama lost 16 men killed and 83 wounded out of 400, for 24.7 percent. The 63rd Tennessee, which the reader will recall was mauled by the Federal artillery in Snodgrass Field, lost 16 killed and 184 wounded, 200 casualties out of 402 men or 49.7 percent. Most of the Tennessee regiment's losses were suffered within the first few minutes of the attack.[8]

There are various estimates of the losses at Chickamauga for both the Federal and Confederate armies. Simply for the purposes of consistency, we have used the statistics supplied by commanding officers in the Official Records.[9]

The reader will recall the so-called "fatigue duty" men from Gracie's command, led by Lt. Hughes, who spent the night of the 19th and part of the day on the 20th building defenses near Chickamauga Creek. This is the group that eventually joined the 6th Florida Regiment and went to the fighting on Horseshoe Ridge.

In his report, Lieutenant John W. A. Sanford of the Legion's 3rd Battalion said, "I have been informed they were attached to Colonel Trigg's brigade. Of the fatigue party, 1 man was killed, and 1 officer and 2 men were wounded."[10]

The Hall family was hard hit by the Federal riflemen. In a September 23, 1863, letter to his uncle, Bolling Hall, Sr., E. Crenshaw Hall related that he had been wounded in the face. "Bolling [Jr.] has a flesh wound in the leg. Tom Brown [Hall] is rather severely wounded in the leg; Jim Crenshaw and Johny are unhurt." He added, "My righ' cheek bone and Jaw bone are broken and near by (possibly nearly) all of my Jaw teeth shot out."[11]

Perhaps the most poignant sentence written about serving in the Civil War was penned by Horace McLean, the 2nd Battalion sergeant. In a letter to his wife, Mary, McLean wrote, "[I] am the proudest fellow that I cam [sic] through the battle safe that I hardly know how to contain myself."[12]

One final comparison for a point of reference: Colonel Robert Bullock, who commanded the 7th Florida Infantry, wrote about the fighting on the 20th: "I am happy to report but few casualties in my command, nearly all of which occurred [on the 19th]."[13]

Few ledger challenges are greater than those dealing with the battlefield. The Official Records are full of good faith efforts by officers in both armies to report accurate casualty numbers. But, truth be told, this is a difficult statistic to keep.

Take, for example, the Confederates in the "fatigue duty" detail. For the sake of simplicity, let us accept Sanford's report that the detail included 50 privates and six officers. These 56 men were separated from their brigade when the brigade was sent up the hills of Horseshoe Ridge.

As we have seen, this detail was still at work building defenses when its members noticed that some of the wounded coming toward the brigade hospital were members of their own battalion. The men of the detail then threw down their tools, according to Fuller, and rushed toward the front line, eventually joining and fighting with the 6th Florida Regiment belonging to Trigg. Two of the men in the detail were apparently killed (one officer and one enlisted) in the fighting. The surviving men of the detail later rejoined their own brigade.

How could Gracie's officers account for the 56 men while compiling their statistics for their reports? Gracie's officers did not know until later that the men of the special detail had gone into battle. And what of Trigg's reports? Should they include the men of the special detail?

Then there is the case of one Private David Cannon. Cannon is said to have been shot through the bowels. Desperately wounded, he made his way into the area where Kelly's and Gracie's men were fighting, where he finally succumbed to his injury. Cannon was buried where he was found, among Gracie's men, and was originally listed as missing by his regiment. Gracie later related the incident to Colonel Finley, mentioning that the private's knapsack identified him as coming from Company A of the 6th Florida.

Wave after wave of Confederate soldiers attacked Horseshoe Ridge on September 20. Soldiers from many, many companies in numerous regiments and brigades from several divisions battered themselves against the stubborn Union defenders. Every one of those commands left dead and wounded comrades on the sides and crests of the ridge. Considering this daunting statistical challenge, amazing work was done.

Numbers are important, and this book is a good-faith attempt to sift through the statistics in the various reports in the Official Records to determine how many soldiers probably went into action with Gracie on that September afternoon. Remember, Preston's report stated that Gracie's Brigade was 2,003 strong. Not every member of Hilliard's Legion, the 43rd Alabama or the 63rd Tennessee was a foot soldier. There were non-combatants, such as surgeons, quartermasters and teamsters, who had duty assignments that kept them away from the front lines. Gracie's report stated that the brigade carried *about* 1,870 into action (the emphasis is the author's). That's a difference of 133 or 7.1 percent.

In his report about the 1st Battalion, Huguley said his command had 260 men, "aggregate," and that 238 members went into action on the 20th. Hall's report said the 2nd Battalion "carried into action 230 aggregate." Sanford's 3rd Battalion report said his battalion "carried into the fight ... 211 enlisted men and 18 officers; aggregate 229." This report also mentioned the 56 men in the fatigue detail, noting that this group eventually became attached to the 6th Florida. But Sanford did not further explain how many of the 56 came from his command. McLennan wrote that the 4th Battalion had "Aggregate carried into the fight, 205." Major John A. Aiken of the 63rd Tennessee wrote that his regiment took 402 "aggregate" into the engagement. Moody, commanding the 43rd Alabama, did not note how many his regiment sent against the Federal troops on Horseshoe Ridge, but the number traditionally used for the strength of the 43rd is 400.

Simple mathematics indicate that the Legion had 902 officers and enlisted men attacking the ridge. Add Aiken's 402 men and Moody's 400 and you have 1,704 men. If you subtract the figure 1,704 from Gracie's estimate that his strength as he attacked the ridge was 1,870, the difference is 166, which could be the number of non-combatants in the brigade. The figure used here for the number of men Gracie led into combat, 1,704, represents the number of men claimed by the commanders of the Legion's four battalions and the two regiments. As those officers had smaller numbers to keep track of and since they did not have to count the brigade-level non-combatants, the author has used that figure.[14]

The reports are clearer about casualties. Gracie said that his brigade lost 90 killed and 615 wounded (705 total). The reports from the battalion commanders indicate that the 1st Battalion lost 24 killed and 144 wounded (168 total), the 2nd lost 16 killed and 75 wounded (91 total), the 3rd suffered four killed and 42 wounded (46 total), the 4th lost 15 killed and 87 wounded (102 total). Moody's 43rd Alabama lost 16 killed and 83 wounded (99 total) and the 63rd Tennessee suffered, as we have seen, 16 killed and 184 wounded (200 total). The battalion and regimental reports add up to 706 killed and wounded.[15]

Sanford's report seems to discount the men and officers in the fatigue party, separating that group from the remainder of his command. He wrote that they did not return to the battalion until after the battle but that they had been attached to Trigg's command. Among the fatigue party, Sanford wrote, one officer and one enlisted man were killed and two enlisted men were wounded.

That would bump the brigade's casualty total to 710.

To make better sense of the bookkeeping, the author decided to accept the statistics in the Official Records and work with the ambiguities. When numbers in various reports do not match up, it makes sense to take the figure listed by the officer lowest in rank, as that man was the closest to the party that performed the grisly job of counting the killed and wounded.

Whatever the actual casualty count was, the Legion men took a savage pounding on their way to pushing elements of the Union army off the brow of Horseshoe Ridge. As the survivors manned the line along the ridge on the morning of September 21, they had no way of knowing what was in front of them. War, more war, and endless uncertainty, that much seemed obvious.

George Washington Sexton, the short-penned diarist who suffered a thigh wound at Chickamauga, described the short-term future in his September 22 entry: "Moved from the battlefield to Missionary Ridge and remained in front of Chattanooga, [two miles] under the guns of the enemy for one month."[16]

With the Yankees gone from the field, the Confederates began to take stock of the frayed remnants of Braxton Bragg's army. There was no front line, no clearly delineated streak following the contours of the land manned by alert Rebels peering into the dark for stray bluecoats. Instead, there were clumps of survivors strewn along the area where the Federals had last been seen.

Groups like the aforementioned soldiers from Company A of the 43rd Alabama inhabited spots roughly in a general direction running slightly southwest to northeast. In those spots, they waited.

After the battle, the cleanup began. Weaponry and wounded were strewn about, intermingled with corpses. Not all of the corpses were human, because many horses were killed as well. One or possibly two horses were killed while Gracie rode them.

Preston wrote:

> The next morning I ordered the burial of the dead. Many of our brave men had fallen in charging the slopes leading to the summit of the ridge. The musketry from the low breastworks of the enemy on the hill attacked by General Gracie had set fire to the dry foliage and scorched and blackened corpses gave fearful proof of the heroism and suffering of the brave men who had stormed the hill. The ground occupied by the enemy's battery was strewn with slain. More to the north, in a wooded dell in front of Kelly and Trig, many dead and wounded of the enemy were found who had fled the combat and sought concealment in its shadows. All the dead along my line, whether of friend or enemy, were buried, and the wounded removed to hospitals.[17]

The winning side is always stuck with the tiring and gruesome work of collecting and tending to the wounded, burying the dead and recovering any useful items cast off during the fighting. Frequently during the American Civil War, the army still holding the field when the fighting was ended would leave the area quickly, seeking to further engage the enemy and leaving the local citizenry to deal with the resulting mess.

As the Confederates held the battlefield after the fighting ended at Chickamauga, the fallen gray backs received more attention than their blue-clad counterparts. Surviving soldiers searched the battlefield in order to find missing comrades, living and dead. The living, obviously, were sent to field hospitals.

John L. Odom, a private in Company F of the 3rd Battalion, wrote after the war: "The next morning our regiment was among those detailed to bury the dead. After getting our own men buried, we buried the enemy. We would dig a pit about 6x8 feet deep; fill the ditch about three-fourths full of the dead, and then cover them with dirt. We were engaged at this for three days and then left for Missionary Ridge."[18]

Bragg reported on September 24 that his army had taken 7,000 prisoners (of whom 2,000 were wounded), 36 pieces of artillery and 15,000 pieces of small arms.[19]

After the fighting at Chickamauga, there was no rush to chase after the defeated foe. McLean, the 2nd Battalion quartermaster, described the cleanup to his wife:

> Most all of the enemies wounded fell into our hands on the battle field owing to our pressing them back so fast which made it quit a task to get them up in anything like due time. I saw some of their wounded that lay on the ground two nights and one day and a piece we captured … and a great many of their infirmary Corps commonally known as liter bearers and we made them assist all they could in gather their wounded I have no ida [sic] but that a good many of the (unclear) wounded burned to death from the woods they were burning all around….[20]

The dead were mainly buried where they fell, their resting places noted with simple wooden markers. Those soldiers recognized by company or regimental buddies had their names carved on the markers. As the battle took place along the border between Tennessee and Georgia, some Confederate soldiers' remains were identified by family or friends and taken or sent home shortly after the battle.

About three years after the battle, a year after the war ended, an effort was made to send the remains of Confederate soldiers from their graves at the battlefield to a Confederate cemetery in Marietta, Georgia. By this time, weather and age had affected the wooden grave markers and, sadder still, grave robbers had had their way with some of the remains. Not all of the Confederate remains that were found at Chickamauga in 1866 could be identified for burial at Marietta.

Worse still, there was a fire at the cemetery about two decades later. The cemetery is located near a railroad and somehow a spark from a passing train ignited a fire, destroying some of the wooden markers above the resting places of the Confederate veterans.

Fallen U.S. Army soldiers fared worse, as was normal for the losing side during that era. We know from Odom's writing that many of the Union dead were not identified when they were buried on the battlefield and, obviously, could not be identified when the remains were moved after the war. The Union remains were reinterred in Federal cemeteries.

In his post-action report, General Preston praised the gallantry of several officers and enlisted men, one of them Private George W. Norris. Norris served in Gracie's Brigade, in Company E of the Legion's 2nd Battalion. Preston wrote: "George W. Norris, of Captain Wise's company, of Hall's battalion, fell at the foot of the enemy's flag-staff, and was buried at the spot where he had so nobly died."[21]

Norris' name appears on the muster roll for Company E of the Legion's 2nd Battalion, but the author has found no reference which indicates where his final resting place might be. He could be among the unknowns at Marietta City. It is especially interesting that Norris drew such high praise from his divisional commander, yet his name is not mentioned in General Gracie's report. As luck would have it, and as noted earlier, the 2nd Battalion's command structure was hammered during the struggle to take Horseshoe Ridge. Lieutenant Colonel Bolling Hall, in command of the 2nd Battalion, fell wounded. Captain Westley D. Walden of Company B assumed command next and fell mortally wounded, as did Lieutenant William F. Fisher, from Company C, who came next. The 2nd Battalion's report was penned by Crenshaw Hall, the battalion's adjutant.[22]

The divisional commander's words carried enough authority to get Norris' contribution to the attack noticed. George W. Norris is included on the Confederate States Army's Roll of Honor. He is also listed among the dead of the 2nd Battalion's Company E in a letter received by Archibald Gracie IV, the General's son.

In a 1908 letter to a 2nd Battalion survivor, Albert Patterson of Jemison, Alabama, Gracie IV wrote, "Comrade [J. J.] Wilson wrote, 'We had five men killed in our Company, Moe Oden [Gracie called the name indistinct], George Norris, Loeb [also called indistinct by Gracie], Jones, Powell Johnson,' and a fifth soldier Wilson could not identify.[23] It turned out that Norris' luck just wasn't running in his favor, even in death. Not only did he die on the hillside of Horseshoe Ridge, but he fell owing the Confederacy for three pairs of shoes, a hat, a jacket and a blanket.[24]

Behind the Legionnaires who manned the front on the slopes of Horseshoe Ridge on September 21, 1863, were the men who lay in the battalion's field hospitals and in areas in between, who even then continued to spill blood for the Confederate cause: The injured, the wounded and the dying.

One of those men was Private Henry Hines.

11

"Come at once
if you wish to see him"

Henry Hines, the farmer from Company F of the Legion's 1st Battalion, was wounded in the left leg by a bullet. He suffered a broken ankle which never healed properly. Like hundreds of his 1st Battalion comrades, Hines somehow made it to the field hospital behind Chickamauga Creek.

Civil War medicine was a gruesome thing to behold, although the sensitivities of the era were somewhat different from those of today. Shaver, a man of his own era, described the 1st Battalion's field hospital colorfully: "Here was presented a scene which surpassed in horror, if possible, the battle-field itself…. At this point was congregated the wounded who had covered a large area of the field. A lurid glare was cast by scores of flaming rail fires upon the pale, agonized features of the many victims of the battle. There was no canopy for the sufferers save the heavens—no couch save the uneven earth—and no pillows save billets of wood."[1]

For Hines, the raging violence of September 20, 1863, marked the beginning of a journey through the medical organization of the Army of Tennessee and the Confederate States of America's version of red tape. That journey would see Hines correctly following the established procedure and yet being marked Absent Without Leave. He would eventually be honorably mustered out of the service and then, after the war, have his name included on a procedural list of Prisoners of War. Hines collected a small Confederate pension from the State of Alabama near the end of his life. He left a widow, having remarried after outliving his first wife. And he limped with every other step he took over his final 41 years. Hines died in 1908.

Hines' post-war story was not unlike those of other former Confederate soldiers. Life was hard for wounded soldiers after the Civil War. The lucky ones who survived both their wounds and their medical treatment returned to civilian life sooner or later.

It appears that Hines made his required doctor's visits and it was eventually determined that he was not physically able to return to the army and the war. He was briefly listed on the Retired Soldiers, Invalid Corps, in the fall of 1864 before he was officially retired from military service on October 24, 1864. But a paperwork problem, stemming from the inaccurate Absent Without Leave notation on some of his service cards, popped up and made trouble for his family.

Here is what happened: Hines, a farmer before the war, married Mary Ard shortly after the war and they struggled to get by. By the time of the 1870 census, Henry and Mary had three children. They valued their real estate holdings at $200 and their personal holdings at $100. Ten years later, the Hineses had eight children (four boys, four girls) and Henry was still farming. The 1880 census lists Henry and Mary plus eight Hines children and includes the information that Mary Ard Hines was ill with consumption (now called tuberculosis).

Sometime after the 1880 census was conducted, Mary Ard Hines died. Henry left farming and worked at a mill; near the end of his life, he was a watchman at the mill. Mary Hines' death left Henry to care for his children. There is family evidence that he may have sent some of the children to live with relatives, a fairly common practice at the time. Henry married Sarah Eddins on August 11, 1902. Sarah had been born in 1874 and was a widow with children of her own when she met Henry Hines. Henry and Sarah may have had a child together, although there is some question about this point. Family histories mention the birth of a son and the 1910 census lists S. Hines as a widow and the head of the household (Henry had been dead for two years) with four children surnamed Eddins and a six-year-old son named Jessie Hines.

Henry Hilliard Hines died June 27, 1908, and it was some time afterward that the conflicting paperwork over his furlough and eventual discharge from the Confederate States Army became a problem. As the Confederate Army veterans aged, former CSA states started offering pensions for the needy former soldiers. In 1867, Alabama began offering pensions for Confederate vets who had lost limbs during the war. That changed in 1886 when the state started offering pensions to the widows of Confederate veterans. Finally, in 1891, Alabama began offering pensions to indigent veterans or their widows. Henry Hines qualified for the fund and began the application process. Eventually he was granted a small sum each month and continued to collect until his death, except for one year when he forgot to complete the reapplication process.

Having outlived two husbands, Sarah J. Hines moved to Florida on

November 1, 1909. Several city directories found online suggest that Sarah supported herself as a dressmaker for several decades. However, she does not seem to have made too much money in that way and she continued to collect Henry's Confederate pension in order to make ends meet.

It appears the Alabama pension board discovered the matter of Henry's mistaken AWOL status in 1914, six years after Henry's passing. The board wrote a letter to Sarah explaining its position on the matter and notifying her that the payments would not continue. The letter said in part, "The records show that H. H. Hines, pvt-Co-23rd Battalion Alabama Sharpshooters C.S.A. was absent without leave Sept-10th-1863-Nothing later of him on record." Sarah was ill at the time the letter from the board arrived and was due to have surgery of some kind. She requested, and was granted, a continuance until she was healthy enough to gather evidence that Henry had not deserted the army.

In shaky handwriting (and uncertain spelling), Sarah Hines wrote to the pension board on May 10, 1914:

> I bage to say I am down sick and have ben for over 4 months not able to be about to atend to any biness at all but if you will give me time to recover I shurley can get profe that my husben was at home on a fer low not able to walk when the ware ended he was Shot down at the battle of Chickey margie and never was able to go back ... if you can give me time to get well anuff to attend to it I am shure that I have as much rite to it as any one ... if I am not in title to it and am not getting it fair I shure don't want it for I don't want nothing only what is rite....[2]

She eventually gathered statements from three men who had known Henry and who swore before a notary that Henry had served honorably but was unable to serve after suffering his wound. One of the three statements was made by John G. Betts, a sergeant in Company F of the 1st Battalion and a comrade of Henry's during the war.

Betts' statement reads in part "that said H. H. Hines was wounded in the battle of 'Chickamauga' and was a cripple for several years after the war." The statement continues, "that H. H. Hines was never regarded as a deserter and in his [Betts'] opinion the said H. H. Hines did not desert the servive [sic] of the Confederate States nor of the state of Alabama."[3]

Curiously, Betts specifically said that Hines served in the "Co. F. 23d Alabama sharpshooters" and does not mention Hilliard's Legion. Remember, the Legion was split up after it was shot to pieces at Chickamauga. Hines and Betts were assigned to the 23rd. Hines was carried on the muster rolls of the 23rd but he did not serve a day in that unit.

Sarah Hines was returned to the rolls and continued to collect Henry's pension until her death at age 82 on May 6, 1957. Sarah's daughters, who were no longer spring chickens themselves, wrote to the pension board with the news and date of Sarah's passing. The board sent the family a check for the final days of her life, May 1–May 6. Ray E. Green, comptroller, wrote, "It was a real privilege to mail Mrs. Hines Confederate pension warrants each month and I shall miss doing so in the future."[4]

Hines' story was representative of southern soldiers, but every wounded man had a story. Bolling Hall, Jr., the lieutenant colonel of the Legion's 2nd Battalion, served with his brothers. Tom Brown Hall was wounded at Chickamauga and, despite his own wound, Bolling Hall telegraphed his father on September 24, 1863, "Tom is very low. Come at once if you wish to see him & bring a good surgeon."[5]

Hall Sr. was a man of influence in Alabama and he had connections in important places. In his papers, kept by the ADAH, there is a note dated September 23, 1863, from Daniel Cram, superintendent of the Montgomery and West Point Railroad, to E. B. Walker, the superintendent of the Western and Atlantic Railroad. Cram's note explained the urgent nature of Hall Sr.'s errand and closed, "If you can give him any assistance in obtaining a passage up your road you will render him as well as myself deeply indebted."

Walker issued papers making it possible for Hall to rush to see his sons, adding, "Conductors will give Major Hall a seat in ladies' car."

There is no evidence that Hall Sr. was able to bring a doctor with him, but he did see his sons shortly after the fighting. Tom Brown Hall succumbed to his wound, although he is not listed among the casualties of the Army of Tennessee. As a university student, Tom had written of his desire to join his brothers and cousin in the war, but he had not yet enlisted. Bolling Jr. knew of Tom's desire but recommended that Tom look to brother James, serving in

Lieutenant Colonel Bolling Hall, Jr., commanding officer, 2nd Battalion, Hilliard's Legion (Alabama Department of Archives and History, Montgomery, Alabama).

the 24th Alabama. Bolling Jr. already had brothers serving with him among the officers in the Legion's 2nd Battalion and thought it unlikely that another Hall would be accepted as an officer. Tom was visiting James when the fighting broke out at Chickamauga, and he was buried on the battlefield with others of the 24th.[6]

If Bolling Hall Sr. did in fact manage to bring a doctor with him when he rushed to the sides of his wounded sons, the Confederate doctors already on site probably welcomed the help. They were simply overwhelmed by the sheer number of patients. That number of men needing attention also included the thousands of wounded Federal soldiers.

Byrd Fitzpatrick Meriwether, a private in Company A of the 1st Battalion, was listed as mortally wounded but he survived the war. Meriwether wrote decades later in *The Confederate Veteran*, "We were ordered to charge the enemy's breastworks, when I was badly wounded and left on the field to die, but was removed on the seventh day and carried to Ringgold, Ga." Meriwether wrote that his father located him in the Ringgold hospital and took him home. After about a year at home, Meriwether related, he returned to the army.[7]

Obviously, a lot of the wounded did not survive. Young S. Childee died the day after the battle. Childee was a private in the 4th Battalion's B Company. Private George Welch, Company A of the 4th Battalion, apparently died of his wounds on September 23, 1863. Alfred Mills, a private in the 4th Battalion's B Company, died of his wounds in Ringgold, Georgia on October 31, 1863. William R. Pate, a private in Company B of the 4th Battalion, died at Chickamauga owing the Confederate States Army $15 for clothing drawn. Private J. B. L. Davis, a private in Company B of the Legion's 1st Battalion, was killed at Chickamauga, having enlisted at the age of 19. His mother, Louisa F. Davis, was eventually awarded $112.57 by the Confederate Treasury Department's Second Auditor's Office. The payment was for her son's final 20 days of service ($7.33) and 351 days' commutation for clothing ($129.18), minus $24.00 in debt to the Army.

William E. Johnson, also a member of the 2nd Battalion's E Company, was killed at Chickamauga. Patrick W. Johnson, a private in the 2nd Battalion's E Company, passed away five days after the end of the fighting at Chickamauga, but while he did not die of wounds, he died of disease. Their similar names and the fact that they served in the same company suggests that they may have been related. If so, it was a difficult week for the family.[8]

12

Consider Some Facts

Finally, you ask yourself what it all meant.

The battle of Chickamauga was a battering, grinding, bloodletting event. For the purposes of mathematics, this book accepts the casualty statistics presented by the Official Records for the final numbers: The Confederates suffered 18,454 total casualties, and the Federals lost 16,170. That makes the grand total 34,624 dead, wounded or missing soldiers for the two days of fighting, plus the skirmishing on the 18th.

Confederate General D. H. Hill may have had trouble following orders, but he was eloquent. Writing for the three-volume series *Battles and Leaders of the Civil War*, volume three, he said, "It seems to me that the élan of the Southern soldier was never seen after Chickamauga—that brilliant dash which had distinguished him was gone forever."[1]

The figures here do not include the army horses and mules that were killed, nor the farm animals and livestock. Crops were ruined and farm buildings were damaged or destroyed. Sawmills refused to accept trees from the battlefield area for decades for fear of ruining a cutting blade by hitting spent lead within the wood of the trees. The author spoke to a resident of the area in 2011 who reported frequently finding Minie balls in her garden more than 145 years after the battle ended.

The Federal Army of the Cumberland already held Chattanooga, the king city of the regional chessboard. The Confederate Army of Tennessee held the field, but did not manage to chase Rosecrans out of Chattanooga. The battle ended with the Federal leadership taking cover in Chattanooga, a city it had controlled before the battle. Rosecrans' willingness to get his army involved in a major attack when he already held an important prize, the city of Chattanooga, has been bait for critics for many decades. His performance on the 20th has drawn legitimate scorn, but his chase after Bragg's retreating army and the bloody fight that resulted does not rate disapproval.

Rosecrans' Commander in Chief, Abraham Lincoln, felt it was more important to destroy the Confederate army than it was to seize a city. It is fair to say that the Army of the Cumberland was following the policy of the War Department and the wishes of the President of the United States when it entered into battle with the Army of Tennessee near the banks of the Chickamauga. Given those circumstances, Rosecrans was correct to engage the enemy. In his report, Rosecrans wrote, "It is proper to observe that the battle of Chickamauga was absolutely necessary to secure our concentration and cover Chattanooga."[2] Indeed, in his report, Rosecrans wrote that his army *won* the battle. Rosecrans wrote that Reynolds' forces captured 500 Confederates on the ridge. "This closed the battle of the 20th," Rosecrans asserted. "At nightfall the enemy had been repulsed along the whole line."[3]

Rosecrans was not the only Federal man to consider Chickamauga a win for the Army of the Cumberland. Sergeant James T. Inman, a member of the 21st Ohio Volunteer Infantry's Company K, said the same thing in a letter he wrote the month after the battle. Inman wrote home from Chattanooga, "I think we were vicktorious [*sic*] for all we wanted was this place and we have got it."[4]

After stopping the Confederates, Rosecrans wrote, Thomas pulled back to Chattanooga. In praising the victory and the victors, the *Montgomery Weekly Advertiser* wrote that the victory would help maintain support for the war within the Confederate public. The paper said, in part, "No less important are its effects upon public sentiment at home. This splendid victory has silenced, in a great measure, the murmurs of the discontented; it has restored the confidence of the timid in our ultimate success."[5]

History has passed harsh judgment on Confederate General Bragg for not mounting a chase after the fleeing Federals on Sept. 21. History could also judge Confederate General James Longstreet for not mounting a chase on the afternoon of the 20th when he had Preston's fresh division available, but historians have largely left Longstreet alone. Before history becomes too judgmental, however, it should consider some facts. As we have seen, Bragg's army was low on mobility, having lost many horses during the battle. Gracie, for example, famously had either one or two mounts shot out from under him during the attack on Horseshoe Ridge. Bragg noted the shortage in a September 29 note to Richmond: "the artillery is much crippled by loss of horses."[6]

Longstreet's men had reached the area of the battle by rail and the horses for that command were not among the first to arrive, so Bragg's command was short of needed horses before the battle even started. Some of Longstreet's force was still arriving on the 21st.

The Confederate survivors of the battle had eaten very little in recent weeks and probably lacked the energy to go back into combat on September 21st. Remember Private Gillian and his pumpkin. Bragg, again in his September 29 report, said, "The question of subsistence should receive early attention as our supplies are nearly exhausted at Atlanta."[7]

A few lucky Confederate regiments were whole enough to give chase to the fleeing Federals. As an example, Trigg's 6th and 7th Florida regiments had low casualty counts during the battle. Those men might have been able to head toward Chattanooga early in the morning of September 21, 1863, but even Trigg's men were likely worn out. One wonders whether two regiments of Confederates would have been strong enough to evict the entire Union Army of the Cumberland from Chattanooga. Bragg's army, on the whole, was not ready for another major engagement on the 21st and the detractors among his commanders ought to have considered their own performances before serving themselves with criticisms of Bragg's.

Consider Daniel H. Hill and Leonidas Polk, for example. Before Chickamauga, during the failure at McLemore's Cove, their laziness and refusal to follow orders cost the Confederates a golden opportunity to severely damage the Union's Army of the Cumberland. Then came the extraordinary mess on the Confederate right before dawn on September 20. James Longstreet, who is to be congratulated for finding time to enjoy a hearty lunch in the midst of a major battle, was another harsh critic of Bragg's. But as we have seen, Longstreet had his own opportunity to perform a maneuver similar to the one he later said Bragg should have made. Longstreet instead rushed Preston's Division toward the guns and destiny waiting atop Horseshoe Ridge.

Was Braxton Bragg a great leader of men whose leadership skills and visionary martial decisions resulted in a great Confederate victory at Chickamauga? No. But as the saying goes, a bad boss is still the boss. The refusal of Bragg's commanders to act with vigor at McLemore's Cove left James Negley's division intact and ready for its feature role in the Chickamauga saga. Thus the failure of Bragg's commanders to follow orders at McLemore's Cove cost Confederate lives a few days later, some of them probably belonging to Gracie's men.

Polk's inability, really his refusal, to be ready to attack on time on the morning of the 20th cost the Confederates five hours of combat time. Consider what might have happened if Horseshoe Ridge had been secured by the Confederates at about 1 p.m. rather than shortly after dark.

Obviously, we'll never know what might have been. What we do know is that Bragg was poorly served by some of his commanders at Chickamauga. Hill, Polk, Longstreet and others have been treated far too kindly by history. After the battle ended, Polk and other commanders refused even the simple military duty of sending post-action reports to Bragg. Bragg wrote to his superiors in the Confederate capital, Richmond, Virginia, on December 28, 1863, "There has been much delay in rendering some of the subordinate reports, and none have been received from Lieutenant-Generals Polk and Hill, and only two from brigades in Longstreet's corps. The absence of these has caused a delay in making up my own, and induced me to defer forwarding the others, hoping that all might be submitted together."[8]

We circle back to General Hill's well worded comment about the effect the high casualty rate at Chickamauga had on the common Confederate soldier, that the élan of the Southern soldier, that spirit that marked the Confederate States Army in the early years of the war, disappeared after September 20, 1863.

Whether or not one accepts Hill's review of the Confederate soldier's waning spirit in the closing years of the war, the fact remains that the spirit of the southern fighters was an important part of the conflict. No

Battle flag of Hilliard's Legion. This flag was carried into battle at Horseshoe Ridge. The author viewed the flag in 2010 (Alabama Department of Archives and History, Montgomery, Alabama).

Federal soldier who heard the Rebel yell ever forgot it. At battles such as Chickamauga and Gettysburg, where the Confederates charged at a fixed Union position, the Rebel effort was always supreme.

If the élan that Hill wrote about did eventually disappear from the Confederate army, it lives on today on the fields and playing courts of the South's athletic teams. Since 1900, 14 southern schools have won college football's national championship. The University of Alabama not only leads the old Confederacy in football championships, it is the national leader. Alabama has won the most consensus titles, eleven. The school claims 16 national championships, since there were multiple champions listed by the various polls through the years.[9] Over the same period, Auburn University, the University of Tennessee, Louisiana State University, the University of Texas, the University of Miami (Florida), the University of Florida, Florida State University and Clemson University have all won national titles.

No, the élan Hill wrote about is still present. Take the Alabama team that won the Bowl Championship Series national title game in January of 2012, for example. Of the 116 players on the roster that season, 48 came from Alabama. Of the others, 56 came from southern states.[10]

The southern spirit is never more obvious than in the grandstands of a Southeastern Conference athletic contest. Every time a football player makes a hard tackle, a softball player strikes a home run or a basketball player slams home a dunk shot, the roar from the assembled crowd emboldens and embodies that spirit.

It is, perhaps, the renewal of the Rebel yell once bellowed by the men of Hilliard's Legion.

13

The End of the Story

Many of the soldiers quoted in these pages were not around for the end of the war. Some were. After Hilliard's Legion was reformed into three different commands (all remaining under Gracie), the survivors of the struggle at Chickamauga found themselves serving in Robert E. Lee's Army of Northern Virginia.

A few notes here, then, about the men whose words described the Legion's efforts on Horseshoe Ridge, whether they played significant roles in that fight or simply had interesting stories. Most of the information below comes from muster rolls and Final Statements of the Legion, the 23rd Battalion Alabama Sharpshooters, the 59th Alabama Infantry Regiment or the 60th Alabama Infantry Regiment. The Final Statements are located at the Alabama Department of Archives in Montgomery. Where other sources were used, they have been noted. In General Bragg's case, the information is available through many sources.

Hilliard's Legion: The Legion was split into two regiments and a battalion on November 25, 1863. The 2nd and 4th Battalions became the 59th Alabama Infantry Regiment, under the command of Col. Bolling Hall. Companies A, B, C and D of the 1st Battalion and the remainder of the 3rd Battalion formed the 60th Alabama Infantry Regiment, commanded by Col. John W. A. Sanford. Companies E, F and G of the 1st Battalion filled out the 23rd Battalion, Alabama Sharpshooters, led by Major Nicholas Stallworth. The newly organized units all served in Gracie's Brigade until Gracie was killed in Virginia in 1864 (see Appendix 2 below). The 23rd, 59th and 60th were with the Army of Northern Virginia when it surrendered. The Legion's flag somehow ended up in the possession of Colonel John W. A. Sanford after the Legion was split up. By then Sanford, a former member of the 3rd Battalion, was with the 60th Regiment. Sanford later gave the flag to Private John B. Fuller. Fuller's son donated the flag to the Alabama Department of Archives and History in 1963. The flag, which is said to have been created out of the wedding trousseau of Mrs. Henry Washington Hilliard, has since been restored.

Clabourn Payne Barganier (5th Battalion, Company D): A private, he was one of nine brothers, five of whom served in the same unit. Four of the five survived the war and lived beyond the turn of the century. Severely wounded at Chickamauga, Clabourn lived until 1933, passing away at either 93 or 94 years of age, the last of the nine brothers. (Muster roll for the 60th Alabama Infantry Regiment, Ancestry.com.)

General Braxton Bragg: Bragg was eventually replaced as the head of the Army of Tennessee by Joseph E. Johnston. Bragg became a military advisor to Confederate President Jefferson Davis. After the war, Bragg served as the superintendent of the New Orleans waterworks, and later he became the superintendent of harbor improvements at Mobile, Alabama. Still later he moved to Texas where he held various railroad jobs. He died in Texas in 1876 at the age of 59.

E. F. Comegys (43rd Alabama): Edward Freeman Comegys originally enlisted as a sergeant but was promoted to lieutenant before taking command of the 43rd Alabama Infantry Regiment as a captain shortly before the end of the war. Comegys was captured by Union forces during the fight at Hatcher's Run in Virginia on March 25, 1865. He was released from Fort Delaware after taking the Oath of Allegiance on June 17, 1865. After returning home, he married the former Susan Harris and the marriage eventually produced six children. The Comegys family moved to Texas where Edward became the superintendent of Denton Public Schools in 1884. He left the Denton schools to take the same job with the Gainesville, Texas, school district in 1890. Edward remained involved in Confederate veteran affairs as an active member of the United Confederate Veterans Post 119 in Texas. He attended at least one reunion of Alabama Confederates, where he met Archibald Gracie IV. The two men corresponded for a time as Gracie researched his father's military career. Comegys died on January 26, 1910. (Confederate pension documents and U.S. Census documents available online. Texas education career available on www.zoominfo.com.)

John W. Cotton (5th Battalion, Company C): Cotton survived the war but died in 1866 at the age of 35.

John Forbes Davenport (1st Battalion, Company D): Killed in action on July 9, 1864, near Petersburg, Virginia.

William T. "Pumpkin" Gillian (1st Battalion, Company D): Surrendered at Appomattox as a member of the 60th Alabama Infantry Regiment. Returned to farming in Alabama after the war. He married Olivia Herlong on December 20, 1867, and their union resulted in nine children, four of whom died at young ages. William died in Alabama on March 24, 1928, at age 86. Olivia died on June 29, 1930. (Census documents, Alabama pension documents, Census of Confederate soldiers.)

James N. Gilmer (1st Battalion Quartermaster and Commissary): The ambrotype image of Gilmer in uniform is probably the clearest surviving picture of a member of the Legion in uniform.

General Archibald Gracie III: Killed in action on December 2, 1864, near Petersburg, Virginia. A day earlier, on Gracie's 32nd birthday, his wife gave birth to a daughter. On a list of wounded members of the 60th Alabama Infantry Regiment, there is the following note: "This space is dedicated to the memory of Gen'l Archie Gracie Jr [*sic*] Brigade Commander who was killed at 10 o'clock Dec 2/64. Shot through the neck and left shoulder by fragments of schrapnel [*sic*] shot while viewing the enemy's works from the trenches at the Crater."

James N. Gilmer, Quartermaster and Commissary, 1st Battalion, Hilliard's Legion. This ambrotype image is possibly the clearest of a member of the Legion in uniform (Alabama Department of Archives and History, Montgomery, Alabama).

The last two words are unclear; the author believes the above is accurate. (*The Truth About Chickamauga*, Morningside [A history of the Gracie family appears in the introduction to the Morningside Edition]. The page noting the wounds for the 60th is available online through the Alabama Department of Archives and History.)

Colonel Archibald Gracie IV: A boy when his father died, Gracie IV began researching his dad and the battle of Chickamauga shortly before the turn of the 20th century. He attended Confederate army reunions and his letters point toward a son trying to learn about the father he didn't know. Gracie IV wrote *The Truth About Chickamauga*, about the battle. The book relates mostly the movement of Union troops atop and around Horseshoe Ridge. He apparently intended to write another book, this one about the Confederate movements or perhaps about his father's career. He traveled to Europe in 1912, then boarded the RMS *Titanic* for a pleasant cruise back to the U.S. He survived the sinking and was among those who stood on an upturned lifeboat for many hours before the rescue. With typical Gracie energy, he gathered stories from fellow survivors while aboard the rescue ship *Carpathia*, then wrote another research classic, *The Truth About the Titanic*. But Gracie IV's health was broken by the harrowing night when the Titanic sank, and he died on December 4, 1912. His last words reportedly were, "We must get them into the boats." His *Titanic* book was published posthumously but Gracie IV lived to see the book's first proofs. (*The Truth About Chickamauga*, Morningside [A history of the Gracie family appears in the introduction to the Morningside Edition].)

Lieutenant Colonel Bolling Hall, Jr. (2nd Battalion): Hall recovered from his Chickamauga wound and returned to his men after the unit had become part of the 59th Alabama Infantry Regiment. But his luck had run out. He was wounded again during the battle of Drewry's Bluff and this time he lost his right leg. Hall did not recover from this second severe wound, and died February 3, 1866. He never married.

Adjutant Crenshaw Hall (2nd Battalion): Wrote the Chickamuaga post-battle report for his wounded brother, Bolling Jr. This Hall brother survived the war and became a cotton buyer in the Montgomery area. He briefly went into business with another Hall brother, Frank, around 1888, when the men operated a coal mine. Crenshaw Hall died on May 20, 1893, at age 55.

Lieutenant John Elmore Hall (2nd Battalion, Company E): Enlisted as a private in 1861 and rose to captain in the 59th by the end of the war. He moved to Colorado after the war and lived there for four years before returning to Alabama, where he died on January 27, 1882, at 40 years of age.

Tom Brown Hall: This Hall brother died at Chickamauga without ever enlisting. He was visiting still another Hall brother in the 24th Alabama Infantry Regiment when the battle broke out. He was killed there and was buried with the men of the 24th. Tom Hall was a student at the University of Alabama at the time of his death. (Regimental notebook in the Hall Family Papers, ADAH.)

Henry Washington Hilliard: After the war, he moved to Atlanta, Georgia. The 1870 Federal Census valued his real estate holdings at $26,000 and his personal estate at zero. Hilliard attempted to return to Congress but was defeated at the polls. He was named the United States

Minister to Brazil, serving in that capacity from 1877 to 1881. He died in Atlanta in December of 1892 at age 85.

Lieutenant David Hughes (43rd Alabama): The man who led what has been named the Hughes Detail, the group from the 43rd Alabama and from the Legion that worked on fatigue duty on the night of September 19/20. The group joined a Florida regiment for the final Confederate attack on Horseshoe Ridge. Hughes was killed by the same shell that killed General Gracie on December 2, 1864, in the trenches near Petersburg. He had been promoted to captain the previous week. (Gracie Papers, January 7, 1908, letter from Gracie IV to Winfield Woolf. See also ADAH Civil War Service Database for information on Hughes and Private John Norwood, who was also killed by the same shell. The ADAH Database listing for Woolf says Woolf was promoted to captain when Hughes was killed.)

Lieutenant John Washington Keyes: A dentist before the war, Keyes joined the Montgomery Rifles in 1861. The Rifles became part of the Legion in 1862. Keyes later served in the 60th Alabama Infantry Regiment before retiring from the service. He later became the surgeon of the 17th Alabama Infantry Regiment. After the war, he joined the group of ex–Confederates who went to Brazil to colonize in that country, lured by the offer of cheap land and other inducements. Keyes became the dentist for Emperor Dom Pedro and the royal family. Interestingly enough, a toothbrush believed to have belonged to the Emperor was unearthed in Brazil in 2013. It seems possible that Keyes and Hilliard could have been in contact while both men were living in Brazil. Keyes returned to Alabama in the late 1870s and settled in Wewahitchka, Florida. He died in Florida in 1892.

Private Daniel Lewis (2nd Battalion, Company F): Died of sickness in an Atlanta hospital on November 3, 1862. His father, Abel Lewis, wrote to the Confederate government on December 4, 1862, in hopes he might speed up the government's payment to Daniel's widow of the money owed Daniel for his service. The payment seems to finally have been issued on March 20, 1865. Descendants of Daniel Lewis and his widow, Martha, say the couple had two daughters. Martha did not survive her husband for very long; she died before 1870. Interestingly, two other pairs of Castleberry and Lewis siblings married during the war era. (1860 U.S. Census found on Ancestry.com; author's correspondence with descendants of Daniel Lewis.)

Private John W. Little (3rd Battalion, Company C): Died October 10, 1862. His father, James Little, was awarded $47.66 for his son's final four months and 10 days of service by the Confederate Treasury's Second Auditor's Office. The award paperwork was dated November 30, 1864.

Private Byrd Fitzpatrick Meriwether (1st Battalion, Company A): Survived the war. After spending seven days left for dead on the Chickamauga battlefield, he was transported to a hospital in Ringgold, Georgia. Meriwether's father located him and they began their journey home to Alabama. Byrd wrote that he

> … had gone as far as Newnan, Ga., when I was so exhausted that we had to stop, and stayed there until I was able to make the journey home, a mere skeleton. After about a year I rejoined my command.… Not having sufficiently recovered from my wounds to return to active service, I was ordered to report to Gen. Gracie … he said he wanted me for one of his couriers but sent me to the division infirmary to remain for several weeks.

Meriwether was eventually assigned to the Commissary Department and was still in the Army when Lee surrendered to Grant, which Meriwether wrote was the saddest day of his life. "My captain lost his leg on the morning of the surrender. We were released on the 12th of April and given the choice of coming home by land or water. I came by water, arriving home on Sunday, May 7, 1865." (ADAH, Regimental History, Alabama Infantry Regiment, 60th: Sketches, staff, etc. SG 24909 Folder 5.)

Colonel Young Marshall Moody (Commander of the 43rd Alabama Infantry Regiment): Moody took command of Gracie's Brigade after Gracie was killed in the trenches in front of Petersburg. Promoted to Brigadier General in March of 1865, Moody was captured at Appomattox Court House on April 8, 1865, and was paroled the next day. He survived the war. Moody moved his family to New Orleans after the surrender at Appomattox. He died of yellow fever on September 18, 1866, in New Orleans.

Private Henry Owens (2nd Battalion, Company E): Served briefly. He died on August 10, 1862, without ever collecting an army paycheck.

Private Wesley M. Parrish (2nd Battalion, Company E): Died in Knoxville on March 9, 1863, owing the Army 50 cents for clothing and a blanket.

Private Thomas Pearce (2nd Battalion, Company E): Served in the Legion and then the 59th Regiment's B Company for a total of 26 months before he was killed at Drewry's Bluff on May 16, 1864. He was owed a $100 bounty granted by the Confederate government. This was done usually for re-enlistment, but he died owing the Army for a pair of pants, two shirts, three pairs of shoes and a blanket.

Brigadier General William Preston: Preston's long record of public service is unique. A Kentucky state legislator and then Congressman during the decade before the war, Preston was the United States Ambassador to Spain when hostilities broke out in 1861. He joined the Confederate

Army after returning from Spain and was a brigadier general by 1862. In 1864, the Confederate government appointed Preston ambassador to Mexico. That post ended with the close of the war and Preston returned to his home state. He served in Kentucky's House of Representatives in 1868 and 1869. Preston died on September 21, 1887, in Louisville at the age of 71.

Private Robert H. Scott (2nd Battalion, Company E): Scott is listed as a deserter in late 1862 in some Confederate paperwork. He must have returned at some point because he was killed at Drewry's Bluff on May 16, 1864.

Major William W. Screws (2nd Battalion): Screws originally served in the 1st Battalion before he was transferred to the 2nd. He was captured during the final weeks of the war at Sailor's Creek and was held as a prisoner of war until June of 1865. After the war, Screws was offered and accepted a partnership in the *Montgomery Advertiser* and wrote editorials for that paper for half a century. He eventually served as Alabama's Secretary of State (1878–1882) before serving as a postmaster at Montgomery (1893–1897). Screws died on August 7, 1913. (The Confederate Veteran, XXI, No. 10, page 504.)

Private George Washington Sexton (1st Battalion, Company D): Survived the surrender and left these final three entries in his war diary:

April 9, 1865	Lee Surrendered
April 10, 1865	Prisoner of War belonging to the Army of North Virginia, who have been this day surrendered by General Lee
April 11, 1865	Started home

Captain Nicholas Stallworth: Stallworth was born to a farm family in Alabama's Conecuh County and attended the University of Alabama prior to the war. He served in Company C of the 1st Alabama Infantry in 1861 and raised Company F of the First Battalion, Hilliard's Legion in 1862. He moved on to the 23rd Battalion, Alabama Sharpshooters when that unit was formed from the remnants of the Legion and he survived the war. Stallworth briefly returned to Alabama when the war ended, but he and his wife Lucy moved to Texas and farmed there for two decades. Stallworth eventually became the Falls County Tax Assessor and Collector. He was a justice of the peace and served as the treasurer of the Texas State Grange. He and Lucy celebrated their 50th wedding anniversary in 1907 before the Major died on Feb. 28, 1909. (Ancestry.com.)

Major Daniel Shipman Troy: Troy survived the war but it wasn't easy. On March 25, 1865, then a member of the 60th Alabama Infantry Regiment, he was shot in the lung during a fight at Hatcher's Run, Virginia. Troy had been given temporary command of the 59th Alabama Infantry Regiment and was leading those men in a charge against a Union position. The initial charge succeeded, but a counterattack by the Federals began pushing the men of the 59th back. The regimental flag bearer was shot down. Troy picked up the 59th's banner and was shot for his trouble by Private George W. Tomkins of the 124th New York Infantry. Tomkins captured the 59th's flag and was later awarded the Medal of Honor. Unfortunately, the citation on Tomkins' award reads that he captured the flag of the 49th Alabama. The 49th was not in Virginia at the time. Troy's wound was a dangerous one but he overcame it and lived until Sept. 27, 1895. (*Alabama Heritage,* Number 63, Winter 2002. Also see the Congressional Library for the citation on Tomkins' Medal of Honor.)

Private James Wilson (2nd Battalion, Company E): Wilson died on July 2, 1864, of wounds he had received at Petersburg the previous June 17. In death, he left behind a substantial debt to the Confederate government. Wilson owed for three jackets, five pairs of pants, four shirts, an overcoat, three pairs of drawers, four pairs of shoes, three pairs of socks and three blankets.

Captain Daniel Shipman Troy, 1st Battalion, Hilliard's Legion, in a post-war image (Alabama Department of Archives and History, Montgomery, Alabama).

Regimental battle flag of the 59th Alabama Infantry. Daniel Shipman Troy was severely wounded while carrying this flag on March 25, 1865. The author has viewed the flag. There do appear to be stains on the flag (Alabama Department of Archives and History, Montgomery, Alabama).

Appendix 1

After Chickamauga

Hilliard's Legion did not survive the year 1863, although its living members kept fighting. Gracie's command was part of Bragg's attempt to do the same thing to Chattanooga that Ulysses Grant did to Vicksburg, Mississippi. Without detailing the differences between Bragg and Grant, and without discussing the differences of their resources, we can say here that Gracie's Brigade was transported to Tennessee in late November to serve with Longstreet.

On November 25, 1863, Special Order 280 XV from the Adjutant General's Office reformed the Legion's four battalions into three new commands: the 59th and 60th Alabama Infantry regiments and the 23rd Alabama Sharpshooters. "The organization known as Hilliard's Alabama Legion is hereby resolved," the special order read.[1]

The 59th was comprised of the 2nd and 4th Battalions. The 60th came from companies A through D of the 1st Battalion and the six companies of the 3rd Battalion. Companies E, F and G of the 1st Battalion became the 23rd Battalion, Alabama Sharpshooters. The three units served together in Gracie's Brigade through the end of the war.

Gracie's Brigade and the men who had formerly served in Hilliard's Legion in particular played a major role at Bean's Station, the site of a nasty fight. After the so-called investment of Knoxville failed, Longstreet moved his force in the direction of Virginia but soon discovered that the Union Army was overextended in its haste to chase the Confederates. Just as Braxton Bragg had attempted to do at both McLemore's Cove and Chickamauga, Longstreet tried to punish his pursuers and the result was the December 14, 1863, fight at Bean's Station.

Divisional commander Brigadier General Bushrod Johnson wrote of Gracie's men, "This force was badly shod and poorly clad," but the former Legion men and their brigade-mates ran into a spot of good luck when Johnson's force seized upon a chance to make some shoes between December 9 and December 13. "Several tan-yards and shoe-shops were taken possession of by my order, and a number of tanners and shoemakers from my command were placed on extra duty preparing leather and shoes for the men."[2]

Early in the battle, seven companies of the 59th Alabama were a part of the force ordered to attack the Union cavalry after a Confederate unit discovered the Union picket line and drove the pickets back to where the Union reserve line had been established.

Again, from Johnson's report: "My leading brigade [Gracie's] was moved up and seven companies of the 59th Alabama Regiment, commanded by Lieut. Col. J. D. McLennan, was advanced as skirmishers, the center moving along the road."[3]

The Confederate cavalry attacked from the left and the combination made things difficult for the Union cause. Johnson's attackers drove the Union line back about two miles and crossed a creek before the next of Gracie's regiments got into the fight. "The Forty-third Alabama Regiment, commanded by Col. Y. M. Moody, was deployed in the rear of the fifth-ninth and moved to the right, extending into the woods on the slope of the mountain on the north side of the valley. As the skirmishers ascended to the top of the hill east of the station, the enemy's artillery opened from three points on the elevations west of the station."[4] The hard-fighting men of the 43rd must have thought that every time they were positioned on the right flank and sent up a hill, someone's cannons opened up. Gracie was wounded as the 43rd was in action, leaving Johnson to note, "I was deprived of his valuable services I was not aware until later in the day, as I had seen him return to the field after having his wound examined."[5]

Eventually an artillery duel ensued and, as the tubers banged away at one another, Longstreet sent Major General Lafayette McLaws' division on an end-around attack upon the Union left. Longstreet sent two companies of the 43rd Alabama to the Confederate right to act as skirmishers in concert with McLaws' attack. Not long after that point, Longstreet ordered Johnson to press his line forward. It turned out Gracie's men were further advanced than Johnson knew. "The line of Gracie's brigade had, however, been somewhat advanced, and was exposed to the fire of the Federals occupying the large hotel building at Bean's Station and firing through loop-holes cut in the wall of the second and third stories," Johnson wrote.[6]

The hotel sheltering the Union forces began to burn—Johnson supposed it was set afire by the Union men to deny its use by the Confederates—and the southern attackers moved forward again:

The advance in Gracie's brigade was made mainly by the Sixtieth Alabama Regiment, under Colonel Sanford, the Fifty-ninth and eight companies of the Forty-third Alabama Regiments moving up as skirmishers on its right and rear. Captain Blakemore, my aide-de-camp, first conveyed to Colonel Sanford the order to advance about the time Johnson's brigade commenced moving. This regiment rushed forward gallantry [*sic*], and with a shout passed the line of the Fifty-ninth and eight companies of the Forty-third Alabama Regiments deployed as skirmishers. In this movement the Sixtieth Alabama Regiment was exposed to the heavy fire of the enemy, concealed in the hotel, and of a line of Federals in the plain west of the hotel, and it consequently halted, and the men attempted to cover themselves by lying on the ground. The deliberate fire delivered with accuracy from the loopholes of the hotel continually struck the men of the Sixtieth Alabama Regiment as they lay immovably on the ground, and when that regiment subsequently arose to advance again on the hotel, under orders conveyed to Colonel Sanford by Lieutenant Moorhead, Gracie's brigade inspector, it left its line marked out by the dead and wounded.[7]

The fighting now included many moving pieces. Johnson's brigade attacked from east of the station and south of Knoxville Road but was subjected to resistance from a cavalry unit and artillery. When elements of Johnson's brigade sought refuge behind a minor undulation in the ground, the Union battery pulled out of the fighting.

The Sixtieth, Johnson wrote,

now arose and advanced on the right of the Knoxville road directly upon the hotel in the face of the fire from that building, and from a line of the enemy extending across the valley south of the hotel, which caused the regiment to take to the shelter of a large stable some 50 yards east of the hotel building, where it continued to return the enemy's fire. In this advance Colonel Sanford was knocked down by a shot, but afterward joined the regiment at the stable, where it had moved under command of Lieutenant Colonel D. S. Troy.[8]

Sometime after the 60th reached the barn, the 59th and 43rd Alabamians deployed to the right of the 60th and attacked the north side of the beleaguered hotel. Two Confederate artillery outfits began firing at what those units believed was a Union stronghold and mistakenly fired twice into the stable. Johnson said two men from the 60th were killed by the friendly artillery fire and three more may have been wounded. The affair eventually ended after Confederate artillery worked over the hotel again. When the fighting was over, three Union soldiers were discovered in the hotel's cellar.

As had been the case at Chickamauga, Gracie's Brigade suffered heavier casualties than might have been expected. Johnson's Brigade lost five soldiers and one officer killed. Five officers were wounded, along with 47 soldiers. Add in two men counted as missing and you get 60 casualties.

Gracie's men lost 24 men killed, counting two officers. The brigade lost 180 men wounded, including nine officers. The reader will recall that two of the wounded officers were Gracie and Sanford. Gracie counted 10 missing for a total of 162 casualties. The fighting at Bean's Station was really just a skirmish, a small piece of the war. But it was deadly.

In a December 16, 1863, note to General S. Cooper, Longstreet mentioned the capture of 68 wagons from the Union force at Bean's Station, specifically mentioning that about 40 of the former Federal wagons were loaded with coffee and sugar. But his next sentence summed up life in the Confederate army in the winter of 1863. Longstreet wrote simply, "We shall be obliged to suspend active operations for want of shoes and clothing."[9]

It is interesting to note how slowly information got around in and around the Confederate Army. On December 31, 1863, Gracie's Brigade included the 41st Alabama Infantry, the 43rd Alabama Infantry and the Legion's four battalions. Hilliard's Legion had been reconfigured into the 59th, 60th and 23rd Sharpshooters on the previous November 25. The organization of forces chart for March 1, 1864, finally shows the 41st, 43rd, 59th and 60th Alabama Infantry Regiments, plus the 23rd Battalion, Alabama Sharpshooters.

After the New Year was born, Gracie's command was involved in the fight at Dandridge on January 17. But the biggest piece of news for the Brigade came in the form of an order from Braxton Bragg, who was by now in Richmond with a staff job. Gracie's Brigade was to move from Buckner's Department, as the Confederates liked to call it, to join Lee's Army of Northern Virginia at Petersburg, Virginia. Bragg's note to Cooper said, "Order by telegraph, move by rail." Gracie was to report to Brigadier General Robert Ransom, Jr. By May 10, the Brigade's strength was said to be 1,578 strong (2,197 aggregate).[10]

For once, in the trenches in front of Petersburg, the Confederate strength was too great. General Bushrod Johnson reported in a June 30 communication to Assistant Adjutant-General Colonel G.W. Brent:

> Gracie's brigade relieved Martin's brigade early last night…. General Gracie reports the "trenches very poorly constructed; too narrow and not sufficiently deep; that there are also some very dangerous points where the enemy have a plunging fire into our ditches." There was not room enough in the lines for the whole of Gracie's brigade, and the Fifty-ninth Alabama Regiment, about 250 effective has been retired to the rear of the railroad.[11]

Still, with his typical energy, Gracie got to work. By August 3, he was still thinking about digging, albeit in a different way. It seems that a private in the 41st Alabama named Thomas Fowler invented a boring instrument that could allow the Confederates to dig into the ground and try to search, or "feel" as Gracie put it, for Union mines. The 41st had been recently transferred to Gracie's command. Gracie notified Bushrod Johnson about the device and asked Johnson to send an engineer to Gracie's area.

As was mentioned earlier, there is an enduring story about Gracie and Confederate General Robert E. Lee in the trenches near Petersburg: that Gracie stood in front of Lee to ensure Lee was not shot while observing Federal lines from Gracie's area. The story was memorialized in the poem *Gracie of Alabama* by Francis O. Tickner (see Appendix 9).

Did this happen? Did Gracie place himself between Lee and the Union lines? Did Lee, surprised, caution the Alabama general with the words, "Why, Gracie, you'll be shot"? Did Gracie reply, basically, "Better me than you"? We do know that Lee visited the Gracie salient on November 2, 1864. General Bushrod Johnson mentions the visit in a communication the next day, November 3.[12]

Lee's most extensive biographer, Douglas Southall Freeman, described the incident in the third volume of his massive four-volume classic:

> One day in November he (Lee) had been on the lines with Gracie who commanded a brigade in Johnson's Division. Being perhaps unfamiliar with the deadliness of the sharpshooting on that part of the front, Lee carelessly stood up on the parapet. Gracie, without a word, instantly interposed his body between that of Lee and the enemy. Both were pulled back over the works before either was hit but Lee never forgot the spirit Gracie exhibited.[13]

Confederate artillery commander Edward Porter Alexander's two books, *Fighting for the Confederacy: The Personal Recollections of General Edward Porter Alexander* and *Military Memoirs of a Confederate*, are considered by most Civil War historians to be solid sources of information. In *Military Memoirs*, Alexander quotes a letter from Colonel Walter Taylor, a member of Lee's staff:

> Gen. Lee was making an inspection along the line occupied by Gen. Gracie's troops; the fire of the enemy's sharpshooters was uncomfortably accurate along there and the orders were against needless exposure. To get a good view, Gen. Lee mounted the parapet or stepped out in front of the works. Of course all who saw it realized his danger but who was to direct his attention to it? Gen. Gracie at once stepped to his side. The minies whistled viciously. Gen. Lee, oblivious to his own danger, quickly realized Gen. Gracie's and immediately removed from the point of danger. That is all, but it showed tact on the part of the latter.

In a December 4, 1864, letter, Taylor again referenced the same incident when reporting Gracie's death. "Gen. Gracie," Taylor wrote, "who showed such tact in getting Gen. Lee to descend from a dangerous position."[14]

It seems probable that *something* happened between Gracie and Lee on November 3. The commander of the Army of Northern Virginia possibly became engrossed in his observations of the enemy lines and briefly lost track of his position. Any photographer would understand how Lee could have become fixated on his observations. Photographers experience the same thing when looking through the viewfinder of a camera.

Remember Colonel Taylor's wording, "But who was to direct his [Lee's] attention to it?" Who indeed? Gracie was a general officer and knew Lee, if only slightly, from the days when Gracie was a cadet at West Point and Lee was the commandant. Further, Lee was visiting Gracie's command. Gracie was the logical man to act.[15]

The story seems to be true and it has an ironic twist of fate. Gracie was killed by an artillery shell a month later while observing the Union lines.

Appendix 2

The Death of Brigadier General Archibald Gracie III

The Petersburg period was bloody and disheartening for all involved, and especially so for the former Legion men still serving with Gracie. The Official Records are replete with daily mentions of men killed, wounded or deserted. The command lost roughly a man or two a day.

The daily division report covering December 2, 1864, issued by Johnson, says that two men were killed and two more were wounded. One of the dead was Brigadier General Archibald Gracie III. He'd had horses shot out from under him at Chickamauga and been wounded at Bean's Station but had always survived. Finally, his luck had run out. Most accounts have an artillery shell exploding while Gracie III observed the enemy with a telescope. The shell somehow broke Gracie's neck.

Archibald Gracie IV, the general's son and researcher, exchanged letters with former Confederate Captain Winfield Wolfe, who told Gracie IV that Wolfe was within 20 feet of General Gracie when Gracie III was killed in the trenches near Petersburg. Two others were killed by the same shell, according to Wolfe.

Also killed were Private John Norwood and Captain David Hughes. Norwood's head was severed, according to Wolfe, and Captain Hughes' head was half severed by the same shell that killed Gracie.[1]

Private Norwood was in Company C of the 43rd Alabama. He was about 27 (age 25 at enlistment March 25, 1862) when he was killed. Norwood was a married farmer and a resident of Hopewell, Alabama.[2]

Captain Hughes enlisted on March 20, 1862. He was elected second lieutenant on December 7, 1862, and later first lieutenant. He was promoted to captain on October 30, 1864, when Captain Buck retired. Wolfe was promoted to captain when Hughes was killed.[3]

There was more fighting to do. Gracie was replaced as commander of the Brigade by Young Moody of the 43rd Alabama. Still, the Brigade would be known from then forward as Gracie's Brigade. Lee's army did not surrender until the following April.

Appendix 3

Affidavits of Privates William T. Gillian and H. T. "Hub" Tillery

Gillian

This is to certify that I, William T. Gillian, was a member of Co. D., 1st Battalion, Alabama Legion, commanded by Major Holt, in the battle of Chickamauga.

On this occasion, after having charged up the hill of Snodgrass Ridge, and driven the enemy from the summit and north through the thick woods, I, with other comrades, pursued them. We pressed through the woods into the open garden south of a log-house, which I intended taking shelter behind. As I double-quicked along I stopped and picked up a small pumpkin, which I put into my haversack.

I had not fired a shot from my gun and had roved but a few steps when I received a wound in my right arm. At this time I was very close to the log-house. I remember seeing there Comrade Hub Tillery, a few paces in front, between me and the log-house, when I turned back on account of my severe wound.

I sliced and ate this pumpkin that night, offering some to my comrades. They laughed at me and joked me about it from that day to the surrender, and called me pumpkin thereafter.

I further recall the fact that Lieut. Gilchrist of our company, just after I was shot, called out: "Come back, you boys, you are getting too far." These were his exact words.

Tillery

This is to certify that I was a member of Company "D," First Battalion, Alabama Legion, commanded by Major Holt in the battle of Chickamauga. That I was a Comrade of William T. Gillian, of the same Company. That I have read the affidavit subscribed to him, describing the incidences on Snodgrass Ridge, and I also subscribe to the accuracy of the statements he has made therein, so far as regards myself, as to the position I occupied at the time he was wounded. I remember seeing the log-house referred to and my taking position behind it. I further recall the fact, also mentioned, that Lieutenant Gilchrist of our Company called out, "Come back boys, you are getting too far."[1]

Appendix 4

Bragg vs. the Office of Commissary-General of Subsistence

Braxton Bragg had detractors everywhere in the Confederate States Army. Even when following through with standard army paperwork for his superiors, Bragg attracted the worst sort of criticism. In a letter dated September 4, 1863, just two weeks before the opening of the Chickamauga firestorm, L. B. Northrop, of the Office of Commissary-General of Subsistence, wrote that Bragg was delusional to believe that the lack of food being supplied to the Army of Tennessee was the primary cause of poor morale within that Army.

A few days earlier, on August 25, 1863, Giles M. Hillyer, Office Chief of Subsistence, Army of Tennessee, wrote Bragg a note summarizing the supply and the resources upon which the Army could depend for food in the near future. Hillyer's note did not bring good news.

"In relation to rice, pease, soap, salt and vinegar," Hillyer wrote, "there is no problem" in the near or long term. He continued, "For breadstuffs, also, I have no fear." But bacon and beef were a problem. "The prospects for a supply beyond October 1 are not merely uncertain, but gloomy indeed. I have only fifteen days' supply on hand after September 1."[1] Hillyer enclosed extracts from officers in the field, giving particulars about the supplies on hand and what could be expected in the near future, which was not enough.

"These estimates are irrespective of any probable increase of the strength of this army. They are also based on the ration of one-third pound of bacon, an amount which I am satisfied cannot further be reduced without great dissatisfaction in the army." Hillyer reported. He added, "I can see no reasonable expectation to feed the army with meats beyond the last of September and that only with the most rigid care and economy."

The strength of the army did increase, of course, when Longstreet and his force of about 12,000 men from the Army of Northern Virginia arrived in advance of and during the fight at Chickamauga.

Hillyer outlined sources of beef in Florida and Alabama but maintained that his office lacked the manpower to collect the cattle, and often the authority as well.

On August 26 Bragg forwarded Hillyer's letter to the Headquarters of the Department of Tennessee, writing, "The morale of this army is being seriously injured by this cause principally, and desertions, some to the enemy, are not uncommon."

The Adjutant and Inspector General's Office, commanded by the Secretary of War, referred the matter to the Commissary-General. Northrop fired back with a far-reaching description of the Confederate States Army's supply difficulties, including a brief history of the issues confronting his office. Then Northrop let Bragg have it.

"General Bragg has fallen into a delusion," Northrup diagnosed. He continued:

> His army has probably many Tennesseans and inhabitants of districts in Mississippi and Alabama which have been yielded to the enemy from the Mississippi east, and the loyal Tennessee having entered the army, and perhaps many also lukewarm, if not disloyal, consider that their families are virtually in the hands of their domestic enemies. Those from the rest of Tennessee and North Alabama and Mississippi know that their homes are actually so. That army has been sufficiently fed to keep the men in good condition. Witness that the Army of Virginia, on less, never was more healthy or efficient than last winter.

Had Bragg kept his army more active, Northrup opined, morale would be better. "Even without those causes an army of men having homes and families not well provided for will be demoralized, while an army with far less rations than his army has had, if operating actively, will not become demoralized."

Northrop got his wish on September 18. Bragg's army became active and three days later the Army of Tennessee had thousands fewer soldiers to supply with beef.

But Hillyer was correct in his prediction that the Army of Tennessee would soon be short of food. Quartermaster Sergeant Horace McLean of the Legion's 2nd Battalion, Company B, wrote to his wife, Mary, in the weeks and months after Chickamauga and left no doubt about whether he and his comrades were properly fed. On October 6, 1863, McLean wrote home from near Chattanooga, "The greatest grumbling that I hear amonge the boys is for want of some thing to Eat our rations ar very short."[2]

Two days later, the Legion's John Elmore Hall wrote to his father that, "Rations are very short throughout the army I don't suppose there has been a pound of bacon brought to the army in seven or eight days Beef (and very poor) is used altogether. Soured meal with once in a while flour spoiled by smoot is what is mostly brought for breadstuffs."[3]

This was eight days into October, shortly after Hillyer predicted the scarcity of beef would begin. Two weeks later, on October 20, McLean told his wife, "Our rations are very poor and of a very inferior quality."

The availability of food eventually improved, according to McLean's letters. But the issue of clothing did not improve. McLean wrote of comrades walking their picket posts on frozen ground without shoes. McLean may have been slightly better off than some of his buddies, as it seems that he had shoes. He wrote that he lacked a coat.

On November 4, McLean wrote his family, "I trust in God that the time is not longe till we can either get out of this place or be better provided for than we have been for the last 40 days."

On Christmas Eve of the same year, now writing from Morristown, Tennessee, McLean said, "At this time our men are in a Dreadful condition in way of clothing & shoes many of them are bare footed and hardly have clothes enough to hide their nakedness."

Appendix 5

The Argument Over Chasing the Union Army Back Toward Chattanooga

The final controversy regarding the fighting at Horseshoe Ridge scarcely involves Hilliard's Legion, but the Legion *could* have been involved.

Victory, that rare and difficult experience for the Army of Tennessee, was accomplished. Full darkness had fallen. The tattered remnants of the Confederate force were clumped in groups where they had stopped fighting. The men were exhausted, many were without ammunition and most were without food or water.

Nobody knew for sure where the Federals were. They were gone, true, but how far? A few hundred yards? A mile? Nobody knew.

James Longstreet certainly did not know where the enemy was. The wing commander was so uncertain of the enemy's location that he declined an order to report to Bragg, the commanding officer of the Army of Tennessee, early the following morning for fear of a possible attack on Longstreet's front.

Longstreet had not attempted a risky night chase of the Army of the Cumberland, but years later he said Bragg should have. In an 1879 newspaper interview, Longstreet, now a post office worker Gainesville, Georgia, said, "If ever there was an occasion that demanded pursuit pell-mell, this was the time. The Federals were rushing back on Chattanooga in the utmost confusion. It was a bright moonlit night and our people were anxious to pursue. We might actually have entered Chattanooga with flying Federals and thus recovered the key to Georgia and East Tennessee. General Bragg declined to follow up this advantage."[1]

Longstreet probably had the authority to issue the pursuit order himself, as wing commander with plenty of room for discretionary decisions. Longstreet might have attempted to cobble together a force with enough muscle and ammunition to chase "pell-mell" after Rosecrans' army.

But Longstreet did not order the chase when asked to by his subordinates. Longstreet met in the darkness sometime after the fighting ended on the 20th with a representative of General Preston. Preston wanted to chase the Yankees toward Chattanooga. Remember, much of Preston's Division had been shot to tatters during the struggle for Horseshoe Ridge, but the 6th and 7th Florida regiments were relatively whole and might have marched off toward Chattanooga.

But for many of the same reasons that George Meade did not immediately rush after Robert E. Lee and the Army of Northern Virginia after the fight at Gettysburg, the Army of Tennessee really could not chase the Army of the Cumberland after the battle at Chickamauga.

Braxton Bragg, the commanding general, wrote in a report later, "Our loss was in proportion to the prolonged and obstinate struggle. Two-fifths of our gallant troops had fallen." Bragg estimated his losses at just under 18,000 men. He also estimated his loss in horseflesh, needed for pulling artillery and wagons, to be about a third of his strength before the battle.[2]

Most of the Confederate soldiers still alive were exhausted. Many were critically low or out of ammunition. The army had not eaten since breakfast. Even water was scarce. Bragg again, from the same report as above: "Exhausted by two days' battle, with very limited supply of provisions, and almost destitute of water, sometime in daylight was absolutely essential for our troops to supply these necessaries and replenish their ammunition before renewing the contest."[3]

Many officers were dead or too badly wounded to fight, requiring at least minimal reorganization of companies, brigades and even regiments. Bragg reported:

> Major-General Hood lost a leg on the 20th, when gallantly leading his command. Brigadier General Preston Smith was killed on the 19th, and Brigadier-Generals B. H. Helm and James Deshler fell on the next day—all gallant soldiers and able commanders. Brigadier-Generals Gregg, McNair, and Adams were severely wounded, the first two not dangerously; the latter is missing. The accounts of him are conflicting, but he probably fell into the hands of the enemy. Brigadier-General Brown was slightly wounded, but is again on duty.[4]

The Legion's 1st Battalion commander, Colonel John H. Holt, was badly wounded and out of action, as was the 2nd Battalion's commander, Lieutenant Colonel Bolling Hall. Captain W. D. Walden, the 2nd Battalion's next in line, was dead, too. So bad was the casualty list among the officers of the 2nd that Lieutenant Crenshaw Hall, the Battalion Adjutant and brother of the original commander, was called upon to write the after-battle report.

True, the Legion's losses were exceptional. But those losses illustrate the point that Longstreet did not have a force capable of racing the Union army into Chattanooga. When he did have an opportunity to do so, earlier in the day, he instead committed Preston's Division to the headlong collision with Horseshoe Ridge. The Rebels won the battle but at a terrible cost.

Bragg's ultimate decision, for which he would later receive great criticism, was not to immediately chase the retreating Rosecrans troops. But his reasoning was solid. In reply to other proposals, such as a move toward Nashville, Bragg reported:

> Such a movement was utterly impossible for want of transportation. Nearly half our army consisted of re-enforcements just before the battle without a wagon or an artillery horse, and nearly, if not quite, a third of the artillery horses on the field had been lost. The railroad bridges, too, had been destroyed to a point south of Ringgold, and on all the road from Cleveland to Knoxville. To these insurmountable difficulties were added the entire absence of means to cross the river except by fording at a few precarious points too deep for artillery and the well-known danger of sudden rises, by which all communication would be cut, a contingency which did actually happen a few days after the visionary scheme was proposed. But the most serious objection to the proposition was its entire want of military propriety. It abandoned to the enemy our entire line of communication and laid open to him our depots of supplies, while it placed us with a greatly inferior force beyond a difficult and at times impassable river, in a country affording no subsistence to men or animals. It also left open to the enemy, at a distance of only 10 miles, our battle-field, with thousands of our wounded and his own, and all the trophies and supplies we had won.[5]

Braxton Bragg was not the finest soldier in the Confederate States Army. His leadership style is open to question. But his decision to spend September 21 putting his army back together after the brutal meat grinder that was the Battle of Chickamauga was probably the right one.

The real question about chasing the fleeing Union troops was about James Longstreet's decision regarding the best use of Preston's Division the previous afternoon. Preston's men were fresh and rested, though mostly untested in battle. They were probably hungry, but their time near the banks of the Chickamauga may have allowed them to fill their canteens during the previous night and they may have had more water than most Confederate units.

Of Preston's soldiers on the morning of the 20th, Gracie's men were fully provisioned for battle, as most had not fired a weapon since arriving in the area. As discussed earlier, some of Preston's men had done some fighting since crossing the creek on the night of the 18th, but most had not.

Unsure of the quality of fighting Preston's Division might produce, Longstreet appealed to Bragg for the use of a division from Polk's reserves. Bragg properly denied the request, eventually forcing Longstreet to use his own reserves, namely the Preston force.

And here was the key moment for Longstreet: The opportunity to show creativity. As the afternoon drew long, the Federal forces on Horseshoe Ridge were under increasing pressure and were less and less capable of mounting any effort other than fighting to hold their positions while also retreating.

Longstreet obviously knew that his men had driven the Union soldiers toward the Ridge by pressuring and collapsing the Union's right flank. While he probably did not know exactly how successful Polk's wing was that afternoon, Longstreet was veteran enough to know his wing had a victory on its hands.

This was the moment to show himself worthy of appointment to a larger command. It was a chance to prove himself ready to take over command of an entire army by displaying the ability to see the bigger picture while commanding one wing. Bragg's illness or some other factor caused Bragg to give Longstreet enough latitude to make important decisions on the spot. In the dysfunctional atmosphere of Bragg's Army of Tennessee, such freedom was tantamount to an invitation to get into trouble with the overall commander. But Longstreet's status within the Confederate Army probably forced Bragg to give his newly arrived general more leeway to make decisions than, say, Polk was allowed to do.

Longstreet could have sent Preston's Division on an end run around the Federal army, first to the north and then east and around the backside of Horseshoe Ridge. Such an attack would have cut off the Federal retreat and bagged a very large number of prisoners.

Further, assuming Preston's men were successful in this theoretical sweep around the back of the Ridge, Preston's Division would have been in perfect position to chase after the fleeing bluecoats the next day.

Or, Longstreet might have sent Preston rushing toward Chattanooga to batter Rosecrans and the retreating, dispirited men of the Army of the Cumberland. Decades later, Longstreet said Bragg should have done exactly that on September 21, one day after Longstreet had his chance.

Instead, James Longstreet simply sent Preston's Division rushing up a steep hill against well-manned defenses. That Gracie and his Brigade were able to force the Union men out of their prepared defensive positions and off the ridge is a testament to their fighting spirit. That they had to do so at all is a testament to something else.

Appendix 6

The Legion's Walk
to Chickamauga

The Legion's march toward the site of the Battle of Chickamauga has been mentioned many times in this book. Below is the report of a Legion company starting with September 1, 1863, and extending through the day after the battle. Where text wasn't entirely legible the author's interpretation is in enclosed in brackets.

Sept. 1st/63 Left Bivouac in Sweet Water Valley marched in the direction of Charleston passed through Athens and camped in [Ricerville]. 2nd Passed through Charleston about noon, and camped at dusk on Hiwassee River 7 miles below Charleston.—3rd Left camp and marched about 12 miles in the night to Georgetown camped there that night.—4th moved 3 miles north of Georgetown and camped. 5th marched back through Georgetown, thence westward in direction of Harrlson's Landing, camped in 3 miles of River. Left camp about sunset on 6th and marched to [Ooltawah] on the Knoxville and Chattanooga RR that night distance about 10 miles. 7th Left camp at Ooltawah about 2 a.m. and marched to Graysville, Ga., by sunrise, thence south and camped near Ringgold, Ga that night. 8th passed through Ringgold and marched thence due west about 12 miles & camped for night in an old "Camp Ground." 9th Sept. Marched 6 or 8 miles westward and camped on a creek in "MacLemores Cove."—10th marched down into the "Cove" and spent the day in forming and changing lines of battle positions etc. Anticipated an engagement with the enemy. Camped that night at foot of Pigeon Mountain.—11th Crossed the Mountain and entered the village of LaFayette, Ga., about noon. Camped near the village that night. 12th moved up the Chattanooga Road 5 miles but returned to Lafayette that evening and camped.

Remained at La Fayette until the 17th Sept. when we were moved up the Chattanooga Road and camped about 10 miles distant. 18th moved during day up to Chickamauga Creek, which we crossed after dark and lay on our arms the remainder of the night.—19th Formed in line of battle Early in day and remained during the entire day in support of artillery without becoming engaged lay near battle field.—20th Sept Still in support of artillery up to 4 p.m. when we were marched down to the left and engaged the enemy in a strong position on the left of the Chattanooga Road since known as "Battery Hill." After a stubborn resistance we succeeded in driving the enemy from the works which we held for about an hour and were at last compelled to fall back for want of ammunition. 21st Spent the day burying our dead.[1]

Appendix 7

The Fifth Battalion
of Hilliard's Legion

The 5th Battalion of Hilliard's Legion was at Chickamauga as well. When the five companies of the 5th were split away from the Legion, the Battalion was paired with the 19th Georgia Cavalry Regiment to form the 10th Confederate Cavalry Regiment. The 5th Battalion seems to have stayed with the bulk of the Legion, first at Camp Mary in Montgomery, Alabama, and then at Loudon, Tennessee, through most of 1862, except for D Company.

The D Company muster roll card for June 1 through September 1, which is dated November 9, noted that, "This company was detached from Hilliard's Legion on the 12 of August 1862 as escort for Gen. [unclear] and served in that capacity through its campaign of Kentucky until Nov. 10, 1862."[1]

Like many of the companies in the Legion's infantry and artillery battalions, some of the men of the 5th Battalion started the war in volunteer companies which were then assigned to regiments (or battalions, such as those in the Legion). Company A was commissioned as the David Clopton Rangers. Company E was originally the Fluie Rangers, commissioned on February 5, 1862. The 5th Battalion merged with the 19th Regiment around the first of the year, 1863.

The wartime letters of John W. Cotton, a private in the 5th Battalion's C Company, have become a staple of researchers studying Alabama units in the war. They were published in 1951 as the book *Civil War Letters of John W. Cotton, Yours Till Death*. The letters were edited by Lucille Griffith and the reader is warned that Cotton did not use periods.[2] Cotton's summation of the 10th Regiment's contribution to the Confederate victory at Chickamauga sheds little light on the exact actions of the 10th, but it is interesting for other reasons.

Cotton wrote to his wife four days after the battle:

I reckon you will here of the big battle we have had before you get this letter I hant got time to rite much about it now but we have given them the worst whipping they have ever had so ther prisoner say we have run them all out of Georgia ... we brought on the fite saturday morning but our regiment hant lost but few men our company hant lost but nary man killed or wounded but I cant see how we all escapted we were suppoting a battery on sunday evening and the yankeys commenced a cross fire on it and the grape shot shells fell around us like hail but we got behind trees and places so none of us did not get hurt they shot off three horses lags clost to us and killed one man and wounded one if I could tell you all I have seen it would make your heart ache to think of it but I could not tell if half as bad as it is.[3]

Still, according to David A. Powell's statistics in his authoritative *The Maps of Chickamauga*, the 10th Regiment lost just two killed and 11 wounded out of 250 men.[4]

In the same letter home quoted above, Cotton related that, "Our cavalry cant do not more good here so we will go back to east Tennessee I think in a few days if we don't start today."[5] Cotton never learned how to spell Chattanooga properly, but his letters were written from that general area until mid–November of 1863. The 10th Confederate Cavalry Regiment ended the war in the Carolina theater, surrendering with General Joseph E. Johnston's command on April 14, 1865, near Durham, North Carolina.

Appendix 8

Charge of Disloyalty

David A. Powell, whose book *The Maps of Chickamauga* does a tremendous job of tracking the paths of the many commands during the battle, charges in that book that Gracie's Brigade, specifically the 2nd Battalion of the Legion, had a become problem to the Rebel cause.

"After Chickamauga," Powell wrote of Gracie's command in *The Maps*, "many of them would be accused of inciting treason and mutiny." Powell also noted that the 63rd Tennessee "shed at least 150 men to desertion in the weeks leading up to the battle."[1]

The second volume of Powell's Chickamauga trilogy, *The Chickamauga Campaign—Glory or the Grave: The Breakthrough, the Union Collapse, and the Defense of Horseshoe Ridge, September 20, 1863,* has more of the same. After discussing the desertion rate in the Brigade during the summer of 1863, specifically in the Legion's 2nd Battalion, Powell wrote about the 70 soldiers in an Alabama home guard outfit who were arrested for mutiny in December of 1863.

Powell wrote that an investigation revealed that the revolt was instigated by men transferred from the battalions of Hilliard's Legion and other troops from Gracie's Brigade just after Chickamauga. The 2nd Battalion was singled out as specifically affected by treason.[2] The source for the allegation seems to be a brief passage in a letter from General James Clanton to, of all officers, General Leonidas Polk that is found in the Official Records. Clanton was an officer in what amounted to a home guard unit in Alabama. Men in Clanton's command were accused of disloyalty by Polk and Clanton responded with a third-person defense.

Clanton wrote to Polk:

In the interview granted me at Meridian in January last you did me and the brigade which I had been commanding great injustice in saying that the mutiny which was threatened at Pollard was the result of a want of discipline, and in contradicting the assertion which I made that the Peace Society, as it was called, originated in General Bragg's army.... The military court at Mobile assert that I arrested more officers and men in my brigade and forwarded to Mobile for trial (from Pollard) than any brigadier in your department. I averaged about sixty prisoners in my guard house for several months before I was ordered from Pollard. Inclosed I send a copy of a certificate of the court at Mobile. General Maury told me in Mobile, in November last, that he arrested in East Tennessee officers, as well as privates, for belonging to this same Peace Society, before he was assigned to duty at Mobile. Governor Watts says that the same society existed in the Army of Tennessee long before it was heard of at Pollard. Information of the fact was forwarded to Richmond whilst he was in the Cabinet ... and he advised the President to send the battalion (Hall's, of Alabama) to the front, the lieutenant-colonel asserting that the purpose of the society were not treasonable, and that he would be responsible for the conduct of his men on the field.[3]

Having been questioned by Polk, Clanton apparently tried to save himself by accusing another unit, specifically the Legion's 2nd Battalion, of spreading the disloyalty disease in the months after the fight at Chickamauga. This smacks of a military career version of the old joke about the Buddy System: If you are attacked by a bear, throw your buddy toward the bear and run. Clanton threw Bolling Hall and his 2nd Battalion at Polk, the bear.

Nor was the Legion alone. The 63rd Tennessee, according to Powell in *The Maps,* lost 150 men or more in desertions during the weeks before Chickamauga. "Despite this," Powell wrote, "the regiment fought reasonably well" at Chickamauga.

In *Glory or the Grave,* Powell cites Georgia Lee Tatum's book, *Disloyalty in the Confederacy,* as a source for the charge of disloyalty against the Legion. Tatum's source for the charge against Gracie's command in general, and the men of the Legion in particular, is the same letter from Clanton to Polk. Powell also wrote in *Glory or the Grave* that the revolt among Clanton's soldiers was spread by members of the Legion and others who were transferred from Gracie's command to Clanton's.[4]

But the muster rolls and the ADAH Civil War Soldiers database do not seem to bear out the idea that there were transfers from Gracie's to Clanton's command. There were Legion men in parts of Alabama in the weeks following their service at Chickamauga. There were plenty of furloughs granted to the wounded after the Battle of Chickamauga, and those wounded seriously enough to be granted a furlough, and who were able, went home for that period. Having seen the elephant, as the saying went at the time, these battered men may have come home unhappy about their condition and the idea that, when healthy again, they were supposed to return to the fighting. Those men may have had a poor attitude about the war, and probably said so if they did. But obviously the Legion's men were not the only Alabamians returning from the front, and men on furlough would not have joined Clanton's command while they were home. Those so badly hurt that they were medically unable to return to the front lines would not have joined Clanton, either.

The possibility of leaving Gracie's Battalion and transferring to a unit closer to home, such as Clanton's, was probably an attractive idea. Clanton's men were not fighting far from home and Gracie's men were. But it was the Confederate Army command structure that approved and disapproved transfer requests, not the individual soldiers.

At least one Confederate office holder gave thought to allowing deserters to change their duty assignment. North Carolina Governor Zebulon B. Vance wrote to Secretary of War James Seddon on July 25, 1863:

> A large number of deserters, say 1,200, are in the mountains and inaccessible wilds of the west. I have found it impossible to get them out, and they are plundering and robbing the people. Through their friends they have made me propositions to come out and enlist for defense of this state alone. Shall I accept it? The effect on the Army might be injurious, but they can never otherwise be made of service or kept from devastating the country. If you advise favorably, I think I can get at least 1,000 effective men.[5]

J. A. Campbell, the Confederate Government's Assistant Secretary of War, wrote an endorsement for Vance's idea and estimated that, "There are 50,000 to 100,000 men who are in some form or other evading duty. Probably there are 40,000 to 50,000 of absentees without leave."[6]

Desertion was rampant throughout the Confederate Army. The Legion's muster cards and letters home from the army make it clear that the government was not paying the soldiers, not feeding them and not clothing them. Letters home from men such as Cotton and Mason make it obvious that Confederate soldiers, like soldiers throughout history, missed their families and were concerned about what was happening back home. The Confederate Government was not giving the men in its armed forces any reason to continue their arduous service and, at the same time, the home front was begging the soldiers for their return.

In May of 1863, Lieutenant Colonel Bolling Hall, Jr., the commander of the Legion's 2nd Battalion, wrote to his father that, "A good many desertions have been going on lately from the Legion." He said later in the same letter that eight would-be deserters had been caught and were awaiting prosecution. Other 2nd Battalion soldiers evaded Hall's efforts and left camp. To pretend that desertion from the army was not an issue for the Confederacy would be silly. But to assume Gracie's Brigade was more guilty of desertion than other units would be equally inaccurate.

Obviously, losing soldiers to desertion hurt the Confederate Army. The northern states had a greater population to draw from to begin with, so losses suffered through the voluntary withdrawal of able-bodied men were costlier for the southern states' cause. Powell and others indicate that the Legion's losses were more severe than those of other Confederate units and even indicate that Legion's roster was rife with traitors to the Confederate cause. However, their primary source of information, Clanton's letter to Polk, also contains verbiage absolving the Legion from accusations of disloyalty. Clanton wrote:

> At Chickamauga the colors of this battalion were pierced by eighty-two balls, and President Davis promoted Lieutenant-Colonel Hall to colonel and the color bearer to a lieutenancy. This [Peace] society existed very generally in Hilliard's legion, now Gracie's brigade. The investigations in the court disclosed the fact that very few members of this society joined for any treasonable purpose, although I sent seventy members to Mobile in irons for trial, yet not one has been shot, and near four months have elapsed.[7]

Clanton may have sent 70 soldiers from his command to Mobile for trial, but he did not send 70 soldiers from Hilliard's Legion, who were under the command of Brigadier General Archibald Gracie, anywhere.

Brian Scott Hilliard, a member of the 150th Civil War Commission, wrote about executions in the *Dalton Daily Citizen*. Hilliard wrote that after Joe Johnston replaced Braxton Bragg as commander of the Army of Tennessee, Johnston tried to stem the flow of desertion with amnesty offers for deserters who returned to the army, just as Bragg had done. When his offer failed to draw back significant numbers of soldiers, Johnston executed 14 men from the 58th and 60th North Carolina Regiments who had been charged with desertion. The executions were held on May 4, 1864. The men were tried and judged guilty in April of that year.[8]

The men of the Legion were split away from the Army of Tennessee at the end of November 1863, and fought effectively with Longstreet's command. Those men followed Longstreet to the Army of Northern Virginia when Longstreet's failed operations in Kentucky and Tennessee ended. The issues Johnston had with his army could not be blamed on Hilliard's Legion. Clanton's accusation against Hall's 2nd Battalion, based upon second-person hearsay, does not ring true.

Jack A. Bunch compiled the *Roster of the Courts-Martial on the Confederate States Armies*, an exhaustive listing of Confederate soldiers who were subjected to a military trial during the Civil War. According to Bunch, 59 members of the original Legion were court-martialed. This includes members of the 59th and 60th infantry regiments, which were filled by Legion men after Chickamauga. Interestingly, no members of the 23rd Battalion, Alabama Sharpshooters are listed in Bunch's roster. The 23rd also was made up entirely of Legion members. In most cases the charges or specifications did not survive the war, but most of the outcomes did.[9]

Before the Legion was consolidated into the 59th, 60th and 23rd, 26 of its members were court-martialed. Daniel E. Lee, a private in the 2nd Battalion's A Company, was acquitted. Lee was the only Legion man acquitted, but seven others had their sentences remitted or disapproved or were not sentenced. Among this second group was Theophilus Arnett of the Legion's 2nd Battalion, Company A. Arnett was accused of desertion and persuading others to do the same.

Eight more were sentenced to company punishment, which meant the accused was returned to his regiment to be punished by the company commander. Five Legion men were confined and limited to a diet of bread and water. Given the uncertain nature of the frequency and quality of the food that the active soldiers were fed in the field, this punishment might not have seemed too bad. Four others were sentenced to hard labor. Private Moses P. May, of Company D, 2nd Battalion, was sentenced to be returned to his company and to be branded with the letter B on his left hip.[10] Gilbert McInish and John Treadwell, both privates in the 2nd Battalion's Company A, were sentenced to death. They were subsequently either pardoned or had their sentences remitted. The record is unclear, but they were not executed.

After the Legion was consolidated, 17 soldiers each from the 59th Alabama and 60th Alabama were court-martialed. From the 59th, J. J. H. Daniel and J. R. Kilpatrick both were sentenced to death, but both were pardoned. John Shaw of the 60th Infantry similarly was sentenced to die but later pardoned.

Finally, James Ray, of the 59th Regiment's Company C, was sentenced to death. According to Bunch, there is no evidence indicating whether the sentence was carried out. There is no evidence that any man serving in Hilliard's Legion was executed for treason, desertion or any other crime.

There were, of course, a few odd cases. Silas Patterson, a private in the 2nd Battalion's Company B, deserted sometime in 1862 and returned to his unit on October 21, 1863. He was tried January 26, 1864, and was sentenced to confinement with bread and water.

Appendix 9

Gracie, of Alabama

Gracie, of Alabama
By Francis Orray Ticknor

On, sons of mighty stature,
And souls that match the best,
When nations name their jewels
Let Alabama rest.

Gracie, of Alabama!
'Twas on that dreadful day
When howling hounds were fiercest,
With Petersburg at bay.

Gracie, of Alabama,
Walked down the lines with Lee,
Marking through mists of gunshot
The clouds of enemy.

Scanning the Anaconda
At every scale and joint;
And halting, glasses level
At gaze on "Dead Man's Point."

Thrice, Alabama's warning
Fell on a heedless ear,
While the relentless lead-storm,
Converging, hurtled near.

Till straight before his Chieftain,
Without a sound or sign,
He stood, a shield the grandest,
Against the Union line!

And then the glass was lowered,
And voice that faltered not

Said, in its measured cadence,
"Why, Gracie, you'll be shot!"

And Alabama answered:
"The South will pardon me
If the ball that goes through Gracie
Comes short of Robert Lee."

Swept a swift flash of crimson
Athwart the Chieftain's cheek,
And the eyes whose glance was "knighthood"
Spake as no king could speak.

And side by side with Gracie
He turned from shot and flame;
Side by side with Gracie
Up the grand aisle of Fame.

The author found this poem online at http://www.poetrynook.com/poem/
gracie-alabama.

Appendix 10

The Reorganization
of Hilliard's Legion

When the Confederate Army reorganized what was left of Hilliard's Legion after the battle of Chickamauga, most of the 1st Battalion was merged with the 3rd Battalion to form the 60th Alabama Infantry Regiment. The 2nd and 4th Battalions merged and became the 59th Alabama Infantry Regiment. Three companies from the 1st Battalion were kept together to form the 23rd Battalion Alabama Sharpshooters. All three commands remained in Brigadier General Archibald Gracie's command. Most companies were renamed within their new units, and the author found it easier to look at the following chart than to try to explain who went where to become what.

The companies of the 5th Battalion, the Legion's cavalry battalion that was merged with the 19th Georgia Cavalry to become the 10th Confederate Cavalry in 1862, and kept its company designations but those changes are included below to be complete.

Old Designation		New Designation	
Battalion	Company	Regiment	Company
First	A	60th	F
	B		H
	C		K
	D		I
	E	23rd Bat. SS	E
	F		F
	G		G
Second	A	59th	F
	B		K
	C		A
	D		G
	E		B
	F		C

(Battalion)	(Company)	(Regiment)	(Company)
Third	A	60th	E
	B		A
	C		B
	D		C
	E		G
	F		D
Fourth	A	59th	I
	B		D
	C		
	D		H
	E		E
Fifth	A	10th Con. Cav.	A
	B		B
	C		C
	D		D
	E		E

Roster of Hilliard's Legion

The information about the soldiers of Hilliard's Legion comes from a variety of sources. Those sources include the Alabama Department of Archives and History's Civil War Soldiers Database, the Legion's Confederate Army muster rolls (available on Ancestry.com) and muster cards (available online at Fold3.com), and the muster rolls for the 59th and 60th Alabama Infantry Regiments (also on Ancestry.com). Much of the information for the 5th Battalion's Company D came from a handwritten list compiled by two veterans of that company, Dr. Lucius Ernest Starr and Colonel John B. Rudolf. In some cases, Legion membership was discovered on tombstones.

It should be noted that, while there is a great deal of information available on some soldiers through the sources listed above, only a minimal amount is available about others. The roster of Legion soldiers is organized on the following pages in this manner: Name, battalion/company, rank at the time of enlistment, date of enlistment, age at enlistment and home county. Military history: Wounded/killed with location and date, other notes. Personal history: Marital status, pre-war occupation.

1st Battalion

Abney, Sylvester S.; 1/C; Private, enlisted 5/12/61 at 19 at Montgomery. Discharged 4/11/65 at Chickamauga, Ga. Co. K, 60th Ala.

Adams, G. W.; 1/D; Private, enlisted at 31 at Lowndes, Ala., absent on detail at Chickamauga and other battles, present at last battle listed. Married, farmer.

Adams, J. R.; 1/G; Sergeant, enlisted 7/3/62 at 23, Montgomery County.

Adams, Marshall; 1/G; Private, enlisted at 18, Montgomery County. Sick furlough (as of 7/3/62 record roll).

Adams, Thomas; 1/G; Private, enlisted at 19, Montgomery County. Surrendered 4/9/65.

Adams, Thomas (M or H); 1/C-G; Private, enlisted at 16, Chambers County, died in camp 6/2/62.

Adams, William A.; 1/C; Private, enlisted at 4/20/62 at 20, Chambers County. Discharged 4/9/62.

Alford, H. J.; 1/G; Private, enlisted 7/3/62 at 27, discharged by surgeon.

Alford, John; 1/G; Corporal, enlisted at 30, Montgomery County. Promoted to Sergeant, surrendered 4/9/65.

Alford, Sylvesta W.; 1/G; Private, enlisted at 18, Montgomery County. Surrendered 4/9/65.

Allen, A. M.; 1/G; Private, enlisted at 35.

Ankles, Theadore; 1/G; Private, enlisted at 35, Montgomery County.

Arington, W.M.; 1/D; Private, enlisted at 32, Lowndes County.

Armstrong, Josiah; 1/B; Private, enlisted at 22 in Butler County.

Armstrong, Thomas K.; 1/A; Private, enlisted 5/10/62. Wounded at Chickamauga (hand), absent next two battles. Single, minister.

Arnold, John W.; 1/AC; Private, enlisted at 24, single, born in Georgia, lived in Montgomery County, Ala. Jockey.

Atchison, William D.; 1/G; Private, enlisted at 25, surrendered 4/9/65. Sick furlough 7/3/62.

Athey, Elijah James; 3/D; Private, enlisted 5/9/62 at 23. Oakley, Ala. Lived 6/4/39–February of 1908, buried Pilgreen Cemetery, Montgomery County, Texas.

Athey, W. C.; 3/D; Private, enlisted 5/9/62 at 18, Montgomery County. Present at Chickamauga, Bean's Station, Drury's Bluff, DoB 12/28/1844–DoD 3/3/1923, buried Ramer Cemetery, Montgomery County.

Athy, William W.; 1/B; Private, enlisted at 22, wounded at Chickamauga (leg).

Austin, John W.; 1/G; Private, enlisted at 17.

Avant (Avaunt?), John A.; 1/C; Private, enlisted at 28, Chambers County.

Bagley, Joseph C.; 1/C; Private, enlisted at 17, Chambers County.

Baine, Thomas J.; 1/F; Private, enlisted at 25, Wilcox County.

Baine, William D.; 1/F; Private, enlisted at 23, Wilcox County.

Baker, Christopher C.; 1/C; Private, enlisted at 5/12/62 at 26. Absent on detail at Chickamauga. Married, physician.

Baldwin, Bird H.; 1/A; Private, enlisted 8/8/62 at 31. Present at Chickamauga. Single, farmer.

Ballard, J.T.; 1/D; Private, enlisted at 31 (32?), Lowndes County. Sick furlough as of 7/2/62.

Barber, George; 1/C; Private, enlisted at 32, Chambers County.

Barfield, William; 1/G; Private, enlisted at 17, Montgomery County. Surrendered with Lee.

Bargainer, Andrew A.; 1/D; Private, enlisted September 1862, Montgomery. Reported absent on furlough from hospital muster roll 10/31/62, present 8/31/64 as member of 60th Alabama, Company I, reported AWOL 2/28/65, Union POW records show paroled 5/30/65. Capture/surrender date, place unknown. Lived 1832–1914.

Bargainer, Barry Columbus; 1/D; Private, lived 9/7/32–11/15/62, died of disease.

Bargainer, Cleburn Payne; 1/D; Private, enlisted in 1862, continued to end of war, Lowndes County, lived 1/10/39–1933.

Bargainer, Hillary Hubert; 1/D; Private, enlisted May 1862 at 28, Lowndes County, served to end of war, lived 6/15/34–6/14/1915.

Bargainer, Lawson Brown; 1/D; Private, lived 8/21/28–2/26/1907.

Barker, Joseph N.; 1/A; 2nd Lieutenant. Wounded at Chickamauga (arm, severe).

Barnett, N. M.; 1/A; Corporal, enlisted at 32, Montgomery County. Replaced by substitute John J. Blair 1/1/63.

Barrett, Benjamin J.; 1/B; Private, enlisted at 36, killed at Chickamauga.

Barrett, Nathaniel W.; 1/D; Sergeant, enlisted 5/5/62, Lowndes County, probably died in hospital 8/1/62.

Barrett, William; 1/B; Private, enlisted at 35.

Bates, W.; 1/D; Private, could be W. D. Bates.

Baxter, William; 1/G; Private, enlisted at 38, Montgomery County.

Beasley, D.C.; 1/E; Private, enlisted at 20, Barbour County.

Beasley, D. J.; 1/E; Private, enlisted at 20, Barbour County.

Beesley, James; 1/B; Private, enlisted at 28, Butler County.

Beesley, John; 1/B; Private, enlisted at 25, Butler County.

Berry, Henry T.; 1/B; Private, enlisted at 29, Butler County.

Berry, W.; 1/B; Private.

Beshears, John D.; 1/A; Private, enlisted at 17, Montgomery County. Wounded at Chickamauga, present at Knoxville, on furlough for Beans Station. Bookbinder.

Betts, John Godbold; 1/F; Sergeant, enlisted at 25, Conecuh County. Wounded at Drewry's Bluff 5/16/64 (hip, lower jaw), survived war.

Beverly, J. E.; 1/D; Private, enlisted at 34, Lowndes County.

Bibb, John D.; 1/A; Private, enlisted 2/21/63? at 16. Wounded at Chickamauga (hip), present at Knoxville. Single, student.

Bibb, Richard; 1/G; Lieutenant. Killed at Chickamauga.

Blair, John; 1/A; Private, enlisted 1/1/63, Troy, Alabama. Substitute for N. M. Barnett. Absent, sick for Chickamauga and later. Blacksmith.

Blair, K. N.; 1/G; Private, enlisted at 17, discharged by Colonel Hilliard.

Blair, W.; 1/D; Private.

Blake, Henry C.; 1/B; Private, enlisted at 19, Butler County, killed at Chickamauga.

Blakey, James; 1/E; Sergeant, enlisted at 30, Barbour County.

Bludworth, John L.; 1/E; Private, enlisted at 33, Barbour County. Surrendered 4/9/65.

Bludworth, William; 1/E; Private, enlisted 5/6/62 at 34. Promoted to Corporal 10/1/62, wounded at Chickamauga, furloughed from hospital.

Bobbet, William; 1/E; Private, enlisted at 22.

Bodie, N. A.; 1/D; Sergeant, enlisted at 25, Lowndes County.

Boggs, Joseph J.; 1/B; Private, enlisted at 38, Butler County.

Boland, Henry M.; 1/A; Private, enlisted in 1862 at 20. Listed both wounded and captured at Chickamauga. Single.

Boler, Alexander H. (or Alascandre H.); 1/C; Private, enlisted at 17, Chambers County.

Boseman, F.; 1/D; Private.

Boseman, J.; 1/D; Private.

Bottoms, J. J.; 1/E; Private, enlisted at 22, Barbour County.

Bottoms, W. H.; 1/E; Private, enlisted at 20, Barbour County.

Bowling, James; 1/B; Private.

Bowling, Joseph; 1/B; Private.

Boyd, Thomas E.; 1/G; Private, enlisted at 18, Montgomery County.

Boyett, Henry; 1/B; Private, enlisted at 35, Butler County, wounded at Chickamauga (arm).

Boykin, Elias; 1/E; Private, enlisted at 40, Barber. Subbed for (first name unclear, possibly R. C.) Johnson, Barbour County. Captured at Chickamauga, sent to Military Prison at Louisville, Kentucky, then paroled at Camp Douglas and sent to Look Out Point for exchange. Exchanged and arrived at City Point, Virginia 3/14/65.

Bradley, J.; 1/D; Private.

Bradley, J. M.; 1/G; Private, enlisted at 34, Montgomery County.

Brame, William Whitman; 1/A; Corporal, enlisted 3/6/62 at 22, Montgomery County. Eligible for Confederate Cross of Honor.

Brandy, Chonic (or Chornick); 1/F; Private, surrendered 4/9/65.

Brantley, Solomon; 1/F; Private.

Brassell, William M.; 1/A; Private, enlisted 4/4/62 (possibly 4/1/62) at 26, Montgomery County. Present at Chickamauga. Single, farmer.

Bridges, David L.; 1/C; Private, enlisted 5/62, Montgomery, wounded at Bean's Station.

Briggs, Levi E.; 1/B; Private, had served previously then reenlisted 6/20/62, Butler County, continued until 9/30/63.

Brooks, Erwin; 1/F; Private, enlisted at 25, Conecuh County.

Broughton, William E.; 1/F; Lieutenant, enlisted at 27, Conecuh County. Promoted to Captain, a recruiting officer.

Browder, Maliciah C.; 1/B; Private, enlisted at 38, Butler County.

Browder, William T.; 1/B; Private, enlisted at 46, Butler County, buried at Confederate Cemetery, East Knoxville, Tennessee.

Brown, Daniel; 1/F; Private, enlisted at 34, Conecuh County.

Brown, David A.; 1/B; Sergeant, enlisted at 22, Butler County.

Brown, Edward; 1/A; Private, enlisted at 20 (born in Canada), listed as deserter at Petersburg.

Brown, Henry; 1/C; Private, enlisted at 24. Present at Chickamauga, arrested at Knoxville, present after. Single, laborer.

Brown, H. P.; 1/B; Private, enlisted at 27, Butler County.

Brown, Isaac; 1/F; Private.

Brown, J.; 1/E; Private.

Brown, James; 1/B; Private.

Brown, John W.; 1/F; Sergeant.

Brown, R.J.; 1/E; Private, enlisted at 25, Barbour County.

Brown, Thomas; 1/E; Private.

Brown, William; 1/E; Private, enlisted at 34, Barbour County.

Brown, William; 1/F; Private, surrendered 4/9/65.

Brown, Winlock; 1/F; Sergeant, enlisted at 25 as 3rd Corporal, Barbour County.

Brunson, Adam; 1/B Private, enlisted at 24, Pike County.

Brunson, Charles; 1/B; Private, enlisted at 24.

Brunson, C. A.;1/C; Private, enlisted at 26, Pike County.

Brunson, Richard; 1/B; Private.

Brunson, William G.; 1/B; Private, enlisted at 19, Pike County.

Bryant, Thomas; 1/G; Private.

Bryant, Thomas; 1/D; Private, could be Thomas H. Bryant.

Burgamy, Robert; 1/F; Corporal, enlisted at 30, Conecuh County.

Burgamy, Thomas; 1/B; Private, enlisted at 30, died in service in Tennessee, date unknown.

Burgamy, William D.; 1/F; Private, enlisted at 23, Conecuh County.

Burgin, J. M.; 1/C; Private, enlisted at 17, Montgomery, discharged by Colonel Hilliard.

Burke, Henry; 1/B; Private, enlisted at 21, Butler County.

Burns, L.; 1/D; Private, Lowndes County.

Burt, R.; 1/D. Private.

Bussey, J. C.; 1/D; Private, enlisted at 19, Lowndes County.

Butler, J.; 1/G; Corporal, later Sergeant in 23rd Alabama Sharpshooters.

Butler, James; 1/D; Private, enlisted May 1861.

Butler, N. B.; 1/G; Private, enlisted at 20.

Butler, T.M.; 1/G; Private, enlisted at 25, Montgomery.

Byrd, J.; 1/G; Private.

Cain, O.; 1/D; Private.

Callens, R.; 1/D; Private.

Camp, L.G.; 1/D; Sergeant, enlisted at 29, Lowndes County.

Candler, Henry; 1/G; Private, enlisted at 28, Montgomery County.

Capps, H. W.; 1/B; 2nd Lieutenant, enlisted at 27, Butler County.

Capps, John W.; 1/B; Private, enlisted 4/5/62, Ranersville, Ala. Died of disease at Cumberland Gap 11/29/62. Married, farmer.

Capps, S. W.; 1/B; Lieutenant, enlisted at 27, wounded at Chickamauga (foot), on roll at Petersburg.

Capps, Thomas A.; 1/B; Private, enlisted at 32, Butler County.

Capps, W.W.; 1/B; Lieutenant, enlisted at 27, Butler County.

Capps, William (W. W. L.); 1/B; Private, enlisted at 29, Pike County.

Carr, John; 1/F; Private, enlisted at 23, Conecuh County.

Carter, William; 1/E; Private, surrendered 4/9/65.

Cawley, Wesley; 1/A; Private, enlisted

10/28/62. Substitute for J. J. Smith, detached for detail 4/28/63.

Chambers, John; 1/G; Private, enlisted at 28, Montgomery.

Chambers, Joseph S.; 1/C; Corporal, enlisted at 18, Chambers County. Promoted to Sergeant of 23rd Sharpshooters, surrendered 4/9/65.

Chance, Isaac; 1/D-G; Private, Enlisted at 40, Montgomery.

Chance, John; 1/E; Private, enlisted at 33, Barbour County.

Chapman, Daniel; 1/F; Sergeant, enlisted at 30, Conecuh County. Died 3/24/65 of pneumonia at Richmond, Virginia General Hospital Howard Grove.

Chapman, John B.; 1/F; Private, enlisted at 19, Conecuh County. Promoted to Corporal, then Sergeant in 23rd Sharpshooters.

Cheatham, G.; 1/D; Private.

Cherry, Charles S.; 1/C; Private, enlisted at 29, Chambers County.

Clancy, Daniel; 1/B; Private, enlisted at 35.

Clancy, Greenwood B.; 1/B; Private, enlisted 4/5/62 at 19, Butler County. Wounded at Chickamauga (arm).

Clancy, Joseph E.; 1/B; Sergeant, enlisted April of 62 at 27. Later Corporal, discharged 7/4/65.

Clancy, Michael A.; 1/B; Private, enlisted at 25, Butler County. Promoted to Sergeant.

Clancy, Thomas B.; 1/B; Private, enlisted at 22.

Clark, David A.; 1/A; Enlisted as Lieutenant, promoted to Captain. Killed at Chickamauga.

Clemens, John A.; 1/C; Private, enlisted 5/12/62, Chambers County. Served with Legion, then in 60th Alabama. Was detached to Division Engineer Corps, paroled 4/16/65 in Lynchburg, VA.

Clements, John B.; 1/B; Private, enlisted at 23, Butler County.

Cloud (or Clowd), William B.; 1/A; Private, enlisted at 17. Absent sick at Chickamauga. Student.

Cobb, J. T.; 1/G; Private, enlisted at 37, Montgomery.

Cobb, Thomas A.; 1/A; Private, enlisted 4/8/62 at 30 (or29), Montgomery. Chickamauga or later. Married, physician. Born in Georgia.

Coker, William J.; 1/G; Private, enlisted at 28, Montgomery.

Cole, William; 1/E; Private.

Coleman, John; 1/E; Sergeant, enlisted at 28.

Collins, E.; 1/G; Private.

Collins, Eli; 1/C; Sergeant.

Connaway, J.; 1/B; Private.

Connor, John H.; 1/A; Private, enlisted at 28, Maryland. Killed at Chickamauga. Carriage trimmer.

Conron, T.; 1/A; Private, enlisted 3/11/62 at 22. Wounded at Chickamauga (finger), absent wounded at Knoxville, present later, deserted at Petersburg. Single, bookkeeper.

Conroy, John; 1/E; Private.

Cooper, John B.; 1/F; Quartermaster Sergeant, Conecuh County.

Copeland, John T.; 1/C; Private, enlisted at 16, Chambers County.

Copps, John; 1/B; Private.

Cowart, George P.; 1/B; Private, enlisted at 38, Butler County.

Cowart, James ; 1/B; Sergeant, enlisted at 36, Butler County.

Cowart, William Y.; 1/B; Corporal, enlisted at 19.

Cox, C.; 1/E; Corporal, enlisted at 25, Barbour County. Also shown as Private.

Cox, John; 1/E; Sergeant, enlisted at 31, Barbour County. Also shown as Lieutenant.

Cramford, Joesph T.; 1/C; See Joseph Crawford below.

Crawford, Joseph Terrell; 1/C; Private, Chambers County. Wounded at Knoxville, discharged 4/11/65.

Crew, Henry H.; 1/E; Private, enlisted at 21, Barbour County. Wounded at Chickamauga (hand, severe). Farmer.

Crusins (also spelled Crusius), Fredrick; 1/A; Sergeant, enlisted 4/7/62. Severely wounded at Chickamauga (both thighs). Painter.

Crysell, L. D.; 1/B; Private, enlisted at 20, Butler County.

Crysell, Semuell; 1/B; Private.

Crysell, William D.; 1/B; Private, enlisted at 22, Butler County.

Dallas, V.; 1/C; Private.

Dalton, M.; 1/A; Private.

Daniel, John W. L.; 1/E; Captain, enlisted at 32, Barbour County.

Davenport, J. J.; 1/D; Private, enlisted at 21, Lowndes County.

Davenport, John F.; 1/G; Private, enlisted at 36, Montgomery County.

Davidson, Whitfield; 1/C; Sergeant.

Davis, B. A.; 1/D; Private, killed at Chickamauga, Confederate Roll of Honor.

Davis, E.; 1/C; Private.

Davis, J. B. L. (or P. B. L. Davis);1/B; Private, enlisted at 19, Butler County. Killed at Chickamauga.

Davis, John; 1/E; Corporal, enlisted at 25, Barbour County.

Davis, R.; 1/D; Private.

Davis, Richard; 1/B; Private, enlisted at 19, Butler County. Wounded at Chickamauga (hand).

Davis, Samuel W. D.; 1/E; Private, enlisted at 20, Barbour County.

Davison, Benjamin; 1/B; Private, enlisted at 40, Butler County.

Daw, Andrew; 1/F; Private, enlisted at 27, Conecuh County.

Daw, William; 1/F; Sergeant, enlisted at 46.

Dawson, J. M.; 1/E; Private, enlisted at 29, Barbour County, rejected by Confederate States Inspecting Surgeon Dillard.

Deas, Eli; 1/G; Private, enlisted at 18, Montgomery County, surrendered 4/9/65.

Deer, John S.; 1/F; Private, enlisted 9/9/62 at Evergreen, Ala. Final muster roll shows him as battalion orderly, captured 4/3/65 at Jarrett's Station, Virginia (possibly while in hospital), imprisoned at Newport News, Virginia; released there 6/24/65 on taking Oath of Allegiance to United States. Description: fair complexion, black hair, blue eyes, 6 feet tall.

Dewberry, Leonard; 1/F; Private.

Diamond, Daniel; 1/F; Private, enlisted at 20, Conecuh County. Brother of Reuben.

Diamond, Reuben; 1/F; Private, enlisted at 25, Conecuh County. Brother of Daniel.

Dickerson, J. L.; 1/G; Private, enlisted at 30.

Dickson, Crayton; 1/E; Sergeant, enlisted at 30, Barbour County.

Dikes, Steve; 1/G; Private.

Dikus, William; 1/B; Private.

Dix, Alexander F.; 1/E; Private, enlisted at 29, Barbour County. Promoted to Sergeant Major.

Dixon, John; 1/C; Private.

Dodson, John; 1/F; Private, enlisted at 32, Conecuh.

Donaldson, W. H.; 1/D; Private, enlisted at 38, Lowndes County.

Dorris, James; 1/A; Private, enlisted at 18, Montgomery.

Dorris, James M.; 1/A; Private, died at Soldiers Home 6/17/62.

Dorris, W. E. L.; 1/A; Private, enlisted at 19, Montgomery.

Dorris, W. W.; 1/A; Private, enlisted at 19, Montgomery.

Dorset, William; 1/D; Private.

Douglas, Edward; 1/F; Private, enlisted at 24, Conecuh County.

Douglass, George; 1/F; Private.

Douglass, F. M.; 1/D; Private, enlisted at 23, Lowndes County.

Dowd, John; 1/C; Private.

Dunkin, John; 1/C; Private.

Echols, John H.; 1/C; Private, enlisted at 19, Chambers County.

Echols, Milton F.; 1/C; Sergeant, enlisted at 22, Chambers County.

Edeker, Augustus; 1/F; Private, enlisted at 18, Conecuh County.

Edikes, Augustus; 1/F; See Edeker, Augustus above.

Eford, J. C.; 1/E; See Efurd, G.

Efurd, G.; 1/E; Private.

Efurd, T.; 1/E; Corporal.

Ethridge, John H.; 1/F; Private, enlisted at 26, Conecuh County.

Ethridge, Louis J.; 1/F; Private, enlisted at 24, Conecuh County.

Eubanks, Thomas; 1/E; Private.

Evans, William; 1/E; Private, enlisted at 30, Barbour County.

Ewing, W.; 1/D; Private, enlisted at 30, Lowndes County.

Fears, Algernon; 1/C; Private, enlisted at 25, Chambers County.

Finch, James M.; 1/C; Private, enlisted at 27, Chambers County. Brother to Jeptha, Thomas.

Finch, Jeptha; 1/C; Private, enlisted at 24, Chambers County. Brother to James, Thomas.

Finch, Thomas C.; 1/C; Private, enlisted at 20, Chambers County. Brother to Jeptha, James.

Fitzmaurice, P.; 1/A; Private, enlisted 7/4/63. Substitute for P. H. S. Gayle. Deserted from camp near Cumberland Gap 8/6/63.

Fitzmaurice, W.; 1/A; Private.

Floyd, Charles ; 1/C; Lieutenant, enlisted at 25, Chambers County, later resigned from service.

Fost, J.; 1/D; Private.

Foster, J.; 1/C; Private.

Fowler, John; 1/B; Private, enlisted 4/5/62, Ranersville, Alabama. Transferred to Company D 7/1/62. Married, farmer.

Freeman, P.; 1/G; Private.

Fuller, H.; 1/A; Private, enlisted at 42, Montgomery.

Fussell, Benjamin; 1/E; Private.

Gafford, J.; 1/D; Private.

Galoway, Eli; 1/F; Private, enlisted at 22, Conecuh County. Farm laborer, brother to Noah.

Galoway, Noah; 1/F; Private, enlisted at 19, Conecuh County. Farm laborer, brother to Eli.

Gandy, E.; 1/C; Private, enlisted at 39.

Gannen, William; 1/E; Private.

Garner, J. W.; 1/D; Private, enlisted at 18, Lowndes County.

Garner, James; 1/F; Private.

Garrett, D. F.; 1/D; Private, enlisted at 22, Lowndes County. Buried in Confederate Cemetery, East Knoxville, Tennessee.

Garrett, John Harrison; 1/D; Private, enlisted at 24, Lowndes County.

Garrett, P.; 1/D; Private.

Gayle, P. H. S.; 1/A; Private, enlisted 5/16/62 at 21, Montgomery. Detached to work in Confederate State Tax Assessor office 5/16/62, returned to command 1/24/63. Furnished P. Fitzmaurice as a substitute.

Gayle, Z. R.; 1/A; Private, enlisted at 21. Killed at Chickamauga.

Geaslin, H.; 1/E; Private, enlisted at 19, Barbour County.

Geesling, N.; 1/E; Private.

Geigler, W.; 1/D; Lieutenant.

Gerry, Alfred; 1/B; Private.

Geter, Alfred; 1/G; Private.

Gibson, James; 1/E; Private, enlisted at 19, Barbour County.

Gibson, James; 1/C; Private, enlisted at 19, Barbour County.

Gibson, Joseph; 1/B; Private.

Gibson, Legget; 1/C; Private, enlisted at 21.

Gibson, William; 1/C; Private, enlisted at 23, Chambers County.

Gideon, Alfred; 1/B; Private, enlisted at 23, Butler County.

Gilbert, L.; 1/D; Private.

Gilchrist, John; 1/D; Sergeant, enlisted at 35. Promoted to Lieutenant.

Gilchrist, Miner; 1/B; Private, enlisted at 34, Butler County, wounded at Chickamauga.

Gilder, Henry; 1/G; Private, enlisted at 33, Montgomery County. Promoted to Corporal.

Gill, J. J.; 1/G; Private, enlisted at 18, Montgomery County.

Gill, Silas; 1/G; Private, enlisted at 19, Montgomery County.

Gill, T. H.; 1/G; Private, enlisted at 21, Montgomery County.

Gillian, W. T.; 1/D; Private, enlisted at 18, Lowndes County. "Pumpkin" Gillian.

Gilmer, N. M.; 1/A; Private, enlisted at 17, killed at Chickamauga.

Giloray, Hugh; 1/E; Corporal.

Godwin, Green; 1/F; Private.

Goodman, J.; 1/G; Private, enlisted at 23, Montgomery County. Deserter.

Gordon, J.; 1/D; Private.

Gordon, E. B.; 1/D; Private, enlisted 16, Lowndes County.

Grattan, P. R.; 1/A; Sergeant, resigned May 1862.

Green, George ; 1/F; Private.

Green, Irving; 1/E; Private, enlisted at 33, Barbour County.

Griffin, R. H.; 1/E; Private, enlisted at 22, Barbour County.

Griffin, Thomas; 1/E; Private, enlisted at 25.

Grigg, K.; 1/A; Sergeant, enlisted at 21, Montgomery County.

Grigg, R. P.; 1/A; Private, enlisted at 19, Montgomery County. Wounded twice at Petersburg.

Guice, George; 1/E; Private, enlisted at 24, Barbour County, later sergeant in 23rd Battalion, Alabama Sharpshooters.

Gunn, Simeon; 1/C; Private.

Gunter, G.; 1/G; Lieutenant.

Guy, Alfred E. ; 1/B; Private, enlisted at 26, Butler County.

Guy, James H. ; 1/B; Private, enlisted at 33, Butler County.

Hall, Daniel; 1/G; Private.

Hall, J. J.; 1/G; Private, enlisted at 18.

Hall, J. M.; 1/E; Lieutenant, enlisted at 28, Barbour County, died in Montgomery.

Hall, John; 1/B; Private.

Hall, Silas; 1/B; Private, enlisted at 21, Butler County, wounded at Chickamauga.

Hall, William; 1/G; Private, enlisted at 27.

Hall, W. J.; 1/E; Private, enlisted at 18, Barbour County.

Hallenquist; 1/G; Private.

Halley, George; 1/E; Private.

Ham, Levi; 1/F; Corporal, enlisted at 24, Conecuh County.

Ham, William H.; 1/F; Private, enlisted at 34, Conecuh County.

Hamill, J.; 1/G; Private, enlisted at 18, Montgomery County.

Hammonds, Duthan A.; 1/F; Private, enlisted at 25, Conecuh County.

Hammonds, Luthan or Luther: See Duthan, Hammonds, above.

Haney, William; 1/G; Private.

Harris, Jesse; 1/A; Private.

Harris, John J.; 1/B; Private, enlisted at 25.

Harris, William; 1/B; Private, enlisted at 48, Butler County.

Haynes, R.; 1/G; Private.

Henderson, Shade W.; 1/B; Private, enlisted at 26.

Henley, John; 1/A; Sergeant Major, originally 4th Sergeant of Company A of First Battalion, promoted June 1862.

Henley, T.; 1/G; Sergeant Major.

Hennessey, Michael; 1/G; Private, enlisted at 47, Montgomery County.

Herlong, Martin; 1/D; Corporal, enlisted at 28, Lowndes County.

Herlong, W.; 1/D; Private, enlisted at 34.

Herring, L.; 1/E; Lieutenant, enlisted at 27 as a sergeant.

Herring, Stephen; 1/E; Private.

Hicks, W. M.; 1/A; Private, enlisted at 40, killed at Hatcher's Run, Virginia.

Higgenbothem, William; 1/C; Private, enlisted at 18, Chambers County.

Hilliard, C.; Staff; Assistant Surgeon.

Hines, Henry H.; 1/F; Private, enlisted 5/14/62 at 23, Conecuh County. Wounded knee or ankle at Chickamauga, did not serve again. Died 6/27/1908.

Hinkman, A.; 1/A; Private.

Hobbs, Timothy; 1/F; Private, enlisted at 27, Conecuh County. Surrendered with Lee.

Holliday, F.; 1/D; Private, enlisted at 25.

Holliday, J.; 1/D; Private.

Holliday, W.; 1/D; Private.

Holman, C.; 1/D; Private.

Holt, E.; 1/G; Private.

Holt, Henry; 1/C; Private, enlisted at 28, Chambers County.

Holt, John B.; 1/C; Private, enlisted at 24, Chambers County.

Holt, John Hackett; 1/Staff Major, later Lt. Colonel, severely wounded at Chickamauga (knee).

Holt, Martin; 1/C; Private.

Holt, Samuel; 1/C; Sergeant.

Hook, J. M.; 1/D; Private, Lowndes County.

Howard, H.; 1/C; Private.

Howell, Henry H.; 1/C; Private, enlisted at 22, Chambers County.

Howell, James; 1/A; Private, joined later.

Howell, John; 1/A; Private.

Howerd, D.; Private, company uncertain.

Hubbard, John; 1/A; Private, enlisted at 34.

Hudman, James; 1/C; Private, enlisted at 21, Chambers County.

Hudman, William E.; 1/C; Corporal, enlisted 4/62 at 18, Chambers County. Promoted to sergeant, captured 4/65 in Virginia.

Hudson, Isaac; 1/C; Private.

Hughes, Daniel; 1/F; Private, enlisted at 36, Montgomery County.

Huguley, George W.; 1/C; Captain, Chambers County.

Hunt, L. J.; 1/E; Corporal, enlisted at 26, Barbour County.

Hutchinson, R. H.; 1/D; Private, enlisted at 47. Also served as private in Company C, 6th Alabama Cavalry Regiment.

Jackson, Henry; 1/B; Corporal, enlisted at 27, Butler County.

Jarvis, Thomas; 1/G; Private.

Jay, John; 1/E; Private, enlisted at 19, Barbour County. Discharged by Confederates States Surgeon Dillard.

Jenkins, James; 1/E; Private, later Corporal in 23rd Battalion, Alabama Sharp Shooters.

Jennings, J.M.; 1/D; Sergeant, enlisted at 28, Lowndes County.

Jeter, William; 1/G; Private, enlisted at 22.

Johns, L.; 1/E; Private.

Johns, T. M.; 1/E; Private, enlisted at 28, Barbour County, discharged by Confederate States Surgeon Dillard.

Johnson, George L.; 1/A; Private, enlisted at 20.

Johnson, M. J.; 1/D; Private, Lowndes County.

Johnson, Smith P.; 1/F; Private, enlisted at 28, Conecuh County.

Joiner, Berry H.; 1/F; Private, enlisted at 23, Conecuh County.

Joiner, Dixon H. L.; 1/F; Private, enlisted at 27, Conecuh County.

Joiner, Jefferson; 1/F; Private, enlisted at 23, Conecuh County, died March 1863.

Joiner, Thomas; 1/F; Private.

Joiner, Wiley; 1/F; Private, surrendered with Lee.

Joiner, William; 1/F; Private, enlisted at 34, Conecuh County.

Joiner, William R.; 1/F; Private, enlisted at 19, Conecuh County.

Joins, J. P.; 1/E; Private, enlisted at 28, Barbour County, discharged by C.S. Inspecting Surgeon Dillard.

Jones, Columbus; 1/A; Private, enlisted at 25.

Jones, George L.; 1/A; Private, enlisted at 18.

Jones, James; 1/A; Private, enlisted January 1862, discharged 4/9/65.

Jones, Mark; 1/G; Private, enlisted at 36.

Jordan, James Edward; 1/B; Private, enlisted 9/9/62.

Jordan, Mathew; 1/B; Private.

Jordan, S.; 1/B; Private.

Jorden, C. D.; 1/G; Private.

Jourdon, Charles; 1/D; Private.

Keadle, William; 1/G; Private, enlisted at 21.

Kennedy, John D.; 1/E; Private, enlisted at 30.

Keyes, George ; 1/A; Private, enlisted at 32.

Keyes, John; 1/A; Lieutenant.

Kief, Michael; 1/A; Private, wounded at Chickamauga (both legs).

Kinard, W. D.; 1/E; Private, enlisted at 33, Barbour County.

King, Samuel; 1/B; Private, enlisted at 32, Butler County.

King, T.; 1/E; Private, enlisted at 33 (or 34), Barbour County. Discharged by Inspecting Surgeon Dillard.

Kirkpatrick, H.; 1/D; Private.

Kirkpatrick, John; 1/D; Private.

Kirkpatrick, O. M.; 1/D; Private, enlisted at 18.

Kirkpatrick, Valentine; 1/D; Private, enlisted at 32 from Lowndes County. Promoted to Sergeant.

Knight, W.; 1/D; Private.

Knighton, Joseph; 1/F; Private.

Kolb, E.; 1/D; Private, enlisted at 17, Lowndes County.

Kyser, William; 1/F; Corporal, enlisted at

30, Conecuh County. Promoted to Sergeant.

Landrum, H. T.; 1/A; Private, enlisted at 16.

Lard, George W.; 1/E; Private, enlisted at 27, Barbour County.

Leaptrot, James; 1/G; Private.

Lee, Alter; 1/E; Private.

Lee, Young; 1/B; Private.

Lester, L.; 1/E; Private.

Lester, William; 1/E; Private.

Letson, Gabriel N.; 1/A; Lieutenant.

Letson, H.; 1/A; Private, "joined later."

Leysath, J. A. (Leyeath? Leyhath?); 1/D; Sergeant, enlisted at 34, Lowndes County.

Loftin, W. M.; 1/D; Private, enlisted at 29. Disabled due to accidental hand wound.

Long, James; 1/B; Private, enlisted at 27, Butler County.

Long, R. B.; 1/B; Sergeant, enlisted at 31, Butler County.

Long, Solomon M.; 1/B; Private, enlisted at 19, Butler County. Wounded at Chickamauga (head).

Lovelace, Welcome; 1/G; Private, enlisted at 37. Montgomery County.

Lowery, George; 1/B; Private.

Lowery, L.; 1/B; Corporal.

Lowery, T. D.; 1/B; Sergeant, enlisted at 26.

Loyd, J. B.; 1/E; Private, enlisted at 27, Barbour County.

Loyd, J. T.; 1/E; Private, enlisted at 25, Barbour County.

Luckey, E. J.; 1/D; Private, enlisted at 33, Lowndes County.

Luckey, T. M.; 1/D; Private, enlisted at 29, Lowndes County.

Luckey, William Hamilton; 1/D; Private, enlisted May 1862 at 18, Lowndes County. Discharged Newport News, Virginia, July 1865.

Mahone, W. A.; 1/A; Private.

Maloy (Malloy?), William A.; 1/E; Private, enlisted at 18, Barbour County.

Manning, William H.; 1/A; Private, enlisted at 18, wounded at Chickamauga (leg).

Marks, S.; 1/G; Private.

Marsh, W.; 1/D; Private, enlisted at 30, Lowndes County.

Martin, Charles L.; 1/B; Private, enlisted at 30, Butler County.

Martin, Green; 1/B; Private, enlisted at 28. Wounded at Chickamauga (head).

Martin, John; 1/E; Private, enlisted at 31, Barbour County.

Martin, W.; 1/D; Private.

Martin, William; 1/A; Private. Killed at Chickamauga.

Martin, Zack; 1/F; Private.

Mashburn, W.; 1/E; Private.

Mason, Benjamin; 1/A; Private, enlisted at 39, wounded at Chickamauga (hand). His letters are at Auburn.

Massey, John; 1 F/S; Adjutant of 1st Battalion, enlisted at 28. Wounded at Chickamauga (chest, ankle), wrote *Reminiscences*.

McCardell, John; 1/A; Corporal, enlisted at 26. Mortally wounded at Chickamauga (leg, died 10/13/63). Married, printer.

McCaskill, John Graham; 1/A; Private, enlisted May of 1862. Wounded in arm in Virginia, surrendered at Appomattox. Born Chesterfield District, S. Carolina 4/8/37.

McCormack, J.; 1/D; Private, enlisted 9/5/62.

McCrosby, E.; 1/A; Private, enlisted at 24, Montgomery County. Rejected for service by inspecting surgeon.

McDaniel, Willis; 1/C; Private, enlisted at 33, Chambers County.

McDonald, John; 1/A; Private, enlisted at 30.

McDonald, Robert; 1/G; Private.

McFarland, Alexander; 1/D; Private, enlisted at 30, Lowndes County.

McFarland, J.C.; 1/D; Private, enlisted at 20, Lowndes County.

McFarland, J.M.; 1/D; Corporal, enlisted at 24, Lowndes County.

McFarland, W. W.; 1/D; Private, enlisted at 28, Lowndes County.

McGill, John; 1/A; Corporal, enlisted at 30.

McGilvary, Hugh; 1/E; Private, enlisted at 26, Barbour County. Promoted to

Corporal 8/3/63, wounded at Chickamauga.

McKleroy, John; 1/A; Private, transferred to become Adjutant of 5th Battalion 6/30/62, from Montgomery.

McLane, James; 1/B; Private.

McMellin, Charles; 1/E; Private, enlisted at 22, Barbour County, wounded at Chickamauga.

McMellin (or McMillan), Farley; 1/E; Private, enlisted at 34, Barbour County.

McNeill, Samuel H.; 1/E; Private, enlisted at 19, Barbour County.

McQueen, J. D.; 1/G; Sergeant, enlisted at 24, Montgomery County.

McWilliams, James; 1/D; Private, Lowndes County.

Meads, Ervin (also shown as Erwin Mead or Meads); 1/F; Private, enlisted at 28, Conecuh County. May have been Color Corporal.

Melear (or Meliar), P. B.; 1/G; Private.

Melear (or Meliar), P. V.; 1/G; Private. Wounded at Chickamauga. Promoted to Corporal 1/12/63, to Sergeant 3/31/1863.

Melton, E.; 1/D; Private, Lowndes County.

Merriwether, B. F.; 1/A; Private, enlisted at 16, Montgomery. Wounded at Chickamauga (lung, arm).

Merriwether, Francis Valentine; 1/A; Private, enlisted at 20, Montgomery. Appears to be cousin of B. F. Merriwether, lived close enough that they were on the same page of the 1850 census.

Micou, William H.; 1/A; Private, enlisted 3/11/62. Promoted to Ordnance Sergeant 8/8/62, was on noncommissioned officers staff, discharged 5/3/65 in North Carolina.

Midleton, W.; 1/G; Captain, enlisted at 34, Montgomery County. Appointed Captain of Company G 6/27/1862, later Captain of Company G in the 23rd Battalion Alabama Sharpshooters. Severely wounded at Dandridge, Tenn. 1/28/64, retired to duty on the Invalid Corps in Charleston, S.C. Paroled at Montgomery, Ala., 6/14/65. Five feet, eight inches, black hair, blue eyes, fair complexion.

Mills, Benjamin; 1/C; Private.

Mills, Charles C.; 1/C; Sergeant, enlisted at 27, Chambers County.

Mills, George T.; 1/C; Private, enlisted at 18, Chambers County.

Mills, John W.; 1/C; Corporal, enlisted at 22, Chambers County.

Michael, J.; 1/D; P:rivate.

Mitchell, L.; 1/C; Private.

Molton, Robert H.; 1/G; Lieutenant, enlisted at 31, Montgomery County.

Monk, John; 1/C; Private, enlisted May 1862 at 32, Chambers County.

Moody, John; 1/A; Private.

Moody, W.; 1/B; Private.

Moore, R.; 1/D; Captain, enlisted at 32, Lowndes County.

Moore, S.; 1/G; Private.

Moore, W; 1/E; Private, enlisted at 24, Barbour County.

Morgan, Robert; 1/B; Private, enlisted at 18, Butler County.

Morgan, Stephen N.; 1/B; Private, enlisted at 20, Butler County.

Morris, James M.; 1/B; Sergeant, enlisted 4/5/62. Wounded at Chickamauga (arm).

Mosley, John; 1/F; Sergeant, enlisted at 27, Conecuh County.

Mosley, W.; 1/G; Private.

Murry, John; 1/C; Private, enlisted at 33, Chambers County. Transferred to Company D, 1st Battalion by Colonel Holt, Special Order 13, 7/17/63. Muster card notes confirm spelling.

Nealy, Benjamin Franklin; 1/C; Private, enlisted March 1862 at 22, Chambers County.

Neese, Ervin (Irwin?); 1/B; Private, enlisted at 23, Butler County.

Neese, Henry Irving; 1/B; Private, enlisted at 24, Butler County, buried Good Hope Cemetery, Neshoba, Mississippi.

Neese, J.; 1/B; Private.

Neese, Men; 1/B; Private.

Newman, C.; 1/C; Private.

Nolan, John H.; 1/C; Sergeant, enlisted at 18, Chambers County.

Nolan, Thomas; 1/C; Private.

Norman, J.; 1/D; Lieutenant.

Norred, Lodric; 1/F; Private, enlisted at

19, Conecuh County. Discharged Nov. 11, 1862.

Norris, James; 1/G; Sergeant, enlisted at 25, Montgomery County.

Northcut, John; 1/B; Private, enlisted at 18, Butler County. Died 10/6/62.

Norton, Lewis Valentine; 1/E; Private, enlisted at 28, Barbour County.

Norvel, D. W.; 1/A; Private, enlisted at 32.

O'Brien, William; 1/C; Private, enlisted at 22, Chambers County.

Odam, William H. H.; 1/B; Private.

Ogborn (or Ogborne), W. H.; 1/A; Private, transferred to 18th Alabama 5/22/62.

Padgett (or Padget), Moses; 1/G; Private, enlisted at 21, died in 1862.

Page, James Andrew; 1/F; Corporal, enlisted at 20, Conecuh County. Wounded at Chickamauga, captured 4/7/65 during retreat from Petersburg to Appomattox, paroled 6/17/65 at Fort Monroe. Lived 8/6/1840–10/30/1923.

Page, John W.; 1/F; Private, enlisted at 18 on 6/1/62, Conecuh County. Wounded at Petersburg, surrendered 4/9/65.

Page, Leroy; 1/F; Private.

Parker, Leonidas W.; 1/C; Private, enlisted at 26, Chambers County.

Partin (or Parting), F. M.; 1/G; Private, enlisted at 38. Discharged for medical disability 12/23/63.

Patterson, A.; 1/A; Private, enlisted at 33. Wounded at Chickamauga (lungs, thigh), died 10/1/63 or 10/6/63 in hospital, Newman, Georgia.

Patterson, J. E.; 1/A; Private, enlisted at 41. Promoted to Sergeant 7/13/62, wounded at Chickamauga (arm).

Patterson, T. B.; 1/D; Private, enlisted at 27, Lowndes County. Promoted to Sergeant 8/22/62, discharged 4/22/63 on surgeon's certificate. Born in Florida, married, farmer.

Paull, E.; 1/A; Quartermaster Sergeant, enlisted at 22, Montgomery County.

Pendelton, T. F.; 1/A; Private, enlisted at 20, Montgomery County.

Perdue, P.; 1/D; Private, enlisted at 19 on 5/5/62, Lowndes County. Transferred to Co. K, 17th Alabama, 10/14/62. Single farmer.

Petty, James; 1/B; Private, enlisted at 24, Butler County. Discharged for disability (probably in) 1862.

Phelps, James; 1/B; Private. Continued with command until transfer to 13th Alabama Regiment 12/25/64.

Phillips, D.; 1/D; Private.

Phillips, James; 1/D; Private.

Phillips, John; 1/D; Corporal, enlisted at 31, Lowndes County.

Phillips, T.; 1/D; Private, enlisted at 30.

Phillips, William; 1/E; Private, enlisted at 19, Barbour County.

Pickens, E.; 1/D; Private.

Pickens, J.; 1/D; Private.

Pickens, W. M.; 1/D; Private, enlisted at 29, Lowndes County.

Picket, T.; 1/E; Private.

Pierce, W. S. G.; 1/C; Private, enlisted at 26, Butler County.

Pitman, J. S.; 1/G; Private, enlisted at 18, Montgomery County.

Pitman, J.W.; 1/B; Private, enlisted at 19, Butler County.

Pitts, Asa; 1/C; Private, enlisted at 17, Chambers County. Pitts, James B. ; 1/C; Private, enlisted at 30, Chambers County.

Pitts, Joseph; 1/C; Private.

Ponder, B. K.; 1/A; Private, enlisted at 24, Montgomery County.

Ponder, James; 1/A; Private, killed at Chickamauga.

Potts, Franklin ; 1/C; Private, enlisted at 20, Chambers County.

Prather, Jabez; 1/C; Private, enlisted at 28, Chambers County, transferred to Signal Corps 3/1/63.

Prickett, S. C. (Samuel Carr?); 1/A; Private, enlisted at 23, Montgomery County.

Prier (or Prior), James; 1/B; Corporal, enlisted at 30, Butler County. Wounded at Chickamauga (thigh, shoulders).

Pugh, James; 1/F; Private.

Quining, John J.; 1/F; Private.

Rabon, Josiah; 1/B; Private, enlisted at 19, Butler County.

Rabon, William R.; 1/B; Private, enlisted at 19, Butler County.

Raleigh, James; 1/A; Private.

Ramsey, B. W.; 1/A; Private, Montgomery County.

Reaves, Ervin; 1/B; Private.

Reaves, Joseph; 1/B; Private.

Reaves, R.; 1/B; Private.

Reed, James; 1/C; Private, enlisted at 22, Chambers County.

Reed, John W. ; 1/C; Private, wounded at Chickamauga.

Reese, W.; 1/C; Private.

Reese, W. S.; 1/A; Private, enlisted 3/24/62. Detailed as wagon master for the Legion 8/8/62, returned to unit 8/2/63, wounded and deserted or was captured at Chickamauga 9/20/63, in hospital in Nashville, Tennessee, prisoner at Camp Morgan, Indiana and asked to take oath of allegiance to the Union and then moved to Philadelphia, Pennsylvania.

Reeves, Christen M.; 1/B; Private, enlisted at 26, Butler County. Killed at Chickamauga.

Reeves, R.; 1/B; Private.

Richburg (or Richberg), Benjamin; 1/B; Private.

Richburg, Josiah; 1/B; Private, died of disease 6/28/63.

Richburg, John W.; 1/B; Private, enlisted at 24, Butler County. Note: Also listed: P. W. Richberg or Richburge.

Ridgeway, Jesse; 1/B; Private, enlisted at 19, Butler County.

Ridgway (or Ridgeway), M.; 1/B; Captain, enlisted at 36, Butler County.

Ridgway (or Ridgeway), Willis; 1/B; Private, enlisted at 27, Butler County.

Roach, John; 1/B; Private.

Roberson, Henry C.; 1/F; Private, died at Big Creek Gap 2/6/63.

Roberson, James; 1/B; Private, enlisted at 30, Butler County, deserted 7/12/63.

Roberts, Nathaniel P.; 1/G; Sergeant, enlisted 5/14/62 at 34, Montgomery County. Killed 7/30/64 near Petersburg. Married.

Robins, George; 1/F; Private.

Robinson, Leggert; 1/C; Private.

Robinson, Sidney; 1/C; Private.

Roemer, E.; 1/A; Corporal.

Rohde, Charles; 1/A; Private, enlisted at 23, Montgomery County. Deserted.

Rooks, Columbus C.; 1/F; Private, enlisted at 27, Conecuh County.

Roper, F. W.; 1/D; Private, enlisted at 20, Lowndes County.

Roper, J. B.; 1/D; Private, enlisted at 30, Lowndes County. Promoted to Sergeant 9/1/62, killed at Chickamauga. Married, farmer.

Roper, J. E.; 1/D; Corporal, enlisted at 28.

Roper, Marlin Pleasant; 1/D; Private, enlisted at 18, Lowndes County. Transferred to 1st Battalion Alabama Artillery, Company B. Captured 8/23/64 at Fort Morgan, paroled at Elmira, New York March 2, 1865. Admitted to Jackson Hospital in Richmond 3/8/65, paroled 3/9/65.

Roper, P. W.; 1/D; Private, enlisted at 22, Lowndes County. Wounded at Chickamauga, returned to service in time to be at Petersburg in early 1864.

Roper, W. F.; 1/D; Private, enlisted 5/5/62 at 18, Lowndes County. Died 7/8/62 after falling from train.

Ross, John; 1/G; Private, surrendered 4/9/65.

Rouse, R.; 1/E; Private.

Russ, J. W.; 1/G; Private, Montgomery County.

Russell, J.; 1/D; Private.

Salter, Abner; 1/F; Private, enlisted at 33, Conecuh County, died as POW at Camp Chase in Columbus, Ohio 2/2/65.

Salter, Jefferson; 1/F; Private, enlisted at 18, Conecuh County.

Salter, Jesse; 1/F; Private.

Salter, Richard; 1/F; Corporal, enlisted at 26, Conecuh County.

Salter, Samuel; 1/F; Sergeant, later Captain in the 23rd Battalion, Ala. Sharpshooters.

Sawyer, L.; 1/D; Private.

Scholl, Jacob; 1/A; Private, enlisted at 23, Montgomery County.

Scipper, E.; 1/G; Private, died of disease 12/31/62.

Scipper, J. H.; 1/B; Private, enlisted at 23, Butler County.

Screws, H. P.; 1/A; Enlisted at 15 at Columbus, Ga., discharged by Colonel Hilliard due to his age, 6/30/62. Later reenlisted, 29th Alabama. Missing after Battle of Nashville December 15/16, 1864. Paroled Greensboro, NC. Born 3/10/47.

Screws, William Wallace; 1/A; Private, enlisted at 23. Transferred to 2nd Battalion, Co. D. Captured at Sailors Creek 4/6/65, released from Johnson Island, Ohio 6/19/65.

Sellers, Josiah; 1/B; Private, enlisted at 36, Butler County.

Sessions, Thomas B.; 1/B; Sergeant, enlisted at 23, Butler County, wounded at Chickamauga (leg, severe).

Sexton, A.; 1/D; Private, enlisted at 26. Deserted 11/15/62. Married, farmer.

Sexton, E. J.; 1/D; Private, enlisted at 24. Absent (sick) for Chickamauga, on furlough for Knoxville, Bean's Station, present at Drewry's Bluff, Petersburg.

Sexton, G. W.; 1/D; Private, Lowndes County. Wounded at Chickamauga, absent (sick) for Knoxville, Bean's Station, present for Drewry's Bluff, Petersburg.

Shaver, Lewellyn; 1/A; Private, historian of 60th Alabama Infantry.

Shaw, Daniel B.; 1/B; Private, enlisted at 18, Butler County.

Shaw, Daniel D.; 1/B; Private, enlisted at 26.

Shaw, John; 1/A; Private, enlisted at 32, Montgomery. Arrested 8/25/63.

Shell, James; 1/F; Private, enlisted at 17, Conecuh County.

Shelley (or Shelly), George; 1/F.

Shelley, William; 1/F; Private, enlisted at 44, Conecuh County.

Sheron, D.; 1/E; Private.

Shipman, John H.; 1/E; Private, enlisted at 24, Barbour County.

Shropshire, J.; 1/C; Private.

Shultz, Frank; 1/G; Private.

Simmons, Frank; 1/G; Private, enlisted at 26, Montgomery County. Discharged.

Skains (or Skain), Newton N.; 1/B; Private, enlisted at 40, Butler County.

Skipper, James; 1/B; Private.

Smith, David E.; 1/B; Private.

Smith, E. Cade; 1/F; Private, enlisted at 29, Conecuh County.

Smith, Fleming; 1/A; Private, Montgomery County. Killed at Bean's Station.

Smith, H. V.; 1/G; Corporal, enlisted at 18, Montgomery County.

Smith, J.; 1/A; Private. Substituted for by Wesley Cawley 10/28/62.

Smith, J.; 1/C; Private, enlisted at 26, Chambers County.

Smith, John W.; 1/C; Lieutenant.

Smith, Joseph; 1/I; Sergeant. Captured at Knoxville, Tennessee, prisoner of war at Camp Chase in Columbus, Ohio.

Smith, R. B.; 1/B; Corporal, enlisted at 33, Butler County.

Smith, Saul; 1/A; Private.

Smith, Stephen; 1/F; Private, enlisted at 17, Conecuh County.

Smith, W. F.; 1/G; Private, enlisted at 28, Montgomery County. Discharged by surgeon.

Snell, Albert; 1/A; Private, Montgomery County.

Snell, John; 1/A; Private.

Sommerville, R. 1/G; Private. Appointed Captain, Assistant Commissary of Subsistence for Hilliard's Legion, officially took position 6/1/62.

Spence, Judson; 1/F; Private, enlisted at 26, Conecuh County. Buried at Confederate Cemetery, East Knoxville, Tennessee.

Spence, Timothy; 1/F; Private.

Spradlin, James; 1/G; Private.

Stallworth, Nicholas; 1/F; Captain, enlisted at 25, Conecuh County. Wounded at Chickamauga, promoted to Major, retired 9/20/64. Lived 3/10/1837 to 2/28/1909. Held county offices in Texas.

Standard, J.; 1/C; Private.

Sterne, P. R.; 1/A; Private, enlisted at 24, Montgomery County. Deserted.

Stevens, Benjamin; 1/F; Private, enlisted at 23, Conecuh County.

Steverson (also Stevenson), John; 1/E; Private, enlisted at 45, Barbour County. Substitute for T. E. Eford. Died 10/15/62 at Tazewell.

Stewart, Eli; 1/E; Sergeant.

Stewart, Jackson; 1/C; Private.

Stewart, James R.; 1/E; Corporal, enlisted at 30, Barbour County. Promoted to Lieutenant, later resigned.

Stewart, James S.; 1/E; Private. Sick, then furloughed from hospital.

Stewart, Jeptha; 1/C; Private.

Still, W. C.; 1/A; Corporal, enlisted at 26, Montgomery County. Wounded at Chickamauga 9/19/63 (hand). Merchant.

Stokes, Andrew; 1/A; Private. Killed at Hatcher's Run, Va.

Strange, J. A.; 1/G; Private, enlisted at 45, Montgomery County.

Strausburger (or Strassburger), H.; 1/A; Corporal, enlisted at 23, Montgomery County.

Stringer, J. R.; 1/D; Private, Lowndes County. Promoted to Corporal.

Stringfellow, Harrison; 1/C; Private, enlisted at 45, Chambers County.

Strother, Cyrus W.; 1/E; Private, enlisted at 25, Barbour County.

Stubbs. J. A.; 1/D; Private, enlisted at 29, Lowndes County.

Stuckey, John; 1/F; Corporal, enlisted at 23, Conecuh County.

Styson, L. M.; 1/D; Private, enlisted at 32, Lowndes County. Discharged due to illness.

Sullivan, Phillip; 1/A; Private.

Sullivan, Risen (or Riser); 1/F; Private, enlisted at 25, Conecuh County.

Swan, George; 1/G; Private.

Swaner, Thomas B.; 1/B; Private, enlisted at 31.

Swaner, William; 1/B; Private, enlisted at 20, Butler County.

Talley, Linsey D.; 1/C; Private, enlisted at 21, Chambers County. Wounded at Petersburg (arm), died 11/30/64.

Talley, Pane; 1/C; Private, enlisted at 16, Chambers County.

Tarbutton (or Tarburton), George A.; 1/B; Sergeant, enlisted at 19. Promoted to Lieutenant.

Tarbutton (or Tarburton), J. M.; 1/B; Lieutenant, enlisted at 22, Butler County. Promoted to Captain. Killed at Chickamauga (knee wound).

Tarver, C.; 1/E; Private.

Tate, Howard; 1/E; Private, enlisted at 38, Barbour County. Substitute for G. J. Terman.

Taylor, Elias; 1/F; Private, enlisted at 30, Conecuh County.

Thomas, Alvin; 1/G; Private.

Thomas, Daniel; 1/B; Private, enlisted at 38, Butler County.

Thomas, David; 1/B; Private, enlisted at 30.

Thomas, William H.; 1/E; Private, enlisted at 26. Detailed to work at Confederate States arsenal in Columbus, Georgia, 10/2/62. Worked there through December of 1863. May have lost use of left leg at Atlanta, Georgia 7/26/64.

Thomason, William; 1/B; Private, enlisted at 27, Butler County.

Thompson, James; 1/G; Private.

Thompson, John; 1/F; Private.

Thompson, R.; 1/B; Private.

Thompson, William; 1/F; Private, enlisted at 30, Conecuh County.

Thorington, Jack; 1/FS; Lieutenant Colonel. Took command of Legion when Colonel Hilliard retired.

Thornton, R. D.; 1/E; Private.

Thurmond, C. J.; 1/C; Private, enlisted at 23, Chambers County. Promoted to Sergeant.

Thurmond, William D.; 1/C; Private, enlisted at 20, Chambers County.

Till, A. D.; 1/D; Private, enlisted 5/5/62, Lowndes Country. Died of disease 7/20/62. Single, farmer.

Till, D. G.; 1/D; Private, enlisted Lowndes County. Discharged 8/1/62.

Till, J. H.; 1/D; Private, enlisted at 25, Lowndes County. Died 7/20/62.

Tillery, Herbert (Hub) Carey; 1/D; Private, enlisted April 1862, Lowndes County. Born 8/20/40.

Tillery, James; 1/D; Lieutenant, enlisted at 31, Lowndes County.

Tillery, M. N.; 1/D; Private, enlisted at 19, Lowndes County.

Todd, Andrew W.; 1/C; Private, enlisted at 26, Chambers County.

Tomlinson, C.; 1/D; Private.

Traimum, George; 1/B; Private.

Troy, Daniel Shipman; 1/A; Captain. Promoted to Major, wounded at Hatcher's Run.

Truitt, Edmond; 1/C; Private, Chambers County.

Truitt, James; 1/C; Private, enlisted at 21, Chambers County.

Truitt, Henry; 1/C; Private, enlisted at 24, Chambers County.

Truitt, Walton; 1/C; Private, enlisted at 28, Chambers County.

Truitt, William H.; 1/C; Private, enlisted 30, Chambers County.

Trye, William T.; 1/B; Private, enlisted at 23.

Tucker, J. W.; 1/D; Private, enlisted at 29, Lowndes County.

Turman, George; 1/E; Private.

Turner, Asberry W.; 1/C; Private, enlisted at 28, Chambers County.

Turner, Henry C.; 1/C; Private, enlisted at 17, Chambers County.

Turnipseed, John; 1/G; Corporal, enlisted at 18. Promoted to Sergeant.

Twit, Walton; 1/C; Private.

Upchurch, A. R.; 1/C; Private. Appointed Color Sergeant 7/1/62.

Upchurch, C.; 1/C; Private.

Upchurch, James K. (or H); Private, enlisted at 22, Chambers County.

Upchurch, Osburn (or Orborne); 1/C; Private, enlisted at 53, Chambers County. Promoted to Sergeant, worked in Confederate government shop in Atlanta, deserted 9/20/63. Wagon maker.

Upshaw, George H.; 1/B; Private, enlisted at 20, Butler County.

Upshaw, Lee; 1/B; Private, enlisted at 40, Butler County.

Vann, Calvin; 1/B; Private, enlisted at 43, Butler County.

Varner, R.; 1/D; Private.

Viard, P.B.; 1/A; Private, enlisted at 18, Montgomery County. Deserted.

Vincent, Columbus; 1/G; Private.

Wadsworth, Francis L.; 1/A; Private, enlisted at 18, Montgomery County. Clerk at brigade headquarters 9/4/63, elected 2nd Lieutenant of 59th Alabama Infantry Regiment 12/10/64, promoted to 1st Lieutenant. Absent with leave granted by General Lee 2/2/65, paroled at Montgomery 5/10/54.

Walker, J. N.; 1/E; Private, enlisted at 37. Substitute for C. H. Tarver. Walker died 9/13/62 at Tazewell Hospital.

Wall, Conrad; Staff; 1st Battalion Surgeon; enlisted 4/14/62, Lowndes County. May have enlisted as Private, 5th Battalion, Company D. Promoted to Surgeon of 60th Alabama Infantry 12/24/64.

Wallace, James; 1/A; Private, enlisted at 25, Montgomery. Deserted.

Waller, Clark (or Clarke); 1/B; Private, enlisted at 27, Butler County.

Walton, James A. (or H); 1/A; Private, enlisted at 24.

Ward, Henry; 1/F; Private.

Ward, James; 1/B; Private, enlisted at 35, Butler County.

Ward, James H.; 1/C; Private, enlisted at 22, Chambers County.

Ward, William; 1/F; Private, enlisted at 22, Conecuh County.

Ware, William H.; 1/A; Sergeant. Promoted to Lieutenant, wounded at Bean's Station.

Warren, Robert; 1/E; Private, enlisted at 33.

Watkins, Michael; 1/A; Private, enlisted at 20, Montgomery County.

Watts, James B. F.; 1/F; Corporal, enlisted at 27, Conecuh County.

Weaver, John; 1/B; Private, enlisted at 25.

Webb, Fortunatus Pope.; 1/C; Private, enlisted at 26, Chambers County. Survived war.

Webb, Joseph F.; 1/G; Private, enlisted at 17, Montgomery County.

Webb, Joseph S.; 1/C; Private, enlisted at 25, Chambers County.

Webb, Joseph L.; 1/C; Private, enlisted at 25, Chambers County.

Webb, Joseph T., 1/C; Private.

Webb, William M.; 1/C; Private, enlisted at 19, Chambers County.

Weeks, T.; 1/G; Corporal, enlisted at 30, Montgomery County.

Wells, Jacob; 1/E; Private, enlisted at 28. Died March 1863 in Jackboro Hospital.

White, C. C.; 1/A; Private, enlisted at Montgomery. Died of disease in East Tennessee.

White, James; 1/E; Sergeant. Elected Lieutenant 7/7/62, appointed acting commissary early 1863, swore oath of loyalty to the United States 6/20/63.

Wight, H.; 1/D; Private.

Wilder, John; 1/A; Private, enlisted at 20, Montgomery. Died at Maynardsville, Tennessee.

Wilkerson, John; 1/A; Private.

Wilkerson, John; 1/E; Private, enlisted at 16, Barbour County. Substitute for R. T. Rouse.

Williams, A; 1/A; Private. Appointed Commander of 2nd Battalion June 1862.

Williams, C.; 1/C; Private.

Williams, E. W.;1/E; Sergeant, enlisted at 30, Barbour County.

Williams, John L.; 1/C; Private, enlisted at 23, Chambers County. Died at home 6/29/62, appears to have died prior to beginning service.

Williams, J. S.; 1/E; Private, enlisted at 28.

Williams, John T.; 1/C; Private, enlisted at 17, Chambers County. Killed at Chickamauga.

Williams, M. C.; 1/G; Private, enlisted at 32, Montgomery County. Discharged.

Williams, R. Henry; 1/D; Lieutenant, enlisted at 30, Lowndes County.

Williams, Thomas; 1/E; Private.

Williams, W. J.; 1/E; Private, enlisted at 24, Barbour County. Dismissed by Inspecting Surgeon.

Williamson, J.; 1/G; Private, enlisted at 27, Montgomery County. Died 7/1/62.

Williamson, S. T.; 1/G; Lieutenant, enlisted at 30.

Williamson, Willis; 1/G; Private, enlisted at 33, Montgomery County. Died 12/5/62.

Willis, George T.; 1/G; Private, enlisted at 34, Barbour County.

Willis, Thomas; 1/E; Private.

Wilson, Joseph; 1/E; Private. Wounded at Chickamauga (shoulder).

Witherington, James; 1/F; Sergeant, enlisted at 25, Conecuh County.

Witherington, William; 1/F; Private.

Wood, Benjamin F.; 1/C; Sergeant.

Wood, Fortunatus P.; 1/C; Private.

Wood, George B.; 1/C; Private, enlisted at 26, Chambers County.

Wood, J.; 1/D; Private, enlisted at 22, Lowndes County.

Wood, James; 1/C; Private.

Wood, John C.; 1/C; Private, enlisted at 18, Chambers County.

Worrell, W. G.; 1/A; Private.

Wright, G. W.; 1/B; Sergeant, enlisted at 34, Butler County.

Wright, John E.; 1/B; Private, enlisted at 26.

Yarbrough, Thomas; 1/C; Private, enlisted at 25.

Yarbrough, Thomas C.; 1/C; Private, enlisted at 19, Chambers County.

Yarborough, William F.; 1/C; Private, enlisted at 23, Chambers County.

Yoll, John; 1/A; Private, Montgomery County. Deserted.

Zeigler, W. H.; 1/D; Lieutenant, enlisted at 27, Lowndes County.

2nd Battalion

Abbott, William; 2/C; Private, enlisted 5/5/62 at 18.

Abrams, William; 2/C; Private.

Adair, Joseph; 2/C; Private.

Aikins, W.; 2/B; Private, enlisted 4/1/62. Elected Sergeant, later detailed to serve as a waggoner on two occasions.

Akins, James W.; 2/B; Private, enlisted at 30, Coosa County.

Akins, John H.; 2/B; Corporal, enlisted 4/1/62 at 17.

Albey, Thomas M.; 2/F; Private, enlisted 4/18/62 at 27. Died in service.

Aldridge, J.; 2/B; Private. Deserted home from Knoxville hospital 11/10/63.

Allen, F.; 2/F; Private.

Allen, Joseph P.; 2/B; Private, enlisted at 32.

Anglin, Francis M.; 2/A; Private, enlisted at 34, Randolph County.

Anglin, John G.; 2/A; Private, enlisted at 27, Randolph County.

Arant, Henry; 2/B; Private, enlisted at 34.

Argoe, Thaddeus; 2/C; Private. Died in Knoxville, Tennessee October 31, 1862.

Arnett, Theophilus H.; 2/A; Private, enlisted 4/5/62 at 24, Randolph County. Deserted 5/30/63, jailed, rejoined 7/10/63.

Arnett, William P.; 2/A; Private, enlisted at Cumberland Gap, Tennessee August 1861 at 27. Paroled at Atlanta 1865.

Arnold, Levi; 2/C; Private, enlisted at 42, Randolph. Detached as teamster by Gracie.

Arnold, William F.; 2/F; Private, enlisted at 35, Coosa.

Atchley, Jeremiah; 2/C; Private.

Atchley, Thomas F.; 2/F Private, enlisted at 26, Coosa.

Atkins, Alsey S.; 2/F; Private, enlisted at 37, Coosa.

Aultmon, Burrell; 2/D; Private, enlisted 5/12/62, Troy, Alabama.

Aultmon, Lorenzo; 2/D; Private, enlisted 5/12/62, Troy, Alabama.

Aultmon, Paul; 2/D; Private. Died 8/17/62 or 8/27/62 in Atlanta, Georgia.

Baggett, Thomas; 2/B; Private, enlisted 4/2/62 at 25. Wounded at Petersburg 7/30/64, paroled at Greensboro, NC. Born 4/22/38 in South Carolina.

Baggett, William; 2/B; Private, enlisted at 28, Coosa.

Bailey, Charles; 2/C; Private, enlisted 5/12/62. Killed at Chickamauga.

Bailey, David E.; 2/D; Private.

Bailey, James; 2/D; Private, enlisted 5/12/62, Troy, Alabama.

Bailey, Robert; 2/C; Corporal, enlisted 5/12/62, Coosa.

Baker, Joshua; 2/A; Private, enlisted at 29, Randolph.

Baltzegar, Daniel; 2/E; Private.

Barbour, Benjamin; 2/E; Sergeant, enlisted 3/16.62 at 21.

Bards, S.; 2/C; Private.

Barggaimer, ??; 2/E; Private. Died 11/16/62, Knoxville, Tennessee.

Barkley, John; 2/F; Private, enlisted at 31, Coosa.

Barnett, C. W.; 2/D; Lieutenant, enlisted 5/12/62, Troy, Alabama. Died 7/17/62.

Barnett, M. R.; 2/B; Private, enlisted at 35, Coosa.

Barrett, B. B.; 2/F; Private, enlisted at 19, Coosa.

Beasley, Isaac; 2/B; Private.

Beasley, Jefferson; 2/B; Private.

Beckett (or Bickett), Wilson; 2/C; Private, enlisted 5/12/62, Coosa. Rejected. May have served later Company A, 2nd Battalion and in 59th Alabama Infantry.

Bell, Joseph B.; 2/F; Private, enlisted at 30, Coosa.

Besinger, Seaborn W.; 2/D; Private, enlisted 5/12/62. Deserted 5/16/62.

Bird, John; 2/F; Private.

Bishop, Jefferson; 2/F; Private.

Black, George L.; 2/C; Private.

Blackman, John P.; 2/C; Private.

Blake, Randolph; 2/E; Private, enlisted 3/16/62 at 40.

Blan, Robert E.; 2/D; Private, enlisted 5/12/62.

Bly, Jonathan; 2/B; Private, enlisted at 30.

Boman, Sanford; 2/D; Private.

Bond, James W.; 2/D; Private, enlisted 5/12/62. Discharged 5/20/62.

Bond, Julien, 2/D; Private, enlisted 5/12/62, Troy. Elected Lieutenant 7/21/62, resigned 11/19/62.

Bond, William M.; 2/D; Private, enlisted 5/12/62, Troy. Discharged 5/20/62.

Booth, George; 2/E; Private, enlisted 4/1/62 at 23.

Bowdoin, William; 2/E; Sergeant, enlisted 3/16/62 at 34.

Box, William; 2/E; Sergeant, enlisted 3/16/62 at 36.

Bradbury, Thomas; 2/B; Private, enlisted

4/30/62 at 30, Coosa. Died 10/1/62, Bean's Station, Tennessee.

Brand, Bryant; 2/A; Private, enlisted at 30, Randolph.

Brand, Thomas; 2/A; Private, enlisted at 19, Randolph.

Brewer, Joel; 2/E; Private, enlisted 3/16/62 at 19, Autauga.

Brewer, Pollard; 2/E; Private, enlisted 3/16/62 at 22, Autauga.

Brewster, L.; 2/A; Private.

Bridges, Joseph; 2/C; Private.

Bridges, Thomas; 2/C; Private.

Bridges, William; 2;C; Private, enlisted at 35, Coosa.

Britnall, William W.; 2/E; Private, enlisted 3/16/62 at 18, Autauga.

Browder, A.; 2/D; Private.

Brown, E.; 2/F; Private, enlisted 5/12/62. Died at Richmond 6/1/64.

Brown, Hilry; 2/A; Private, enlisted at 31, Randolph.

Brown, Hiram; 2/E; Private, enlisted 4/1/62 at 26, Autauga.

Brown, Isaac; 2/A; Private, enlisted at 23, Randolph.

Brown, W.; 2/D; Private, enlisted 8/15/62. Deserted 8/18/62.

Brown, William; 2/F; Private.

Brown, William R. O.; 2/A; Private, enlisted at 38, Randolph. Fifer.

Brumbelow, James H.; 2/A; Private, enlisted 4/14/62 at 31. Deserted.

Bryant, F. L.; 2/F; Private, enlisted at 32, Coosa.

Bryant, George W.; 2/C; Sergeant, Coosa.

Bryant, Thomas; 2/A; Private. Died 8/31/63.

Bullard, J. T.; 2/B; Private, enlisted at 23, Coosa.

Burdell, J.; 2/E; Private.

Burgess, James M.; 2/D; Private, enlisted 5/12/62.

Burgess, Richard; 2/D; Corporal, enlisted 5/12/62.

Burk, J.; 2/D; Private.

Burk, James; 2/F; Corporal, enlisted at 18. Substitute for Thomas J. Yarbrough.

Burkes; 2/C; Private.

Burns, W.; 2/B; Firefighter.

Burroughs, John; 2/B; Lieutenant, enlisted at 39.

Burson, Joseph; 2/A; Private.

Burton, William T.; 2/B; Private, enlisted at 31, Coosa.

Bussey, John F.; 2/E; Private, enlisted at 35, Coosa.

Butler, James; 2/B; Private, enlisted at 18.

Caldwell, James R.; 2/F; Private, enlisted at 33, Coosa.

Callaway, William B.; 2/C; Private. Promoted to Sergeant.

Cannon, John.; 2/C; Private.

Carden, Benjamin; 2/F; Private, enlisted at 26.

Carden, Elijah; 2/F; Private, enlisted at 27.

Carlisle, John; 2/C; Private.

Carlisle, Edmond; 2/C; Sergeant.

Carlisle, Jesse; 2/D; Private.

Carpenter, J.; 2/D; Private, enlisted 5/12/62. Rejected for physical disability.

Carroll, A. Green; 2/F; Private. Died 11/13/62.

Carroll, Henry B.; 2/F; Private, enlisted at 23, Coosa.

Caspeuter, John D.; 2/D; Private. Rejected for physical disability.

Castleberry, Jeremiah; 2/F; Private, enlisted at 26, Coosa.

Castleberry, Joseph; 2/F; Corporal, enlisted at 23, Coosa.

Catching, Joshua; 2/C; Private, Tallapoosa. Died 8/1/62, seven months pay due him.

Chitty, Hansford D.; 2/E; Private, enlisted 3/16/62 at 30, Autauga.

Clark, John J.; 2/B; Private, enlisted at 26, Coosa.

Coker, Noah; 2/E; Corporal, enlisted 3/16/62 at 24, Autauga. Later, Sergeant Major.

Coley, Thomas Turner; 2/A; Private, enlisted at 19, Randolph.

Coley, William S.; 2/A; Private, enlisted at 25. Rejoined from desertion 5/30/63.

Collier, U. M.; 2/B; Private, enlisted at 21, Coosa. Died 8/20/62.

Collins, Arthur A.; 2/C; Corporal, Coosa.

Conaway, J.; 2/B; Private, enlisted at 26.

Conaway, John T.; Private, enlisted 5/5/62 at 19, Coosa.

Conaway, W.H.; Private, enlisted at 22, Coosa.

Conaway, Willis M.; 2/B; Private, enlisted 4/12/62 at 22, Coosa.

Connell, Henry; 2/E; Private, enlisted 4/1/62 at 29.

Cook, John; 2/E; Private, enlisted 3/16/62 at 20, Autauga.

Cooper, Alphonse; 2/E; Musician, enlisted 3/16/62 at 18, Autauga.

Copland, J. W.; 2/A; Private.

Cotton, David; 2/F; Private, enlisted at 23, Coosa.

Cotton, James M.; 2/F; Private, enlisted 3/26/62 at 25, Coosa. Later promoted to Sergeant.

Cotton, Merrell J.; 2/F; Private, enlisted at 28, Coosa.

Cowart, John; 2/F; Private.

Cowart, Wiley, 2/F; Corporal, enlisted at 25, Coosa.

Cranford, James; 2/F; Private, enlisted at 26.

Crawford, Francis M.; 2/E; Private, enlisted 3/16/62 at 22, Autauga.

Crawford, Joseph H.; 2/E; Private, enlisted 3/16/62 at 25, Autauga.

Cross, H. J.; 2/B; Private, enlisted at 23, Coosa.

Crowder, Joseph; 2/A; Private.

Crumpler, Lewis H., 2/F; Captain, enlisted at 20, Coosa.

Cullins, T.S.; 2/A; Private. Joined company 8/28/63.

Culver, William C.; 2/B; Private, enlisted at 18, Coosa. Killed at Chickamauga.

Curlee, William D.; 2/B; Corporal, enlisted at 18, from Coosa.

Darsey, Joseph L.; 2/F; Private, enlisted on about 4/14/62 at 40, Coosa. Died 10/7/63. Married.

Davenport, Samuel; 2/E; Private, enlisted 3/16/62 at 27, Autauga.

Davie, William R.; 2/F; Lieutenant, enlisted at 19.

Davis, John; 2/A; Private, enlisted 4/5/62 at 23. Died at home 10/5/62.

Davis, John Mener; 2/A; Private, enlisted at 32, Randolph.

Davis, William Thomas; 2/A; Private, enlisted at 25, Randolph.

Davis, Wilson L.; 2/A; Sergeant, enlisted at 28.

Deloney, W. G.; 2/B; Lientenant, enlisted at 43.

Dendy, James; 2/D; Sergeant, enlisted 5/12/62, Troy, Alabama.

Dennis, A. B.; 2/E; Private, enlisted 7/1/62 at 16, Autauga. Discharged by Certificate of Disability. Discharged 10/18/62.

Dennis, Andrew Jackson; 2/E; Private, enlisted 3/16/62 at 36, Autauga.

Dennis, Jesse M.; 2/E; Private, enlisted 3/16/62 at 19, Autauga.

Dennis, John; 2/E; Private, enlisted 3/16/62 at 17.

Dennis, John W.; 2/A; Private, enlisted at 18, Randolph. Died 7/1/62.

Dennis, Levi; 2/E; Private, enlisted 3/16/62 at 21, Autauga.

Dennis, Samuel; 2/A; Private.

Dennis, Seaborn; 2/E; Private, enlisted 3/1/62 at 27, Autauga.

Dickey, Andrew J.; 2/D; Private, enlisted 8/15/62. Discharged 6/25/63.

Dickey, Joshua D. W.; 2/D; Private, enlisted 5/12/62, Pike.

Dickey, Owen M. M.; 2/D; Private, enlisted 5/12/62.

Dickey, Henderson D.; 2/D; Private, died 6/15/62.

Dillard, John H.; 2/C; Captain, Tallapoosa.

Dillard, W.; 2/D; Private, enlisted 8/15/62.

Dixon, John; 2/F; Assistant Surgeon, enlisted 3/26/62 at 28. Paroled 4/9/65.

Dobson, William; 2/C; Private.

Doster, William H.; 2/B; Private, enlisted at 30, Coosa.

Dowles, J.; 2/D; Private.

Driver, James; 2/E; Private, enlisted 4/1/62 at 42, Autauga.

Driver, Jessee (Jeper); 2/C; Private, enlisted 5/12/62. Died 9/6/62 at Chattanooga, Tennessee.

Driver, Richard H.; 2/E; Private, enlisted 3/16/62. Died 12/10/62 in Knoxville, Tennessee of pleuritis.

Dukes, John N.; 2/D; Private, enlisted

5/12/62, Pike. Died at Chattanooga 2/20/63.

Dupree, T.; 2/E; Private.

Durden, Francis M.; 2/F; Private, enlisted at 28.

Edwards, James E.; 2/E; Private, enlisted 3/16/62 at 40, Autauga.

Eilands, Jefferson; 2/E; Private, enlisted 3/16/62 at 20, Autauga.

Eilands, Uriah; 2/E; Private.

Estes, Elliott E.; 2/B; Private, enlisted at 25, Coosa.

Favors, Archibold; 2/B; Private, enlisted at 25, Coosa.

Favors, Willis; 2/B; Private, enlisted at 19, Coosa.

Fiquett, Charles M.; 2/F; Private, enlisted at 22, Coosa.

Fiquett, Wilson L.; 2/F; Private, enlisted at 27, Coosa.

Fisher, William F.; 2/C; Sergeant, enlisted 5/12/62. Elected Lieutenant 11/1/62, died 9/20/63 at Chickamauga.

Folmar, Ephraim; 2/D; Private.

Folmar, John; 2/D; Sergeant.

Foster, William; 2/F; Private.

Fountain, Green; 2/A; Private, enlisted at 31, Randolph.

Freeman, Charles J.; 2/A; Private, enlisted at 19, Randolph. Died 5/4/62.

Freeman, Eli Jackson; 2/A; Private, enlisted at 18, Randolph.

Freeman, John; 2/A; Private, Randolph. AWOL 8/63.

Freeman, Levi W.; 2/A, Private, enlisted 4/5/62, Randolph. Left Chickamauga, Tennessee hospital 11/22/63, surrendered April 1865, died 1902.

Furguson, Manuel; 2/C; Private, Coosa.

Futral, Etheldred; 2/C; Private, enlisted 5/12/62, Tallapoosa.

Gay, Walter B.; 2/F; Private, enlisted at 24, Coosa.

Gibbons, R.; 2/E; Private.

Gibbons, William B.; 2/E; Private, enlisted 3/16/62 at 19, Autauga. Died of disease 6/16/63 in Morristown, Tennessee.

Gibson, L.; 2/C; Private.

Giles, Leander T.; 2/F; Private, enlisted at 31, Coosa. Killed at Chickamauga.

Gillespie, David; 2/F; Private, enlisted at 18, Coosa.

Gillespie, James; 2/F; Private.

Gillespie, Thomas; 2/F; Private.

Gillespie, William H.; 2/F; Private, enlisted at 21, Coosa.

Ginwright, C.; 2/D; Sergeant.

Ginwright, J.; 2/D; Private.

Ginwright, Jesse; 2/D; Private.

Ginwright, R.; 2/D; Private.

Girdner, Clairborn (or Clayborn, Clairborne, Clairbun); 2/F; Private, enlisted at 25, Coosa.

Glenn, T. J.; 2/B; Private, enlisted at 29, Coosa.

Glenn, William F.; 2/B; Private, enlisted at 31.

Goetter, Joseph; 2/B; Private.

Goodwin, B.; 2/F; Private.

Gordan (or Gordon), William D.; 2/C; Private. Enlisted 8/13/63, killed at Chickamauga 9/20/63.

Goss, William D.; 2/E; Private, enlisted 3/16/62 at 21, Autauga. Later Sergeant. Wounded at Drewry's Bluff (left hip).

Gothard, Ira; 2/C; Private.

Goza, Alpheus; 2/C; Lieutenant.

Gray, Jesse M.; 2/E; Private, enlisted 3/16/62 at 20, Autauga.

Gray, Levin D.; 2/E; Private, enlisted 3/16/62 at 22, Autauga. Died at Montgomery, Alabama 4/10/62.

Gray, Plesant M.; 2/E; Private, enlisted 3/16/62 at 24, Autauga. Killed at Drewry's Bluff 5/10/64.

Green, Alexander; 2/D; Private, enlisted 5/12/62.

Green, John; 2/A; Private, enlisted 1862. Transferred to 1st Alabama Infantry, Company A in 1863.

Green, Silus J.M.; 2/F; Private, enlisted 3/29/62 at 30.

Green, Zaba H.; 2/F; Private, enlisted at 30, Coosa.

Greer, William T.; 2/E; Private, enlisted 3/16/62 at 18, Autauga.

Gresham, F.L.; 2/B; Corporal, Coosa.

Griffin, Joseph J.; 2/D; Private, enlisted 5/12/62.

Groff, W.; 2/D; Private.

Gullidge, J. W. E.; 2/B; Private.

Gullidge, Robert H.; 2/B; Private, enlisted 4/28/62 at 25, Coosa. Elected Lieutenant 11/9/63, promoted to Captain 10/10/63.

Guy, Dennis; 2/D; Private.

Hackney, Thomas; 2/C; Private, enlisted 5/12/62, Tallapoosa.

Haines, William L.; 2/C; Private.

Hall, Jr, Bolling; 2/E; Captain, enlisted 3/16/62 at 24, Autauga. Later Lieutenant Colonel.

Hall, Crenshaw, 2/E; Adjutant.

Hall, John E.; 2/E; Lieutenant.

Ham, James; 2/F; Private, enlisted 3/29/62 at 24. Deserted at Strawberry Plains, Tennessee 8/19/63, rejoined from desertion 9/28/63.

Ham, Thomas L.; 2/F; Private, enlisted at 18, Coosa.

Hamilton, Samuel; 2/F; Private, enlisted at 27, Coosa.

Hankins, Jesee; 2/A; Private, enlisted at 18, Randolph. Died 6/7/62.

Hanna, Asariah; 2/C; Private, enlisted 5/12/62, Tallapoosa.

Hannan, Kinney M.; 2/C; Private, enlisted 5/12/62, Tallapoosa.

Hardagree, Jonathan; 2/F; Private.

Hardel, J. E.; 2/B; Private.

Hardel, W. T.; 2/B; Private. Served as a nurse in a hospital in Catoosa Springs, Georgia in March 1863.

Hardy, William F.; 2/B; Private, enlisted at 26, Coosa.

Harper, David; 2/E; Private, enlisted 4/1/62 at 42, Autauga.

Harrell, E.; 2/D; Corporal, enlisted 5/12/62. Detached to become brigade wagoner 11/62, later detailed to ordnance train of Buckner's Division.

Harris, Wilson G.; 2/B; Private, enlisted at 30, Coosa.

Harrison, Gaines L.; 2/D; Corporal, enlisted 5/12/62.

Harrison, Henry; 2/D; Private.

Harvey, John; 2/F; Private.

Harwell, Emmet; 2/C; Private.

Harwell, Jeremiah; 2/C; Private, Coosa.

Harwell, Russell; 2/C; Private, Coosa.

Hawes, Abel J.; 2/F; Private, enlisted at 24, Coosa.

Hawkins, Jesse; 2/A; Private.

Hawkins, John O.; 2/C; Private.

Hays, Leander; 2/E; Musician, enlisted 3/16/62 at 40, Autauga.

Head, Benjamin; 2/A; Private, enlisted at 22, Randolph.

Head, John; 2/A; Private, enlisted at 19, Randolph.

Head, Thomas E.; 2/A; Lieutenant, enlisted at 32, Randolph.

Head, Thomas E.; 2/A; Private, Randolph.

Henderson, Newton H.; 2/B; Private, enlisted 5/11/62 at 33, Coosa.

Hendrick (also filed as Hendricks), John; 2/A; Captain, enlisted at 27, Randolph.

Henley, John; 2/G; Captain.

Henry, Wiley; 2/A; Private, enlisted at 23.

Herren, Miles; 2/F; Private.

Hester, George W; 2/F; Private, enlisted at 20, Coosa.

Hesten, M.; 2/C; Private.

Heyns, W.; 2/C; Private.

Hiett, William H.; 2/C; Private, enlisted 5/12/62. Promoted to lieutenant by order of Jefferson Davis for distinguished valor and skill displayed at Chickamauga, killed at Petersburg 8/23/64. Incorrectly listed as Robert Y. Hiett in the OR.

Higgenbotham, J. T.; 2/A; Private, enlisted 5/10/62.

Hill, John H.; 2/A; Private, enlisted at 19, Randolph.

Hill, L.; 2/D; Private.

Hill, Thomas; 2/D; Private, enlisted 5/12/62, Pike.

Hill, William Manuel; 2/A; Private, enlisted 4/5/62, Randolph.

Hilyer, Henry H.; 2/F; Private, enlisted at 25, Coosa.

Hobgood, H. H.; 2/A; Private, enlisted at 26, Randolph. Originally 5/A.

Holland, John F.; 2/E; Private, enlisted 3/16/62 at 22, Autauga.

Holly, Joseph S.; 2/E; Private, enlisted 3/16/62 at 36.

Holman, D. B.; 2/B; Private, enlisted at 33, Coosa.

Holms, Thomas; 2/B; Private, enlisted at 40, Coosa.

Homes, Gideon; 2/F; Private.

Hooten, Drewry Flowers; 2/A; Private, enlisted at 35. Later sergeant.

Horn, Isaac H.; 2/D; Private.

Horn, James F.; 2/F; Private, enlisted at 24, Coosa.

Horn, Oliver; 2/D; Private, enlisted 5/12/62.

House, Anthony C.; 2/C; Private, enlisted 5/12/62. Later corporal, captured at Petersburg 6/17/64, released in Elmira, New York 6/19/65.

House, George V.; 2/C; Private, Coosa.

House, William E.; 2/C; Private.

Howard, James; 2/E; Private, enlisted 3/1/6/62 at 50, Autauga.

Howard, William S.; 2/E; Private, enlisted 3/16/62 at 27 (age uncertain), Autauga.

Hubbard, Alfred; 2/E; Corporal, enlisted 3/16/62 at 33, Autauga.

Hubbard, Henry B.; 2/E; Private, enlisted 3/16/62 at 23, Autauga.

Hubbard, Miles H.; 2/E; Private, enlisted 3/16/62 at 21, Autauga. Died of disease, Knoxville, Tennessee, 12/22/62.

Huckeba, Charles B.; 2/A; Private, enlisted 4/5/62 at 23, Randolph.

Huckeba, F. M.; 2/A; Private, enlisted 2/28/63.

Hudman, William F.; Private, enlisted at 36, Coosa.

Hudson, J. F. M.; 2/B; Private, enlisted at 23, Coosa.

Hudson, William; 2/A; Private.

Huey, R. E.; 2/D; Private, enlisted 5/12/62, Pike. Rejected for physical disability.

Hughes, Jonathan; 2/C; Corporal, enlisted at 41, Randolph. Died 8/3/62.

Hull, James M.; 2/B; Private, enlisted at 26, enlisted 4/1/62.

Hull, Nathaniel; 2/F; Private, enlisted 4/1/62 at 18, Autauga.

Hull, Thomas; 2/B; Lieutenant, enlisted at 35.

Hunt, James T.; 2/E; Private, enlisted 3/16/62 at 20, Autauga.

Hunt, Joseph; 2/A; Private, enlisted at 18, Randolph.

Huoy, R. E.; 2/D; Private, enlisted 3/12/62, discharged 5/20/62.

Hurt, James A.; 2/D; Private, enlisted 5/12/62, rejected for physical disability 5/20/62.

Hurt, J. D.; 2/D; Private, enlisted 8/15/62, Montgomery.

Hurt, O. J.; 2/D; Private, enlisted 8/15/62. May have deserted or transferred to the 45th Alabama Infantry.

Hutson, John; 2/C; Private, enlisted 5/12/62, Coosa. Died 9/10/62.

Jacks, B. F.; 2/B; Private, enlisted at 19, Coosa.

Jacks, John A.; 2/B; Private, enlisted 4/28/62 at 27, Coosa. Detailed as Brigade Wagoner by General Gracie 4/17/63.

Jacks, John; 2/B; Private.

Jackson, William; 2/B; Private, enlisted at 21, Coosa.

Jeams, William; 2/C; Private, enlisted 7/10/63. Soon after went to hospital in Cassville, Ga.

Jefcoat, Elijah H.; 2/D; Private, enlisted 8/10/62, Pike. Furloughed home from Knoxville, Tennessee hospital 8/20/63, died at home about 9/28/63.

Jefcoat, Samuel F.; 2/D; Private, enlisted 5/2/62, Pike.

Jenks, William; 2/C; Private.

Jenright, Readus; 2/D; Private.

Jinks, John; 2/C; Private, enlisted 5/12/62, Tallapoosa.

Jinright, Calvin; 2/D; Private, enlisted 5/14/62. Later sergeant.

Jinright, Jefferson; 2/D; Private, enlisted 5/12/62.

Johns, Levi; 2/D; Private, enlisted 5/12/62. Appointed Musician, deserted 9/25/63 from near Chattanooga.

Johns, William W.; 2/D; Private, enlisted 5/12/62.

Johnson, Alexander C.; 2/E; Private, enlisted 3/16/62 at 28, Autauga. Later sergeant.

Johnson, Daniel J.; 2/E; Private, enlisted 3/16/62 at 42, Autauga. Wounded at Chickamauga 9/19/63. Farmer.

Johnson, Henry A.; 2/E; Private, enlisted 3/16/62 at 20, Autauga.

Johnson, John; 2/E; Private, enlisted 7/18/63, Autauga. May have deserted 9/16/63.

Johnson, Louis; 2/D; Private.

Johnson, Patrick W.; 2/E; Private. Died of disease 9/25/63.

Johnson, Paul J.; 2/E; Private, enlisted 3/16/62 at 42.

Johnson, Stephen C.; 2/E; Private, enlisted 3/16/62 at 25, Autauga. Died of wounds at Petersburg 6/23/64.

Johnson, William E.; 2/E; Private, enlisted 3/16/62 at 27, Autauga.

Johnson, William Q.; 2/E; Private, enlisted 3/16/62 at 28, Autauga.

Johnson, William S.; 2/E; Private, enlisted 3/16/62 at 30.

Jones, Ethan W.; 2/E; Lieutenant, enlisted 3/16/62 at 25, Autauga. Killed by shell fragment at Petersburg 10/4/64.

Jones, George; 2/C; Private, enlisted 2/17/63, Coosa. Wounded at Chickamauga.

Jones, Henry; 2/E; Private, enlisted 4/1/62 at 20, Autauga.

Jones, Henry; 2/F; Corporal, enlisted 3/26/62.

Jones, Hernton; 2/B; Private, enlisted 4/2/62. Deserted 8/20/63 at Strawberry Plains, Tennessee.

Jones, Jesse G.; 2/E; Private, enlisted 3/16/62 at 24, Autauga.

Jones, John N.; 2/F; Private, enlisted at 24, Coosa.

Jones, L. A.; 2/C; Private, enlisted 8/13/63. Wounded at Chickamauga.

Jones, M. D.; 2/B; Private, enlisted at 20, Coosa.

Jones, Seaborn C.; 2/E; Private, enlisted 3/16/62 at 30, Autauga. Killed at Chickamauga.

Jones, William A.; 2/D; Private, enlisted 8/15/62. Deserted 8/16/62.

Jones, William H.; 2/F; Private, enlisted 3/29/62 at 18. Later sergeant, wounded at Chickamauga.

Jones, William P.; 2/D; Private, enlisted 12/20/62. Confederate Honor Roll at Chickamauga.

Jones, Young A.; 2/C; Corporal, enlisted 5/12/62. Later sergeant, wounded at Chickamauga.

Jordan, Asa; 2/C; Private, enlisted 2/10/63, Coosa.

Jordan, John H.; 2/C; Private, enlisted 2/19/63, Coosa. Died 8/3/63 at Strawberry Plains, Tennessee.

Jordan, John T.; 2/D; Private, enlisted 5/12/62, Pike.

Jordan, John W.; 2/D; Private, enlisted 5/12/62, Pike.

Jordan, Joshua E.; 2/D; Private, enlisted 5/12/62.

Jordan, W.; 2/D; Sergeant, enlisted 5/12/62.

Kelley, F.; 2/B; Private, enlisted 1/1/63, Coosa. Deserted 9/19/63.

Kelley, William C.; 2/F; Private, enlisted 3/26/62 at 35, Coosa.

Kemp, Solomon A.; 2/A; Private, enlisted 6/28/63, Randolph. Wounded at Chickamauga.

Kemp, William J.; 2/E; Private, enlisted 3/16/62 at 20, Autauga.

Kenedy, John A. H.; 2/A; Private, enlisted at 30, Randolph. Deserted sometime after 8/31/63, rejoined 11/13/63.

Kenedy, Linsey Alexander; 2/A; Private, enlisted 4/13/62, Randolph.

Kerr, David; 2/A; Corporal, enlisted 4/5/62 at 34, Randolph. Later lieutenant. Wounded at Bean's Station 12/14/63, killed 5/16/64.

Kilpatrick, Isiah; 2/F; Private, enlisted at 19, Coosa.

Kilpatrick, James; 2/F; Private.

Kilpatrick, John; 2/F; Private.

Kilpatrick, Sanford R.; 2/F; Corporal, enlisted at 23, Coosa.

Kimbriel, J.; 2/F; Private.

Kinard, L. D.; 2/F; Private, enlisted 1/1/63. Appointed corporal 10/31/63.

King, Francis M.; 2/C; Sergeant, enlisted 5/12/62, Tallapoosa. Appointed sergeant 10/20/63.

Kittley, William; 2/A; Private, Randolph. Died 10/12/62.

Knight, Isaac; 2/B; Private, enlisted at 40, Coosa.

Knowles, Samuel; 2/D; Private, enlisted 5/12/62, Pike.

Ladd, Reuben; 2/C; Private. Attached to three hospitals as a nurse, died in 1863.

Laurence, Wade; 2/D; Private, enlisted 5/12/62. Deserted 5/14/62.

Lawrence, Ervin Y.; 2/D; Sergeant, enlisted 5/12/62.

Lawrence, Samuel N.; 2/D; Private, enlisted 5/12/62.

Leach, Malcom; 2/C; Private, enlisted 3/3/63, Coosa.

Lee, Daniel; 2/A; Private, enlisted at 32, Randolph.

Lee, Isom L.; 2/F; Lieutenant, enlisted at 30.

Lee, John M.; 2/F; Sergeant, enlisted at 26, Coosa.

Lee, Stanmore B.; 2/D; Private, enlisted 5/12/62.

Lester, John T.; 2/F; Private, enlisted at 18, Coosa.

Lester, Wilson; 2/F; Private, enlisted 3/29/62.

Levi, John T.; 2/C; Private.

Levi, Quillin; 2/C; Private.

Levi, Theadore; 2/C; Private, Tallapoosa.

Lewis, Daniel; 2/F; Private, enlisted at 25, Coosa.

Lewis, Edward; 2/E; Private, enlisted 2/63.

Lewis, Jacob; 2/A; Private, enlisted at 30, Randolph.

Lewis, James M.; 2/E; Private, enlisted 3/16/62 at 36, Autauga.

Lewis, John; 2/B; Private, enlisted at 22, Coosa.

Lewis, Jonathan C.; 2/E; Private, enlisted 3/16/62 at 39, Autauga. Died of disease 12/12/62.

Lewis, William; 2/F; Private, enlisted at 18, Coosa.

Lewis, William H.; 2/E; Lieutenant, enlisted 3/16/62 at 26, Autauga.

Lindsey, Martin; 2/C; Private, enlisted 5/12/62.

Little, Enoch; 2/F; Private, enlisted at 23, Coosa.

Little, J. J.; 2/B; Private, enlisted 7/8/62. Mustered in 10/1/62 as substitute for J. M. Wilson. Deserted 9/22/62.

Little, James; 2/F; Private, enlisted at 22, Coosa.

Liverett, Thomas; 2/A; Private, enlisted 11/12/63.

Logan, James A.; 2/F; Private, Coosa.

Logan, John; 2/F; Private, enlisted 4/11/63.

Long, Alexander; 2/E; Private, enlisted 3/16/62 at 19.

Long, J. B.; 2/D; Private, enlisted 5/12/62, Pike.

Long, J. D.; 2/D; Private, enlisted 5/12/62. Deserted 5/14/62.

Long, J. H. D.; 2/D; Private, enlisted 5/12/62, Pike. Deserted 5/14/62.

Long, William E.; 2/B; Private, enlisted at 16, Coosa.

Love, William Lucus; 2/A; Private, enlisted 4/13/62 at 35, Randolph. Later sergeant.

Lowery (or Lowry), James M.; 2/B; Private, enlisted at 32, Coosa. Deserted 10/3/63, took Oath of Allegiance 5/25/65.

Malloy, Patrick; 2/D; Private, enlisted 8/16/62.

Maloy, W.; 2/D; Private, enlisted 8/5/62. Deserted 8/20/62.

Marlow, James W.; 2/E; Private, enlisted 3/16/62 at 18, Autauga. Died of disease 7/6/62.

Martin, John; 2/B; Private, enlisted at 36, Coosa.

Martin, P. M.; 2/B; Private, enlisted at 21, Coosa.

Martin, Robert Y.; 2/F; Private, enlisted at 28, Coosa.

Masingal, J. A.; 2/B; Private, enlisted at 30, Talladega.

Maudling, William W.; 2/E; Private, enlisted 3/16/62 at 38, Autauga.

Mauk, William; 2/A; Lieutenant, enlisted 3/5/62 at 28, Randolph. Resignation accepted 7/25/63, cited hemorrhaging in his lungs.

May, Andrew; 2/C; Private, enlisted 9/27/62.

May, J.; 2/D; Private.

May, John M.; 2/A; Private, enlisted at 32, Randolph.

May, John; 2/A; Private. Could be John W. May.

May, Moses P.; 2/D; Private, enlisted 5/12/62. Deserted, prisoned, convicted by court-martial, sentenced to be returned to company, branded with letter B on left hip.

May, Wade; 2/D; Private, enlisted 8/14/62.

Mayfield, David M.; 2/A; Private, enlisted at 24, Randolph.

Mayfield, William S.; 2/A; Private, enlisted at 28, Randolph.

McBurnett, Elbert; 2/A; Private, enlisted at 19, Randolph.

McClain, Hamilton, 2/A; Private, enlisted at 39, Coosa.

McColloch, James; 2/A; Private, enlisted 4/5/62.

McDermid, James; 2/C; Private, enlisted 2/25/63, Coosa. Died 11/30/63.

McDonald, James L.; 2/F; Sergeant, enlisted at 18, Coosa.

McDowell, Elihu; 2/A; Private.

McDowell, John; 2/B; Private, enlisted at 18.

McGrady, C.; 2/B; Private, enlisted at 20, Coosa.

McGrady, J. P.; 2/B; Private, enlisted at 20.

McGrady, James W.; Corporal, enlisted at 29.

McGrady, William C.; Sergeant, enlisted at 25, Coosa. Promoted 10/10/63.

McIntyre, Edward Legare; 2/D; Captain, enlisted 5/12/62, Pike.

McKinney, Joseph; 2/D; Private, enlisted 5/12/62, Pike. Died 6/10/62.

McLean, H.; 2/B; Private, enlisted 4/12/62. Promoted to quartermaster sergeant 5/6/62.

McLeroy, James; 2/A; Private, enlisted 7/7/62. Substitute for H. C. Owens.

McInish, Gilbert; 2/A; Private, enlisted at 51, Randolph.

McInnish, Allen D.; 2/A; Private. Court-martialed, rejoined from desertion 7/10/63, AWOL after 12/4/63, POW and released after taking Oath of Allegiance 12/12/63.

McNealy, David; 2/C; Private, Coosa. Rejected.

McPherson, Archibald; 2/A; Private.

McPherson, Napleon B.; 2/A; Private, enlisted at 27, Randolph.

McSwain, John; 2/A; Private, enlisted at 27, Randolph.

McSwain, Rufus; 2/B; Sergeant, enlisted at 22, Coosa.

Meeks, Jeremiah; 2/C; Private, enlisted 5/30/63. Transferred to hospital with dislocated knee 9/6/63.

Meherg, William A.; 2/B; Private, enlisted at 23, Coosa.

Meherg, Willis A.; 2/B; Private, enlisted at 23, Coosa.

Miears, Thomas; 2/E; Sergeant, enlisted 3/16/62, Autauga. Wounded at Chickamauga.

Miller, James; 2/F; Private, enlisted 3/26/62, Coosa.

Miller, James H.; 2/F; Private, enlisted 3/29/62, Coosa.

Miller, John; 2/E; Private, enlisted 4/1/62 at 46, Autauga.

Miller, Thomas; 2/F; Private, enlisted 4/7/62 at 18.

Miller, William W.; 2/F; Private.

Milurs, Thomas A.; 2/E; Private, enlisted 3/16/62 at 26, Autauga.

Mitchell, Thomas J.; 2/F; Private, enlisted 3/26/62 at 24, Coosa. Killed at Chickamauga.

Mitchell, William F.; 2/D; Private, 5/12/62, Pike. Died at Cumberland Gap 9/29/62.

Monfee, James; 2/E; Private, enlisted 3/16/62, Autauga. Named orderly for commander of 2nd Battalion 3/18/63.

Monroe, J. A.; 2/B; Private.

Moody, Lewis; 2/D; Private, enlisted 5/12/62, Pike.

Mooney, Samuel N.; 2/D; Private, enlisted 5/12/62, Pike.

Moore, Lunsford; 2/E; Corporal, enlisted 3/16/62 at 25, Autauga.

Moore, Moses; 2/E; Private, enlisted 3/16/62 at 38, Autauga.

Moore, William; 2/E; Private, enlisted 3/16/62 at 27.

Morgan, J.; 2/D; Private, enlisted 6/30/62. Died 9/26/62.

Morgan, Timothy; 2/A; Private, enlisted 4/5/62 at 37.

Morgan, William C.; 2/F; Private, Coosa.

Morris, Elias; 2/B; Private, enlisted at 26, Coosa.

Morris, John; 2/B; Private, enlisted 4/2/62 at 25.

Morris, Samuel; 2/B; Private, enlisted at 52, Coosa.

Morris, W.; 2/B; Private, enlisted 3/1/63. Wounded at Chickamauga.

Morrison, Samuel E.; 2/F; Private, enlisted at 30, Coosa.

Morton, Thomas; 2/A; Private, enlisted 4/13/62. Rejected, elbow anchylosis.

Moses, John W.; 2/A; Private, enlisted at 23, Randolph.

Motes, Jesse E.; 2/D; Private, enlisted 5/12/62.

Motes, William; 2/E; Private, enlisted 3/16/62 at 25, Autauga. Deserted 9/16/63.

Motes, William; 2/E; Private, enlisted 3/16/62. Deserted 9/16/63.

Mount, F. M.; 2/D; Private, enlisted 8/8/62.

Mount, J.; 2/D; Private, enlisted 8/1/62, Lee County, Georgia. Discharged due to disability, chronic rheumatism.

Mount, S.; 2/D; Private.

Muldrew, James P.; 2/A; Private, enlisted 5/7/62, Randolph. Transferred to Ferrel's Artillery 8/1/62.

Mulkey, James; 2/A; Private, enlisted 3/5/62 at 19, Randolph. Listed as absent sick, left at Chickamauga, probably wounded.

Mulkey, John; 2/A; Private, enlisted 3/5/62 at 30, Randolph.

Mulkey, Marion (Mims); 2/A; Private. Died in 1862.

Mulkey, Seaborn; 2/A; Private, enlisted 8/31/62, Randolph.

Mulloy, Levi; 2/A; Private, enlisted 8/31/62, Randolph. Possibly wounded at Chickamauga.

Munfee, James; 2/E; Private, enlisted 3/16/62 at 20, Autauga.

Murrah, Silas; 2/F; Private, enlisted 3/25/62 at 35.

Murrer, Thomas; 2/E; Private, enlisted 3/16/62 at 28, Autauga. Died at Cumberland Gap 10/5/62.

Nelson, Alfred B.; 2/E; Musician, enlisted 3/16/62 at 18, Autauga. Died of disease 2/2/62 or 2/20/62.

Nelson, John H.; 2/E; Private, enlisted 3/16/62 at 24, Autauga.

Nelson, John M.; 2/E; Private, enlisted 4/1/62 at 18, Autauga.

Nelson, Robert H.; 2/E; Corporal, enlisted 3/16/62 at 28, Autauga. Promoted to sergeant.

Nelson, Thomas A.; 2/E; Private, enlisted 3/16/62 at 21, Autauga. Died of disease 2/3/63.

Nelson, W. D.; 2/E; Private, enlisted 3/16/62 at 28, Autauga.

Nesbit, Robert; 2/F; Private, enlisted at 22, Coosa.

Nesbit, Stephen N.; 2/F; Private, enlisted 5/7/62 at 26, Coosa.

Nesbit, William J.A.; 2/F; Private, enlisted 3/29/62 at 32, Coosa.

Newman, Richard; 2/A; Private, enlisted at 27, Randolph.

Nolen, Andrew J.; 2/F; Private, enlisted at 25, Coosa.

Nolen, Francis M.; 2/F; Private, enlisted 3/26/62.

Nolen, Thomas J.; 2/F; Private, enlisted at 32, Coosa.

Norris, Alexander T.; 2/E; Private, enlisted 3/16/62 at 19, Autauga.

Norris, F. M.; 2/E; Private, enlisted 7/16/63, Autauga.

Norris, George C.; 2/E; Musician, enlisted 3/16/62 at 18.

Norris, George W.; 2/E; Private, enlisted 3/16/62 at 22, Autauga. Killed at Chickamauga, cited by Preston, Roll of Honor.

Nummy, James A.; 2/E; Private, enlisted 4/1/62 at 30, Autauga.

Oats, Aaron; 2/E; Private, enlisted 3/16/62 at 20, Autauga. Died at Knoxville 11/29/62

Oats, Isaiah; 2/E; Private, enlisted 3/16/62 at 24, Autauga.

Oden, George H.; 2/E; Private, enlisted 3/16/62 at 23, Autauga.

Oden, Peter; 2/E; Private, enlisted 3/16/62 at 31. Promoted to lieutenant 7/1/62, died 10/6/62.

Oslen, Alva J.; 2/F; Private, enlisted at 21, Coosa.

Oswald, J. F.; 2/D; Private.

Owens, Henry; 2/A; Private, enlisted 3/16/62 at 21, Autauga. Died 8/10/62 without ever collecting a paycheck.

Palmer, John W.; 2/F; Private, enlisted at 35, Coosa.

Palmer, William E.; 2/F; Private, enlisted 3/26/62 at 21. Deserted, captured 9/9/63, released after taking Oath of Allegiance.

Parish, Henry M.; 2/E; Private, enlisted 3/16/62, Autauga.

Parish, Jesse B. H. 2/E; Private, enlisted 3/16/62 at 33, Autauga.

Parish, Wesly M.; 2/E; Private, enlisted 3/16/62 at 28, Autauga. Died at Knoxville 4/9/63.

Paschal, M. B.; 2/B; Private, enlisted at 21.

Patterson, Albert; Private, enlisted at 19, Coosa.

Patterson, Felix; 2/B; Private, enlisted at 23, Coosa.

Patterson, James; 2/B; Corporal, enlisted 3/1/62 at 29, Coosa. Elected corporal 3/29/62 (note date). Finished service as a private.

Patterson, Silas; 2/B; Private, enlisted 4/1/62 at 35, Coosa. Deserted, rejoined 10/21/63.

Paul, Edward; Field/Staff; Quartermaster Sergeant, enlisted 3/6/62.

Pearce, Thomas; 2/E; Private, enlisted 3/16/62 at 36, Autauga. Died at Drewry's Bluff 5/26/64.

Pearce, T.; 2/E; Private.

Pearson, George; 2/C; Private, enlisted 5/12/62.

Pearson, John G.; 2/C; Private, Tallapoosa.

Penton, R. S.; 2/F; Private, enlisted at 27, Coosa.

Perkins, J. F.; 2/B; Private, enlisted 10/1/62, Coosa.

Phillips, Joel; 2/B; Private, enlisted at 43, Coosa.

Phillips, John D.; 2/A; Private, enlisted 5/15/62, Randolph.

Pike, William T. F.; 2/A; Private, enlisted at 19, Randolph. Wounded at Chickamauga, died 9/30/63.

Plunkett, Elisha; 2/F; Private, enlisted at 40, Coosa.

Polk, Phillip M.; 2/C; Private, enlisted 5/12/62, rejected.

Pond, Joseph; 2/F; Private, enlisted 3/29/62 at 30. Promoted to lieutenant 7/1/62.

Pool, John L.; 2/D; Sergeant, enlisted 5/12/62.

Popewell, Alfred; 2/E; Private, enlisted 3/16/62 at 18, Autauga. Discharged 2/18/63 at Knoxville. Born 2/7/44.

Porter, George W.; 2/C; Sergeant, enlisted 5/12/62, Tallapoosa. Rejected.

Porter, John H.; 2/C; Lieutenant, enlisted 5/12/62.

Porter, Thomas J.; 2/C; Private. Deserted December 1863, took Oath of Allegiance to United States in Knoxville, Tennessee. Sent to Camp Nelson, Kentucky until he could go home. Hospitalized with smallpox at Camp Nelson 2/10/64.

Posey, James W.; 2/B; Corporal.

Posey, Jasper; 2/E; Private, enlisted 3/16/62 at 21, Autauga.

Posey, John T.; 2/B; Sergeant, enlisted at 22, Coosa.

Posey, William M; 2/B; Corporal, enlisted 4/1/62 at 22. Wounded at Chickamauga.

Powell, Joseph; 2/D; Private, enlisted 5/12/62, Pike.

Powell, Robert; 2/F; Private, enlisted 3/21/62 at 26. Deserted 6/27/63.

Powell, Stephen; 2/D; Private, enlisted 5/12/62, Pike.

Presnel, John; 2/A; Private, enlisted 11/13/63.

Pruett, Wiley; 2/B; Private, enlisted 4/29/62 at 24. Deserted from hospital 9/21/63, returned 10/12/63.

Pruitt, Francis M.; 2/D; Lieutenant, enlisted 5/12/62.

Pruitt, George A.; 2/D; Private, enlisted 5/12/62.

Pruitt, John; 2/D; Private, enlisted 5/12/62. Deserted from hospital 9/17/63, rejoined 10/9/63.

Pruitt, W.; 2/D; Corporal, enlisted 1/5/63.

Pure, F.; 2/D; Private.

Pure, Thomas; 2/D; Private, enlisted 5/12/62. Deserted 9/17/63, rejoined 10/9/63.

Ramsey, John A.; 2/F; Private, enlisted at 25, Coosa.

Ramsey, William; 2/F; Private, enlisted at 18, Coosa.

Randall, John H.; 2/A; Private, enlisted at 34, Randolph.

Randall (or Randle), Smiley; 2/A; Corporal, enlisted at 26, Randolph.

Raney, Joshua J.; 2/A; Private, enlisted 5/15/62. Deserted, rejoined.

Raney, Josiah T.; 2/A; Private, enlisted 4/5/62 at 19, Randolph.

Ray, George W.; 2/E; Private, enlisted 4/1/62 at 31.

Ray, James; 2/F; Private, enlisted at 18, Coosa.

Ray, James (some paperwork lists first name as Duncan) D.; 2/A; Private, enlisted 4/8/62, Montgomery. Elected corporal 8/15/62. Died of disease 5/19/63.

Ray, John R.; 2/A; Private, enlisted 9/15/62, Randolph. Rejoined from desertion 7/10/63, wounded at Chickamauga. Farmer.

Ray, Samuel T.; 2/C; Private. Rejected.

Ray, Sion W.; 2/A; Private, enlisted 4/5/62 at 26, Randolph. Died 10/26/62.

Riddick, John F.; 2/D; Private, enlisted 5/12/62.

Riddick, Elisha; 2/D; Private, enlisted 5/12/62.

Reaves, Stephen E. A.; 2/A; Lieutenant, enlisted 4/5/62 at 24, Randolph. Elected captain 11/12/62, wounded at Bean's Station 12/14/63.

Reaves, George W.; 2/C; Corporal, enlisted 5/12/62.

Roberson, Allen R.; 2/F; Private, enlisted 5/19/63.

Roberson, John; 2/F; Private, enlisted 4/29/62.

Roberson, Samuel; 2/F; Private, enlisted at 23, Coosa.

Roberson, Sanford; 2/B; Private, enlisted at 29, Coosa.

Roberson, Westley; 2/F; Sergeant, enlisted 4/26/62 at 25.

Roberson, William H.; 2/C; Private, enlisted 5/12/62, Coosa. Died 8/27/62.

Roberson, William M.; 2/B; Private, enlisted 4/29/62 at 32, Coosa. Appointed corporal after Chickamauga.

Robinson, William F.; 2/D; Private, enlisted 5/12/62.

Robinson, William H; 2/C; Private, Coosa.

Rodgers (also Roggers), James Henry; 2/A; Private, enlisted at 25, Randolph. Deserted, rejoined.

Rogers, J. W.; 2/B; Private, enlisted at 28, Coosa.

Rogers, P. H.; 2/B; Private, enlisted at 32, Coosa.

Rollins, James; 2/A; Private, enlisted at 26, Randolph.

Rollins, John; 2/A; Private, enlisted at 26, Randolph.

Rollins, John; 2/E; Private, enlisted 3/16/62, Autauga.

Ross, John A.; 2/E; Private, enlisted 3/16/62 at 22, Autauga.

Roy, David; 2/E; Private, enlisted 3/16/62 at 37, Autauga.

Roy, Hansford Duncan; 2/E; Private, enlisted 4/1/62 at 37. Died 5/19/63.

Roy, John W.; 2/E; Private, enlisted 3/16/62 at 27, Autauga.

Roy, Joseph; 2/E; Private, enlisted 3/16/62 at 22, Autauga.

Rush, James F.; 2/F; Private, enlisted at 36, Coosa.

Russ, James W.; 2/B; Private, enlisted 5/7/62 at 35, Coosa. Deserted, rejoined, then wounded at Chickamauga.

Ryal, H.; 2/D; Private, enlisted 5/12/62, Pike.

Sample, William; 2/F; Private, enlisted at 18, Coosa. Later corporal.

Sanders (or Saunders), Jere; 2/D; Private, enlisted 5/12/62, Troy. Deserted 5/14/62.

Sanders (or Saunders), Jonathan; 2/F; Private, enlisted at 30, Coosa.

Sanders (or Saunders), William T.; 2/D; Private, enlisted 5/12/62, Troy.

Sandford, John H.; 2/B; Private, enlisted 5/14/62 at 47, Montgomery. Deserted, rejoined, killed at Petersburg.

Sandlin, B. J.; 2/F; Private, enlisted 9/23/63.

Sanford, G. W.; 2/B; Private, enlisted 6/12/62.

Saunders, John; 2/D; Private, enlisted 5/12/62.

Saxon, George W.; 2/C; Private, enlisted 5/12/62. Died 8/29/62.

Saxon, James H.; 2/C; Private, Tallapoosa.

Scaggs, G. W.; 2/F; Private, enlisted at 43, Coosa.

Scarbro (or Scarbrough), Micajah; 2/C; Private, enlisted 7/17/62. Substitute, died of typhoid fever 1/3/63.

Scogin, James Abel; 2/B; Private, enlisted 4/3/62 at 16, Montgomery. Discharged 11/15/62 (general disability and under-age), commanding officer refused to accept the discharge and initially listed Scogin AWOL. Discharge later ac-cepted. Farmer.

Sconyers, Francis M.; 2/F; Private, en-listed at 18, Coosa.

Sconyers, Miles; 2/F; Private, enlisted 3/26/62 at 23, Coosa. Died 11/2/62.

Scott, L.; 2/E; Private, enlisted 3/5/63, Autauga.

Scott, Robert; 2/E; Private, enlisted 3/16/62 at 26, Autuaga. Appointed Color Guard 8/4/63, wounded at Chickamauga, killed at Drewry's Bluff 5/16/64.

Screws, William; 2/D; see William Wal-lace Screws, 1/A.

Scroggins, George B.; 2/F; Private, en-listed at 22, Coosa.

Sellers, John M.; 2/D; Private, enlisted 5/12/62. Died at Cumberland Gap 3/4/63.

Sellers, Samuel J.; 2/D; Corporal, enlisted 5/12/62, Troy.

Sharp, J. H.; 2/B; Private, enlisted 3/6/62 at 18.

Sharp, James J.; 2/B; Private, 4/1/62, Coosa. Died 6/14/64.

Sharp, Wilburn J.; 2/B; Private. Died on furlough at home 6/11/63.

Sharp, William J.; 2/F; Private, enlisted at 22, Coosa.

Shaw, Lewis L.; 2/I; Orderly Sergeant, en-listed at 37, Coosa.

Shepard, John; 2/D; Private, enlisted 5/12/62, Troy. Deserted 5/12/62.

Shirey, William; 2/A; Private, enlisted at 18, Randolph.

Shoemake, Amos B.; 2/E; Private, enlisted 4/1/62 at 28. Death date uncertain, could be 5/23/62.

Shoemake, James R.; 2/E Private, enlisted 4/1/62 at 18, Autauga. Died of disease 8/4/63.

Shumake, Robert B.; 2/E; Private, enlisted 3/16/62 at 21, Autauga.

Shewmake, W.W.; 2/E; Private, enlisted 3/16/62 at 23, Autauga.

Simms, Burcley; 2/F; Private, enlisted at 36.

Simms, Oliver K.; Private, enlisted 3/29 or 26/62 at 28.

Sims, J. D.; 2/D; Private, enlisted 8/18/62 at 22. Deserted or taken prisoner Crab Orchard, Kentucky 10/13/62. Died 11/20/62.

Sims, John L.; 2/D; Private, enlisted 8/8/62. Died at home, date unverified.

Slaughter, N. J.; 2/A; Private.

Small, James; 2/D; Private, enlisted 5/12/62, Pike.

Small, John E.; 2/D; Private, enlisted 5/12/62, Pike.

Small, William C.; 2/D; Private, enlisted 8/8/62, Montgomery. Died 10/6/62 at Cumberland Gap.

Smith, Albert; 2/F; Private, enlisted at 22, Coosa.

Smith, Andrew J.; 2/C; Private, enlisted 2/12/63.

Smith, Andrew J.; 2/C; Private, enlisted 5/12/62. Later corporal.

Smith, B. B.; 2/F; Private, enlisted at 23, Coosa.

Smith, B. T.; 2/F; Private, enlisted 9/23/13, Coosa. Deserted to enemy while on picket duty 10/14/63, took Oath of Al-legiance, released from Louisville, Ken-tucky.

Smith, Doctor R.; 2/F; Private, enlisted 3/26/62.

Smith, Hampton; 2/F; Private, enlisted 3/26/62 at 26, Coosa.

Smith, Harrison; 2/F; Private, enlisted 9/23/63.

Smith, Henry N.; 2/C; Private, enlisted 5/12/62. July–August 1863 detached duty as recruiting officer, killed at Chickamauga.

Smith, James; 2/A; Private, enlisted 7/5/62, Randolph.

Smith, Jesse J.; 2/F; Private, enlisted at 32, Coosa.

Smith, John W.; 2/E; Private, enlisted 4/20/62 at 20, Autauga.

Smith, Kitchen (Kinchin) S.; 2/A; Private, enlisted 4/5/62 at 22, Randolph.

Smith, Oliver F.; 2/A; Private, enlisted at 21.

Smith, Starlin; 2/A; Private, Randolph.

Snider, Benjamin F.; 2/F; Private, enlisted 4/4/63. Paroled at Appomattox 4/9/65, again at Montgomery, Alabama 5/25/65.

Snider, George; 2/F; Corporal, enlisted 3/26/62. Died 5/23/62.

Snider, Robert M.; 2/F; Sergeant, enlisted 3/26/62 at 28, Coosa. Reduced in rank 6/13 or 31/63, wounded at Chickamauga (both legs). Farmer.

South, J.; 2/A; Private. Randolph.

Spain, Benjamin D.; 2/B; Private, enlisted at 35, Coosa.

Sparks, William; 2/A; Sergeant, enlisted at 42, Randolph.

Spence, Andrew; 2/A; Private, enlisted at 18, Randolph.

Spigener, Joel; 2/B; Private, enlisted at 28.

Spigener (or Springer), Socrates; 2/B; Sergeant, enlisted at 19.

Stalnaker, Joseph; 2/E; Private, enlisted 3/16/62 at 35, Autauga. Discharged, pneumonia, 10/22/62.

Stalnaker, William; 2/E; Private, enlisted 3/16/62 at 17, Autauga.

Stanley, Allen R.; 2/F; Private, enlisted at 22, Coosa.

Stanley, William J.; 2/B; Private, enlisted at 47, Coosa.

Stephens, J.; 2/B; Private, enlisted at 26.

Stephens, William A.; 2/D; Private, enlisted 5/12/62.

Stephens, William M.; 2/F; Private, Coosa.

Stewart, Aaron G.; 2/E; Lieutenant, enlisted 3/16/62 at 34, Autauga.

Stewart, Allen M.; 2/C; Private, enlisted 5/12/62.

Stitt, William W.; 2/A; Sergeant, enlisted 4/23/62 at 29, Randolph.

Stone, Henry J.; 2/C; Private, enlisted 12/1/62.

Stone, James C.; 2/C; Lieutenant, enlisted 5/12/62. Resigned 10/31/62 due to chronic rheumatism.

Stone, W. B. J.; 2/F; Private, enlisted 5/13/62.

Strain, John; 2/A; Private.

Street, Raleigh W.; 2/C; Private, enlisted 5/12/62. Died 8/28/62.

Strickland, Mathew; 2/E; Private, enlisted 3/16/62 at 28.

Stross, G.; 2/D; Private, enlisted 8/15/62. Deserted 10/13/62.

Strother, John; 2/C; Private, enlisted 2/21/63. Deserted or captured 7/4/63, discharged 5/15/65.

Stroud, Jeremiah; 2/F; Private, enlisted 9/23/63.

Stubblefield, William Thomas; 2/F; Captain, enlisted 3/26/62 at 40. Promoted to major 6/25/62. Resigned 5/8/63.

Sudduth, James F.; 2/A; Private, enlisted at 23, Randolph.

Sullivan, Joseph; 2/E; Private, enlisted 8/28/63, Montgomery. Deserted 9/9/63.

Tankersley, John; 2/C; Private, enlisted 5/12/62, Tallapoosa.

Taylor, E.; 2/B; Private, enlisted at 37, Coosa.

Tekell, J.; 2/B; Private, enlisted at 40, Coosa.

Temples, Columbus M.; 2/E; Private, enlisted 3/16/62 at 19, Autauga. Captured at Chickamauga 9/20/63, discharged 6/13/65.

Thomas, George; 2/E; Private, enlisted 3/16/62 at 32, Autauga.

Thomas, George M.; 2/F; Private, enlisted at 25, Coosa.

Thomas, James F.; 2/F; Private, enlisted 3/29/62 at 32, Coosa. Died 4/18/63.

Thomas, John H.; 2/A; Private, enlisted at 25, Randolph.

Thomas, Samuel L.; 2/C; Private, enlisted 5/12/62.

Thomas, Stephen; 2/C; Private, enlisted 5/12/62.

Thomas, William M.; 2/B; Private, enlisted at 27, Coosa.

Thomas, William N.; 2/B; Private, enlisted at 23, Montgomery.

Thompson, James P.; 2/C; Private, enlisted 5/12/62.

Thompson, Wilson B.; 2/C; Private.

Thornton, L. C.; 2/A; Private.

Thornton, Seaborn; 2/A; Private.

Thornton, Wiley T.; 2/A; Private, enlisted

4/5/62, Randolph. Later corporal. Fatally wounded at Bean's Station.

Tiner, James W.; 2/D; Private, enlisted 5/12/62. Later corporal.

Tomlin, Sherrod; 2/C; Private, enlisted 2/12/63. Captured at Tullahoma 7/1/63. Died at Camp Chase, Columbus, Ohio.

Traywick, J. C.; 2/B; Private, enlisted at 30, Coosa.

Treadwell, John; 2/A; Private, enlisted 8/31/62, Randolph. Deserted, court-martialed, sentenced to death (not carried out), rejoined.

Turnham, T.; 2/F; Private.

Varner, J. W..; 2/B; Private, enlisted at 37, Coosa.

Varnon, David H.; 2/F; Private, enlisted 3/26/62 at 32, Coosa.

Veal, Benjamin; 2/A; Private, enlisted 7/5/63, Randolph.

Vernon, Eleizer R.; 2/F; Private, enlisted 3/26/62 at 32.

Vinson, Edward B.; Sergeant, enlisted 3/16/62 at 22, Autauga.

Vinson, Henry G. W.; 2/A; Private, enlisted at 24, Randolph.

Vinson, John R.; 2/E; Sergeant, enlisted 3/16/62 at 24, Autauga.

Walden, W.D.; 2/B; Captain, enlisted at 43.

Walker, George; 2/D; Private, enlisted 5/12/62, Pike.

Walker, William; 2/B; Private, enlisted 1/26/63.

Walton, J.; 2/D; Private.

Wates, John W.; 2/B; Private, enlisted 5/1/62 at 26.

Watkins, John; 2/C; Private, enlisted 3/5/63.

Weaver, Jeremiah; 2/B; Private, enlisted 4/3/62 at 32, Coosa. Married.

Weldon, E.; 2/E; Private, enlisted 7/1/63, Autauga.

Weldon, Floyd W.; 2/A; Private, enlisted at 18, Randolph.

Whetstone, David; 2/F; Private, enlisted 3/24/62 at 28.

White, James C.; 2/C; Private, enlisted 5/12/62. Rejected.

White, James W.; 2/D; Private, enlisted 5/12/62, Pike.

White, Seaborn J.; 2/D; Corporal, enlisted 5/12/62 at 21, Pike. Single.

Whitehead, Francis W.; 2/C; Sergeant, Tallapoosa. Died 10/3/62.

Whitton (or Whitten), Alfred; 2/A; Private, enlisted 5/6/62 at 29, Randolph. Served as teamster at various times during war.

Wilkins, Ephram; 2/C; Private, enlisted 5/12/62.

Williams, Andrew W.; Private, enlisted in 1st Battalion 5/16/62, Montgomery. Appointed quartermaster of 2nd Battalion 6/27/62, commanded division wagon train 7/63–8/63, later captain.

Williams, E. Y.; 2/B; Private, enlisted 4/7/62 at 27, Coosa. Killed at Petersburg 7/30/64.

Williams, Eli; 2/B; Private, enlisted at 27, Georgia. Died at Richmond 12/13/64.

Williams, H. J.; 2/B; Private, enlisted 1/1/63, Coosa. Captured at Chickamauga, died at Camp Douglas, Illinois 11/1/63 (typhoid fever).

Williams, Jeremiah; 2/E; Private, enlisted 3/16/62 at 22, Autauga.

Williams, R.; 2/D; Private.

Williams, Robert L.; 2/E; Private, enlisted 3/16/62 at 30, Autauga.

Williams, Squire; 2/D; Sergeant, enlisted 5/20/62, Montgomery.

Williams, Uriah; 2/C; Private, enlisted 4/5/62.

Willingham, J. F.; 2/A; Private.

Wilson, Griffin; 2/A; Private, enlisted 6/15/63.

Wilson, Jacob; 2/A; Private, enlisted at 17, Randolph.

Wilson, James; 2/E; Private, enlisted 3/16/62 at 31, Autauga. Wounded at Petersburg 6/17/64, died 7/2/64.

Wilson, Jasper N.; 2/F; Private, enlisted 3/29/62 at 24, Coosa.

Wilson, John J.; 2/E; Private, enlisted 3/16/62 at 20, Autauga.

Wilson, W. J.; 2/B; Private, enlisted at 26, Coosa.

Wilson, William; 2/F; Sergeant, enlisted at 28, Coosa.

Wingard, William A.; 2/D; Private, enlisted 5/12/62, Pike.

Wingard, Zachariah; 2/D; Private, enlisted 5/12/62, Pike.

Wingler, P.; 2/D; Private, enlisted 8/2/62. Deserted 8/8/62.

Wise, John F.; 2/E; Lieutenant, enlisted 3/16/62 at 32. Later, captain of Company E.

Wolf, John C.; 2/C; Private.

Wolf, John W.; 2/C; Private, enlisted 2/13/63.

Wolf, Peter M.; 2/C; Private, enlisted 2/2/62; wounded at Chickamauga.

Wolf, Phillip; 2/C; Private, enlisted 5/12/62, Georgia. Farmer.

Wood, Isaac M.; 2/D; Private, enlisted 5/12/62, Pike. Rejected for physical disability.

Works, Benjamin J.; 2/C; Private, Coosa.

Worthy, T. J.; 2/B; Private, enlisted at 29, Coosa.

Wright, Judson C.; 2/C; Private, Talladega.

Wright, Lewis M.; 2/F; Private, enlisted 3/26/62 at 40, Coosa. Rejoined from desertion 10/12/63.

Wyatt, Benjamin F.; 2/E; Private, enlisted 3/16/62 at 23, Autauga. Deserted 9/16/63.

Wyatt, Thomas J.; 2/E; Private, enlisted 3/16/62 at 22, Autauga. Discharged for disability 11/23/62.

Wyatt, William P.; 2/E; Private, enlisted 3/16/62 at 18, Autauga.

Yann, Garrett; 2/E; Private, enlisted 4/1/62 at 29, Autauga. Deserted, rejoined 10/9/63.

Yarbrough, George T.; 2/F; Private, enlisted 3/26/62 at 22, Coosa.

Yarbrough, Seaborn; 2/F; Private, enlisted at 25, Coosa. Subbed out by James P. Burk.

Young, Elijah; 2/A; Private, enlisted 4/5/62 at 19, Randolph. Listed as deserter sometime after 8/31/63, rejoined 11/13/63. Discharged 4/9/65.

Young, Isaac C. L.; 2/A; Private, enlisted 4/5/62 at 23, Randolph.

Young, James W.; 2/A; Private, enlisted 4/13/62 at 23, Randolph. Died at Tazewell, Tennessee 9/18/62.

Young, Robert; 2/A; Private, enlisted 4/13/62 at 26, Randolph.

Young, William Leftvich; 2/A; Drummer, enlisted 4/23/62 at 19, Randolph. Later private.

3rd Battalion

Adams, Elias; 3/B; Private, enlisted 4/7/62 at 21, Pike. Died 6/15/62 at Montgomery.

Adams, Marshall; 3/B; Private, enlisted 5/14/62 at 18. Transferred from 1st Battalion 8/1/63.

Adams, Robert B.; 3/E; Private, joined as recruit 7/31/63 at Cumberland Gap.

Adams, William H.; 3/E; Private, enlisted 7/3/62 at 26, Pike.

Allen, John J.; 3/B; Private, enlisted at 24, Pike.

Allen, William B.; 3/F; Private, joined 6/4/62 from Company C, 45th Alabama.

Amerson, Francis M.; 3/B; Private, enlisted 4/7/62 at 20, Pike. Discharged 3/23/63 by Board of Examination (lost use of left arm).

Amerson, William; 3/D; Private. Died 6/17/62 at Montgomery.

Anderson, Bartlett C.; 3/B; Private, enlisted 4/7/62. Died 7/26/62 at Chattanooga.

Armstrong, Aries; 3/A; Private, enlisted 3/10/62 at 24, Montgomery.

Armstrong, William; 3/A; Private, enlisted 8/11/62.

Arnold, George C.; 3/A; Private, enlisted 8/11/62. Died at Drewry's Bluff 5/9/64.

Arrington, James N.; 3/B; Lieutenant, enlisted 4/7/62 at 27, Pike. Resigned 10/27/62.

Athey, Elijah; 3/D; Private.

Athey, William Champion; 3/D; Private, enlisted 5/12/62. Wounded at Drewry's Bluff, captured 4/6/65, paroled at Newport News 7/1/65.

Averett, James; 3/F; Private, enlisted 5/9/62. Died as POW 1/28/64.

Bailey, George; 3/A; Corporal, enlisted 4/10/62. Resigned 7/25/62, discharged 11/4/62.

Baker, D. M.; 3/A; Private, enlisted 3/10/62 at 25, Montgomery.

Baker, Joseph; 3/A; Private, enlisted 3/10/62 at 23, Montgomery.

Baker, Thomas; 3/A; Private, enlisted 5/5/62.

Barlow, Daniel M.; 3/B; Private, enlisted at 36, Pike.

Barlow, James E.; 3/B; Private, enlisted 4/7/62 at 38, Pike. Detached as blacksmith 5/7/63, sick in hospital (rheumatism), detailed as shoemaker 8/20/64, later listed physically disabled.

Barnhill, Owen C.; 3/E; Private, enlisted 1862.

Bartlett, Joseph H.; 3/B; Private, enlisted 4/7/62. Died 6/14/62.

Battle, John M.; 3/E; Private, enlisted 5/14/62 at 32, Pike. Died 4/20/63 in Knoxville.

Baygents, James F.; 3/B; Private, enlisted 4/7/62. Later corporal, sergeant.

Baygents, Rufus F.; 3/B; Private, enlisted 4/7/62 at 37, Pike.

Bays, Zachariah; 3/E; Private, enlisted 5/14/62, Pike. Appointed sergeant 3/4/63.

Bean, Aaron (or Abran) W.; 3/E; Private, enlisted 9/20/62.

Bean, James F.; 3/E; Private, enlisted 5/14/62 at 34, Pike. Died 1/4/63.

Bean, Thomas F.; 3/E; Lieutenant, enlisted at 26, Pike. Resigned due to ill health 12/23/62.

Beasley, John; 3/F; Private, Georgia. Later Lieutenant.

Belle, Alexander E.; 3/F; Corporal, enlisted 5/9/62, Georgia. Later reduced to private.

Berry, Elijah A.; 3/D; Private, enlisted 5/9/62. Died 10/1/62.

Berry, Giles; 3/E; Private, enlisted 5/14/62.

Berry, James W.; 3/B; Private, enlisted 4/7/62 at 21, Pike. Sick, then detached for hospital duty 11/18/62.

Betton, Nathan T.; 3/B; Private, enlisted 4/7/62 at 21, Pike. Discharged 8/21/62 due to ill health. Farmer.

Bishop, John E.; 3/B; Private, enlisted 4/7/62 at 18, Pike. Died 8/22/63 in Tennessee.

Blackman (or Blackmon), Benjamin E.; 3/C; Private.

Blackman, Frank H.; 3/C; Private, enlisted 5/3/62. Died 2/24/64.

Blackman, James J.; 3/C; Private, enlisted 5/5/62 at 29, Coosa.

Blackmon, John R.; 3/C; Private, enlisted 5/3/62. Died 9/20/62.

Blan, Robert; 3/B; Private, enlisted 4/7/62 at 35, Pike. Later sergeant major, then private again.

Blankenship, Henry; 3/C; Private, enlisted 5/3/62 at 28, Coosa.

Blankenship, John; 3/C; Private, enlisted 5/3/62 at 31.

Blankenship, Miles Green; 3/C; Private, enlisted 5/3/62 at 27, Coosa. Lived 12/1/34–2/21/1908. Teamster 6/30/63–8/31/65.

Blaylock, James (or John) W.; 3/A; Private, enlisted at 18, Montgomery.

Bledsoe, George W.; 3/B; Private, enlisted 4/7/62 at 28, Pike. Discharged 11/12/62.

Bledsoe, John L.; 3/B; Private, enlisted 4/7/62 at 24, Pike. Died at 99. Appointed sergeant 7/1/63.

Bledsoe, William M.; 3/B; Private, enlisted 4/7/62 at 21.

Boatright, George T.; 3/B; Captain, enlisted 4/7/62 at 35, Pike.

Boland, J. W.; 3/F; Private, enlisted 7/1/62, Georgia.

Bonds, Marion; 3/C; Private, enlisted at 28, Coosa.

Bonds, Sugar J.; 3/C; Private, enlisted 5/3/62 at 30, Coosa. Died 11/30/62.

Bonner, Wyatt H.; 3/E; Private, enlisted 5/14/62. Died 4/15/63.

Bonner, Wyatt J.; 3/E; Private, enlisted 7/17/62. Briefly assigned teamster duty.

Bowden, Jacob; 3/B; Corporal, enlisted 4/7/62 at 20, Pike.

Bowden, Noah; 3/B; Private, enlisted 5/31/62 at 19, Montgomery.

Bowden, Richard D.; 3/B; Private, enlisted at 20, Pike. Lived 4/11/1842–9/4/1927.

Bowden, Simeon; 3/B; Private, enlisted 12/1/62. Died 4/10/63 at Knoxville, Tennessee.

Brackin, James; 3/A; Private, enlisted 3/10/62 at 24, Montgomery.

Brackin, Josiah; 3/A; Sergeant, enlisted 3/10/62 at 26.

Bradley, William J. P. (also W. J. Bradly or Bradley); 3/C; Private, enlisted 5/3/62 at 18, Coosa.

Braswell, James E. D.; 3/E; Private, enlisted 5/14/62 at 25, Pike.

Braswell, William; 3/E; Private, enlisted 5/14/62 at 32, Pike.

Brazile, John; 3/C; Private, enlisted 3/6/63.

Britton, J. M. (Mat); 3/C; Private, enlisted 5/14/62 at 23, Coosa. Later sergeant.

Britton, William H.; 3/C; Private.

Broadway, J. M.; 3/D; Private.

Brock, J. E.; 3/C; Private. Transferred to command 5/31/62, discharged 10/30/62.

Brooks, Lucius D.; 3/B; Private, enlisted at 31, Pike.

Brown, Mark A.; 3/B; Corporal, enlisted at 25, Pike.

Brown, Thomas J.; 3/C; Private, enlisted 5/3/62 at 29, Coosa.

Browning, William; 3/G; Private, enlisted 6/10/62.

Broxton (or Broxson), Noah; 3/A; Private, enlisted 3/11/62. Died at Bean's Station early 1863.

Bryan, Jasper J.; 3/B; Private, enlisted 4/7/62 at 30, Pike. Died 10/17/62.

Bryan, Washington M. C.; 3/B; Private, enlisted 7/7/62.

Burks, Jeremiah; 3/C; Private, enlisted 5/3/62 at 23, Coosa. Detailed as teamster 8/30/63.

Butt, James; 3/F; Lieutenant, enlisted 5/9/62, Georgia.

Byrd, George B.; 3/B; Private, enlisted at 21, Pike.

Byrd, William C.; 3/B; Private, enlisted 4/7/62 at 25, Pike. Captured 3/25/65, paroled 6/23/65.

Byrd, William H.; 3/A; Private, enlisted 4/21/62. Died 6/21/62.

Campbell, William A.; 3/A; Private, enlisted 3/10/62 at 22, Montgomery.

Cannon, John; 3/C; Private, enlisted 5/3/62 at 33, Coosa.

Cannon, W.; 3/A; Private.

Carmichael, David; 3/F; Private, enlisted 5/9/62, Georgia.

Carmichael, George L.; 3/F; Private, enlisted 6/12/62.

Carter, Jefferson A.; 3/A; Private, enlisted 3/10/62 at 17, Montgomery. Died 8/30/62 at Tazewell.

Catrett, Benjamin L.; 3/E; Private, enlisted 4/3/62 at 25, Pike.

Catrett, Isreal; 3/E; Private, enlisted 7/3/62 at 50, Pike.

Catrett, John Thomas; 3/E; Private, enlisted 5/14/62 at 29, Pike.

Catrett, John; 3/E; Private, enlisted 7/3/62 at 35, Pike. Died 12/20/62.

Chancelor (or Chancerlor), James; 3/E; Private. Substitute for E. B. Salter 3/2/63.

Chesser, John C.; 3/E; Private, enlisted at 28, Pike. Died 6/25/62.

Clark, Daniel; 3/B; Private, enlisted 4/7/62 at 20, Pike.

Clark, Hosea W.; 3/B; Private, enlisted 4/7/62 at 27, Pike. Died 12/7/62 at Knoxville, Tennessee.

Clark, John H.; 3/A; Private, enlisted 3/10/62 at 20, Montgomery.

Clary, J. S.; 3/B; Private, enlisted Montgomery. Died 1/13/63.

Clayton, J. (or J. W.); 3/F; Private, enlisted 9/1/62. Substitute for L. B. Duck. Discharged due to illness 9/1/63. Farmer.

Cochran, David W.; 3/B; Private, enlisted 4/7/62 at 21, Pike. Died 10/18/62.

Cochran, James B.; 3/A; Private, enlisted 3/10/62. Died 6/14/62.

Cockran, Thomas J.; 3/B; Sergeant, enlisted 4/7/62. Later private. Died 4/17/63 at Strawberry Plains.

Collins, James B.; 3/E; Private, enlisted 7/3/62 at 18, Pike. Died 9/20/62 at Tazewell.

Collinsworth (or Collisworth), Whitson; 3/E; Private, enlisted 5/14/62.

Cook, Arch B.; 3/F; Private, enlisted 6/12/62. Wagon master 9/1/13–10/31/63.

Cook, Benjamin; 3/F; Corporal, enlisted 5/9/62.

Cook, Hatch; 3/F; Captain, enlisted 5/9/62. Promoted to major 6/26/62. Later Major of 60th Alabama. Killed at White Oaks Road 3/31/65.

Cook, James; 3/F; Private, enrolled 6/12/62, Georgia. Teamster 7/1/63–8/15/63.

Cook, Turner H.; 3/B; Private, enlisted 4/7/62 at 20. Died 3/12/63.

Cooper, Benjamin; 3/F; Private, enrolled 5/9/62, Georgia. Substitute for Lafayett Mullin.

Cooper, William; 3/F; Private, enrolled 5/9/62. Discharged 10/6/62.

Cox, James B.; 3/B; Private, enlisted 4/7/62 at 21, Pike. Died 6/28/62.

Crawford, Charles A.; 3/B; Private, enlisted 6/10/62. Died 5/27/63 (typhoid pneumonia).

Crawford, John M.; 3/C; Private, enlisted 5/3/62 at 17, Coosa.

Crenshaw, D. C.; 3/D; Private, enlisted 5/2/62.

Crew, Elisha; 3/C; Private, enlisted 5/3/62 at 18, Coosa. Paroled at Appomattox.

Croswell, J.; 3/D; Private. Teamster 7/1/63–10/31/63.

Crow, William C.; 3/C; Private, enlisted at 34, Coosa. Replaced by substitute Frank Davis.

Daniel, John; 3/A; Private, enlisted 3/10/62 at 45, Montgomery. Died at home on furlough 6/14/62.

Daniels, James; 3/E; Private, enlisted 5/14/62 at 25, Pike.

Darby, Samuel T.; 3/E; Private, enlisted 5/14/62 at 25, Pike. Appointed sergeant 4/21/63.

Davis, A. J.; 3/F; Private, enrolled 5/9/62, Georgia. Died 7/14/62.

Davis, Frank; 3/C; Private, enlisted 5/3/62. Replaced William C. Crow as substitute.

Deese, Eli; 3/A; Private, enlisted 4/29/62. Died 6/16/62.

Dixon, John T.; 3/B; Private, enlisted 4/7/62 at 28, Pike.

Dixon, William; 3/E; Private, enlisted 5/14/62. Died 10/5/62.

Dodd, John; 3/F; Private, enrolled 6/12/62, Georgia. Extra duty as hospital steward.

Dodson, F. C.; 3/C; Private, enlisted 5/3/62 at 20, Coosa.

Douglass, James; 3/A; Private, 3/10/62 at 28, Montgomery. Detailed teamster 8/22/63.

Dozier, George W.; 3/E; Private, enlisted 7/3/62 at 27, Pike. Substituted for by Daniel McDonal 7/3/62.

Dozier, John P.; 3/C; Sergeant, enlisted 5/14/62 at 34, Pike. Selected sergeant 2/24/63.

Dudley, Andrew A.; 3/B; Private, enlisted 4/7/62 at 17, Pike.

Duncan, James M.; 3/B; Private, enlisted at 26, Pike. Captured at Chickamauga.

Duncan, Julius M.; 3/E; Private, enlisted 5/14/62 at 33, Pike. Detached service 9/1/62 to death 5/24/63.

Dunn, John T.; 3/B; Private, enlisted 4/7/62 at 23, Pike. Discharged due to disability 4/22/63.

Dupree, John; 3/F; Private, enlisted 5/9/62.

Eagerton, James C.; 3/B; Private. Killed at Bean's Station 12/14/63.

Edwards, Lemuel W.; 3/F; Private, enlisted 5/9/62.

Edwards, William F.; 3/E; Private, enlisted 5/9/62.

Ellis, Francis; 3/E; Sergeant, enlisted 7/3/62 at 20, Pike. Elected sergeant 12/14/62.

Ellison, John; 3/D; Private, enlisted 5/9/62. Died 11/9/62. Married.

Ellitt, James H.; 3/E; Private, enlisted 12/3/62.

Elmore, Levi; 3/A; Private, enlisted 3/10/62 at 30, Montgomery.

Emerson, Frank; 3/D; Private.

Enzor, Peyton; 3/D; Private, enlisted 5/9/62. Later sergeant.

Epperson, Jessie M.; 3/C; Private, enlisted 5/3/62 at 32, Coosa. Deserted at Chattanooga 11/13/62, tried 1/16/63, jailed, returned to company.

Evans, Hosea L.; 3/E; Private, enlisted 5/14/62. Killed at Chickamauga.

Evans, J. L.; 3/D; Private, enlisted 5/9/62.

Falconer, Joseph; 3/D; Private, enlisted at 21. Died 1/15/63 at New Market. Farmer.

Falkner, John; 3/D; Corporal.

Falkner, Joseph; 3/D; Private.

Fallin, Edward R.; 3/F; Private, enlisted 5/9/62, Georgia.

Faulk, Phillip; 3/F; Corporal, enlisted 7/3/62 at 29, Pike.

Fielder, Thomas; 3/E; Private, enlisted 7/3/62 at 28, Pike.

Flowers, Avinder; 3/B; Private, enlisted 4/7/62 at 34, Pike.

Flowers, Joseph; 3/B; Private, enlisted 4/7/62 at 19, Pike. Died 9/15/62.

Floyd, Benjamin F.; 3/F; Private, enlisted 5/9/62, Georgia.

Forbus, Thomas; 3/C; Private, enlisted 5/3/62. Captured at New Market 6/21/63.

Ford, B. H.; 3/C; Private, enlisted at 23 from Coosa.

Ford, Wiatt.; 3/C; Private, enlisted at 30, Coosa. Appointed sergeant 1/25/63.

Forniss, J.; 3/D; Private.

Foslers, T.; 3/C; Private, enlisted at 19, Coosa.

French, J. M.; 3/D; Private, enlisted 5/9/62. Died 8/7/64 in Chattanooga.

Fuller, Daniel M.; 3/B; Musician, enlisted 4/7/62 at 46, Pike. Died 4/23/63 of typhoid fever in Knoxville, Tennessee.

Fuller, Daniel W.; 3/D; Private.

Fuller, George R.; 3/F; Private, enrolled 5/9/62. Discharged due to disability.

Fuller, John B.; 3/D; Private, enlisted 1/10/63. Later sergeant. Paroled 4/9/65.

Fuller, John S.; 3/F; Private, enlisted 5/9/62. Suffered gunshot wound 8/10/62. Substitute for John Mullin.

Gafford (or Garrard), Benjamin; 3/F; Private, enlisted 5/9/62, Georgia. Died 1/27/63.

Garner, C. F.; 3/D; Private, enlisted 11/30/62.

Garrett, Thomas G.; 3/C; Private, enlisted 5/20/63.

Germany, John; 3/E; Corporal, enlisted 5/14/62 at 24, Pike.

Gholston, R.; 3/D; Private, enlisted 5/9/62.

Gibson; F.; 3/D; Private, enlisted 5/4/62. Discharged due to disability 12/7/62.

Gilmore, William; 3/A; Lieutenant, enlisted 3/10/62. Resigned 6/18/63 due to physical disability.

Golden, Benjamin R.; 3/B; Private, enlisted 4/7/62 at 29, Pike.

Goolsby, Wooten; 3/B; Private, enlisted 4/7/62 at 31, Pike.

Gordon, D.A.J.; 3/A; Private, later corporal.

Grace, Noel H.; 3/A; Private, enlisted 3/10/62.

Graham, G.; 3/C; Private, enlisted 11/8/62.

Graham, John T.; 3/C; Private, enlisted at 27, Coosa. Detailed as nurse at hospital in Knoxville, Tennessee.

Graham, Julius C.; 3/C; Private, enlisted 5/3/62 at 18, Coosa.

Graham, R. H.; 3/C; Private, enlisted 5/3/62 at 25, Coosa.

Granberry (or Granbery), M.Y.; 3/A; Corporal, enlisted 3/10/62 at 37, Montgomery. Later private.

Graves, James (Senior); 3/B; Private, enlisted 4/7/62, Pike.

Graves, James M.; 3/B; Private, enlisted at 16, Pike. Died 6/7/62.

Graves, Joseph; 3/B; Private, enlisted 4/7/62 at 23, Pike.

Graves, Newton; 3/B; Private, enlisted 4/7/62 at 21, Pike.

Graves, Richard; 3/F; Private, enlisted 5/9/62.

Gray, Thomas J.; 3/E; Private, enlisted 7/3/62 at 26, Pike. Extra duty as teamster.

Gray, Walter; 3/D; Private, enlisted 5/9/62. Killed at Bean's Station 12/14/63.

Greathouse, W. W.; 3/B; Private. Died in service.

Grice, Lemuel M.; 3/B; Private, enlisted 4/7/62 at 25, Pike.

Griffin, Joseph J.; 3/B; Private, enlisted 4/7/62 at 30, Pike.

Griggs, Maclamare; 3/B; Private, enlisted 4/7/62 at 27, Pike. Died 9/17/62.

Grimes, J. T. (Thomas E. Grimes on some lists); 3/C; Private, enlisted at 27, Coosa.

Grimes, J. T.; 3/C; Private, enlisted at 27, Coosa.

Grimes, Thomas E.; 3/C; Private, enlisted at 24.

Gunton, Noah; 3/B; Private, enlisted 7/2/62. Died 7/26/62.

Hacker, John; 3/E; Private, enlisted 9/26/62. Died 12/10/62.

Hales, William M.; 3/C; Corporal, enlisted 5/3/62, age at enlistment uncertain, could be 28 (or 33), Coosa.

Hall, Daniel; 3/B; Private, enlisted 4/7/62 at 28, Pike.

Hall, John A.; 3/B; Private, enlisted at 30, Pike.

Harbard, E.G.; 3/C; Private.

Hardin, William H.; 3/E; Private, enlisted 5/14/62, Pike. Died at home 2/23/63.

Harper, Erastus M.; 3/E; Private, enlisted 5/14/62. Captured at New Market 6/21/63.

Harris, Benjamin F.; 3/E; Sergeant, enlisted 5/14/62 at 22, Pike. Died 6/24/63.

Harris, Ezekiel B.; 3/E; Private.

Harris, George Henry; 3/E; Sergeant, enlisted 5/14/62. Deserted 6/18/63.

Harris, James W.; 3/E; Private, enlisted 5/14/62.

Harrison, John C.; 3/F; Private, enlisted 5/9/62, Georgia.

Hartley, Ellison; 3/A; Private, enlisted 3/10/62. Died 5/25/62.

Hartley, Isaac; 3/A; Private, enlisted 3/6/62, Montgomery. Detached as teamster 4/30/63, captured 1/10/64, sent to Camp Chase, Ohio 1/20/64, forwarded to Louisville, Kentucky 2/11/64 for exchange, back to Camp Chase 2/14/64, sent to Rock Island, Illinois 2/15/64.

Hartley, James; 3/A; Private, enlisted 3/10/62.

Harvel (or Harvil), C.; 3/D; Private.

Harvel, Samuel; 3/A; Private. Substituted for James M. Salter 1/19/63. Died 3/26/63.

Head, W.; 3/E; Captain, enlisted 7/3/62 at 35, Pike. Resigned 1/26/63.

Hearn, James; Private, enlisted 6/12/62. Detailed as teamster 8/28/63.

Heith, William A.; 3/B; Private, enlisted at 24, Pike. Died 11/26/62 at Knoxville, Tennessee.

Helton, John; 3/C; Private, enlisted 5/3/62 at 18, Coosa.

Helton, Robert; 3/F; Private, enlisted 8/1/63.

Hendrix, Nathan A.; 3/B; Private, enlisted at 24, Pike.

Hickman, Willis C.; 3/A; Private, enlisted 3/10/62.

Hicks, C.; 3/D; Private.

Hicks, Charles R.; 3/C; Sergeant, enlisted at 29, Coosa.

Hicks, Henry; 3/D; Private, enlisted 5/9/62. Died 7/8/62.

Hicks, J. D.; 3/D; Private.

Hicks, Nimrod J.; 3/C; Private, enlisted 5/3/62 at 22, Coosa. Deserted 7/28/62, apprehended 2/18/63, jailed.

Hicks, W.; 3/D; Private, enlisted 5/9/62.

Hinton, Richard; 3/F; Private, enlisted 8/1/63. Discharged 10/24/63.

Hix, Mason; 3/A; Sergeant, enlisted 3/25/62, Florida. Resigned as sergeant 7/23/62, remained as private. Served as guard at Libby Prison 9/1/63–10/31/63.

Hodge, Riley; 3/D; Private, enlisted 5/4/62.

Hodges, Coleman H.; 3/A; Private, enlisted 3/10/62. Died at Tazewell 9/7/62.

Hodges, Floyd; 3/A; Private, enlisted 8/11/62. Served as nurse at hospital 11/1/62–12/31/62.

Hodges, Foreman; 3/A; Private, enlisted 8/11/62.

Hodges, Jordan; 3/A; Private, enlisted 3/10/62.

Hodges, Joseph; 3/A; Private, enlisted 3/10/62, Montgomery. May have been wounded 4/3/65 (right arm), furloughed 4/8/65.

Hodges, Lemuel; 3/A; Private, enlisted 3/10/62 at 23. Killed at Drewry's Bluff 5/16/64.

Hodges, Reddin; 3/A; Private, enlisted 3/10/62.

Hodges, Thomas; 3/A; Private, enlisted 3/10/62.

Hodges, Wiley; 3/A; Private, enlisted 8/11/62.

Holland, Aaron K.; 3/A; Private, enlisted 4/26/62. Died 12/14/62.

Holland, George W.; 3/A; Private, enlisted 4/26/62. Served as teamster 7/63.

Holland, J.A.; 3/A; Private, enlisted 3/10/62 at 19.

Holt, Orrin J.; 3/F; Private, enlisted 5/9/62, Georgia.

Holton, John W.; 3/D; Private, enlisted 5/9/62. Died 7/22/62.

Holton, Thomas; 3/D; Private.

Hood, David R.; 3/F; Private, enlisted 5/9/62.

Hooks, William J.; 3/E; Private. Substituted R. T. Tate 6/14/62.

Howard, Edward; 3/A; Private. Exchanged for Jerry Thurmond 10/1/62.

Howard, William S.; 3/F; Sergeant, enrolled 5/9/62, Georgia.

Howell, John; 3/D; Private.

Hubard (or Hubbard), C. G. (or E. G.); 3/C; Private, enlisted at 32, Coosa.

Hudgins, Frank; 3/D; Private, enlisted 5/63.

Huffham. J.W.; 3/D; Private.

Huffman, D. Morgan; 3/D; Sergeant. Later lieutenant.

Huffman, Jacob H.; 3/D; Private.

Hughes, John E.; 3/A; Private, enlisted 3/10/62.

Hughs (or Hughes), Daniel; 3/C; Corporal, enlisted 5/3/62 at 31, Coosa.

Hughs, Eli D.; 3/B; Private, enlisted 4/7/62 at 27, Pike.

Hutcherson, Samuel; 3/C; Private, enlisted 7/27/62. Deserted 8/28/62.

Hutcherson, W. P.; 3/C; Private. Substituted for A. J. Taylor. Deserted, retaken 1863.

Hutto, Joseph; 3/A; Private, enlisted 3/10/62 at 24, Montgomery.

Hyman, Stephen C.; 3/E; Private, enlisted 7/3/62 at 28, Pike.

Ivey, Samuel; 3/E; Private, enlisted 7/3/62 at 25, Pike.

Jackson, A. J.; 3/D; Private, enlisted 5/9/62. Substitute for John R. Jackson.

Jackson, Benjamin; 3/D; Corporal.

Jackson, Ellis; 3/A; Private, enlisted 3/10/62 at 26. Detailed as teamster 7/1/63–10/31/63.

Jackson, Enoch; 3/C; Private, enlisted 5/3/62. Substituted for by his brother H. C. Jackson.

Jackson, H. C.; 3/C; Private, substituted for his brother Enoch Jackson.

Jackson, J. L.; 3/C; Private, enlisted 5/9/62.

Jackson, John R.; 3/D; Sergeant, enlisted 5/9/62.

Jackson, John W.; 3/A; Private, enlisted 3/31/62. Attached to hospital 12/1/62 as nurse.

Jackson, L.; 3/D; Private.

Jackson, Roderick Sheppard; 3/B; Private, enlisted 4/7/62 at 25, Pike. Listed sick, then as nurse at hospital 5/6/63–6/30/63. Later captured.

Jackson, Samuel; 3/A; Private, enlisted 3/31/62. Discharged at 49 years due to disability. Farmer.

Jackson, W. H.; 3/F; Private, enlisted 8/1/63.

Jacobs, J. F.; 3/C; Private, enlisted 5/3/62 at 20.

Jacobs, Moses; 3/C; Private, enlisted 5/3/62 at 20, Coosa.

James, A. S.; 3/Staff; Adjutant.

Jeffcoat, D. W.; 3/D; Private, enlisted 5/9/62.

Jernigan, John W.; 3/B; Private, enlisted 4/7/62 at 30, Pike. Appointed corporal 1/1/63.

Johnson, H. C.; 3/C; Private, enlisted 8/8/62.

Johnson (or Johnston), Isaac Spain; 3/C; Private, enlisted 5/3/62 at 20, Coosa. Farmer.

Johnson, Jesse; 3/F; Private, enlisted 5/9/62, Georgia. Taken as substitute for James Bennett.

Johnson, John; 3/A; Private, enlisted 4/21/62. Died 6/26/62.

Johnson, William H.; 3/B; Private, enlisted 4/7/62 at 35, Pike. Left sick at Cumberland Gap 8/9/63, later attached to hospital at La Grange, Ga.

Johnson, William W.; 3/B; Private, enlisted 4/7/62 at 23, Pike.

Jones, Amos; 3/D; Private, enlisted 5/9/62. Later sergeant.

Jones, H. B.; 3/C; Private, enlisted at 25, Coosa.

Jones, James; 3/A; Private, enlisted 3/10/62 at 20.

Jones, James; 3/D; Private.

Jones, Jarrett J.; 3/D; Private, enlisted 5/12/62.

Jones, John; 3/A; Private, enlisted 3/13/63.

Jones, Lewis; 3/D; Private, enlisted 9/1/62.

Jones, Thomas; 3/C; Private, enlisted 5/3/62 at 31, Coosa. Deserted 7/1/62.

Jones, Warren; 3/A; Private, enlisted 3/10/62 at 18.

Jones, William; 3/D; Private, enlisted 5/9/62.

Jones, Yell; 3/D; Private, enlisted 3/25/62. Died in Knoxville 4/12/63.

Jordan, Joseph; 3/D; Private, enlisted 5/9/62.

Kiley, Thomas J.; 3/F; Private, enlisted at 16. Single, farmer.

Kirkland, A.; 3/A; Private, enlisted 5/1/62. Detailed as teamster.

Kirkland, F. Marion; 3/A; Private, enlisted 3/10/62. Later corporal, Company E, 60th Alabama. Surrendered 4/9/65, paroled 4/10/65.

Kirkland, Henry; 3/A; Private, enlisted 3/10/62.

Kirkland, James L.; 3/E; Corporal, enlisted 5/14/62. Extra duty as nurse 5/22/63–7/1/63.

Kirkland, James M.; 3/A; Private, enlisted 3/10/62.

Kirkland, Micajah; 3/A; Private, enlisted 3/10/62 at 31. Killed at Chickamauga, voted to Roll of Honor.

Kirkland, Mason; 3/A; Private, enlisted 3/10/62 at 24. Died in hospital, Tazewell, 9/20/63.

Kirkland, William; 3/A; Private.

Kirkland, William Jasper; 3/A; Private, enlisted 3/10/62. Died at Bean's Station 1/3/64.

Knowles, George S.; 3/B; Private, enlisted 4/7/62 at 20, Pike.

Knowles, Green B.; 3/B; Private, enlisted at 53, Pike. Died 6/7/62.

Knowles, L. A.; 3/A; Private, enlisted 3/10/62 at 22.

Knowles, Patrick (or Patric) H.; 3/B; Private, enlisted 4/7/62 at 18, Pike.

Knowles, Thomas J.; 3/B; Private, enlisted 4/7/62 at 32, Pike.

Knowles, Samuel; 3/A; Elected lieutenant 3/5/62, commission ended 7/26/62 due to surgeon's certificate. Later lieutenant in 60th Alabama.

Knowles, William T.; 3/B; Private, enlisted 4/7/62 at 26, Pike. Extra duty as teamster 7/1/63–10/31/63.

Laborous (also Labourous), Joseph A.; 3/A; Private, enlisted 3/10/62.

Lane, W. A. M.; 3/D; Private, enlisted 5/9/62. Died in service.

Laney, Miner; 3/E; Private, enlisted 5/14/62. Died 1/5/63.

Lanton, Edmund; 3/A; Private, enlisted 3/10/62 at 18, Montgomery.

Lanton, Theophilus; 3/A; Private, enlisted 4/8/63.

Lanton, Thomas; 3/A; Private, enlisted 3/10/62 at 16.

Lawrence, Crawford B.; 3/B; Private, enlisted 4/7/62 at 18, Pike. Captured, later exchanged.

Lawrence, J. A.; 3/D; Private, enlisted 5/9/62. Died 3/28/63 (diarrhea).

Lawrence, Marshall T.; 3/B; Sergeant, enlisted at 21, Pike.

Layfield, Levin; 3/F; Private, enlisted 6/12/62, Georgia. Substitute for S. Rothschild. Died 10/24/63.

Leak, W. C.; 3/D; Private, 5/9/62. Died 11/20/62.

Leddon, Alfred M.; 3/B; Private, enlisted 4/7/62 at 30, Pike. Died 3/8/63 in Knoxville, Tennessee.

Lee, John H. (or J. A.); 3/C; Private, enlisted at 22, Coosa.

Lee, Thomas; 3/C; Private, enlisted 3/6/63.

Lennard, John B. 3/C; Lieutenant, enlisted 5/3/62 at 28, Coosa. Detached as provost marshal a Cumberland Gap 7/12/63.

Leplie, R. A.; 3/C; Private.

Leslie, George W.; 3/F; Corporal, enlisted 5/9/62, Georgia.

Leslie, John J.; 3/F; Private, enlisted 5/9/62, Georgia. Detailed as a hospital nurse for three months. Died 1/8/64.

Leslie (also Lesslie), Robert A.; 3/C; Private, enlisted at 31, Coosa.

Leslie, William M.; 3/F; Private, enlisted 5/9/62, Georgia.

Leslie, William N.; 3/F; Private, enlisted 5/9/62, Georgia. Became battalion color guard in summer 1863.

Lewis, A. J. (or A. S.); 3/D; Private, enlisted 5/9/62.

Lewis, Henry R.; 3/E; Private, enlisted 5/14/62. Roll of Honor at Chickamauga.

Lewis, James F.; 3/F; Private, enlisted 5/9/62, Georgia. Transferred to Company C, 9th Georgi Battalion, 7/1/62.

Lide, Carney W.; 3/D; Private, enlisted 5/9/62.

Lindsey (or Lidsy), J. W.; 3/C; Private, enlisted 5/3/62 at 18, Coosa.

Linsey, Thomas J.; 3/B; Private, enlisted 7/1/62 at 17, Montgomery. Served as teamster 11/25/62–6/20/63, returned to company.

Linton, Aaron E.; 3/E; Private, enlisted 5/14/62. Detailed as nurse 3/3/63.

Lisenby, A. L.J.; 3/A; Private, enlisted 4/21/62. Sent to hospital at Loudon, Tennessee 11/14/62. Detailed as nurse and wood chopper 6/4/62.

Lisenby, John H.; 3/A; Private, enlisted 4/21/62. Sent to hospital at Knoxville, Tennessee 11/62, died ½.62 (laryngitis, severe respiratory infection).

Little, James A.; 3/C; Private, enlisted 5/3/62 at 19, Coosa.

Little, John W.; 3/C; Private, enlisted at 21, Coosa. Died 10/10/62.

Liveoak, James J.; 3/C; Private, enlisted 5/3/62 at 26, Coosa. Captured in Lexington, Kentucky hospital 10/17/62, died 11/19/62.

Liveoak, William; 3/C; Private, enlisted 5/3/62 at 28. Died 6/3/62.

Livings, John L.; 3/E; Private, enlisted 5/14/62 at 21, Pike. Died 7/8/62.

Livings, Thomas S.; 3/E; Private, enlisted 5/14/62 at 24. Deserted 11/21/64, took Oath of Allegiance 11/25/64.

Livingston, Joseph R.; 3/B; Private, enlisted 9/1/62, Tennessee. Died 4/24/63 Knoxville, Tennessee.

Locke, Elias H.; 3/B; Private, enlisted 4/7/62 at 18, Pike. Detached to guard prisoners on way to Vicksburg, Mississippi 1/63–2/63, detached guard detail 3/25/63.

Lockhart, Robert B.; 3/F; Lieutenant. Promoted to captain 6/25/62. Detached to Commissary Department 3/12/63. Promoted to commandant of post at Morristown, Tennessee 8/4/63 by Major General Buckner.

Lominack, George, 3/A; Private, enlisted 3/10/62.

Long, Benjamin; 3/F; Private, enlisted 5/9/62.

Long, Benjamin Franklin; 3/C (or D); Private, enlisted 1/10/62. Wounded at Drewry's Bluff, discharged 4/9/65.

Long, James B.; 3/E; Private, enlisted 5/14/62 at 32, Pike.

Long, John H. D.; 3/E; Private, enlisted 5/14/62. Appointed sergeant 12/62. Killed at Chickamauga.

Luckie, J. B.; Staff; Surgeon.

Lumpkin, John W.; 3/E; Private, enlisted 5/14/62 at 32, Pike. Died 9/24/62.

Lyon, George W.; 3/F; Private, enlisted 5/9/62, Georgia.

Lynn, William B.; 3/F; Private, enlisted 5/9/62, Georgia.

Madden, D.; 3/A; Private, enlisted 3/10/62. Promoted to lieutenant 8/26/62.

Maddox, James H.; 3/B; Private, enlisted 4/7/62. Extra duty as hospital attendant.

Maddox, John B.; 3/B; Private, enlisted 4/7/62.

Mahoney, Charles A.; 3/B; Private, enlisted 4/7/62 at 25, Pike.

Mahoney, Daniel A.; 3/B; Private, enlisted at 27, Pike.

Malloy, Charles Shockley; 3/D; Lieutenant, 5/9/62. Became adjutant, granted leave of absence due to extreme emaciation due to typhoid pneumonia 12/15/63. Discharged 4/9/65.

Malloy, William; 3/D; Private. Later sergeant.

Mansell, D. M.; 3/D; Private.

Market, Stephen; 3/A; Private, enlisted 3/10/62 at 28. Promoted to sergeant 7/7/62.

Marrow, Thomas A.; 3/B; Private, enlisted 4/7/62 at 30, Pike.

Martin, Benjamin F.; 3/B; Private, enlisted 4/7/62 at 18, Pike.

Martin, Edward Y.; 3/B; Private, enlisted 4/7/62 at 25, Pike.

Martin, James M.; 3/C; Private, enlisted 5/3/62 at 26, Coosa. Died in service.

Martin, James; 3/B; Private, enlisted 8/4/63.

Martin, Washington L.; 3/B; Corporal, enlisted 4/7/62 at 28, Pike. Later sergeant, then reduced to private.

Matheson, Alexander; 3/A; Private, enlisted 3/16/62.

Mathews, George; 3/A; Private, enlisted 3/10/62 at 20. Died 6/6/62.

Maull, James; 3/F; Private, enlisted 5/9/62 at 27, Georgia. Married, farmer.

Maull, John; 3/F; Private, enlisted 10/10/62, Georgia. Died or was discharged, date uncertain. Co. D Muster for 60th Alabama shows discharge 11/10/63. Muster cards show both death and discharge 4/1/64.

May, Allen C.; 3/E; Private, enlisted 5/14/62 at 32, Pike.

McBrier, G. L.; 3/C; Private, enlisted at 32, Coosa.

McCarty, Nathan; 3/A; Private, enlisted 3/10/62 at 22, Montgomery.

McCloud, John; 3/C; Private, enlisted 5/3/62 at 26. Special detail 6/63–8/63.

McRiry (or McCrary), Aurelius B.; 3/E; Private.

McCreless, John; 3/E; Lieutenant, enlisted 5/14/62. Promoted to captain 2/28/63.

McDonal, Daniel; 3/E; Private, enlisted 6/28/62 at 17. Substituted for George W. Dozier 7/3/62. Single, farmer.

McEachin (or McEchin), Peter; 3/D; Captain, enlisted 5/9/62.

McKalister (or McAlister), D. L.; 3/C; Sergeant, enlisted at 23, Coosa.

McKnoir, D. B.; 3/C; Private, enlisted at 19, Coosa.

McLendon, Isaac; 3/B; Private, enlisted at 28, Pike.

McLendon, Zacariah G.; 3/B; Private, enlisted at 30, Pike.

McLeod, James; 3/E; Private, enlisted 5/14/62 at 29, Pike. Died 8/12/62.

McLoud, John; 3/C; Private, enlisted at 26.

McMichael, John C.; 3/B; Private, enlisted 4/7/62 at 35, Pike.

McNair, W. B.; 3/C; Private, enlisted 5/3/62.

McNeel, Ira; 3/B; Private.

Merideth (or Meredith), Hillman; 3/E; Private, enlisted 7/3/62 at 38, Pike.

Merritt, Julius C.; 3/B; Private, enlisted 4/7/62 at 19, Pike.

Messer, Miles P.; 3/C; Private.

Miller, John H.; 3/D; Private, enlisted 5/9/62. Died 2/8/63.

Miller, William; 3/A; Private, enlisted 3/10/62 at 46.

Mills, James E.; 3/A; Private, enlisted 3/10/62 at 22, Montgomery. Died 4/9/62.

Mills, Josiah B.; 3/A; Private, enlisted 3/11/62.

Mills, William Wright; 3/A; Private, enlisted 3/10/62.

Monk, William R.; 3/A; Private, enlisted 3/10/62. Captured at Petersburg 1/65, took Oath of Allegiance.

Moody, T.; 3/D; Private, enlisted 6/27/62.

Moore, James W.; 3/E; Private, enlisted at 25, Pike. Died 9/6/62.

Moore, Joseph J.; 3/B; Private, enlisted at 36, Pike.

Morgan, J. E. A.; 3/C; Private.

Morris, Isaac; 3/A; Private, enlisted 3/10/62.

Morris, James; 3/A; Private, enlisted 3/10/62 at 20. Died 6/6/62.

Mullin, Harrison H.; 3/F; Sergeant, enlisted 5/9/62, Georgia. Elected lieutenant 7/25/62.

Mullin, James M.; 3/F; Private, enlisted at 30. Discharged 12/1/62. Married, farmer.

Murray, James W.; 3/D; Private. Died 1/1/64.

Nelson, James T.; 3/C; Private, enlisted at 29, Coosa.

Newberry, James P.; 3/C; Private, enlisted 5/9/62 at 27 (or 22).

Newberry, William; 3/F; Private, enlisted 5/9/62 at 17. Discharged 10/3/62.

Newman, Henry J.; 3/C; Private, enlisted 5/3/62 at 17.

Niblet, Burns; 3/F; Private, enlisted at 26. Deserted 5/9/62. Married, farmer.

Niblet, Walker; 3/F; Private, enlisted 5/9/62 at 26. Deserted 6/18/62. Married, farmer.

Niblet, William F.; 3/D; Private, enlisted 5/9/62.

Nichols, Jefferson; 3/A; Private, enlisted 3/18/62. Promoted to corporal 8/26/62.

Nichols, John; 3/A; Private, enlisted 4/21/62. Discharged 10/2/62.

Nolen, Abner A.; 3/C; Private, enlisted 5/3/62 at 24, Coosa.

Nolen, H. H.; 3/C; Private.

Nolen, Isaac A.; 3.C; Private, enlisted at 19, Coosa. Discharged 8/10/62.

Nolen, Richard S.; 3/C; Private, enlisted 5/3/62 at 26, Coosa.

Norden, Able B.; 3/E; Private, enlisted 5/14/62.

Norden, Martin J.; 3/E; Private, enlisted 9/13/62.

North, Richard T.; 3/E; Private, enlisted 7/3/62 at 33, Pike. May have been discharged, shown as suffering extreme emaciation with articular rheumatism, winter 1863.

Odom, John; 3/F; Private, enlisted 5/9/62 at 24, Georgia. Appointed sergeant 7/25/62. Single, farmer.

Odom, William; 3/F; Private, enlisted 7/13/62 at 22. Transferred from Company C, 9th Battalion, Georgia Volunteers. Married, farmer.

Ogletree, John; 3/C; Private, enlisted 5/14/62 at 28, Coosa. Detached as teamster 9/1/63–10/31/63.

Ogletree, Joshua P.; 3/B; Private, enlisted 4/7/62 at 29, Pike. Teamster from 8/1/62.

Oliver, J. C.; 3/C; Private, enlisted 8/26/62.

Oliver, William G.; 3/F; Private, enlisted 6/10/62 at 28. Wounded at Chickamauga, deserted 12/22/63. Single, farmer.

Osborn, George C.; 3/F; Sergeant, enlisted 5/9/62, Georgia.

Osborn (or Osburn), Hiram P.; 3/E; Private, enlisted 5/14/62 at 31, Pike. Died 5/9/63 (pneumonia).

Outler, John A.; 3/E; Private, enlisted 9/13/62.

Owen, George F.; 3/F; Private, enlisted 5/9/62 at 30, Georgia. Deserted 9/16/62.

Owen, Henry M.; 3/F; Private, enlisted at 30, Georgia. Deserted 9/16/62.

Owens, Edward B.; 3/B; Private, enlisted 4/7/62 at 18, Pike. Detached as teamster 4/30/63, later returned to company.

Owens, James W.; 3/B; Private, enlisted 2/25/63.

Owens, Samuel A.; 3/B; Private, enlisted 4/7/62 at 20, Pike.

Owens, William T.; 3/B; Sergeant, enlisted at 21, Pike.

Palmer, Robert A.; 3/C; Sergeant, enlisted 5/3/62 at 36, Coosa. Deserted 11/25/62 at Chattanooga, apprehended 1/16/63, reduced to private 1/23/63, pay deducted, returned to company.

Parks Jr., Eli; 3/B; Musician, enlisted at 28, Pike.

Parrish, Joseph; 3/E; Private, enlisted 5/14/62, Pike.

Patrick, James J.; 3/F; Private, enlisted at 18. Single, farmer.

Patrick, James W.; 3/F; Sergeant, enlisted 5/9/62, Georgia.

Patrick, John; 3/F; Private, enlisted at 20. Single, farmer.

Patrick, William A.; 3/F; Private, enlisted 5/9/62 at 22. Severely wounded at Drewry's Bluff. Single, farmer.

Patrick, William D.; 3/F; Private, enlisted 6/12/62 at 18. Single, farmer.

Patridge, Isaih (or Isaiah); 3/A; Private, enlisted 5/8/62.

Patterson, James W.; 3/C; Private, enlisted at 26, Coosa. Captured 6/21/63.

Paul, George W.; 3/B; Private, enlisted 4/7/62 at 21, Pike.

Paul, John R.; 3/B; Private, enlisted 4/7/62 at 27. Died 11/6/62.

Pepper, John W.; 3/F; Private, enlisted at 17. Substitute for I. L. McGirigh, wounded at Chickamauga. Single, farmer.

Perry, John; 3/A; Captain, enlisted 3/10/65.

Phillips, Martin; 3/C; Private. Died 8/22/63 (pneumonia).

Pierce, Edward W.; 3/B; Private, enlisted at 23, Pike.

Pierce, John W.; 3/B; Private, enlisted 4/7/62 at 23, Pike.

Pierson, Seabourn; 3/D; Sergeant, enlisted 3/25/62.

Pippen, R.; 3/A; Sergeant, enlisted 3/25/62. Promoted to lieutenant 7/5/62.

Pippen, William B.; 3/A; Private, enlisted 9/11/62.

Pitts, L. B.; 3/A; Private.

Pitts, Noel; 3/E; Private, enlisted 5/14/62 at 25, Pike.

Poner (or Powers), Morris C.; 3/C; Corporal, enlisted at 21, Coosa.

Power, James F.; 3/C; Private, enlisted 5/3/62 at 32.

Pritchett, Elmore; 3/D; Private, enlisted 5/9/62.

Pritchett, James; 3/E; Corporal, enlisted 5/14/62. Killed at Bean's Station.

Pritchett, Richard; 3/D; Private, enlisted 7/12/62.

Pryor (Pryer), Philip W.; 3/F; Private, enlisted 6/12/62 at 18. Single, farmer.

Pugh, Alexander M.; 3/D; Private, enlisted 5/9/62.

Pugh, Jesse; 3/D; Private, enlisted 5/17/62. Died 9/6/62.

Purvis, Vinson E.; 3/B; Private, enlisted 1/16/63. Deserted 5/20/63.

Quillin, Elisha; 3/D; Private, enlisted 2/9/63.

Radford, Arnold S.; 3/B; Private, enlisted 9/1/62, Tennessee.

Radford, William J.; 3/B; Private, enlisted at 34, Montgomery.

Raley, Irwin; 3/B; Private, enlisted 4/7/62 at 19, Pike. Died 6/7/62.

Raley, J. W.; 3/D; Private, enlisted 5/9/62.

Rayfield, John W.; 3/C; Corporal, enlisted 5/3/62 at 30, Coosa. Listed with Provost Guard at La Grange, Georgia, 12/31/63.

Reeves, Francis; 3/E; Private, enlisted 5/14/62. Died 4/20/63.

Reeves, James L.; 3/E; Private, enlisted 5/14/62. Died 6/9/63.

Reeves, Joseph; 3/E; Private, enlisted 4/5/62.

Reffin, Henry J.; 3/F; Private, enlisted at 17. Single, farmer.

Revel, Alfred; 3/D; Private, enlisted 5/9/62.

Revel (or Revels), Steven (or Stephen); 3/E; Private, enlisted 5/14/62. Died 12/16/62.

Richardson, Robert J.; 3/C; Private, enlisted 5/3/62 at 19, Coosa. Brother is William D. Richardson of same company.

Richardson, William D.; 3/C; Private, enlisted 5/3/62 at 21, Coosa. Brother is Robert J. Richardson of same company.

Ridley, Robert; 3/B; Private, enlisted at 45, Pike. Discharged due to disability 8/63.

Riley, Thomas L.; 3/F; Private, enlisted 5/9/62. Died 11/25/62.

Ritch, Andrew; 3/E; Private, enlisted 5/14/62.

Rob, John A.; 3/B; Private, enlisted at 24, Pike.

Robbins, Edward; 3/D; Private, enlisted 5/9/62.

Robbins, George W.; 3/C; Private, enlisted 5/3/62 at 26, Coosa. Discharged due to disability. Farmer.

Robbins, Jethro; 3/D; Corporal, enlisted 5/9/62.

Robbins, L.; 3/D; Private, enlisted 1/24/63.

Robbins, Thomas C.; 3/C; Private, enlisted 5/3/62 at 29, Coosa. Died at Knoxville, Tennessee 3/2/63.

Roberson (or Robinson), John A.; 3/C; Private, enlisted at 21.

Roberson, James; 3/C; Private, enlisted at 28, Coosa.

Roberson, Jones; 3/C; Private, enlisted 4/5/62. Deserted 7/12/62.

Roberts, John; 3/C; Private, enlisted 5/3/62 at 19, Coosa. Died 10/20/62.

Roberts, William; 3/C; Lieutenant, enlisted 5/3/62 at 27.

Robinson, J. A.; 3/C; Private.

Robinson, James T.; 3/C; Private, enlisted 5/3/62, Coosa. Furnished Minyard Yarbrough as substitute 4/14/63.

Rodgers, Thomas A.; 3/B; Sergeant, enlisted in Company G, 1st Alabama 2/13/61, reenlisted 1/16/62 and transferred to Legion 4/25/62.

Rodgers, Thomas O.; 3/D; Private, enlisted 5/9/62. Died 6/20/62.

Rogers, Thomas; 3/F; Private, enlisted 5/9/62, Georgia. Substitute for Sowell Woolfolk.

Ronie, Solomon; 3/A; Private, enlisted 3/10/62 at 21.

Ronie, William; 3/A; Private, enlisted 3/10/62. Died 4/27/62.

Ross, John A.; 3/B; Private, enlisted 4/17/62 at 24, Pike. Transferred to 1st Battalion, Company G 7/31/63. Wounded at Chickamauga.

Rotton, David C.; 3/E; Private, enlisted 5/14/62 at 29, Pike.

Ruffin, H. J.; 3/F; Private, enlisted 6/10/62. Detached as commissary guard 4/27/63.

Rushing, S. J.; 3/D; Private, enlisted 7/7/62.

Rushing, T. A.; 3/D; Private, enlisted 6/27/62.

Rushing, Thomas J.; 3/D; Lieutenant, enlisted 5/9/62. Resigned 10/29/62.

Rushton, James C.; 3/E; Private, enlisted 5/14/62 at 31, Pike.

Rushton, Moses; 3/D; Private, enlisted 5/9/62. Killed at Bean's Station.

Rowden, Jacob; 3/B; Corporal.

Salter, Columbus C.; 3/C; Private, enlisted 5/3/62 at 20, Coosa.

Salter, Enoch P.; 3/E; Sergeant, enlisted 5/14/62 at 31, Pike. Discharged by substitute 3/2/63.

Salter, J. G.; 3/C; Private, enlisted 1/18/63.

Salter, James M.; 3/E; Sergeant, enlisted 5/14/62 at 35, Pike. Discharged by substitute 1/19/63.

Salter, Robert Y.; 3/C; Private, enlisted 5/3/62 at 26, Coosa.

Sanders, James; 3/A; Private, enlisted 3/10/62 at 28. Died 6/6/62.

Sanders, James R.; 3/E; Private, enlisted 5/14/62.

Sanders, John; 3/A; Private, enlisted 3/10/62 at 26.

Sanders, John A.; 3/B; Private, enlisted 7/1/62 at 20, Montgomery.

Sanders, Joseph; 3/A; Private, enlisted 3/10/62 at 16. Discharged 4/10/63.

Sanders, William T.; 3/B; Private, enlisted 7/1/62 at 18, Montgomery.

Sanford, J. W. A.; Staff; Lieutenant Colonel, transferred from Third Alabama Infantry as captain, elected lieutenant colonel 3/25/62. Promoted to colonel of 60th Alabama Infantry 11/25/63.

Scaife, Jesse F.; 3/F; Private, enlisted 5/9/62 at 27. Promoted to sergeant 4/1/64. Single, lawyer.

Schley, William; 3/F; Private, enlisted 5/9/62 at 23. Single.

Scoggins, John; 3/D; Private, enlisted 5/9/62.

Scott, Thomas S.; 3/A; Private, enlisted 3/31/62.

Scroggin, J. B.; 3/F; Private.

Sharp, Josephus; 3/D; Corporal, enlisted 5/9/62.

Shaver, H. A.; 3/D; Private.

Shelly, Malachi P.; 3/A; Private, enlisted 3/13/63.

Shelly, Mark; 3/A; Private, enlisted 3/10/62 at 26, Montgomery.

Shelly, Jr., Reubin; 3/A; Private, enlisted 3/10/62 at 25, Montgomery. Discharged by surgeon's certificate of disability 8/18/62.

Shelton, Andrew J.; 3/C; Private, enlisted at 26, Coosa.

Sheppard, George; 3/A; Private (Fifer), enlisted 3/10/62 at 40, Montgomery.

Sheppard, John F.; 3/A; Private, enlisted 4/22/62.

Sheppard, Lewis; 3/A; Private, enlisted 3/10/62 at 23.

Shirah, James M.; 3/F; Private, enlisted 5/9/62, Georgia.

Shirah, Viles M.; 3/F; Private, enlisted at 24. Killed 12/21/64 at Petersburg. Married, farmer.

Shirley, James K.; 3/E; Private, enlisted 5/14/62, Pike. Appears to be brother of Sidney A. Shirley.

Shirley, Sidney A.; 3/E; Private, enlisted 5/14/62, Pike. Appears to be brother of James K. Shirley.

Sholar, Edward (or Edmund); 3/A; Private, enlisted 3/10/62 at 22, Montgomery.

Shropshire, George; 3/C; Private, enlisted 1/18/63.

Shurley, William E.; 3/F; Private, enlisted

at 20, Georgia. Wounded at Chickamauga. Single, farmer.

Simmons, Austin S.; 3/B; Lieutenant, enlisted at 25, Pike.

Simmons, Benjamin J.; 3/F; Private, enlisted 5/9/62 at 25, Georgia. Died
11/24/63 of disease. Single, farmer.

Simmons, Eugene N.; 3/F; Corporal, enlisted 5/9/62, Georgia.

Simmons, Frank; 3/G; Private, enlisted
7/3/62 at 26, Montgomery.

Simmons, Harrison M.; 3/F; Private, enlisted 5/9/62 at 22. Single, farmer.

Simmons, Jasper P.; 3/F; Private, enlisted
5/9/62 at 21, Georgia. Killed at Petersburg 7/30/64. Single, farmer.

Skean, William H.; 3/A; Private, enlisted
3/10/62 at 18, Montgomery. Died
5/11/62.

Skinner, Jonathan L.; 3/E; Private, enlisted 5/14/62 at 25, Pike. Deserted
6/18/63, returned 7/28/63.

Smart, C. R.; 3/D; Private. Substituted for
by John Walter.

Smart, Frank; 3/D; Private.

Smart, Henry; 3/D; Private, enlisted
5/9/62. Detailed as teamster.

Smith, Bednego; 3/F; Private, enlisted
5/9/62 at 19, Georgia. Deserted
12/22/63, rejoined 8/10/64.

Smith, Henry B.; 3/B; Private, enlisted
4/7/62 at 34, Pike.

Smith, J.; 3/E; Private.

Smith, James; 3/B; Private.

Smith, Jesse B.; 3/C; Private, enlisted
5/3/62 at 23. Died 10/25/62.

Smith, John A.; 3/B; Private, enlisted
4/7/62 at 23, Pike. Detached to guard
duty 3/1/63.

Smith, John A.; 3/C; Private, enlisted
5/3/62 at 21, Coosa.

Smith, Marion G.; 3/C; Private, enlisted
5/3/62 at 20, Coosa.

Smith, Thomas H.; 3/C; Captain, appointed 5/3/62 at 27, Coosa.

Smith, William R.; 3/B; Private, enlisted
12/1/62. Died 1/29/63.

Smothers, William; 3/A; Private, enlisted
3/16/62 at 19. Died 6/27/62.

Smothers, Wilson B.; 3/A; Private, enlisted 3/10/62 at 21.

Snelgrove, William; 3/A; Private, enlisted
3/10/62 at 23. Discharged by surgeon's
certificate 8/10/62. Farmer.

Snow, John M.; 3/F; Private, enlisted
5/9/62 at 26, Georgia. Died 11/15/62.
Married, farmer.

Spirey (or Spiry), Josiah S.; 3/C; Private,
enlisted 5/3/62 at 22.

Spivy, R. D.; 3/C; Private, enlisted 5/3/62.

Standenmire, Hilliard G.; 3/C; Private,
enlisted 5/3/62 at 24.

Stewart, Hiram A.; 3/C; Private, enlisted
5/3/62 at 20.

Stewart, John A.; 3/E; Private, enlisted
5/14/62 at 23. Attached to hospital
after sick furlough, returned to company 8/25/63. Married, farmer.

Stilwell, George; 3/F; Private, enlisted
5/9/62 at 18. Single, farmer.

Stilwell, Jacob B.; 3/F; Private, enlisted at
34. Wounded at Bean's Station. Married, farmer.

Stilwell, John; 3/F; Private, enlisted
5/9/62.

Stokes, James; 3/A; Lieutenant, enlisted
3/10/62 at 32, Montgomery. Promoted
to captain 7/30/62.

Stokes, John W.; 3/A; Musician, enlisted
3/10/62 at 18. Also shown as private.

Strickland, Sampson B.; 3/B; Private, enlisted 12/1/62. Detached as teamster.

Strupper, Thomas J.; 3/F; Private, enlisted
6/12/62 at 17, Georgia. Deserted to
enemy 9/14/62. Single, student.

Sullivan, Daniel; 3/D; Private, enlisted
5/9/62. Detached as teamster.

Summerford, H. W. (or W. H.); 3/A; Private, enlisted 3/10/62 at 26.

Sweat, W.; 3/D; Private, enlisted 5/9/62.
Died 11/20/62.

Tally, George W.; 3/A: Private, enlisted
3/10/62 at 25, Montgomery. Brother of
James F. Tally, son of John Tally.

Tally, James F.; 3/A; Private, enlisted
3/10/62 at 18. Brother of George W.
Tally, son of John Tally.

Tally, John; 3/A; Private, enlisted 3/10/62
at 48, Montgomery. Discharged 12/8/62.
Carpenter. Father of James F. Tally,
George W. Tally.

Taquino, Alexander A.; 3/F; Private, enlisted 11/1/63 (24 days later, Company D, 60th Alabama Regiment), Georgia. Deserted 11/20/64.

Tanton, Charles; 3/B; Private, enlisted at 18, Pike.

Tate, R. T.; 3/E; Private, substituted for William J. Tate 6/14/62.

Tatom, Ithamar; 3/B; Private, enlisted at 26, Pike. Killed at Bean's Station 12/14/63.

Taylor, A. J.; 3/C; Private, enlisted 5/14/62 at 19, Coosa. Substituted Samuel Hutcheson and deserted 8/18/62.

Taylor, Calhoun C.; 3/B; Private, enlisted at 23, Pike. Died 12/1/62 in Atlanta.

Taylor, David; 3/A; Private, enlisted 6/9/62.

Taylor, Fredrick; 3/A; Private, enlisted 6/9/62.

Taylor, Hails; 3/; Private (original enlistment), enlisted 4/26/61 Company F, 3rd Regiment, Alabama Infantry but refused to be mustered in. Enlisted 3/7/62 at 22 in Goldthwaite's Battery, Alabama Light Artillery and transferred to 3rd Battalion, Hilliard's Legion 4/27/63 as sergeant major. Wounded at Murfreesboro (thigh) 12/31/62 (while serving with Goldthwaite's Battery).

Taylor, Henry L.; 3/A; Sergeant, enlisted 3/10/62 at 19.

Taylor, Seaborn; 3/A; Private, enlisted 3/10/62 at 20, Montgomery. Guard at Libby Prison 9/1/63–10/31/63, wounded at Petersburg 1/13/65. Lived 7/10/1842–6/1/1928.

Terrell, James A.; 3/C; Sergeant, enlisted 5/3/62 at 30. Died 6/10/62.

Thomas, Ezeriah N.; 3/C; Private, enlisted 5/3/62 at 26, Coosa.

Thomas, Micajah C.; 3/C; Private, enlisted 5/3/62 at 27.

Thomas, N. H.; 3/C; Private, enlisted 10/24/62.

Thomas, William; 3/C; Private. Substituted for G. W. Walker 10/24/62, listed as deserter 11/23/62 but was discharged due to disability 7/27/63.

Thompson, James W.; 3/C; Sergeant, enlisted 5/3/62 at 34, Coosa. On detached service 1/63–2/63.

Thompson, James S.; 3/E; Private, enlisted 9/13/62.

Thompson, P. F.; 3/A; Lieutenant, enlisted 3/10/62 at 47. Died 6/26/62.

Thompson, William L.; 3/C; Lieutenant, enlisted 5/3/62 at 28 (also listed at 33), Coosa.

Thorington, W. H.; 3/C; Private, enlisted 5/14/62 at 21, Coosa. Captured 6/21/63 at New Market.

Thrower, Miles; 3/B; Private, enlisted 4/7/62 at 27, Pike. Died 6/12/62.

Thurman, Emanuel; 3/A; Private, enlisted 3/10/62 at 19, Montgomery. Died 5/17/63. Appears to be brother of William H. H. Thurman.

Thurman, Jeremiah; 3/A; Private, enlisted 8/22/62. Substitute in place of Thomas Jones.

Thurman, William H. H.; 3/A; Private, enlisted 3/10/62 at 21. Appears to be brother of Emanuel Thurman.

Thweatt, Thacker; 3/F; Private, enlisted 5/9/62 at 30. Discharged 10/27/62. Single, clerk.

Tiller, Benjamin S. L.; 3/A; Private, enlisted 3/10/62 at 20. Promoted to corporal 8/22/62.

Tiller, H. F.; 3/A; Musician, enlisted 4/21/62. Promoted to sergeant 7/25/62.

Tiller, James M.; 3/A; Corporal, enlisted 3/10/62 at 20. Later private.

Tiller, Thomas E. H.; 3/A; Private, enlisted 3/10/62 at 21. Killed at Bean's Station.

Timmons, Jesse L.; 3/D; Private, enlisted 5/9/62.

Timmons, Moses; 3/D; Private. Died 8/7/62.

Tomma (also shown as Tomme), Van B. (or Martin V. B.); 3/B; Private, enlisted 4/7/62 at 22, Pike. Died 6/12/62. Married.

Towler, William W.; 3/F; Private, enlisted 6/12/62 at 28, Georgia. Wounded at Drewry's Bluff.

Townsend, John H.; 3/C; Private, enlisted 5/3/62 at age uncertain, may have been 21 or 19, Coosa. Died 11/28/62 at Loudon, Tennessee.

Tracy (or Trace), Jean (or John) N.; 3/F;

Private, enlisted 5/9/62 at 29, Georgia. Laborer.

Trawick, Robert E.; 3/F; Private, enlisted 3/10/62 at 22. Died 9/13/62.

Truitt, William P.; 3/F; Private, enlisted 6/10/62.

Turner, Amos J.; 3/E; Private, enlisted 5/14/62 at 21, Pike.

Turner, Joseph R.; 3/A; Private, enlisted 3/10/62 at 24.

Turner, Thomas T.; 3/E; Private, enlisted 5/14/62 at 18, Pike. Died 1/21/63.

Underwood, R. R.; 3/D; Private, enlisted 5/9/62. Discharged 6/22/62.

Vardeman, James M.; 3/C; Private, enlisted 5/2/62 in 5/C, transferred to 3/C on 2/1/63.

Verstille, Henry W.; 3/F; Private, enlisted 12/1/62 at 35. Married, lawyer.

Wade, Charles R.; 3/F; Private, enlisted 10/10/62 at 30. Single, farmer.

Walker, G. W.; 3/C; Private, enlisted 5/14/62 at 28, Coosa. Substituted William Thomas 10/24/62, listed as deserter 11/23/62 but was discharged due to disability 7/27/63.

Walker, John W.; 3/B; Private, enlisted 4/7/62 at 30.

Wall, John W.; 3/D; Private, enlisted 5/9/62 at 30, Pike. Promoted to quartermaster sergeant 1/25/63.

Waller, James S.; 3/A; Sergeant, enlisted 3/15/62 at 25. Wounded at Chickamauga, discharged 4/13/65.

Waller, Samuel D.; 3/B; Sergeant, enlisted at 21, Pike.

Walter, E.; 3/D; Private.

Walter, John; 3/D; Private, enlisted 5/9/62.

Walter, T. L.; 3/D Private, enlisted 5/9/62, Pike. Died 8/25/62. Married.

Ward, Joseph; 3/A; Private, enlisted 3/10/62 at 19.

Ward, Ruffin; 3/E; Private, enlisted 7/3/62 at 33, Pike.

Ward, Wiley; 3/A; Private, enlisted 8/11/62.

Warner, John W.; 3/E; Private, enlisted 5/14/62 at 18, Pike.

Watson, Paramore R.; 3/A; Drummer, enlisted 3/10/62 at 34, Montgomery. Subsequently listed as private.

Watson, William; 3/D; Private, enlisted 5/9/62. Later ordinance sergeant.

Weaver, George W.; 3/D; Corporal, enlisted 5/9/62, Montgomery. Captured 9/9/63 at Cumberland Gap (may have been serving as nurse in hospital) by 104th Ohio, sent to Louisville, Kentucky to Camp Douglas, Illinois, swore Oath of Amnesty (date uncertain), discharged 6/13/65.

Welch, Charles P.; 3/C; Private, enlisted 5/3/62 at 28, Coosa.

Wells, Daniel E. B.; 3/A; Private, enlisted 4/21/62. Died 4/2/63.

Wells, John W.; 3/A; Private, enlisted 3/10/62 at 21, Montgomery.

West, Andrew J.; 3/F; Private, enlisted 5/9/62 at 44. Discharged 10/6/62. Married.

West, James K.; 3/F; Private, enlisted at 40, Georgia. Captured 10/20/62. Married.

West, William; 3/F; Private, enlisted 5/9/62 at 17. Died 12/1/62. Single.

Whatley, Lewis; 3/D; Lieutenant, enlisted 5/9/62.

Whiddon, John; 3/A; Private.

White, Archibald; 3/A; Private, enlisted 4/1/62. Promoted to corporal 8/26/62. Discharged by certificate of disability 3/9/65. Farmer.

White, Benjamin F.; 3/B; Private, enlisted 9/1/62. Captured 11/9/62 at Danville, Kentucky.

White, Edward B.; 3/B; Private, enlisted 4/7/62 at 28, Pike. Detached as courier for Col. Thorington, 6/3/63, later courier for B. G. Gracie while in 60th Alabama.

White, George A.; 3/F; Private, enlisted 5/9/62 at 18, Georgia. Killed at Bean's Station 12/14/62. Single, student.

White, Henry M.; 3/A; Private, enlisted 3/10/62 at 27, Montgomery.

White, Rufus F.; 3/E; Private, enlisted 7/3/62 at 34, Pike. Discharged due to physical disability.

Whitehead, Henry; 3/A; Private, enlisted 3/10/62 at 25.

Whitehead, Robert; 3/A; Private, enlisted 3/10/62 at 20, Montgomery.

Wilkins, T. J.; 3/D; Private, enlisted 5/9/62. Quartermaster Clerk 7/13/63–10/31/63.

Williams, Henry; 3/F; Private, enlisted 5/9/62 at 33, Georgia. Died 6/26/64. Married, farmer.

Williams, Jonathan; 3/B; Corporal, enlisted 4/7/62 at 24, Pike. Later sergeant.

Williams, Leonard; 3/D; Private. Died 9/27/62.

Williams, Lewis D.; 3/A; Private, enlisted 5/2/62. Teamster 7/1/63–10/31/63.

Williams, Samuel; 3/D; Private, enlisted 5/9/62.

Williams, Simeon A.; 3/B; Lieutenant, enlisted 4/7/62 at 27, Pike.

Williams, Thomas D. 3/F; Sergeant, enlisted 5/9/62, Georgia.

Williams, William N.; 3/E; Private, enlisted 5/14/62 at 34, Pike.

Williford, George W.; 3/E; Private, enlisted 9/13/62.

Williford, Henry W.; 3/E; Private, enlisted 7/29/63.

Wilson, Joseph D.; 3/D; Private, enlisted 5/9/62. Captured 6/21/63.

Wilson, Meredith (or Meriday); 3/E; Private, enlisted 5/14/62 at 24, Pike.

Wilson, Robert; 3/F; Private, enlisted 6/25/62 at 22. Deserted 10/12/62, returned by end of next muster roll period. Married, farmer.

Wilson, S.; 3/D; Private, enlisted 5/9/62.

Windsor, William A.; 3/A; Private, enlisted 4/22/62.

Wooten, John L.; 3/A; Private, enlisted 3/10/62. Died 12/10/63.

Yarbrough, Minyard; 3/C; Private, enlisted 4/14/63. Substituted for James F. Robinson.

4th Battalion

On September 1, 1862, about 81 members of Company A of this battalion (three officers and 78 privates) were transferred to Company D of the same battalion by order of Colonel Hilliard. On September 14, 1862, members of this battalion's Company B were transferred to Company E of this battalion. Where possible, these transfers have been noted here.

Adams, Nipper; 4/B; Private, enlisted 4/30/62.

Alford, W.; 4/D; Private, enlisted 9/6/63.

Allums, L. Ed; 4/B; Private, enlisted 4/30/62. Killed at Chickamauga.

Anderson, John W.; 4/B; Private, enlisted in Hilliard's Legion 4/3/62 (transferred from Clanton's Legion).

Anderson, Johsua; 4/B; Private, enlisted 4/30/62, Barbour.

Anderson, William A.; 4/A; Private, enlisted 4/7/62 at 31. Died 12/6/62 (typhoid fever).

Anderson, William W.; 4/B; Private, enlisted 4/30/62. Wounded at Chickamauga. Born 3/16/43.

Andrews, John; 4/B; Private, enlisted 4/30/62.

Applin, Stephen; 4/B; Private, enlisted 4/30/62. Teamster.

Armstrong, John M. (or A); 4/A; Private, enlisted 4/7/62.

Arnold, John M.; 4/A; Private.

Baker, T.; 4/B; Private.

Baker, W. V. P.; 4/B; Private, enlisted 4/30/62. Promoted to corporal 9/14/62, transferred from 4/B to 4/E same date. Died 1/9/63.

Barnes, Jasper; 4/B; Private, enlisted 4/30/62. Promoted to corporal 9/14/62. Wounded at Chickamauga.

Barnes, T.; 4/B; Quartermaster Sergeant.

Barnes, William; 4/B; Private, enlisted 4/30/62.

Barrett, Daniel; 4/A; Private, enlisted 4/8/62.

Beasley, Asa; 4/B; Corporal, enlisted 4/30/62. Killed at Petersburg 7/30/64.

Bell, John; 4/D; Private, enlisted 9/6/63. Muster card says company never received Bell.

Bell, William; 4/A; Private, enlisted 4/8/62 at 31. Transferred to 4/D 9/1/62.

Benbow, M. T. G.; 4/A; Private, enlisted 3/24/62. Transferred to 4/D 9/1/62. Detached as Signal Corps.

Bivins, James T.; 4/B; Private, enlisted 4/30/62. Promoted to corporal 1862, sergeant 3/1/63.

Bludworth, T.; 4/E; Private.

Bolling, John; 4/C; Private, enlisted 3/24/62. Paroled 6/6/65. Note: Various records show last name as Bolin, Robin.

Bonner, Robert A.; 4/D; Private, enlisted 3/1/63. Captured 3/25/65, paroled 6/9/65.

Boyette, Denson; 4/A; Private, enlisted 3/13/62 at 23. Discharged by Hilliard 5/6/62, yet shown on muster cards later, mostly shown sick and in hospitals.

Boyette, James L.; 4/A; Private, enlisted 3/13/62 at 33.

Boyette, Thomas; 4/A; Private, enlisted 4/6/63. Deserted 9/17/63.

Boykin, F. A.; 4/A; Sergeant, enlisted 3/13/62 at 42. Promoted to lieutenant 9/1/62, detailed to gather winter clothing. Resigned 11/27/62, discharged 3/13/63 by surgeon's certificate (general disability).

Bozeman, J. C.; 4/A; Private, enlisted 3/12/63. Left in charge at Clinch River 4/28/63, provost guard starting 9/9/63.

Bradley, T.; 4/A; Private.

Branning, James; 4/B; Private, enlisted 4/30/62. Transferred to 4/E on 9/14/62.

Bray, W. Joseph; 4/B; Private, enlisted 4/30/62, Jackson. Transferred to 4/E on 9/17/62. Deserted 10/30/63, Oath of Allegiance 12/63.

Brewer, Samuel W.; 4/B; Private, enlisted 4/30/62. Transferred to 4/E on 9/14/62. Died 11/18/62.

Brewer, William; 4/B; Private, enlisted 4/30/62. Promoted to corporal (date unknown), sergeant 9/14/62, transferred to 4/E on 9/14/62. Died 12/27/62.

Bridges, William A.; 4/B; Private, enlisted 7/24/62. Wounded at Chickamauga.

Brock, J.; 4/B; Private.

Brown, Jesse D.; 4/B; Private, enlisted 4/30/62. Died of wounds 9/21/63.

Brown, Samuel; 4/B; Private.

Brown, W.; 4/B; Private, enlisted 4/30/62. Transferred to 4/E on 9/14/62, died 2/15/63.

Buford, Jefferson; 4/B; Corporal, enlisted 4/30/62. Promoted to sergeant, reduced to private 3/1/63, detailed for hospital duty 5/8/63, later returned to company.

Burns, John W.; 4/A; Private, enlisted 5/5/62. Listed as sergeant for one pay period, detached to Signal Corps 2/14/63.

Burns, Samuel; 4/A; Private, enlisted 3/26/62, Butler. Transferred to 4/D on 9/1/62, promoted to corporal.

Camie, C. H. L.; 4/C; Private. Discharged 3/1/63 (hepitities [sic], general disability).

Campbell, Angus; 4/A; Private, enlisted 3/13/62 at 20. Died 5/18/62. Single.

Campbell, J. A. F.; 4/E; Private, enlisted 8/12/63.

Campbell, Terry D.; 4/D; Private, enlisted 9/27/62.

Cannon, Allen; 4/A; Private, enlisted 3/13/62 at 23. Wounded at Chickamauga.

Caraway, J. A.; 4/C; Private.

Caraway, J. H.; 4/C; Private.

Carter, Joe U.; 4/A; Private.

Chancy, David; 4/E; Private, enlisted 2/15/63.

Chancy, James; 4/E; Private, enlisted 3/15/63.

Chancy, John; 4/B; Sergeant, enlisted 4/30/62. Transferred to 4/E on 9/14/62.

Childree, Asa A; 4/B; Private, enlisted 4/30/62. Died 1/12/63 (chronic diarrhea).

Childree, James F.; 4/B; Private, enlisted 4/30/62.

Childree, Young L.; 4/B; Private, enlisted 4/30/62. Died of wounds suffered at Chickamauga 9/22/63.

Churchwell, Jesse; 4/A; Private, enlisted 3/13/62 at 27. Transferred to 4/D on 9/1/62.

Claighorn, F. T.; 4/A; Private.

Clark, Charles; 4/E; Private, enlisted 11/12/62. Died 2/16/63.

Clayton, N. B.; 4/A; Private, enlisted 2/15/63. Captured 6/21/63 at New Market.

Clements, Chamer; 4/D; Private.

Clements, J. A.; 4/D; Private. Killed at Chickamauga.

Clements, T. H.; 4/D; Private.

Cobern, David F.; 4/B; Private, enlisted 4/30/62 at 18, Barbour. Killed at Chickamauga.

Coddey (or Cody), Frank M.; 4/D; Private, enlisted 8/6/62.

Coddey (or Cody), George W.; 4/D; Private, later corporal. Transferred to 4/D, died 11/25/63.

Coker, George L.; 4/A; Private, enlisted 3/3/62. Transferred to 4/D on 9/1/62. Distant ancestor of Jake Coker, the starting quarterback for the 2015 Alabama Crimson Tide national football championship team.

Collins, R.; 4/E; Private.

Compton, M. S.; 4/D; Private, enlisted 9/6/63.

Cox, John H.; 4/B; Private, enlisted 10/1/62. Wounded at Chickamauga.

Creamer, James J.; 4/A; Private, enlisted 5/10/62, Butler. Wounded at Chickamauga.

Crowell, Levi; 4/A; Private, enlisted 3/13/62 at 23. Transferred to 4/D on 9/1/62. On special duty as teamster.

Crowell, M. J.; 4/A; Private, enlisted 3/13/62 at 36, Butler. Transferred to 4/D on 9/1/62.

Daniel, E. J.; 4/A; Private, enlisted 3/13/62 at 24, Butler. Transferred to 4/D on 9/1/62. Later sergeant.

Daniel, J.; 4/A; Private, enlisted 3/24/62, Butler. Transferred to 4/D on 9/1/62. Promoted to corporal, captured 4/3/65 at Richmond, took Oath of Allegiance 6/25/65.

Daniel, J. V. P.; 4/B; Private, enlisted 4/30/62, Barbour. Discharged 5/29/62.

Daniel, Joe G.; 4/A; Private, enlisted 3/13/62 at 18, Butler. Transferred to 4/D on 9/1/62.

Daniel, John A.; 4/A; Lieutenant, enlisted 3/13/62 at 37. Resigned 9/7/62, surgeon's certificate.

Daniel, John H.; 4/A; Private, enlisted 3/24/62 at 24, Butler. Transferred to 4/D on 9/1/62.

Daniel, T. J.; 4/A; Private.

Daniel, W. Z.; 4/D; Private, enlisted 2/28/63.

Daniel, Zachariah; 4/A; Lieutenant, enlisted 3/13/62 at 34, transferred to 4/D on 9/1/62.

Davis, James A. M.; 4/A; Private, enlisted 3/13/62 at 28, Butler. Detailed as nurse.

Day, John R.; 4/B; Private, enlisted 4/30/62 at 41, Dale. Transferred to 4/E on 9/14/62.

Dean, Ab. T.; 4/B; Private, enlisted 2/12/63. Detailed as blacksmith 6/8/63.

Dean, J. Thomas; 4/B; Private, enlisted 7/10/62.

Dillard, John M.; 4/A; Private, enlisted 3/13/62 at 27. Detached to work on fortifications.

Dudley, W.; 4/A; Private, enlisted 3/13/62 at 27, Butler. Transferred to 4/D on 9/1/62.

Duebose, James F.; 4/E; Private, enlisted 10/1/62. Died 2/11/63.

Dukes, James; 4/A; Private, enlisted 3/13/62 at 25.

Dukes, W.; 4/E; Private, enlisted 8/12/63. Wounded at Chickamauga.

Durr, P. T.; 4/B; Private, enlisted 4/30/62 at 32. Later corporal, promoted to sergeant 9/14/62, transferred to 4/E 9/14/62. Died 4/19/63.

Dykes, Henry; 4/E; Private, enlisted 7/4/63. Captured 12/3/63, sent to Kentucky, sent to Camp Chase 12/15/63, returned to Kentucky, sent to Rock Island, died at Rock Island 2/25/64 (pneumonia).

Dykes, John W.; 4/B; Private, enlisted 4/30/62. Transferred to 4/E on 9/14/62. Captured 12/6/63, sent to Camp Chase 12/15/63, sent to Rock Island 12/31/63. Next appears on roster at General Hospital, Liberty, Virginia 1/11/64.

Emerson, J. C.; 4/B; Corporal, enlisted 4/30/62. Promoted to sergeant 9/14/62.

Emerson, John; 4/B; Private, enlisted 12/6/62.

Evans, Joseph F.; 4/A; Private, enlisted 4/1/62, Butler. Killed at Chickamauga.

Evans, William A.; 4/A; Private. Died in service.

Farrell, Michael; 4/C; Private, enlisted 3/13/62 at 23. Detached to guard smallpox patients 8/3/63.

Flinn, R.; 4/B; Private, enlisted 1/7/62. Discharged by substitution (Warren C. Scroggins) 1/7/63.

Flournoy, Francis M.; 4/B; Private, enlisted 4/30/62.

Flower, William B.; 4/A; Private, enlisted 3/13/62 at 22, Butler. Transferred to 4/D on 9/1/62.

Flowers, J. R.; 4/D; Private, enlisted 2/28/63.

Flowers, Stephen M.; 4/A; Private, enlisted 3/13/62 at 31, Butler. Died 6/6/62.

Flowers (or Flower), W. B.; 4/A; Private, enlisted 3/13/62 at 22. Transferred to 4/D 9/1/62.

Foreman, James; 4/E; Private, enlisted 11/15/62. Wounded at Chickamauga.

Foreman, John; 4/B; Private, enlisted 4/30/62 at 34. Promoted to corporal 9/14/61, transferred to 4/F, discharged 11/21/62.

Fountain, John J.; 4/E; Private, enlisted 11/15/62.

Foust, Hilery; 4/D; Private, enlisted 2/28/63.

Foust, James; 4/D; Private, enlisted 2/28/63. Detached as teamster 5/10/63. Died 10/4/63.

Foxworth, J.C.; 4/B; Private, enlisted 4/30/62 at 27, Dale. Wounded at Chickamauga.

Foxworth, Levi; 4/B; Private, enlisted 4/30/62. Dale. Discharged 7/9/62 (disability).

Frazier (or Frazer), W.D.; 4/A; Private, enlisted 4/1/62 at 18.

Fuller, J. H.; 4/A; Private, enlisted 3/13/62 at 22, Butler. Wounded at Chickamauga.

Fuller, J. M.; 4/A; Private, enlisted 3/13/62. Died 6/22/63 (typhoid fever).

Fuller, J. N.; 4/A; Private, enlisted 3/13/62 at 19, Butler.

Fuller, Jerry M.; 4/A; Private. Died 6/22/63.

Fuller, Jr., Joseph C.; 4/A; Private, enlisted 3/13/62 at 27.

Glasgow, James; 4/A; Captain, enlisted 3/13/62 at 38. On detached service for recruiting. Resigned 8/4/63.

Godwin, William; 4/E; Private.

Goggans, Blueford M.; 4/A; Private, enlisted 5/11/62. Wounded, probably at Chickamauga.

Grubbs, William W.; 4/B; Corporal, enlisted 4/30/62. Detached as teamster, driving ambulance.

Gunter, John; 4/A; Private, enlisted 3/13/62 at 19.

Gunter, Moses; 4/A; Private, enlisted 4/9/62 at 23, Butler. Later corporal, then sergeant..

Hall, Glover; 4/A; Private, enlisted 5/15/62. Transferred to 4/D on 9/1/62, promoted to sergeant, detailed for recruiting.

Hall, Robert; 4/A; Private, enlisted 3/13/62 at 24. Transferred to 4/D on 9/1/62.

Hall, W. A.; 4/B; Private, enlisted 4/30/62. Transferred to 4/E on 9/14/62, captured 12/7/63 (in hospital), died in prison 12/13/63.

Hamilton, John F.; 4/A; Private, enlisted 5/16/62. Transferred to 4/D on 9/1/62. Died 10/10/62 (typhoid fever), married.

Hamrick, J. H.; 4/A; Private, enlisted 4/1/62 at 19, Butler. Transferred 9/1/62.

Hamrick, William; 4/A; Private, enlisted 3/24/62. Detached to guard smallpox patients, later corporal.

Harbin, William P.; 4/D; Private, enlisted 11/16/62. Detached as courier for Colonel Thorington.

Harper, H. H.; 4/C; Private, enlisted 4/30/62, Barbour. Died 7/10/62.

Harper, James B.; 4/B; Private, enlisted 4/30/62 at 20, Barbour. Died 12/8/62.

Harper, Wade; 4/B; Private, enlisted 10/1/62.

Harrell, Louis; 4/A; Lieutenant, enlisted 3/13/62 at 40. Transferred to 4/D on 9/1/62, promoted to captain. Resigned 7/4/63 (rheumatism).

Harris, S. L.; 4/A; Private, enlisted 2/25/63. Discharged (provided a substitute).

Harvill, John; 4/A; Private, enlisted 3/13/62 at 25. Died 7/30/62 (rubeola).

Harville, Evan E.; 4/A; Private, enlisted 3/13/62 at 18, Butler. Transferred to 4/D on 9/1/62.

Hays, A. W.; 4/C; Private, enlisted 4/30/62 at 20, Barbour. Transferred to 4/C and exchanged for Dempsey Odom.

Hays, Bartlett; 4/A; Private, enlisted 3/13/62 at 17, Butler. Extra duty as Battalion drummer, died 11/23/63.

Head, James; 4/A; Private, enlisted 4/7/62 at 22.

Helms, William; 4/B??; Private, enlisted 4/30/62. Died 9/8/62 (measles).

Herring, Thomas; 4/B; Private, enlisted 4/30/62 at 20, Dale. Discharged 7/25/62 (chronic diarrhea), reenlisted 3/2/63.

Herring, W. W.; 4/B; Sergeant, enlisted 4/30/62. Transferred to 4/C and demoted to private.

Herring, William J.; 4/B; Sergeant, enlisted 4/30/62. Died 3/10/64.

Hill, Bishop T.; 4/D; Private, enlisted 3/13/62 at 19, Butler. Transferred to 4/D on 9/1/62, killed at Drewry's Bluff 5/16/64.

Hill, C. T; 4/D; Private, enlisted 9/6/63. Died 4/24/64.

Hill, John M. (or H.); 4/D; Private, enlisted 9/1/63. Died 12/2/63.

Hilliard, C. B.; Asst. Surgeon; appointed by President 4/25/61. Transferred to hospital in Richmond.

Hilliard, H. W.; Colonel, took rank 4/24/62. Resigned 12/1/62.

Hilliard, William; 4/E; Private, enlisted 8/12/63.

Hilliard, William P.; Captain and Adjutant.

Hodges, H.; Asst. Surgeon.

Holder, Thomas; 4/B; Private, enlisted 4/30/62 at 21. Died 11/18/62. Married.

Holley, William; 4/A; Private, enlisted 4/1/62 at 19. Detailed as teamster. Wounded, probably at Chickamauga.

Hood, John; 4/A; Private, enlisted 4/7/62 at 23, Butler. Died 4/28/63 (typhoid fever).

Howard, H.; 4/E; Private. Received in exchange for Jerry Thurman. Deserted 10/30/63.

Huey, George W.; 4/B; Sergeant, enlisted 4/30/62 at 28, Barbour. Promoted to sergeant major 9/14/62. Died 8/7/63.

Hughes, G. W.; 4/B; Private, enlisted 4/20/62. Transferred to 4/E on 9/14/62. Detached as teamster 9/63.

Hurst, Thomas J.; 4/B; Corporal, enlisted 4/30/62 at 20, Barbour. Promoted to sergeant 9/14/62.

Ingraham, A. H.; 4/A; Private, enlisted 4/7/62 at 26, Butler.

Ingraham, Green B.; 4/A; Private, enlisted 3/24/62 at 20, Butler.

Ingraham, H. H.; 4/A; Private, enlisted 4/7/62.

Ingraham, James A. (or H.); 4/A; Private, enlisted 9/10/62.

Ingraham, Jesse; 4/A; Private, enlisted 4/7/63.

Ingraham, Nathaniel; 4/A; Private, enlisted 3/24/62 at 58, Butler. Transferred to 4/D on 9/1/62. Died 11/18/62.

Ingram, Eli H.; 4/A; Private, enlisted 3/13/62 at 23. Sent to field hospital 9/20/63.

Jackson, Daniel H.; 4/A; Private, enlisted 5/6/62, Troy. Transferred to 4/D on 9/1/62. Killed at Chickamauga.

Jackson, N. T.; 4/B; Private, enlisted 4/30/62. Later sergeant, lieutenant 9/14/62. Transferred to 4/E on 9/14/62. Died 11/23/62.

Jacobs, W. J.; 4/E; Private, enlisted 11/15/62.

Jacobs, William; 4/E; Private.

James, A. B.; 4/B; Private, enlisted 4/30/62. Transferred to 4/E on 9/14/62.

James, D. M.; 4/E; Private, enlisted 8/12/63.

James, Robert A.; 4/A; Private, enlisted 3/27/62 at 26, Butler. Transferred to

4/D on 9/1/62, extra duty as teamster. Killed at Drewry's Bluff.

Jefcoat, Benjamin C.; 4/A; Private, enlisted 8/6/62. Transferred to 4/D on 9/1/62. Died 11/2/62.

Jefcoat, Eligah A.; 4/D; Private, enlisted 2/29/63, Butler. Captured 6/21/63.

Jefcoat, Eligah G.; 4/D; Private, enlisted 2/28/63.

Jefcoat, James (or Jasper) J.; 4/A; Private, enlisted 8/6/62. Transferred to 4/D on 9/1/62. Captured 12/3/63, sent to Camp Chase 12/15/63, sent to Rock Island 12/31/63.

Jefcoat, John P.; 4/D; Private, enlisted 2/28/63. Captured 6/21/63.

Jill, Jesse; 4/A; Private.

Johnson, Alex; 4/C; Private, enlisted 4/30/62, Barbour.

Johnson, James; 4/A; Corporal, enlisted 3/13/62 at 26, Butler. Later sergeant, elected lieutenant 8/11/63. Transferred to 4/D on 9/1/62.

Johnson, John; 4/A; Private, enlisted 3/13/62 at 33, Butler. Later sergeant.

Johnson, Zachariah; 4/B; Private, enlisted 4/30/62. Died 9/62, date uncertain.

Jones, Cullin; 4/B; Private, enlisted 4/30/62 at 32, Dale. Detailed to work in hospital, furloughed from hospital, returned to unit, wounded at Chickamauga.

Jordan, Turner E.; 4/A; Sergeant, enlisted 3/13/62 at 42, Butler. Demoted to private, discharged 12/9/62 (surgeon's certificate).

Jordan, William; 4/C; Private, enlisted 3/13/62 at 41, Butler. Briefly a corporal, returned to private. Killed at Chickamauga.

Keith, R. W.; 4/A; Private, enlisted 4/10/62. Later reexamined and excused.

Kelley, A. J.; 4/D; Private, enlisted 8/18/63.

Kemp, Henry; 4/B; Private, enlisted 4/30/62 at 30, Coffee.

Kent, H. H.; 4/D; Private, enlisted 2/1/63.

Kent, Randolph; 4/D; Private, enlisted 11/16/62.

Kent, T. G.; 4/D; Private, enlisted 11/16/62.

King, John Quincy.; 4/A; Private, enlisted 4/8/62 at 24, Butler.

King, John; 4/B; Private, enlisted at 34, Dale. Extra duty as teamster.

Kirkland, George W.; 4/A; Private, enlisted 4/22/62, Butler.

Kirkland, W. F.; 4/A; Private, enlisted 4/22/62.

Kitchens, Elias; 4/D; Private, enlisted 2/28/63. Deserted 6/9/63.

Knight, W.; 4/A; Private, enlisted 5/5/62.

Knight, W. F. S.; 4/B; Private, enlisted 5/5/62. Died 11/4/62.

Kolb, R. F.; 4/C; Captain. Later, Kolb's Battery, Light Artillery.

Laird, William; 4/A; Private, enlisted 3/13/62 at 38, Butler. Compiled 181 days of extra duty, died 10/14/63 of wounds suffered at Chickamauga.

Lang, James; 4/B; Lieutenant, enlisted 4/30/62 at 24, Barbour. Promoted to captain 9/14/62, wounded at Chickamauga.

Langford, F. M.; 4/E; Private, enlisted 8/12/63.

Langford, George Blair; 4/B; Private, enlisted 5/18/62 at 18, Dale. Transferred to 4/E on 9/14/62, detached as teamster, discharged 4/26/65. DoB 7/21/43, DoD 3/15/1927.

Langford, J. A. B.; 4/B; Private, enlisted 4/30/62 at 18. Detached as teamster, transferred to 4/E on 9/14/62.

Lawrence, W. C.; 4/E; Private, enlisted 11/15/62.

Lawrence, Wade; 4/A; Private, enlisted 5/15/62. Extra duty as ambulance driver.

Leard, Patrick; 4/A; Private, enlisted 3/13/62 at 33, Butler. Transferred to 4/D on 9/1/62. Shown as Retired/Invalid Corps.

Lee, Ancil (or Ansel); 4/D; Private, enlisted 2/28/63. Brother of Jackson Lee, Martin Lee.

Lee, Jackson; 4/A; Private, enlisted 3/13/62 at 27, Butler. Killed at Chickamauga. Brother of Ancil Lee, Martin Lee.

Lee, Martin; 4/A; Private, enlisted 3/13/62 at 23, Butler. Killed at Chickamauga. Brother of Jackson Lee, Ancil Lee.

Lewis, Charles; 4/E; Private, enlisted 11/15/62.

Lewis, E.; 4/A; Private, enlisted 3/30/62 at 25, Coosa. Married, died 11/3/62.

Lewis, W. Arch; 4/B; Private, enlisted 3/30/62

Linton, D. W.; 4/D; Private, enlisted 11/16/62.

Loftin, J. W.; 4/E; Private, enlisted 5/1 or 30/63.

Loftin, T. J.; 4/B; Private, enlisted 4/30/62. Transferred to 4/E on 9/14/62.

Loftin, W.; 4/B; Private.

Logan, James; 4/B; Private, enlisted 4/30/62. Transferred to 4/E on 9/14/62. Died 12/21/62. Married.

Logan, James; 4/C; Private.

Long, Hardy; 4/D; Private, enlisted 2/28/63.

Long, T. E.; 4/B; Private, enlisted at 22. Barbour.

Lowery, James C; 4/A; Private, enlisted 3/27/62 at 25, Butler. Transferred to 4/D on 9/1/62.

Lowery, James M.; 4/A; Private, enlisted 4/7/62 at 27, Butler. Detailed on hospital duty.

Marlow, John G.; 4/A; Private, enlisted 3/27/62 at 18, Butler. Transferred to 4/D on 9/1/62.

Marlow, Silas; 4/A; Private, enlisted 4/9/62 at 26, Butler. Transferred to 4/D on 9/1/62. Discharged 6/4/64 (right leg).

Martin, John; 4/B; Private, enlisted 4/30/62. Transferred to 4/E on 9/14/62, promoted to corporal 1/4/63.

Martin, Neal; 4/A; Private, enlisted 4/2/62 at 28. Detached as wagoner 8/13/62.

Mash, John M. (or S.); 4/A; Private, enlisted 4/8/62. Transferred to 4/D on 9/1/62. Detached to hospital 10/1/63–12/31/63.

Massey, William; 4/A; Private, enlisted 3/24/62 at 16. Transferred to 4/D on 9/1/62.

Maugham, B.; 4/A; Private, enlisted 3/24/62 at 17, Butler. Detailed as teamster, detailed to guard commissary at Morristown, Tennessee 5/1/63.

McAdams, Elijah W.; 4/A; Private, enlisted 8/6/62. Transferred to 4/D on 9/1/62.

McAdams, J. W. F. (or W. J. F.); 4/D; Private, enlisted 7/21/63.

McCormick, John; 4/B; Sergeant, enlisted 4/30/62. Promoted to Adjutant 9/9/62.

McGough, James; 4/A; Private, enlisted 5/16/62. Transferred to 4/D on 9/1/62.

McKinney, Solomon; 4/B; Private, enlisted at 22, Dale.

McLean, A. P.; 4/B; Private, enlisted 4/30/62 at 23, Dale. Transferred to 4/E on 9/14/62.

McLean, C. C.; 4/B; Private, enlisted 4/30/62 at 28, Barbour. Died 11/1/62 (pneumonia).

McRae, John J.; 4/B; Private, enlisted 4/30/62 at 31. Later corporal.

Messick, George; 4/B; Private, enlisted 4/30/62 at 30, Barbour. Promoted to sergeant 9/14/62.

Miller, Abram; 4/B; Private, enlisted 4/30/62 at 22, Dale. AWOL from enlistment date, later listed as deserter. Transferred to 4/E on 9/14/62 without being present.

Miller, James L.; 4/B; Private, enlisted 2/3/63.

Miller, James W.; 4/B; Private, enlisted 4/30/62 at 33, Barbour. Died in service 8/62.

Miller, John T.; 4/A; Private, enlisted 3/24/62 at 18. Transferred to 4/D on 9/1/62. May have been POW, paroled 5/24/65.

Miller, John; 4/B; Private, enlisted 4/30/62.

Mills, Alfred; 4/B; Private, enlisted at 20, Dale. Died of wounds 10/31/63.

Mills, William; 4/D; Private, enlisted 3/13/62 at 32. Transferred to 4/D 9/1/62. Died at Richmond 6/5/64.

Mitchell, John M.; 4/A; Private, enlisted 5/10/62, Montgomery.

Mitchell, S.; 4/A; Private.

Moats, H. D.; 4/D; Private, enlisted 7/1/62. Transferred to 4/D on 9/1/62. Died 10/16/63.

Moody, Henry; 4/B; Private, enlisted 7/24/62. Transferred to 4/E on 9/14/62. Died 1/27/63.

Moody, Joel; 4/A; Private, enlisted 3/28/62 at 24, Butler. Transferred to 4/D 4/1/62.

Moody, R. L.; 4/D; Private, enlisted 8/17/63.

Moody, Solomon; 4/E; Private, enlisted 7/24/62. Died 4/25/63.

Moody, William,; 4/D; Private, enlisted 11/16/62.

Morgan, Charles; 4/A; Private, enlisted 3/13/62 at 24, Butler. Detached as teamster.

Morgan, Ira B.; 4/A; Private, enlisted 8/26/62. Detached to build fortifications. Died of Chickamauga wounds 9/24/63.

Morgan, Rufus H.; 4/A; Private, enlisted 3/9/62, Butler. Detailed to work on fortifications. Captured 4/7/65, paroled 6/25/65. DoB 6/17/39.

Morgan, T.; 4/A; Private.

Morgan, William Washington; 4/A; Private, enlisted 4/15/62, Butler. Paroled 6/65. DoB 8/25/42.

Morris, A. J.; 4/B; Private, enlisted at 32, Barbour. Discharged 7/25/62 (substitution).

Newby, F. B.; 4/B; Private, enlisted 4/30/62, Barbour. Promoted to corporal 9/14/62, transferred to 4/E on 9/14/62. Died 1/63.

Newby, J. S.; 4/B; Sergeant, enlisted 4/30/62 at 24. Transferred to 4/E on 9/14/62. Promoted to corporal 1/9/63, to sergeant 4/19/63. Wounded 1864.

Newby, P.; 4/E; Private, enlisted 8/12/63. Died 10/27/63.

Nobles, Daniel P.; 4/B; Private, enlisted 4/30/62. Detached as blacksmith.

O'Daniel, J. W.; 4/E; Private, enlisted 11/15/62. Promoted to corporal 4/19/63. Wounded at Chickamauga.

Odom, Dempsey; 4/B; Private, enlisted 3/30/62. Wounded at Chickamauga.

Odom, Elijah; 4/A; Private, enlisted 3/13/62 at 45, Butler.

Parish, James A.; 4/A; Private, enlisted 4/1/62 at 33, Butler. Hung by bushwhackers using telegraph wire and shot seven times 10/22/62. Married.

Passmore, John R. A.; 4/B; Sergeant, enlisted 4/30/62.

Pate, William R.; 4/B; Private, 4/30/62. Killed at Chickamauga.

Payne, John; 4/B; Private, enlisted 4/30/62 at 20. Transferred to 4/E on 9/14/62. Captured 6/21/63.

Payne, Reason; 4/B; Private, enlisted 4/30/62 at 21. Transferred to 4/E 9/14/62. Wounded 9/23/63.

Peacock, J. A.; 4/E; Private, enlisted 4/30/62 at 20.

Peacock, J. F.; 4/E; Private, enlisted 4/30/62. Transferred to 4/E on 9/14/62.

Peacock, James D.; 4/B; Private, enlisted 11/15/62. Died 3/24/63.

Peacock, John P.; 4/E; Private, enlisted 2/15/63.

Peacock, Louis (or Lewis) L.; 4/E; Private, enlisted 4/30/62.

Peacock, P. C.; 4/B; Private, enlisted 4/30/62, Barbour. Discharged 7/9/62 (disability).

Peacock, W. J.; 4/B; Sergeant, enlisted 4/30/62. Promoted to sergeant major 7/1/62, to lieutenant by election 9/15/62. Transferred to 4/E 9/14/62. Wounded at Chickamauga.

Perrett (or Perritt), John; 4/A; Private, enlisted 3/13/62 at 16, Butler. Transferred to 4/D on 9/1/62.

Perry, John; 4/A; Private, enlisted 4/22/62. Killed at Chickamauga.

Pettis, J. W. C.; 4/B; Corporal, enlisted 4/30/62 at 31. Transferred to 4/E on 9/14/62.

Pettry, Jackson; 4/A; Private, enlisted 3/24/62 at 17, Butler. Transferred to 4/D on 9/1/62.

Petty, W. R.; 4/D; Private, enlisted 8/28/63.

Phillips, Curtis; 4/B; Private, enlisted 4/30/62. Transferred to 4/E on 9/14/62.

Phillips, I. J. L.; 4/B; Private, enlisted 4/30/62. Transferred to 4/E on 9/14/62. Wounded at Chickamauga.

Phillips, John W.; 4/B; Private, enlisted 4/30/62. Transferred to 4/E on 9/14/62.

Phillips, N. R.; 4/B; Private, enlisted 4/30/62. Promoted to sergeant 9/14/62, transferred to 4/E on 9/14/62.

Pierce, A.; 4/B; Private, enlisted 4/30/62 at 22.

Pierce, William; 4/B; Private, enlisted 4/30/62, Barbour. AWOL from date of organization of company, listed as deserter 10/30/63.

Pipkin, C. S.; 4/B; Sergeant, enlisted 4/30/62. Elected lieutenant 6/2/62. Detached for recruiting 12/9/62, later returned to company.

Pippin, Elias; 4/E; Private, enlisted 11/15/62.

Pope, Bryant; 4/E; Private, enlisted 2/15/63 but reported 5/2/63. Killed at Chickamauga.

Pouncy, Calvin; 4/A; Private, enlisted 4/1/62 at 24, Butler. Transferred to 4/D on 9/1/62, detailed as butcher 8/11/63.

Powell, Jacob; 4/B; Private, enlisted 4/30/62 at 30. Transferred to 4/E on 9/14/62.

Powell, John C.; 4/B; Private, enlisted 4/30/62 at 29. Transferred to 4/E on 9/14/62.

Powell, W. R.; 4/E; Private, enlisted 8/12/62.

Redding, William A.; 4/B; Private, enlisted 4/3/62 at 23. Discharged 7/25/62 (surgeon's certificate, disability). Farmer.

Reed, Harrison; 4/E; Private, enlisted 7/4/63.

Reeves, William N.; 4/C; Captain. Later major, then lieutenant colonel. Resigned 5/26/63.

Rhodes (or Rhods), Anderson; 4/A; Private, enlisted 3/13/62 at 39, Butler. Transferred to 4/D on 9/1/62.

Rhodes, F. M.; 4/D; Private, enlisted 2/1/63.

Rhodes, Joseph; 4/A; Private, enlisted 4/8/62 at 28. Captured 6/21/63.

Richardson, Bryant; 4/B; Private, enlisted 12/10/62. Died 1/15/62 (brain fever).

Roach, Green; 4/A; Private, enlisted 4/7/62 at 22, Butler. Transferred to 4/D on 9/1/62. Died 10/24/63.

Robinson, John B.; 4/A; Private, enlisted 3/25/62 at 22. Wounded while on picket duty.

Rogers, Isaac; 4/D; Private, enlisted 2/28/63.

Rogers, Nathaniel; 4/D; Private, enlisted 2/28/63, Butler. Captured 6/21/63.

Rogers, Robert J.; 4/A; Private, enlisted 5/10/62. Butler. Transferred to 4/D on 9/1/62. Detached for duty in Ordinance Department.

Russell, J. R.; 4/C; Sergeant, enlisted 4/30/62 at 19, Barbour.

Russell, John; 4/A; Private, enlisted 5/16/62, Butler. Killed at Chickamauga.

Rutledge, Augustus; 4/D; Private, enlisted 7/21/63.

Rutledge, Dudley; 4/A; Private, enlisted 3/13/62 at 15, Butler. Transferred to 4/D on 9/1/63.

Rutledge, Henry H.; 4/A; Sergeant, enlisted 3/13/62 at 19, Butler. Promoted to lieutenant to captain.

Rutledge, Ulysses C.; 4/A; Private, enlisted 3/24/62 at 16, Butler. Transferred to 4/D on 9/1/62.

Rylander, Edward P.; 4/A; Private, enlisted 1862 (date uncertain). Died 5/29/62.

Sanders (or Saunders), C. M.; 4/C; Private, enlisted at 30. Later corporal.

Sanders, James; 4/D; Private, enlisted 9/27/62.

Scott, Starkey; 4/A; Private, enlisted at 3/24/62 at 28, Butler. Also shown in 1/D.

Scroggins, George; 4/B; Private, enlisted 12/1/62. Put on detached service with Signal Corps 2/1/62.

Scroggins, Warren C.; 4/B; Private, enlisted 1/7/62. Substituted for R. Flinn. Killed at Chickamauga.

Segler, T. F.; 4/B; Private, enlisted 4/30/62 at 33.

Shehane (or Shehan), F. M.; 4/B; Private, enlisted 4/30/62 at 18, Barbour. Discharged 7/25/62 (disability).

Shows, Cornelius; 4/A; Private, enlisted 4/8/62 at 24, Butler. Deserted 8/15/62 (or 8/20/62).

Shows, Jacob; 4/D; Private, enlisted 2/28/63. Deserted 9/17/63.

Shows, Warren J.; 4/D; Private, enlisted

3/13/62 at 31, Butler. Transferred to 4/D on 9/1/62.

Sikes, J. A.; 4/D; Private, enlisted 8/28/63. Deserted after first muster.

Sikes, Thomas A.; 4/A; Sergeant, enlisted 3/13/62 at 30, Butler. Transferred to 4/D on 9/1/62, later demoted to private.

Simmons, James; 4/B; Private, enlisted 2/12/63. Wounded at Chickamauga.

Skipper, Jacob; 4/E; Private, enlisted 8/12/63.

Smith, Henry; 4/B; Private, enlisted 4/30/62.

Smith, Hezekiah; 4/B; Private, enlisted 12/14/62. Wounded at Chickamauga.

Smith, James F.; 4/B; Private, enlisted 4/30/62 at 18.

Smith, James W.; 4/D; Private, enlisted 4/30/62.

Smith, Robert G.; 4/B; Private, enlisted 4/30/62 at 20.

Snell, W. J.; 4/E; Private, enlisted 2/15/63.

Snow, W. M.; 4/B; Private, enlisted 4/30/62 at 27, Barbour. Transferred to 4/E on 9/14/62.

Sowell, D.; 4/E; Private, enlisted 8/12/63.

Spradley, Bryant E.; 4/A; Private, enlisted 5/11/62. Elected lieutenant 2/19/64, wounded at Petersburg, captured 4/3/65, sent to Old Capitol Prison, took Oath of Allegiance and released 6/20/65.

Spradley, Warren A.; 4/A; Private, enlisted 4/8/62 at 24. Died 3/3/63.

Stokes, John; 4/B; Corporal, enlisted 4/30/62 at 21. Later private.

Stokes, S. G.; 4/E; Private. Served 10 days, died 10/14/62.

Stough, G. P.; 4/A; Private, enlisted 4/1/62 at 20, Lowndes.

Stough, George W.; 4/A; Private, enlisted 4/7/62 at 25. Detailed as blacksmith 6/8/63.

Stough, James A.; 4/A; Private, enlisted 4/1/62 at 19.

Stough, Michael M.; 4/A; Private, enlisted 4/1/62 at 31. Wounded at Chickamauga.

Stough, Robert N. (or W.); 4/A; Private, enlisted 4/7/62 at 33, Butler. Elected lieutenant 6/15/63, killed 6/17/64.

Stough, Simeon; 4/A; Private, enlisted 3/13/62 at 24, Lowndes.

Stough, William F; 4/A; Private, enlisted 3/24/62 at 19, Butler. Wounded at Chickamauga.

Street, W. M.; Staff; Assistant Surgeon, resigned 4/28/63.

Strickland, Jackson; 4/E; Private, enlisted 10/3/62.

Stubbs, James M.; 4/B; Private, enlisted 4/30/62. Transferred to 4/E on 9/14/62, promoted to sergeant 11/23/62.

Stuckey, John J.; 4/B; Private, enlisted 4/30/62. Transferred to 4/E on 9/14/62, died 4/24/63.

Stuckey, W. D. A. N.; 4/B; Private, enlisted 4/30/62 at 30, Dale. Transferred to 4/E on 9/14/62, promoted to sergeant 12/27/62, took Oath of Allegiance 6/17/65, released from Point Lookout same date.

Stuckey, William H.; 4/B; Private, enlisted 4/30/62 at 29. Elected lieutenant 6/2/62, transferred to 4/E 9/14/62 and promoted to captain on same day. Detailed to recruiting duty 8/8/63. Wounded at Chickamauga.

Summerlin, W. E.; 4/D; Private, enlisted 9/27/62.

Swain, Thomas; 4/E; Private, enlisted 11/15/62. Died 12/12/63. Married.

Taylor, G. W.; 4/B; Private, enlisted 8/23/62. Transferred to 4/E on 9/14/62.

Taylor, Thomas; 4/D; Private, enlisted 3/24/62 at 41, Butler. Left on retreat from Kentucky, hung by bushwhackers 10/22/62.

Terry, Oscar; 4/A; Private, enlisted 3/24/62 at 21. Later sergeant.

Thomas, John A.; 4/A; Private, enlisted 3/24/62 at 33. Died 11/5/62.

Thomas, S.; 4/A; Private.

Thomas, W. L. (or W. S.); 4/D; Private, enlisted 9/27/62.

Thrower, George W.; 4/A; Private, enlisted 3/13/62 at 18, Butler.

Thrower, Starling J.; 4/A; Corporal, enlisted 3/13/62 at 25, Butler. Later sergeant.

Thrower, Stephen S.; 4/A; Private, enlisted 3/13/62 at 23, Lowndes.

Thrower, William M.; 4/A; Private, enlisted 5/16/62. Listed as corporal for one muster period.

Thurman, Jerry; 4/B; Private, enlisted 8/25/62. Substitute for Thomas H. Jones. Traded places with Edward Howard of 4/E.

Tompkins, Uell H.; 4/A; Corporal, enlisted 3/13/62 at 20, Butler. Detailed to Signal Corps 3/18/63, rank changed to private.

Trawick, W. J.; 4/B; Private, enlisted 4/30/62. Substitute for A. J. Morris. Transferred to 4/E 9/14/62.

Turlington, J. M.; 4/B; Private, enlisted 4/30/62 at 23, Barbour. Transferred to 4/E on 9/14/62.

Turlington, R. S.; 4/B; Corporal, enlisted 4/30/62. Later private, transferred to 4/E on 9/14/62. Killed at Chickamauga, Honor Roll.

Turner, John B.; 4/A; Private, enlisted 4/30/62. Teamster.

Walker, A.; 4/C; Private, enlisted 4/30/62 at 28, Barbour. Promoted to quartermaster sergeant 7/1/62.

Walker, W. H.; 4/A; Private, enlisted 3/4/63.

Ward, G.; 4/B; Corporal. Later private, transferred to 4/E on 9/14/62.

Welch, George T.; 4/A; Private, enlisted 3/27/62 at 20. Transferred to 4/D on 9/1/62, died 9/23/63 of wounds at Chickamauga.

West, Joseph; 4/A; Private, enlisted 3/13/62 at 18, Butler. Died 6/12/62.

White, W.; 4/A; Private, enlisted 3/4/63.

Wiggins, James L.; 4/A; Private, later lieutenant. May have been transferred to 4/E on 9/14/62.

Wiggins, R. E.; 4/B; Private, enlisted 4/30/62 at 31, Dale. Transferred to 4/E on 9/14/62.

Williams, James; 4/B; Private.

Williamson, E. M.; 4/A; Private, enlisted 4/7/62 at 19. Died 8/22/62.

Williamson, Green; 4/B; Private, enlisted 4/30/62, Barbour.

Williamson, John W.; 4/A; Private, enlisted 5/15/62.

Williamson, Seth; 4/B; Private, enlisted 4/30/62 at 19.

Williamson, William W.; 4/A; Private, enlisted 3/27/62 at 25.

Windham, D. B.; 4/E; Private, enlisted 11/15/62. Wounded at Chickamauga.

Wingo, Allen; 4/A; Private, enlisted 4/1/62 at 51. Discharged (surgeon's certificate) about 12/1/62.

Wise, S. J.; 4/D; Private, enlisted 9/8/63.

Woods, J. G.; 4/B; Private, enlisted 4/30/62. Transferred to 4/E on 9/14/62. Killed 12/14/62 at Bean's Station.

Woods, S. H.; 4/E; Private, enlisted 8/12/63. Died 10/27/63.

Woods, W. A.; 4/E; Private, enlisted 10/4/62. Died 12/14/63.

Wooril (or Woorill), F. W.; 4/B; Private, enlisted 4/30/62. Extra duty as teamster. Died in service.

Wooril (or Woorill), H. T. M.; 4/D; Private, enlisted 4/30/62. Detached as teamster, died of wounds at Chickamauga.

Wooril (or Woorill), John L. B.; 4/B; Private, enlisted 7/5/63 but entry into service was delayed due to smallpox. Joined 4/15/63. Died in service in fall of 1863.

Wooril (or Woorill), Louis D.J.; 4/D; Private enlisted 4/30/62.

Wyrosdick, F.; 4/D; Private, enlisted 2/1/63, Butler. Died 1/26/64 (meningitis).

Wyrosdick, Thomas A.; 4/D; Private, enlisted 3/13/62, Butler. Transferred to 4/D on 9/1/62.

Yaw, Green; 4/B; Private, enlisted 4/30/62. Died 7/27/62.

Youngblood, G. H.; 4/B; Private, enlisted 4/30/62 at 21, Dale. Promoted to corporal, transferred to 4/E 9/14/62.

5th Battalion

Abney, Samuel; 5/D; Sergeant, enlisted 4/24/62, Bibb.

Adair, Benjamin P.; 5/C; Private, enlisted at 23, Talladega.

Adair, Edward M.; 5/C; Private, enlisted at 33, Talladega.

Adair, John D.; 5/C; Private, enlisted at 33, Talladega.

Adams, Allen; 5/E; Private, enlisted at 24, Talladega.

Adams, Charles W.; 5/D; Private, enlisted 4/26/62, Lowndes.

Adams, James M.; 5/A; Private, enlisted at 50, Chambers.

Adams, James; 5/E; Private, enlisted at 20, Talladega.

Adams, Joel J.; 5/A; Private, enlisted at 22, Chambers.

Adams, John; 5/E; Private, enlisted at 22, Talladega.

Adams, W.H.; 5/E; Sergeant, enlisted at 38, Tallapoosa.

Adkinson, Lafayette; 5/D; Private, enlisted 4/21/62, Lowndes.

Akkins, William; 5/C; Corporal, enlisted at 26, Coosa.

Alenzo, Terry; 5/A; Sergeant, enlisted at 27, Chambers.

Alexander, Lindsey W.; 5/C; Private, enlisted at 38, Tallapoosa.

Anderson, Andrew; 5/D; Private, enlisted 4/8/62, Lowndes.

Arington, David; 5/B; Private, enlisted at 25, Randolph.

Ashmore, Thomas T. (or S.); 5/A; Private, enlisted at 41, Chambers.

Atkins, William G.; 5/A; Private, enlisted at 27, Chambers.

Averheart, Patrick H.; 5/D; Private, enlisted 5/29/62, Lowndes.

Baily, Johnathan; 5/B; Private, enlisted at 25, Randolph.

Baird, Isaac; 5/C; Lieutenant, enlisted at 37, Talladega.

Baker, Andrew J.; 5/B; Private, enlisted at 21, Randolph.

Baker, Thomas S.; 5/A; Private, enlisted at 26, Chambers.

Baker, William D.; 5/A; Private, enlisted at 30, Chambers.

Baker, William H.; 5/A; Private, enlisted at 21, Chambers.

Ball, J. B.; 5/E; Private, enlisted at 26, Talladega.

Banister, J. Y.; Private, enlisted at 18, Talladega.

Barlow, B. F.; 5/D; Private, enlisted 4/26/62, Lowndes.

Barnes, Aramanus L.; 5/C; Sergeant, enlisted at 37, Coosa.

Barnes, J. R.; 5/E; Private, enlisted at 23, Chambers.

Barnes, N. T.; 5/E; Captain, enlisted at 36, Tallapoosa.

Barnett, Francis M.; 5/C; Private, enlisted at 26, Coffee.

Barnett, Joberry (or James) E.; 5/C; Farrier, enlisted at 40, Coosa.

Bates, Francis M.; 5/A; Private, enlisted at 23, Chambers.

Bates, William N.; 5/A; Private, enlisted at 25, Chambers.

Bennett, J. T.; 5/E; Corporal, enlisted at 21, Randolph.

Bennett, Oliver; 5/A; Private, enlisted at 29, Chambers.

Bennett, Seburn (or Seaborn); 5/A; Private, enlisted at 40, Chambers.

Berry, James T.; 5/A; Private, enlisted at 25, Chambers.

Bishop, J. G.; 5/E; Private, enlisted at 23, Talladega.

Bishop, Stephen; 5/A; Private, enlisted at 38, Chambers.

Bittle, J. E.; 5/E; Private, enlisted at 32, Talladega.

Bittle, John; 5/E; Private, enlisted at 46, Talladega.

Blair, A. J.; 5/E; Corporal, enlisted at 25, Tallapoosa.

Blair, J. L.; 5/E; Private, enlisted at 21, Tallapoosa.

Blair, L. G.; 5/E; Private, enlisted at 22, Tallapoosa.

Blair, Richard; 5/E; Private, enlisted at 18, Tallapoosa.

Blake, Joseph H.; 5/C; Private, enlisted at 30, Talladega.

Boggs, Anderson J.; 5/A; Private, enlisted at 21, Chambers.

Boggs, Joseph M.; 5/A; Private, enlisted at 26, Chambers.

Bowen, Zacariah; 5/B; Private, enlisted at 18, Randolph.

Braddy (or Brady), John H.; 5/C; Private, enlisted 5/5/62, Blount. Deserted 3/15/65, took Oath of Allegiance 4/7/65.

Brady, James A.; 5/C; Private, enlisted at 24, Talladega. Later corporal.

Brantley, Thomas K.; 5/B; Private, enlisted at 26, Randolph.

Brewer, Burrel P.; 5/A; Private, enlisted at 28, Chambers.

Brewer, J.J .; 5/E; Corporal, enlisted at 26, Talladega.

Brewer, James M.; 5/A; Private, enlisted at 25; Chambers.

Britton, Jas.; 5/A; Private, enlisted at 20, Chambers.

Britton, William B. C.; 5/A; Private, enlisted at 18, Chambers.

Brown, W. D.; 5/E; Private, enlisted at 20, Talladega.

Bruce, Junius J.; 5/C; Private, enlisted at 26, Tallapoosa.

Bruner, Julius J.; 5/D; Private, enlisted 4/22/62, Lowndes.

Bryant, David A.; 5/C; Musician, enlisted at 35, Tallapoosa.

Buchanan, William; 5/B; Private, enlisted at 19, Randolph.

Bullard, Alonzo J.; 5/C; Private, enlisted at 18, Coosa.

Bullard, William P.; 5/C; Private, enlisted at 26, Coosa.

Bullock, Josiah M.; 5/D; Private, enlisted 5/14/62, Conecuh.

Bullock, William P.; 5/D; Private, enlisted 4/26/62, Lowndes.

Bunneau, John B.; 5/D; Private, enlisted 4/26/62, Lowndes.

Burke, George W.; 5/C; Private, enlisted at 33, Tallapoosa.

Butler, Peter; 5/D; Private, enlisted 5/7/62, Lowndes.

Buzbee, T. J.; 5/D; Private, enlisted 5/14/62, Montgomery.

Calaway, J. A.; 5/E; Private, enlisted at 20, Talladega.

Camp, Tolaver B.; 5/B; Sergeant, enlisted at 29, Randolph.

Campbell, Aaron W.; 5/D; Private, enlisted 4/15/62, Bibb.

Campbell, Alva; 5/D; Private, enlisted 4/15/62, Bibb.

Campbell, G. W.; 5/E; Lieutenant, enlisted at 30, Tallapoosa.

Canant, James H. (or N.); 5/C; Private, enlisted at 26, Talladega. Later lieutenant.

Carden, Owen H. R.; 5/C; Private, enlisted at 42, Tallapoosa.

Cargile, J. R.; 5/E; Private, enlisted at 33, Talladega.

Casey, James H.; 5/D; Private, enlisted 5/13/62, Montgomery.

Chandler, R. N.; 5/E; Private, enlisted at 24, Talladega.

Chandler, T. B.; 5/E; Private, enlisted at 18, Talladega.

Channel, Edward W.; 5/C; Private, enlisted at 18, Tallapoosa.

Cheek, S. F.; 5/E; Private, enlisted at 30, Talladega.

Clayton, Elijah M.; 5/C; Corporal, enlisted at 40, Coosa.

Clemons, Anderson M.; 5/B; Lieutenant, enlisted at 28, Chambers.

Clowers, J. W.; 5/D; Private, enlisted 5/14/62, Montgomery.

Cochran, Ellison J.; 5/A; Private, enlisted at 45, Chambers.

Coker, A. J.; 5/C; Private.

Coker, Marion J.; 5/C; Private, enlisted at 33, Talladega.

Cole, William B.; 5/B; Private, enlisted at 35, Randolph.

Collins, George W.; 5/C; Private, enlisted at 32, Tallapoosa.

Connel, Jones B.; 5/B; Private, enlisted at 18, Randolph.

Cook, Simeon; 5/A; Private, enlisted at 19, Chambers.

Cotton, John W.; 5/C; Private, enlisted at 31, Coosa. War letters became the book, *Yours 'till Death.*

Cox, Samuel A.; 5/A; Lieutenant, enlisted at 36, Chambers.

Craft, Cornelius; 5/E; Private, enlisted at 17, Chambers.

Craft, Robert; 5/E; Private, enlisted at 56, Talladega.

Craig, William H.; 5/C; Private, enlisted at 27, Tallapoosa.

Creamer, Robert H.; 5/A; Private, enlisted at 16, Chambers. Substituted for Jas. M. (Jackie) Griffin.

Cullins, D. A.; 5/E; Musician, enlisted at 22, Talladega.

Curl, John; 5/A; Private, enlisted at 33, Chambers.

Daniel, Hartford M.; Private, enlisted at 22, Randolph.

Daniel, Thomas J.; 5/B; Private, enlisted at 24, Randolph.

Daniel, William D.; 5/B; Private, enlisted at 24, Randolph.

Davidson, Joseph P.; 5/D; Private, enlisted 4/19/62, Lowndes.

Dean, Bewford L.; 5/C; Private, enlisted 4/1/62 at 29, Tallapoosa.

Dean, William; 5/D; Private, enlisted 5/14/62, Montgomery.

Dearing, John C.; 5/A; Private, enlisted at 42, Chambers.

Deason, Felix; 5/C; Private, enlisted at 18, Coosa.

Deason, James H. (or A.); 5/C; Private, enlisted at 36, Coosa.

Deason, Martin R. (or V.); 5/C; Private, enlisted at 20, Coosa.

Deason, William N.; 5/C; Private, enlisted at 22, Coosa.

Deloach, Charles A.; 5/A; Private, enlisted at 20, Chambers.

Deloach, Thomas J.; 5/A; Private, enlisted at 27, Chambers.

Dixon, Joseph H.; 5/A; Private, enlisted at 19, Chambers.

Duke, Bethel; 5/B; Private, enlisted at 23, Randolph.

Duke, William T.; Private, enlisted at 29, Randolph.

Earnest, Lafayette; 5/D; Private, enlisted 4/30/62, Lowndes.

Epison, William J.; 5/E; Private, enlisted at 18, Talladega.

Espey, George; 5/D; Private, enlisted 4/7/62, Bibb.

Estes, James L.; 5/A; Private, enlisted at 22, Chambers.

Estes, Miles H.; 5/A; Private, enlisted at 29, Chambers.

Evans, George W.; 5/C; Private, enlisted at 38, Talladega.

Evans, Marion S.; 5/C; Private, enlisted at 26, Talladega.

Fannin, William H.; 5/A; Corporal, enlisted at 18, Chambers.

Farly, Christopher C.; 5/A; Private, enlisted at 25.

Farr, Isaac; 5/A; Private, enlisted at 33, Chambers.

Faster, Nicholas T.; 5/B; Private, enlisted at 18, Randolph.

Faster, William H.; 5/B; Private, enlisted at 23, Randolph.

Faster, William; 5/B; Private, enlisted at 34, Randolph.

Fincher, Jeremiah; 5/B; Private, enlisted at 23, Randolph.

Finley, Josiah C.; 5/B; Private, enlisted 24, Randolph.

Fleming, Robert Q.; 5/D; Private, enlisted 4/28/62, Bibb.

Forman (or Foreman), W. P.; 5/E; Private, enlisted at 20, Talladega.

Fortner, Thomas A.; 5/D; Private, enlisted 4/7/62, Lowndes.

Fowler, John W.; 5/A; Private, enlisted at 18, Chambers.

Fowler, W. S.; 5/E; Private, enlisted at 23, St. Clair.

Fuller, George W.; 5/A; Private, enlisted at 25, Chambers.

Fuller, Phillip; 5/E; Private, enlisted at 18, Randolph.

Fuller, Sidney; 5/E; Private, enlisted at 17, Randolph.

Galloway, Franklin M.; 5/C; Private, enlisted at 21, Talladega.

Galloway, Washington M.; 5/C; Private, enlisted at 19, Talladega.

Gann, William; 5/B; Private, enlisted 3/11/62 at 36, Randolph.

Garrett, Jessey H.; 5/B; Bugler, enlisted at 24, Chambers.

Garrett, John W.; 5/B; Corporal, enlisted at 21, Chambers.

Garrett, Theoppolis (or Theoffaleis or Theophilus); 5/B; Bugler, enlisted at 23, Chambers.

Garrett, William R.; 5/A; Private, enlisted at 18, Chambers.

Germany, J. T. (or J. Y.); 5/E; Private, enlisted at 24, Tallapoosa.

Gilchrist, J. M.; 5/E; Private, enlisted at 20, Talladega.

Gilchrist, J. V.; 5/E; Private, enlisted at 22, Talladega.

Goodgain, Floyd N. (or M.); 5/C; Sergeant, enlisted at 20, Coosa.

Gordon, James C.; 5/D; Corporal, enlisted 4/19/62, Lowndes.

Grady, John D.; 5/A; Private, enlisted at 19, Chambers.

Graham, Jesse H.; 5/A; Private, enlisted at 31, Chambers.

Grant, William; 5/D; Private, enlisted 4/11/62, Lowndes.

Gray, Winston W.; 5/A; Sergeant, enlisted at 20 (or 25), Chambers.

Green, James; 5/B; Private, enlisted at 25, Randolph.

Green, M. M.; 5/E; Private, enlisted at 23, Talladega.

Green, William; 5/C; Private, enlisted at 17, Coosa.

Griffin, Thomas M.; 5/A; Private, enlisted at 30.

Guthrie, John; 5/C; Private, enlisted at 29, Tallapoosa.

Hagan, James H. (or N.); 5/C; Private, enlisted at 27, Coosa.

Hall, Right S.; 5/D; Private, enlisted 4/7/62, Lowndes.

Hall, William J.; 5/A; Private, enlisted at 18, Chambers.

Halladay, Charles A.; 5/A; Private, enlisted at 18, Chambers.

Hancock, Andrew J.; 5/C; Private, enlisted at 25, Tallapoosa.

Hancock, John W. W.; 5/C; Private, enlisted at 34, Tallapoosa.

Hanna, James J.; 5/C; Private, enlisted at 20, Coosa.

Hansberger, J.S.; 5/D; Private, enlisted 4/24/62, Bibb.

Harlan, Thomas J. 5/C; Private, enlisted at 18, Talladega.

Harris, David; 5/E; Private, enlisted at 23, Talladega.

Harris, George W.; 5/B; Private, enlisted at 24, Randolph.

Harris, John M.; 5/A; Private, enlisted at 27, Chambers.

Harris, W. E. P.; 5/D; Private, enlisted 5/12/62, Lowndes.

Harris, William V.; 5/A; Private, enlisted at 31, Chambers.

Harrist, Reuben C.; 5/A; Private, enlisted at 36, Chambers.

Hartigan, William; 5/D; Private, enlisted 5/10/62, Lowndes.

Hawkins, Henry; 5/D; Private, enlisted 4/19/62, Lowndes.

Haygood, Daniel M.; 5/D; Private, enlisted 5/14/62, Montgomery.

Haygood, George H.; 5/D; Corporal, enlisted 4/7/62, Lowndes.

Haygood, Gideon; 5/A; Private, enlisted at 34, Chambers.

Hays, Thomas J.; 5/A; Private, enlisted at 30, Chambers.

Head, J. E.; 5/E; Private, enlisted at 18, Talladega.

Hendon, George B.; 5/A; Private, enlisted at 20, Chambers.

Hendon, James A. T.; 5/A; Private, enlisted at 24, Chambers.

Hendrich, J. L.; 5/E; Lieutenant, enlisted at 37, Tallapoosa.

Henry, Thomas; 5/B; Private, enlisted at 24, Randolph.

Hester, Allen; 5/B; Private, enlisted at 29, Randolph.

Hester, Lewallen; 5/B; Private, enlisted at 23, Randolph.

Hicks, James W.; 5/C; Private, enlisted at 22, Tallapoosa.

Hicks, Thomas J.; 5/C; Private, enlisted at 20, Tallapoosa.

Higgins, Joseph L.; 5/A; Private, enlisted at 19, Chambers.

Hindsman, Andrew; 5/C; Private, enlisted at 22, Coosa.

Hix, Mathew; 5/B; Private, enlisted at 47, Randolph.

Hobgood, Hezekiah; 5/A; Private, enlisted 3/10/62 at 26, Chambers. Transferred to 2/A 7/1/62. Deserted 8/16/62.

Hogan, Patrick; 5/D; Private, enlisted 5/5/62, Lowndes.

Holcombe, A. G.; 5/E; Private, enlisted at 18, Talladega.

Holland, James W.; 5/D; Private, enlisted 5/14/62, Montgomery.

Horn, Francis M.; 5/B; Private, enlisted at 29, Randolph.

Hovie, James C.; 5/C; Private, enlisted at 20, Talladega.

Howell, Eli; 5/A; Private, enlisted at 19, Chambers.

Howell, Joseph H.; 5/A; Private, enlisted at 18, Chambers.

Huckabee, Willis G.; 5/D; Sergeant, enlisted 4/19/62, Lowndes.

Hudson, Martin V.; 5/A; Private, enlisted at 24, Chambers.

Hudson, William C.; 5/A; Private, enlisted at 29, Chambers.

Huggins, James; 5/A; Private, enlisted at 22, Chambers.

Hughes, J. G.; 5/E; Private, enlisted at 22, Talladega.

Hurst, Henry E.; 5/A; Private, enlisted at 32, Chambers.

Ingram, J. J.; 5/E; Private, enlisted at 23, Talladega.

Jacobs, William S.; 5/C; Private, enlisted at 22, Talladega.

James, D. G.; 5/E; Musician, enlisted at 25, Chambers.

James, James T.; 5/B; Private, enlisted at 24, Randolph.

Jerman, Floyd; 5/A; Private, enlisted at 25, Chambers.

Johnson, Burrel H.; 5/D; Private, enlisted 4/14/62, Montgomery.

Johnson, Frederick S.; 5/A; Private, enlisted at 24, Chambers.

Johnson, Green C.; 5/A; Private, enlisted at 23, Chambers.

Johnson, William L.; 5/D; Private, enlisted 4/26/62, Lowndes.

Johnson, William S.; 5/C; Private, enlisted at 23, Tallapoosa.

Joiner, J. J.; 5/D; Private, enlisted 5/14/62, Montgomery.

Joiner, N. R.; 5/D; Private, enlisted 5/14/62, Montgomery.

Joiner, S. J.; 5/D; Private, enlisted 5/15/62, Montgomery.

Jones, B. W.; 5/D; Private, enlisted 4/11/62, Lowndes.

Jones, James; 5/E; Private, enlisted at 19, Randolph.

Jones, Jesse T; 5/B; Private, enlisted 3/11/62 at 38, Randolph.

Jones, William H.; 5/D; Lieutenant, enlisted 4/26/62, Lowndes.

Jordan, C. C.; 5/E; Private, enlisted at 18, Talladega.

Jordan, Isaac; 5/B; Private, enlisted at 23, Randolph.

Jordan, J. B.; 5/E; Private, enlisted at 20, Talladega.

Jordan, Richard A; 5/B; Private, enlisted at 21, Randolph.

Jordan, Samuel; 5/D; Private, enlisted 5/5/62, Lowndes.

Kennon, R. B.; 5/D; Private, enlisted 4/30/62, Bibb.

King, A. J.; 5/E; Private, enlisted at 46, Talladega.

King, Henry T.; 5/B; Private, enlisted at 30, Randolph.

King, W. B.; 5/E; Private, enlisted at 30, Talladega.

Kirby, Marion S.; 5/A; Private, enlisted at 25, Chambers.

Kittley, Thomas; 5/B; Private, enlisted at 23, Randolph.

Knight, Thomas, A.; 5/D; Lieutenant, enlisted 4/7/62, Lowndes.

Lachey, James M.; 5/C; Sergeant, enlisted at 29, Talladega.

Lancaster, John W. D.; 5/A; Private, enlisted at 22, Chambers.

Landrum, Charles D.; 5/B; Private, enlisted at 19, Randolph.

Langford, James; 5/D; Private, enlisted 4/26/62, Lowndes.

Lanier, William; 5/B; Private, enlisted at 18, Randolph.

Lawler, L. W.; 5/E; Private, enlisted at 25, Talladega.

Lawler, Thomas; 5/B; Private, enlisted at 22, Randolph.

Lawler, William; 5/B; Private, enlisted at 22, Randolph.

Lawrence, Joel S.; 5/A; Private, enlisted at 24, Chambers

Lawrence (or Laurence), Lenard H.; 5/A; Corporal, enlisted at 22, Chambers.

Leach, W. W.; 5/D; Private, enlisted 4/12/62, Lowndes.

Ledbetter, G. W.; 5/E; Private, enlisted at 23, Talladega.

Lee, John M.; 5/D; Private, enlisted 5/7/62, Lowndes.

Lee, William; 5/C; Lieutenant, enlisted at 29, Tallapoosa. Died 8/14/62.

Lesley (or Lepley), William M.; 5/C; Private, enlisted at 26, Coosa.

Links, Wiley; 5/C; Sergeant, enlisted at 40, Tallapoosa.

Lumsden, Jesse M.; 5/C; Corporal, enlisted at 35, Talladega.

Madden, R. P.; 5/D; Private, enlisted 5/10/62, Lowndes.

Magnan, David; 5/A; Private, enlisted at 20, Chambers.

Magnan, John H.; 5/A; Private, enlisted at 24, Chambers.

Magnan, William H.; 5/A; Private, enlisted at 21, Chambers.

Malone, C. B.; 5/E; Lieutenant, enlisted at 36, Tallapoosa.

Maples, Edward B.; 5/D; Private, enlisted 5/8/62, Montgomery.

Martin, W. C.; 5/E; Sergeant, enlisted at 29, Tallapoosa.

Martin, William; 5/C; Private, enlisted at 18, Coosa.

Mason, George E.; 5/A; Private, enlisted at 29, Chambers. Born 2/27/27, died 1/15/1908 at Confederate Memorial Park, Alabama.

Mathew, Alexander; 5/B; Private, enlisted at 19, Randolph.

Mathew, John E.; 5/B; Private, enlisted at 23, Randolph.

Maxwell, James; 5/B; Private, enlisted at 47, Randolph.

Maxwell, William C.; 5/B; Private, enlisted at 24, Randolph.

May, Jacob; 5/E; Private, enlisted at 18, Talladega.

Maynard, James; 5/D; Lieutenant, enlisted 4/7/62, Lowndes.

McAllister, James; 5/C; Private, enlisted at 26, Tallapoosa.

McCaskill, A.J.; 5/D; Private, enlisted 5/13/62, Montgomery.

McClendon, James; 5/C; Sergeant, enlisted at 26, Tallapoosa.

McClerkin, S. P.; 5/E; Sergeant, enlisted at 18, Tallapoosa.

McCloud, Norman; 5/D; Private, enlisted 5/1/62, Dallas.

McCloud, William; 5/C; Private, enlisted at 19, Tallapoosa.

McConathey (also McConatha), James; 5/E; Private, enlisted 2/5/62 at 51, Talladega. Discharged 11/14/62. Farmer.

McCowen, Augustus D.; 5/A; Private, enlisted at 32, Chambers.

McDaniel, Alexander; 5/B; Sergeant, enlisted at 24, Chambers.

McDaniel, Berdyne; 5/E; Private, enlisted at 18, Talladega.

McDonald, Napoleon; 5/B; Private, enlisted at 19, Randolph.

McGahee, David; 5/B; Private, enlisted at 20, Randolph.

McGehee, George W.; 5/A; Private, enlisted at 27, Chambers. Died 7/2/62.

McKelvey (or McElvie), John; 5/C; Private, enlisted at 18, Tallapoosa.

McKelvey, Joseph N.; 5/C; Private, enlisted at 39, Tallapoosa.

McKinney, Joseph T.; 5/A; Private, enlisted at 31, Chambers.

McKnight, Charles B.; 5/A; Private, enlisted at 32, Chambers.

McQueene, Alexander; 5/D; Private, enlisted 4/11/62, Lowndes.

Merriel, Robert; 5/B; Private, enlisted at 31, Randolph.

Merriwether, John A.; 5/D; Sergeant, enlisted 4/30/62, Lowndes.

Middlebrooks, James M.; 5/C; Blacksmith, enlisted at 34, Tallapoosa.

Miller, William; 5/B; Sergeant, enlisted 3/11/62 at 34, Randolph.

Mills, Wilson; 5/D; Private, enlisted 5/14/62, Montgomery.

Mize, J. G.; 5/E; Farrier, enlisted at 31, Calhoun.

Mobley, Jacob F.; 5/A; Private, enlisted at 33, Montgomery.

Mooney, John A.; 5/C; Private, enlisted at 22, Georgia.

Moore, Abraham B.; 5/A; Private, enlisted at 28, Chambers.

Moore, Andrew J.; 5/B; Private, enlisted at 19, Randolph.

Moore, James C; 5/B; Corporal, enlisted 3/11/62 at 28, Randolph.

Moore, M. D.; 5/E; Private, enlisted at 22, Talladega.

Moorer, Edgar D.; 5/D; Private, enlisted 4/29/62, Lowndes.

Moorer, Frederick; 5/D; Private, enlisted 4/26/62, Lowndes.

Moorer, Henry J.; 5/D; Corporal, enlisted 4/12/62, Lowndes.

Moses, Linton L/; 5/D; Musician, enlisted 5/14/62, Montgomery.

Motes, R. C.; 5/D; Private, enlisted 4/11/62, Lowndes.

Music, William; 5/B; Sergeant, enlisted at 22, Randolph.

Nall, E. L.; 5/E; Private, enlisted at 25, Talladega.

Nance, Thomas H.; 5/D; Private, enlisted 5/2/62, Montgomery.

Neighbors, J. B.; 5/E; Private, enlisted at 18 Calhoun.

Nelson, Esau L.; 5/E; Private, enlisted at 25, Talladega.

Nelson, James T.; 5/B; Private, enlisted at 26, Randolph.

Nepper, Jacob C.; 5/B; Private, enlisted at 32, Randolph.

O'Neil, Calvin W.; 5/C; Private, enlisted at 41, Coosa.

Obrian (or Obriant), Charles; 5/B; Private, enlisted at 18, Randolph.

Omalue (or Omaelue, Omalie, Omelia), John; 5/A; Private, enlisted at 25, Chambers.

Owens, W. Y.; 5/E; Private, enlisted at 18, Talladega.

Page, William F.; 5/A; Private, enlisted at 24, Chambers.

Parker, Henry C.; 5/B; Sergeant, enlisted at 18, Chambers.

Parnell, Benjamin; 5/B; Private, enlisted at 21, Randolph.

Partridge, William H.; 5/C; Private, enlisted at 38, Tallapoosa.

Patterson, Daniel; 5/C; Private, enlisted at 22, Tallapoosa.

Patterson, J. M.; 5/E; Private, enlisted at 22, Talladega.

Patterson, John W.; 5/C; Private, enlisted at 33, Talladega.

Peake, John S.; 5/D; Sergeant, enlisted 4/19/62, Lowndes.

Pearce, J. N.; 5/E; Private, enlisted at 34, Talladega.

Pepper, Andrew (or Andrews or A. J. or Andres); 5/A; Private, enlisted at 38, Chambers.

Perdue, Andrew W.; 5/D; Corporal, enlisted 4/19/62, Lowndes.

Perdue, S. M.; 5/D; Private, enlisted 4/26/62, Lowndes.

Perdue, William; 5/D; Private, enlisted 4/15/62, Baldwin.

Phillips, J. K. P.; 5/E; Private, enlisted at 18, Talladega.

Phillips, James R. 5/A; Lieutenant, enlisted at 41, Chambers.

Phillips, W.; 5/E; Private, enlisted at 23, Talladega.

Pittman, E. R.; 5/D; Private, enlisted 4/19/62, Lowndes.

Pope, John B.; 5/C; Bugler, enlisted at 37, Tallapoosa.

Porterfield, W. M.; 5/D; Private, enlisted 4/26/62, Lowndes.

Power, Robert F.; 5/A; Private, enlisted at 30, Chambers.

Price, Duke P.; 5/B; Farrier, enlisted at 32, Chambers.

Prichard, John C.; 5/B; Private, enlisted at 25, Randolph.

Prichett, W.; 5/E; Private, enlisted at 18, Talladega.

Pricket, George; 5/B; Private, enlisted 3/11/62 at 21, Randolph.

Pricket, John W.; 5/B; Private, enlisted at 18, Randolph.

Prickett, J. L.; 5/E; Sergeant, enlisted at 25, Tallapoosa.

Pruitt, W. W.; 5/D; Private, enlisted 5/10/62, Lowndes.

Rast, M. J. D.; 5/D; Private, enlisted 4/26/62, Lowndes.

Reaves, J.; 5/E; Private, enlisted at 18, Talladega.

Reese, Milton E.; 5/B; Lieutenant, enlisted at 22, Chambers.

Reynolds, John W.; Private, enlisted at 24, Talladega.

Richardson, William A.; 5/D; Blacksmith, enlisted 4/26/62, Lowndes.

Richardson, William H.; 5/D; Private, enlisted 3/13/62, Lowndes.

Roberts, R. R.; 5/D; Private, enlisted 4/12/62, Montgomery.

Robinson, John H.; 5/A; Sergeant, enlisted at 27. Mustered by mistake, sent to Richmond, belonged to Company C, 14th Alabama.

Robinson, Thomas J.; 5/D; Private, enlisted 4/19/62, Lowndes.

Rogers, John W.; 5/C; Private, enlisted at 27, Tallapoosa.

Rone, Mathew F.; 5/C; Private, enlisted at 25, Coosa.

Rudolph (or Rudulph), John B.; 5/D; Captain, enlisted 4/7/62, Lowndes.

Rufsill, W. W.; 5/E; Private, enlisted age/date uncertain, Talladega.

Runyan, Hiram; 5/C; Private, enlisted 5/8/62 at 25, Talladega. Later quartermaster, transferred to Company K, 24th Alabama Infantry Regiment.

Ruple, William C.; 5/D; Private, enlisted 4/12/62, Lowndes.

Russell (or Russel), James T.; 5/C; Private, enlisted at 28, Tallapoosa.

Russell, James R.; 5/A; Private, enlisted at 22, Chambers.

Salley, Franklin B.; 5/D; Private, enlisted 5/15/62, Montgomery.

Salmon, Jacob L.; 5/A; Private, enlisted at 34, Chambers.

Scott, William; 5/A; Private, enlisted at 23, Chambers.

Self, D. R.; 5/E; Private, enlisted at 18, Calhoun.

Sentel, Augustus D.; 5/C; Private, enlisted 7/2/62 at 44, Talladega.

Sentel, Augustus; 5/C; Private, enlisted 7/2/62 at 19, Talladega.

Sexton, Allen; 5/B; Private, enlisted at 18, Randolph.

Sexton, William B.; 5/B; Private, enlisted at 34, Randolph.

Shanks, Robert T.; 5/D; Private, enlisted 4/17/62, Lowndes.

Shanks, William L.; 5/D; Private, enlisted 4/7/62, Lowndes.

Shaw, Oliver; 5/C; Private, enlisted at 22, Coosa.

Sherard, William D.; 5/B; Private, enlisted at 48, Randolph.

Sherard, William; 5/B; Private, enlisted at 18, Randolph.

Shirie, John; 5/B; Private, enlisted 3/11/62 at 18, Randolph.

Simmons, Holman; 5/C; Private. enlisted at 22, Talladega.

Simmons, Robert A.; 5/C; Private, enlisted at 24, Talladega.

Slaughter, M. M.; F/S; Major, Battalion commander.

Slaughter, Martin G.; 5/C; Captain, enlisted at 40, Talladega.

Smallwood, Thomas N.; 5/A; Private, enlisted at 32, Chambers.

Smedley, Thomas; 5/A; Private, enlisted at 18, Chambers.

Smith, Bryant G.; 5/D; Private, enlisted 5/14/62, Montgomery.

Smith, David E.; 5/A; Private, enlisted at 28, Chambers. Furnished substitute 6/25/62.

Smith, George W.; 5/B; Private, enlisted at 26, Randolph.

Smith, J. B.; 5/E; Sergeant, enlisted at 29, Tallapoosa.

Smith, Joshua; 5/D; Private, enlisted 5/14/62, Montgomery.

Smith, Monroe M.; 5/C; Corporal, enlisted at 24, Tallapoosa.

Smith, Phillip R.; 5/C; Private, enlisted at 22, Talladega.

Smith, Seborn W.; 5/A; Corporal, enlisted at 26, Chambers.

Smith, Thomas J.; 5/A; Private, enlisted at 32, Chambers.

Smith, William G.; 5/B; Private, enlisted at 25, Randolph.

Smith, William H.; 5/A; Private, enlisted at 23, Chambers.

Smith, William T.; 5/B; Captain, enlisted at 25, Chambers.

Soles, Joseph M.; 5/D; Musician, enlisted 5/2/62, Lowndes.

Solly, A. J.; 5/E; Private, enlisted at 42, Talladega.

Solly, W. J.; 5/E; Private, enlisted at 18, Talladega.

South, Henry J.; 5/E; Private, enlisted at 25, Talladega.

Spinks, John E.; 5/A; Private, enlisted at 30, Chambers.

Sprewell, Samuel; 5/E; Private, enlisted at 33, Talladega.

Starr, Lucius E.; 5/D; Sergeant, enlisted 4/24/62, Bibb.

Stearns, William F.; 5/C; Lieutenant, enlisted at 46, Tallapoosa.

Stewart, Thomas A.; 5/D; Private, enlisted 4/21/62, Lowndes.

Street, Andrew J.; 5/E; Private, enlisted at 18, Talladega.

Strickland, J. W.; 5/D; Private, enlisted 5/8/62, Lowndes.

Strickland, James L.; 5/A; Blacksmith, enlisted at 28, Chambers.

Strickland, Samuel; 5/B; Private, enlisted at 18, Randolph.

Striplin, William M.; 5/E; Private, enlisted at 18, Randolph.

Suggs, McKinley; 5/C; Private, enlisted at 34, Talladega.

Sullivan, Franklin M.; 5/D; Private, enlisted 4/7/62, Lowndes.

Sully, Thomas J.; 5/D; Private, enlisted 4/30/62, Montgomery.

Tacket, Henry; 5/B; Private, enlisted at 22, Randolph.

Tanner, Jarris M.; 5/D; Private, enlisted 4/12/62, Lowndes.

Tarwater, Y. A.; 5/E; Private, enlisted at 19, Talladega.

Tate, Samuel C.; 5/B; Private, enlisted at 27, Randolph.

Tavar, Peter; 5/A; Private, enlisted at 23, Chambers.

Taylor, Arlington H.; 5/E; Private, enlisted at 18, Talladega.

Taylor, Thomas J.; 5/A; Private, enlisted at 38, Chambers.

Taylor, William L.; 5/A; Corporal, enlisted at 27, Chambers. Farrier.

Tenant, Charles H.; 5/B; Corporal, enlisted at 22, Randolph.

Tenant, William; 5/B; Private, enlisted at 20, Randolph. Died 12/28/62.

Tendal, James W.; 5/B; Private, enlisted at 22, Randolph.

Thigpen, James N.; 5/A; Private, enlisted at 18, Chambers.

Thompson, Andrew J.; 5/B; Lieutenant, enlisted at 35, Chambers.

Thompson, Gideon; 5/D; Private, enlisted 4/10/62, Bibb.

Thompson, J. B.; 5/D; Private, enlisted 5/14/62, Montgomery.

Thompson, J. R.; 5/E; Private, enlisted at 26, Talladega.

Tiller, Stephen H.; 5/A; Private, enlisted at 31, Chambers.

Tinney, Thomas; 5/B; Private, enlisted at 23, Randolph.

Tittle, William; 5/B; Private, enlisted at 18, Randolph.

Todd, John F.; 5/D; Private, enlisted 4/26/62, Lowndes.

Todd, Lewis J.; 5/D; Farrier, enlisted 4/26/62, Lowndes.

Tomlinson, Daniel W. (or M); 5/A; Private, enlisted at 20, Chambers.

Tomlinson, William C.; 5/A; Private, enlisted at 21, Chambers.

Towns, J. W.; 5/E; Private, enlisted at 25, Calhoun.

Trammel, James M.; 5/A; Private, enlisted at 51, Chambers.

Traylor, Jeremiah M.; 5/B; Private, enlisted at 20, Randolph. Believed to be brother of Migamon Traylor.

Traylor, Migamon (Megamine or Myamin) B.; 5/B; Private, enlisted at 23, Randolph. Married. Believed to be brother of Jeremiah Traylor.

Turner, William A.; 5/C; Private, enlisted at 30, Tallapoosa.

(Unknown), William; 5/B; Private, enlisted at 22, Randolph. Died 5/11/62.

Vardaman, James M.; 5/C; Musician, enlisted at 20, Coosa.

Vardaman, John F.; 5/C; Private, enlisted at 27, Coosa.

Veal, Jaret M.; 5/B; Private, enlisted at 38, Randolph.

Veal, William H.; 5/A; Private, enlisted at 28, Chambers.

Waganon, L. H.; 5/E; Corporal, enlisted at 19, Randolph.

Wall, Conrad; 5/D; Private, enlisted 4/19/62, Lowndes.

Waller, Elbert D.; 5/A; Lieutenant, enlisted at 40, Chambers.

Waller, John D.; 5/A; Private, enlisted at 18, Chambers.

Ward, William J.; 5/A; Private, enlisted at 34, Chambers.

Ware, J. B.; 5/E; Private, enlisted at 18, Randolph.

Ware, W. P.; 5/E; Private, enlisted at 16, Randolph.

Waters, T. H.; 5/E; Private, enlisted at 18, Talladega.

Watson, W.; 5/E; Private, enlisted at 18, Talladega.

Weaver, John T.; 5/B; Corporal, enlisted at 30, Randolph.

Webb, M.; 5/E; Private, enlisted at 18, Talladega.

Whatley, Danam (or Ornam); 5/A; Sergeant, enlisted at 21, Chambers.

Whited, A. R.; 5/E; Private, enlisted at 26, Talladega.

Whited, Davis; 5/C; Private, enlisted at 61, Talladega. Married.

Whitlock, William B.; 5/A; Private, enlisted at 38, Chambers.

Williams, J. Y.; 5/E; Private, enlisted at 21, Talladega.

Williams, James B.; 5/A; Private, enlisted at 42, Chambers.

Williams, Warren M.; 5/D; Private, enlisted 4/7/62, Lowndes.

Williams, William S.; 5/A; Private, enlisted at 22, Chambers.

Wilson, Asa P.; Private, enlisted at 27, Coosa.

Wilson, John R.; 5/C; Private, enlisted at 26, Talladega.

Wilson, R. B.; 5/E; Private, enlisted at 30, Talladega.

Wood, James B.; 5/A; Private, enlisted at 326, Chambers.

Woodson, James M.; 5/B; Private, enlisted at 26, Randolph.

Woodson, John A.; 5/B; Private, enlisted at 21, Randolph.

Woodson, Mathew P.; 5/B; Private, enlisted at 36, Randolph.

Wright, Cicero H.; 5/A; Private, enlisted at 22, Chambers.

Wright, John R.; 5/B; Private, enlisted at 22, Randolph.

Wyatt, Robert; 5/A; Private, enlisted at 26, Chambers.

Yancey, William W.; 5/B; Private, enlisted at 18, Randolph.

Zeigler, Frank A.; 5/D; Private, enlisted 4/25/62, Lowndes.

Chapter Notes

Introduction

1. The citation on the Medal of Honor includes an inaccurate notation, as will be shown.

Chapter 1

1. www.timeanddate.com. Accessed July 28, 2016.

2. From Bragg's Chickamauga report in *The War of the Rebellion: A Compilation of the Official Records of the Union and Confederate Armies*, Series I, Volume 30, Part II, Report 236, page 21. From here on, *Official Records* (OR).

Chapter 2

1. 1860 United States Census, Census Slave Schedule, Division 1, Montgomery, page 43.

2. Accessed at the Alabama Department of Archives and History. Hereafter, ADAH.

3. *Ibid.*

4. *Ibid.*

5. Massey, *Reminiscences, giving sketches of scenes through which the author has passed and pen portraits of people who have modified his life*, p. 167. From here on, Massey.

6. Much of the Legion's pre–Chickamauga history is explained by a Historical Memoranda for the 60th Regiment, Alabama Volunteers found in the Gracie Brigade folder at the Chickamauga/Chattanooga National Military Park.

7. Massey, page 164.

8. The author found an image of this letter online and first read it that way. Since then the Auburn University Libraries Special Collections & Archives Department has emailed images of the Benjamin Mason Papers to the author. The original Benjamin Mason Papers are held at Auburn. From here on, Mason Papers.

9. Mary Allin Loftis Civil War Letters, 1861–1865, ADAH. From here on, Loftis Letters. The author has not found either L. W. Moore or L. S. Reaves on the roster of the 3rd Battalion.

10. The Legion roster at the back of this book lists the soldiers who served in the Legion. The death dates are listed for those who died while in uniform.

11. Mason Papers.

12. Loftis Letters.

13. J. E. B. Stuart, the Confederate cavalry commander, ranked 13th in the same class at West Point. John Pegram was tenth. George Washington Custis Lee graduated first in the same class.

14. Archibald Gracie IV, son of the General, spent nearly a decade researching the battle of Chickamauga. Because a number of veterans on both sides of the fight were still living, Gracie IV was able to assemble a great number of first-hand accounts of the battle. He wrote *The Truth About Chickamauga*, which was published in 1911. The fourth Gracie's biggest claim to fame was as a survivor of the ill-fated maiden voyage of the RMS *Titanic*. Gracie IV reportedly gathered accounts from other survivors after they were rescued by the steamer *Carpathia* and turned those notes into another book, *The Truth About the Titanic*. Gracie IV died late in 1912 of complications from illnesses caused by his harrowing night standing on an upturned life boat after the *Titanic* sank.

15. Massey, pages 176–177.

16. Shaver, *A History of the Sixtieth Alabama Regiment*. From here on, referred to as Shaver. See also the Historical Memoranda

about the 60th Alabama Infantry Regiment, ADAH. Shaver's book was published in 1867. Two months after Chickamauga, the remainder of the Legion was split into three new units, the 23rd Battalion, Alabama Sharpshooters and the 59th and 60th infantry regiments. The 2nd and 4th Battalions formed the 59th Regiment.

17. The spelling here is as transcribed. Letter headed "Near Chattanooga" and "This September the 30, 1863" in Civil War Letters of John Forbes Davenport, 1st Battalion, Hilliard's Alabama Legion and 23rd Alabama Sharpshooters. Transcripts in Gracie's Brigade First Battalion file, Chickamauga Chattanooga National Military Park. From here on, Davenport Letter.

18. Mason Papers.

19. *Ibid.*

20. Hall Family Papers, ADAH. This is a very large compilation of papers and letters. The author studied them at the ADAH but the collection is available online through the ADAH. Letters cited generally can be found in this collection by searching for letters dealing with the Civil War. From here on, Hall Family Papers.

21. Hall Family Papers.

Chapter 3

1. The Confederates lost 9,865 killed and wounded, the Federals lost 13,244. NPShistory.com/park_histories, Stones River National Battlefield, Historic Resource Study, p. 34. Accessed March 10, 2017.

2. The author found Woodworth's essay *In Their Dreams* in a book edited by Woodworth, *The Chickamauga Campaign*. The Confederate manpower advantage at McLemore's Cove is discussed on page 64.

3. Davenport Letter.

4. Hall Family Papers.

5. Massey, page 181.

6. From the diary of George Washington Sexton. Transcripts in Gracie's Brigade First Battalion file, Chickamauga National Military Park. From here on, Sexton Diary.

7. The statistics and biographical information on these soldiers came from various sources. They include the muster rolls for the Legion (available online through the ADAH via Ancestry.com), the Final Statements paperwork (available at the ADAH) and the ADAH's Civil War Soldiers Database for Alabamians that fought for the Confederacy during the

Civil War. In some cases among the soldiers cited here, all three sources were used.

Chapter 4

1. Preston's report, OR, Series I, Volume 30, Part II, report 392, page 413.

2. *Ibid.*

3. McLennan's report, OR, Series I, Volume 30, Part II, report 398, page 427.

4. Aiken's report, OR, Series I, Volume 30, Part II, report 399, page 428.

5. Massey, pages 182–183.

6. Shaver, page 13.

7. Huguley's report, OR, Series I, Volume 30, Part II, report 395, page 424.

8. Preston's report, OR, Series I, Volume 30, Part II, report 392, page 413.

9. Preston's report, OR, Series 1, Volume 31, Part II, report 392, page 414.

10. *Ibid.*

11. Preston's report, OR, Series I, Volume 30, Part II, report 392, page 413.

12. Johnson's report, OR, Series 1, Volume 30, Part II, report 412, page 456.

13. Archibald Gracie Papers, ADAH. From here on, Gracie Papers.

14. Gracie, *The Truth about Chickamauga*, page 373.From here on, *The Truth.*

15. Shaver, pages 14–15.

16. Letter from Horace McLean to his wife, Mary. It is part of a collection of McLean's letters home during the war. The collection is held at the Auburn University Libraries Special Collections & Archives Department. The letter quoted here is undated, as the portions still existing appear to begin with the second page. However, on the fourth existing page, McLean mentions that he and his comrades are about three miles away from Chattanooga and have what he calls "shelling and picket fighting" daily. McLean's battlefield experiences quoted here and elsewhere in this book could only have come from the fight at Chickamauga. From here on, McLean Letters.

17. Massey, page 184.

18. The two nights Davenport referred to are those of September 19 and September 20. Davenport Letter.

19. Shaver, page 14.

Chapter 5

1. Bragg's report is very lengthy and includes various communications with com-

manders in the field. For simplicity the author has listed the page number in the volume without the report number. OR, Series I, Volume 30, Part II, page 33.

2. Longstreet's report, OR, Series I, Volume 30, Report 340, page 287.

3. Bragg's report, OR, Series I, Volume 30, Part II, page 33. Longstreet's report, OR, Series I, Volume 30, Part II, Report 340, page 287.

4. Massey, pages 184–185.

5. Gracie was well known to many of the war's highest profile commanders. He was a West Point classmate of J. E. B. Stuart and Custis Lee. There is a story, memorialized by a poem, according to which Gracie noticed Robert E. Lee standing above the Confederate breastworks at Petersburg, about a year after the fight at Chickamauga. Gracie, the story goes, attempted to convince the commander of the Army of Northern Virginia to drop down into a safer position. Lee did not move and, according to the story, Gracie stood and inserted himself between Lee and the prospective path of Union projectiles. When Lee protested that Gracie might be shot, Gracie is said to have told Lee "Better me than you," or words to that effect. The poem is *Gracie, of Alabama* by Francis O. Ticknor. See Appendix 9.

6. Bishop, *Van Derveer's Brigade at Chickamauga.*

7. Shaver, pages 15–16.

8. Aiken's report, OR, Series I, Volume 30, Part II, report 399, page 428.

Chapter 6

1. More on this subject later.

2. Other sources discuss Kershaw's attack more completely. See Powell, *The Maps of Chickamauga,* pages 190–214; Cozzens, *This Terrible Sound,* pages 424–462. See Gracie's *The Truth* for an in-depth examination of the Federal defense of Horseshoe Ridge.

3. One of the funniest things the author ever heard came from a licensed battlefield guide at Gettysburg, who said he is sometimes asked why the monuments there are not marked by bullets from the battle. Suffice it to say that there are no bullet marks on the South Carolina monument at Chickamauga.

4. Clark's death is described in accounts from both sides and is an important note as regards Gracie's Brigade in general and the Legion in particular. The incident is discussed more fully in a later chapter.

Chapter 7

1. Longstreet's report, OR, Series I, Volume 30, Part II, report 340, page 289.

2. Longstreet, *From Manassas to Appomattox, Memoirs of the Civil War in America,* pages 386–387.

3. The author read Robertson's essay in Woodworth (Ed.), *The Chickamauga Campaign.*

4. Longstreet's Report, OR, Series I, Volume 30, Part II, report 340, page 289.

5. There are many sources for Gracie's march up the LaFayette Road. Perhaps the best visual aid is found in Powell and Friedrichs' *The Maps of Chickamauga,* page 191.

6. The reader can easily approach Horseshoe Ridge along the same path the Gracie and Kelly commands did. The simplest way would be to drive along Glenn-Kelly Road and park near the sign indicating the small pathway toward the spot where Hood suffered his wound. From those woods, turn north and walk toward the hill where the South Carolina Monument is perched. Standing at the Monument and facing the trees, the reader would be near the left flank of Gracie's formation.

7. Aitken's report, OR, Series I, Volume 30, Part II, report 389, page 428.

8. Preston's report, OR, Series I, Volume 30, Part II, report 392, page 415.

9. Kershaw's report, OR, Series I, Volume 30, Part II, report 424, page 502.

10. From the author's conversation with James Ogden, Chickamauga National Military Park Historian.

11. Massey, page 186.

12. *The Montgomery Weekly Advertiser,* October 7, 1863.

13. Affidavit in the Archibald Gracie Papers, copy unsigned, dated January, 1908. The formation can be pieced together through reading several sources, including Gracie's report, OR, Series I, Volume 30, Part II, page 421; Moody's report, OR, Series I, Volume 30, Part II, page 423; Huguley's report, OR, Series I, Volume 30, Part II, page 424; Hall's report, OR, Series I, Volume 30, Part II, page 425; Sanford's report, OR, Series I, Volume 30, Part II, page 426; McLennan's report, OR, Series I, Volume 30, Part II, page 427; and Aiken's report, OR, Series I, Volume 30, Part II, page 428.

14. Buckner's report, OR, Series I, Volume 30, Part II, report 367, page 358.

15. McLennan's report, OR, Series I, Volume 30, Part II, report 398, page 427.

16. Gracie's report, OR, Series I, Volume 30, Part II, report 393, page 421.

17. Isaac Cusac letter to E. A. Carman, March 13, 1909. MMS 1404, Center for Archival Collections, Bowling Green State University. From here on, Cusac Letter.

18. Preston's report, OR, Series I, Volume 30, Part II, report 392, page 415.

19. Massey, page 186.

20. Preston's report, OR, Series I, Volume 30, Part II, report 392, page 416.

21. Aitken, OR, Series I, Volume 30, Part II, report 399, page 429.

22. Moody's report, OR, Series I, Volume 30, Part II, report 394, page 423.

23. *Ibid.*

24. Aitken's report, OR, Series I, Volume 30, Part II, report 399, page 429.

25. The author has stood in the area where the 63rd's left flank split from the right flank of the Legion's 2nd Battalion. The confusion is understandable.

26. Shaver, page 16.

27. May 4, 1903, letter from H. H. Bargainer to Thomas N. Davis. The letter came from ADAH box 49, folder 10, containing information about the 60th Alabama Infantry Regiment, but the material is not generally open for viewing. The author found Bargainer's letter among the material photocopied and available on www.ancestry.com.

28. *Reminiscences of the Boys in Gray, 1861–1865*, page 573. The author found a photocopy in the Legion's file at the Chickamauga National Battlefield Park.

29. Wood's report, OR, Series I, Volume 30, Part I, report 136, page 638.

30. J. W. Bishop, *Van Derveer's Brigade at Chickamauga.*

31. Hall's report, OR, Series I, Volume 30, Part II, report 396, page 425.

32. Gracie's report, OR, Series I, Volume 30, Part II, report 393, page 421.

33. Moody's report, OR, Series I, Volume 30, Part II, report 394, page 423.

34. Horace McLean Papers, Auburn University Libraries Special Collections & Archives Department.

35. Hall's report, OR, Series I, Volume 30, Part II, report 396, page 425.

36. The best source for Hall's military history is the Hall Family Papers at the ADAH.

37. Letter from Ben Fitzpatrick to John A. Campbell, dated September 4, 1864. Hall Family Papers, ADAH.

38. Gracie letter to Nicholas Stallworth, May 20, 1907, Gracie Papers.

39. *The Montgomery Weekly Advertiser,* October 7, 1863.

40. April 24, 1863 letter from Bolling Hall, Jr., to his father. Hall Family Papers, ADAH.

41. *The Montgomery Weekly Advertiser,* October 7, 1863.

42. Gracie's report, OR, Series I, Volume 30, Part II, report 393, page 422.

43. Gracie Papers, ADAH.

44. McLennan's report, OR, Series I, Volume 30, Part II, report 398, page 427.

45. Gracie Papers, ADAH.

46. *Ibid.*

47. The book was adopted for the U.S. Army by future Confederate president Jefferson Davis when Davis was the Secretary of War for the United States in the 1850s.

48. Gracie Papers, ADAH.

49. *Ibid.*

50. Davenport Letter.

51. *Ibid.*

52. Moody's report, OR, Series I, Volume 30, Part II, report 394, page 423.

53. Gracie's report, OR, Series I, Volume 30, Part II, page 421.

54. *Ibid.*

55. Longstreet report, OR, Series I, Volume 30, Part II, report 340, page 289.

56. Reports of Longstreet (report 340), Huguley (395), Hall (396) and Sanford (397), OR, Series I, Volume 30, Part II.

57. McLennan's report, OR, Series I, Volume 30, Part II, report 398, page 427.

58. Preston's report, OR, Series I, Volume 30, Part II, report 392, pages 413 and,420.

59. Young's report, OR, Series I, Volume 30, Part II, report 394, page 424.

60. Kelly's report, OR, Series I, Volume 30, Part II, report 405, page 442.

61. Stoughton's report, OR, Series I, Volume 30, Part I, report 40, page 381.

62. *The Truth*, page 311.

63. *Ibid.*

64. Gracie Papers, ADAH.

65. *Ibid.*

66. *Ibid.*

67. Maxwell's report, OR, Series I, Volume 30, Part II, report 401, page 433. Maxwell's "corn-field" was along today's Glenn-Kelly Road.

68. The casualty statistics for both sides, officers and enlisted men, are all available in

the Official Records. The Federal casualty reports can be found in OR, Series I, Volume 30, Part I. The Confederate casualty reports can be found in OR, Series I, Volume 30, Part II.

Chapter 8

1. The information on Hines, Mason, Kief and Jenkins is available on the Legion's muster rolls (ADAH) and in the ADAH's Civil War soldiers database (available at the Department's website). Also, in Mason's case, Mason Letters. In Hines' case, a collection of research done by descendants.

2. Cusac Letter.

3. Trigg's report, OR, Series I, Volume 30, Part 2, report 400, page 431.

4. Cusac Letter.

5. Trigg's report, OR, Series I, Volume 30, Part 2, report 400, page 432.

6. Gracie Papers, ADAH.

7. McMahan letter, Official Records, Series 1, Volume 30, Part I, page 390. Negley's response shifted McMahan to Brigadier General J. M. Brannan for answers, saying that the 21st was under Brannan's command by that point in the fighting. Brannan's response to McMahan's subsequent query quarreled with Negley's statement that the 21st Ohio covered Brannan's retreat, saying that Brannan did not retreat before McMahan and the others were captured. The author wonders if Brannan might have been captured along with McMahan had Brannan still been on the ridge when Trigg and Kelly ordered their pincer movement at the remaining defenders.

8. OR, Series I, Volume 30, Part I, report 44, page 387. Table of losses, page 390.

9. Fuller letter, Gracie Papers.

10. Trigg's report, OR, Series I, Volume 30, Part II, report 400, page 432.

11. Longstreet's report, OR, Series I, Volume 30, Part II, report 340, page 289.

12. The author believes Union officers like Stoughton, some of whom had been defending the ridge for much of the afternoon and early evening, had a much more difficult challenge to determine when specific events happened during the battle for Horseshoe Ridge. Preston, Gracie, Kelly and Trigg had a much tighter period of time to concern themselves with when writing their reports. Their time citations seem clearer, possibly for that reason. Gracie and Kelly must have had it easiest of all because they did not go into action

until they left the Poe and Brotherton area at about 4 p.m. Trigg's men were more active and had more to keep track of.

13. *Untold History: The Battle of Chickamauga*, Bowling Green State University Center for Archival Collections, MMS 1211. This is a sketch of the actions of the 21st written by George S. Canfield and read during the 1908 reunion of Company K. The author found the transcription online.

14. The Gracie Papers are replete with references to the statements of men from Company A of the 43rd. But the clearest references are in a November 22, 1907 letter to Wolfe, then living in Atlanta, and in a March 20, 1908 letter to E. F. Comegys, then of Gainesville, Texas.

15. Beatty's report, OR, Series I, Volume 3, Part I, report 36, page 366.

16. Hindman's report, OR, Series I, Volume 30, Part II, report 41, page 305.

Chapter 9

1. Both quotes above come from Vantine's report, found in McMahan's report, OR, Series I, Volume 30, Part I, report 44, page 395.

2. Kelly's report, OR, Series I, Volume 30, Part II, report 405, starts on page 441.

Chapter 10

1. Gracie's report, OR, Series I, Volume 30, Part II, p. 421.

2. Preston's report, OR, Series I, Volume 30, Part II, report 392. See also reports 393–399. The casualty numbers in the battalion and regimental reports are slightly different from those in Preston's and Gracie's reports. Other sources include the bi-monthly muster cards for the period covering the battle for the Chickamauga loss information, and the Confederate Combined Service Records, which are available at the ADAH. The Confederate muster rolls for the company leave a few clues and are available at the ADAH. A final source is the ADAH Civil War Soldiers Database.

3. Richard Slotkin, *The Long Road to Antietam: How the Civil War Became a Revolution*, page 303.

4. Most of the information is available in the ADAH Hilliard's Legion files, which are available online. The author used the bi-monthly muster cards for the period covering the battle for the Chickamauga loss information; the Confederate Service Records, which

are available at the ADAH; the Confederate muster rolls for the company, which also leave a few clues; and the ADAH Civil War Soldiers Database.

    5. Gracie letter to Nicholas Stallworth, May 20, 1907, Gracie Papers.

    6. Wood's report, OR, Series I, Volume 30, Part I, report 136, page 641. Wood's statistics are found on pages 643–645.

    7. *Ibid.*

    8. Moody's losses can be found in his report, OR, Series I, Volume 30, Part II, report 394, page 424. Aiken's report, OR, Series I, Volume 30, Part II, report 399, page 429.

    9. Powell's *The Maps of Chickamauga* includes casualty statistics that differ slightly from the OR.

    10. Sanford's report, OR, Series I, Volume 30, Part II, report 397, page 427.

    11. Hall Family Papers, ADAH.

    12. McLean Papers.

    13. Bullock's Report, OR, Series I, Volume 30, Part II, report 403, page 438.

    14. Preston's report, OR, Series I, Volume 30, Part II, report 392, page 413, page 420.

    15. See reports of Moody (394), Huguley (395), Hall (396), Sanford (397), McLennan (398), and Aiken (399), OR, Series I, Volume 30, Part II, starting on page 420.

    16. From the diary of George Washington Sexton.

    17. Preston's report, OR, Series I, Volume 30, Part II, report 392, page 418.

    18. Odom's story appears in *Reminiscences of the Boys in Gray 1861–1865*, pages 572–573.

    19. Bragg's report, OR, Series I, Volume 30, Part 2, page 24.

    20. McLeanPapers, undated, page 3.

    21. Preston's report, OR, Series I, Volume 30, Part II, report 392, page 416.

    22. Hall's report, OR, Series I, Volume 30, Part II, page 425.

    23. Letter from Archibald Gracie IV to Albert Patterson, April 28, 1908, Gracie Papers, ADAH.

    24. Deceased Soldiers Accounts, Alabama Infantry Units, ADAH.

Chapter 11

    1. Shaver, page 18.

    2. The matter of Hines' pension can be found in the Alabama Confederate pension documents, available through the ADAH. Hines' service to the Confederate Army is delineated in Hines' service cards. The author

obtained the service cards for Hines and a number of other Legion members through the Reference Department of the United Daughters of the Confederacy.

    3. Alabama Confederate pension documents.

    4. The Henry Hines story was gathered from numerous sources, including Sarah Hines' application for the pension from Florida. The pension application was found online. Privately held family sources, where the author was unable to verify the information, are labeled as such.

    5. Telegraph from Bolling Hall, Jr., dated September 24, 1863, Hall Family Papers, ADAH.

    6. The story of Tom Brown Hall is related through letters in the Hall Family Papers at the ADAH. The notes involving railroad men Cram and Walker are dated September 23, 1863.

    7. *The Confederate Veteran*, May 1903, page 219.

    8. The information for these soldiers came from several sources including the Legion's company muster rolls (held by ADAH but available online), Final Statement paperwork (ADAH) and the ADAH Civil War Soldiers Database (available online).

Chapter 12

    1. D. H. Hill, "Chickamauga—The Great Battle of the West," *Century Illustrated Monthly Magazine*, Volume XXXIII, page 962.

    2. Rosecrans' Report, OR, Series I, Volume 30, Part I, report 3, page 62.

    3. *Ibid.*

    4. Inman's letter is part of the Weddell Family Papers at Ohio's Bowling Green State University Center for Archival Collections, MS 484 mf.

    5. The *Montgomery Weekly Advertiser*, October 7, 2016.

    6. Bragg's report, OR, Series I, Volume 30, Part II, report 236, page 25.

    7. *Ibid.* See also Appendix 4.

    8. Bragg's report, OR, Series I, Volume 30, Part II, report 236, page 36.

    9. There is a connection between the Legion and the Alabama football program. Jake Coker, the starting quarterback on the Crimson Tide's 2015 national championship team, is an indirect descendant of George L. Coker, a private in the 4th Battalion's Company A and, later, D. The author exchanged emails

with Betty L. Coker of Mobile, Alabama in January of 2016 to confirm the link between the soldier and the quarterback.
   10. cfbstats.com. Accessed August 6, 2016.

Appendix 1

   1. The order appears in the OR in several places. The reorganization details are best covered in Part 2, Volume I, Serial 13, starting on page 899.
   2. Johnson's report, January 1864, OR, Series I, Volume 31, Part I, report 74, page 531.
   3. *Ibid.*
   4. *Ibid.*
   5. *Ibid.*
   6. *Ibid.*
   7. *Ibid.*
   8. *Ibid.*
   9. OR, Series I, Volume 31, Part III, page 837.
   10. OR, Series I, Volume 36, Part II, page 988 (see table).
   11. OR, Series I, Volume 40, Part II, page 703.
   12. OR, Series 1, Volume 42, Part I, page 908.
   13. D. S. Freeman, *R. E. Lee: A Biography*, volume 3, page 531, note 40.
   14. Both letters are quoted in *Military Memoirs of a Confederate*, page 586.
   15. Gracie and Lee first met when Gracie III was a cadet at West Point and Lee was the superintendent. In the trenches near Petersburg, Lee may have recalled that Gracie was brought to Lee's attention at West Point when the younger man was involved in an altercation with another cadet. Gracie had repeatedly kicked the other man's heels when the two were marching in formation one day and the other cadet took exception. The two fought and Gracie was losing when they were separated by others. The other cadet rushed away to avoid punishment, but Gracie was later brought to Lee's office. The other cadet came to Lee's office at the same time Gracie was brought there and, eventually, neither man was disciplined.

Appendix 2

   1. Gracie Papers, letter of January 7, 1908, to Wolfe.
   2. Civil War Service Database, ADAH. See listings for Wolfe, Norwood and Hughes.
   3. *Ibid.*

Appendix 3

   1. Both affidavits are found in the Gracie Papers, available by microfilm through the ADAH.

Appendix 4

   1. The letters quoted for Bragg, Northrop and Hillyer are all found in the Official Records. Hillyer's letter to Bragg, OR, Series I, Volume 30, Part IV, page 547. Northrop's reply, page 549 ("General Bragg … delusion," page 550).
   2. McLean's quotes can be found in the Horace McLean [Co. "K"] Papers 1862–1881.
   3. Hall's quotes can be found in the Bolling Hall, Jr., papers, among other Civil War themed letters.

Appendix 5

   1. The story quoted above appeared in several newspapers of the era. The author found it online. The reader is reminded that the moon reached its first quarter on September 20 and would not have reflected as much light as Longstreet would lead one to believe.
   2. OR, Series I, Volume 30, Part II, Report 236, page 35.
   3. OR, Series I, Volume 30, Part II, Report 236, page 34.
   4. OR, Series I, Volume 30, Part II, Report 236, page 24.
   5. OR, Series I, Volume 30, Part II, Report 236, page 37.

Appendix 6

   1. From the ADAH file on Hilliard's Legion, Box/Folder M1/14, record of events for August 1 to September 30, 1863.

Appendix 7

   1. The D Company muster roll is held at the ADAH. It is available for viewing through Ancestry.com.
   2. Lucille Griffith, *Yours Till Death: Civil War Letters of John W. Cotton.* From here, *Yours Till Death.*
   3. *Yours Till Death*, page 85.
   4. *The Maps*, page 279.
   5. *Yours Till Death*, page 85.

Appendix 8

1. *The Maps*, page 226.
2. Powell, *Glory or the Grave*, pages 573–574.
3. OR, Series 1, Volume 39, Part II, page 588.
4. Tatum, *Disloyalty in the Confederacy*, pages 64–65; Powell, *Glory or the Grave,* page 574.
5. OR, Series IV, Volume 2, page 674.
6. *Ibid.*
7. OR, Series 1, Volume 39, Part II, page 588.
8. Executions in the Army of Tennessee at Dalton, May 15, 2014, daltondailycitizen.com. Accessed August 18, 2016.
9. Bunch, *Roster of the Courts-Martial in the Confederate States Armies.*
10. Muster cards for Moses P. May, found on Fold 3.com, accessed October 2, 2016.

Bibliography

Source Materials

Archibald Gracie Papers. Alabama Department of Archives and History (ADAH). LPR 142, Box 1 and Box 2, M2002–0301 and M2002–0302.

Benjamin Mason Papers. Auburn University Libraries Special Collections & Archives Department. Record Group 48.

Bishop, J. W. "Van Derveer's Brigade at Chickamauga." *Glimpses of the Nation's Struggle: Papers Read before the Minnesota Commandery of the Military Order of the Loyal Legion of the United States, 1903–08.* Minneapolis, 1909.

Civil War Letters of John Forbes Davenport. 1st Battalion, Hilliard's Legion file, Chickamauga and Chattanooga National Military Park (CCNMP).

Diary of George Washington Sexton. Transcript in Gracie's Brigade, 1st Battalion file, CCNMP.

Hall Family Papers. ADAH.

Hardee's Rifle and Light Infantry Tactics, 1855.

Historical Memoranda for the 60th Regiment, Alabama Volunteers. Gracie's Brigade folder, CCNMP.

Horace McLean Papers. Auburn University Libraries Special Collections & Archives Department. Record Group 679. Available online.

Isaac Cusac letter to E. A. Carman, March 13, 1909. Center for Archival Collections, Bowling Green State University. MMS 1404.

Mary Allin Loftis Civil War Letters, 1861–1865. ADAH.

Reminiscences of the Boys in Gray, 1861–1865. Hilliard's Legion file, CCNMP.

Samuel Hollingsworth Stout Papers 1837 (1860–1865)—1902. Center for American History, University of Texas at Austin. The portion of the collection viewed by the author was listed as stored in the Microfilm area on the second floor of SRH unit 2 at UT–Austin as of January12, 2012. The author viewed this portion of the Stout Papers on microfilm at the Auburn University Library with the assistance of the Auburn Special Collections & Archives Department.

Untold Story: The Battle of Chickamauga. Center for Archival Collections, Bowling Green State University. MMS 1211.

Weddell Family Papers. Center for Archival Collections, Bowling Green State University.

Maps

Chickamauga and Chattanooga National Military Park Georgia/Tennessee. National Park Service, US Department of the Interior. This map was part of an informational sheet distributed at the CCNMP Visitors Center.

Map of preliminary survey of the Vidito Roads from the Vidito house on Dry Valley to the Snodgrass House and Lafayette road, both roads. CHCH Acc Cat 3262.0002.0004. Map produced by E. E. Betts, Assistant Engineer. Chickamauga Chattanooga National Military Park.

Noon to night September 20th 1863 Map of the battlefield of Chickamauga, drawn by Edward E. Betts, C.E., park ranger for the Chickamauga and Chattanooga National Park Commission.

Websites

www.civilwarvirtualtours.com/chickamauga/sept20.html

www.daltondailycitizen.com, *Executions in*

the Army of Tennessee at Dalton, May 15, 2014, accessed August 18, 2016.
www.NPS.gov
www.timeanddate.com

Books

Bunch, Jack A. *Roster of the Courts-Martial in the Confederate States Armies.* Shippensburg, PA: White Mane Books, 2001.
Cozzens, Peter. *This Terrible Sound: The Battle of Chickamauga.* Urbana: University of Illinois Press, 1992.
Gracie, Archibald. *The Truth About Chickamauga.* Dayton, OH: Morningside, 1987.
Griffith, Lucille. *Yours Till Death: Civil War Letters of John W. Cotton.* University of Alabama Press, 1951.
Longstreet, James. *From Manassas to Appomattox: Memoirs of the Civil War in America.* New York: Barnes & Noble Books, 2004.
Massey, John. *Reminiscences, giving sketches of scenes through which the author has passed and pen portraits of people who have modified his life.* Reprint from the collections of the University of California Libraries [Nashville, TN: M. E. Church, South, 1916].
Powell, David A. *The Chickamauga Campaign—Glory or the Grave.* El Dorado Hills, CA: Savas Beatie, 2015.
Powell, David A. *Failure in the Saddle: Nathan Bedford Forrest, Joseph Wheeler, and the Confederate Cavalry in the Chickamauga Campaign.* New York: Savas Beatie, 2010.
Powell, David A. *The Maps of Chickamauga.* New York: Savas Beatie, 2009.
Shaver, Lewellyn Adolphus. *A History of the Sixtieth Alabama Regiment: Gracie's Alabama Brigade.* Sabin Americana, 2012 [Montgomery, AL: Barrett & Brown Publishers, 1867].
Spruill, Matt. *Guide to the Battle of Chickamauga.* Lawrence: University Press of Kansas, 1993.

Slotkin, Richard. *The Long Road to Antietam: How the Civil War Became a Revolution.* New York: Liveright Publishing, 2013.
Tatum, Georgia Lee. *Disloyalty in the Confederacy.* University of North Carolina Press, 2013.
The Union Army: A History of Military Affairs in the Loyal States, 1861–65—Records of the Regiments in the Union Army—Cyclopedia of Battles—Memoirs of Commanders and Soldiers. Madison: Federal, 19083
War of the Rebellion: Official Records of the Union and Confederate Armies, Series 1, Volume 30, Parts 1–4, Serial 50–54. Washington, DC, 1901.
Watkins, Sam R. *Company Aytch; or, A Side Show of the Big Show: A Memoir of the Civil War.* (Ruth Hill and Fulton McAllister, Eds.). Nashville, TN: Turner Publishing Company, 2011.
White, William Lee. *Bushwhacking on a Grand Scale: The Battle of Chickamauga, September 18–20, 1863.* El Dorado Hills, CA: Savas Beatie, 2013.
Woodworth, Steven E. (Ed.). *The Chickamauga Campaign.* Carbondale: Southern Illinois University Press, 2010.
Yeary, Mamie. *Reminiscences of the Boys in Gray 1861–1865.* Dallas, TX: Smith and Lamar Publishing Company, n.d.

Periodicals

Alabama Monument at Chickamauga. *The Confederate Veteran,* May 1913, page 212.
Daily State Sentinel, May 11, 1862. ADAH.
First Alabama Battalion Reminiscences. *The Confederate Veteran,* May 1903, page 219.
Montgomery Daily Advertiser, March 8, 1863. ADAH.
William Wallace Screws. *The Confederate Veteran,* October 1913, page 504.

Index

Numbers in **bold italics** indicate pages with illustrations